EVOLUTION, ORDER AND COMPLEXITY

Evolution, Order and Complexity reflects the current interest in the relation between the natural and the social. Its central concern, running through all the contributions in this collection, is a desire to overcome the nature/society dichotomy and to move beyond the sterile debate between anti-naturalists and crude naturalists.

Against neo-Darwinian theories, the contributors argue that the complexity of both social and natural phenomena precludes reductionist and mechanistic modes of analysis. As the chapters in this volume demonstrate, it is indeed possible to explore the relations between, and the unity of, the social and natural worlds without reducing one to the other.

Evolution, Order and Complexity brings together specialists in biology, ecology, philosophy, economics, neuropsychology and other fields to give new impetus to the dialogue between natural and social scientists. Together they show that the two branches of science are not mutually exclusive, but are part of a complex continuum.

This is a bold and challenging book; its scope and its often insightful conclusions make it required reading for both natural and social scientists.

This volume is one to the last projects initiated and coordinated by **Kenneth E. Boulding**, late Professor Emeritus of Economics at the University of Colorado at Boulder. Boulding was one of the founding fathers of general system theory and wrote numerous books throughout his prolific career. **Elias L. Khalil** is Assistant Professor of Economics at Ohio State University and Visiting Scholar at the University of Chicago.

T0371908

ROUTLEDGE FRONTIERS OF POLITICAL ECONOMY

EVOLUTION, ORDER AND COMPLEXITY

Edited by
Elias L. Khalil and Kenneth E. Boulding

LONDON AND NEW YORK

First published 1996
by Routledge
2 Park Square, Milton Park, Abingdon, Oxfordshire OX14 4RN

Simultaneously published in the USA and Canada
by Routledge
a division of Routledge, Taylor & Francis
711 Third Avenue, New York, NY 10017

First issued in paperback 2015

Routledge is an imprint of the Taylor and Francis Group, an informa business

© 1996 Elias L. Khalil and Kenneth E. Boulding

Typeset in Garamond by
J&L Composition Ltd, Filey, North Yorkshire

British Library Cataloguing in Publication Data
A catalogue record for this book is available from the British Library.

Library of Congress Cataloging in Publication Data
Evolution, order, and complexity/edited by Elias L. Khalil and
Kenneth E. Boulding.
p.   cm.
Includes index.
1. Social evolution. 2. Evolution (Biology) 3. Social sciences–
Philosophy. I. Khalil, Elias L., 1957–. II. Boulding, Kenneth
E., 1910–1993.
GN360.E89 1996
303.4–dc20   95–33146
CIP

ISBN 13: 978-1-138-86610-2 (pbk)
ISBN 13: 978-0-415-13728-7 (hbk)

Dedicated to the memory of
Kenneth Boulding

CONTENTS

CONTENTS

CONTRIBUTORS

Kenneth E. Boulding (d. 1993) sometime Distinguished Professor of Economics, Emeritus, University of Colorado at Boulder; author of *The Structure of a Modern Economy: The United States, 1929–1989*, 1993.

John H. Campbell Associate Professor at School of Medicine, UCLA, Visiting Professor at Oxford University and the Australian National University; editor of *Creative Evolution*, 1993.

Vilmos Csányi Professor and chair of the Department of Ethology, a member of the Hungarian Academy of Sciences and the International Union of Biological Sciences Commission for Education; serves on the editorial boards of *Acta Biologica Hungarica, Life and Science*, and *World Future*; author of *Evolutionary Systems and Society: A General Theory of Evolution*, 1989.

Jean-Pierre Dupuy Professor of Social and Political Philosophy, Director of Research at CNRS at the Ecole polytechnique, Paris, and Department of Political Science, Stanford University; author of *Introduction aux sciences sociales, Logique des phénomènes collectifs*, 1992.

Niles Eldredge Chairman and Curator of the Department of Invertebrates, American Museum of Natural History, New York; author of *The Miner's Canary: Unraveling the Mysteries of Extinction*, 1994, and *Reinventing Darwin*, 1995.

Hermann Haken Professor Dr. Dr. h.c. mult. of Theoretical Physics at the University of Stuttgart; author of *Information and Self-Organisation*, 1988.

Hubert Hendrichs Professor Dr. of Ethology at the University of Bielefeld; author of *Lebensprozesse und wissenschaftliches Denken. Zur Logik der Lebendigkeit und ihrer Erstarrung in den Wissenschaften*, 1988.

Elias L. Khalil Assistant Professor of Economics at Ohio State University; author of several articles; recipient of the Alexander von Humboldt Research Award for 1995–96.

CONTRIBUTORS

Henri Marie Laborit (d. 1995) sometime Professor and Director of the Laboratoire d'Eutonologie at Hospital Boucicaut; recipient of the Albert Lasker Prize of the American Public Health Association and the Anokhine Prize of Academy of Sciences, USSR; author of *Les Récepteurs Centraux et la Transduction des Signaux*, 1990.

Howard H. Pattee Professor of Systems Science and Director of Graduate Studies, T. J. Watson School of Engineering, State University of New York at Binghamton; author of "Measurement-Control Heterarchical Networks in Living Systems," *International Journal of General Systems*, 1991.

Karl H. Pribram Professor Emeritus, Stanford University, James P. and Anna King University Professor and Eminent Scholar, Commonwealth of Virginia; author of *Brain and Perception: Holonomy and Structure in Figural Processing*, 1991.

Gregory B. Stock Visiting Senior Fellow, the Woodrow Wilson School of Public and International Affairs; author of *Metaman: The Merging of Humans and Machines into a Global Superorganism*, 1993.

Robert E. Ulanowicz Professor at the Center for Environmental and Estuarine Studies Chesapeake Biological Laboratory; recipient of the Frederocj C. Hettinger Memorial Award (1964); author of *Growth and Development: Ecosystems Phenomenology*, 1986.

Milan Zeleny Professor of Management Systems; recipient of the Georg Cantor Award, Erskine Fellowship, Alexander von Humboldt Research Award, and Norbert Wiener Award; serves on the editorial boards of *Computers and Operations Research, Future Generations Computer Systems, Fuzzy Sets and Systems, General Systems Yearbook,* and *Human Systems Management;* author of *Autopoiesis, Dissipative Structures and Spontaneous Social Orders*, 1980.

PREFACE

At the last stage of preparing the manuscript, Kenneth Boulding fell ill. After a long bout with cancer, he passed away on 18 March, 1993, at the age of eighty-three, at his home in Boulder, Colorado. This has left many friends and colleagues with a great void. Although he left behind him over forty volumes and eight hundred articles, people who came to know him closely, to feel his vivid excitement over big ideas and the little things in life, and to note his diligent work towards world peace realize that he died prematurely.

The idea of the volume was born out of a conversation with Boulding at the 1990 meeting of the Society for the Advancement of Socio-Economics at George Washington University in Washington, DC. Two themes emerged from the conversation. First, how amazing that so many diverse forms (ranging from human to nonhuman entities) in nature are, at deeper levels, similar in one way or another. The casual observation of uniformity differs greatly from the drive which informs much of neo-Darwinism. Namely, neo-Darwinians generally start with the notion of how amazing that entities in nature are so different from each other.

Second, most social scientists (the orthodox as well as the heterodox) uncouple most human phenomena from nature. They assume that natural forms are commanded by external and given forces which do not allow intentionality, the role of habits, and the relevance of context. Such an assumption leads, put simply, to the presentation of nonhuman natural phenomena as no different from the artificial realm with includes tools and machines. Boulding and I agreed that the dichotomy should not be penciled along the social realm, on one hand, and the natural realm understood as articificial, on the other. Rather, the dichotomy should be drawn along the social and natural realms, on one side, and the artificial, on the other.

So we invited contributors to write essays which challenge one of the most trenchant assumptions in modern social and economic theories, the natural/social dichotomy. The essays should add a unique voice to an expanding choir calling for the relevance of natural sciences (both physical and biological) to the study of human action, cultural institutions, and social organization. The essays do not attempt a systematic treatment of such a vast topic. It is hoped that the different contributions would converge into a broadly defined intellectual space which would facilitate greater dialogue between natural and social scientists. The contributors, in different ways, argue for the pertinence of the naturalist approach on the bases that the organism is creative, capable of learning, and that its behavior is somewhat context-dependent – very much what most social scientists have stressed about the supposed uniqueness of human behavior.

The thesis that human behavior is unique has informed a great number of methodological positions in the social sciences. Such a thesis is usually contravened by old-style crude naturalist contentions like the ones touted by most sociobiologists. The main character of the contributions here is that they, implicitly or explicitly, criticize the autonomy-of-social-science thesis, but without falling back on crude naturalism. They do not reduce social phenomena to some given genetic information or map them according to supposed mechanistic laws. Rather, the contributors generally argue that natural dynamics and biological entities are as complex as higher level social dynamics and organizations. The complexity perspective may elucidate the unity of social and biological phenomena without resorting to reductionist and mechanistic accounts.

The idea of complexity promises to supersede the barren debate between biological determinism and social determinism. The contributions try to show how biological and social processes are isomorphic. To put it metaphorically, cultural schemes and social organizations could be seen as biological phenomena at a higher level, while biological taxonomic traits and organizations could be viewed as sociocultural phenomena at a lower level.

We would like to invite social scientists to take a fresh look at contributions offered by maverick biologists and others that promise to open new vistas beyond the sterile debate between anti-naturalists and crude naturalists. Boulding had the chance to read and comment on all the invited chapters. Unfortunately, he was not able to work on the organization of the volume. I would like to acknowledge the help of two anonymous readers, the editorial team at Routledge, Vivian Wilson and Thomas Foster, as well as the technical assistance of Carole Brown, Patricia Markley, and Yolanda Allen.

E. Khalil

INTRODUCTION

In the first chapter, "Social theory and naturalism: An introduction," Elias Khalil attempts to defend naturalism understood as the natural/human continuity thesis. First, he distinguishes naturalism from crude naturalism in order to avoid diverse misuses of biological metaphors and, hence, eschew the strong reservation which deconstructionists, ranging from Michel Foucault to Mary Douglas, have expressed towards naturalism. Second, he delineates between two radically different orders: chaotic order as typified by ecosystems and markets, on one hand, and organizational order as displayed by organisms, firms, and states, on the other. Third, he maintains that there are, at least, three different strains of non-crude naturalism related to organizational order: First, "metaphysical naturalism" entails that nonhuman organisms are, in varying degrees, as intentional/purposeful as humans. Second, "phenomenist naturalism" maintains that institutions and taxonomic traits define the identity (nature) of the agent and, hence, are assumed in everyday decisions or neo-Darwinian adaptation. Third, "ontological naturalism" regards social organization as an individual and, hence, cannot be reduced to the strategies of members which could extend to the genome level.

The following chapter, "Interfacing complexity at a boundary between the natural and social sciences," is by Karl H. Pribram. Pribram's concern with complexity is part of the ontological problem of the relations among the different levels of hierarchy. He starts with the behavioral account of Skinner who recognizes two gaps which, according to Skinner, only brain science can fill. The first gap is between the environment and the stimulated behavior. The second gap is between the consequences of behavior and the resulting *change* (the problem of memory). For Pribram, the first gap allows us to argue that as much as the environment has a pattern which "affords" the organism to perceive it (à la Gibson's ecological theory of perception), the organism has a predisposition to select its environment. Furthermore, the second gap allows us to maintain that the resulting change is not a mere reaction to traces of memory, but rather the memory is organized in a way which encourages change in a certain direction.

Pribram summarizes numerous experiments in his laboratory and others which confirm the ways he fills the two gaps, viz., particular neural cells are actively selecting and organizing (tuning). The experiments show that neural processes resulting from stimuli could be described as Fourier holographic-like frequencies where the inputs are transformed into patterns which can be modeled, as suggested by D. Gabor, as sets of convolutional integrals. Gabor used the mathematics of Heisenberg's quantum approach which he also applied earlier to measure the minimum uncertainty of communication among persons. Thus, put simply, the same quanta mathematics about information may account for behavior at the particle, neural, and person levels. This suggests that to understand the brain/behavior relationship and fill the gaps recognized by Skinner, we need to invoke data from both the environment and neural levels. It seems that invariant, deep information identity – which underpins cross-level processes – holds the key for superseding the brain/mind dichotomy. The primacy should be attributed neither to the mental nor to the neural – nor for that matter to equal division between them. Rather, processes at both levels are the instantiations of, or informed by, the same quanta of information à la Gabor's elementary functions. At the end, Pribram reflects on the ramifications of the cross-level isomorphism of the invariant, Platonian-like quanta information with regard to the free will/determinism problem.

In his chapter, "The autonomy of social reality: On the contribution of systems theory to the theory of society," Jean-Pierre Dupuy argues that the contemporary theories in logic, cognitive science, artificial intelligence, and game theory have bearings on fundamental issues in the humanities and the social sciences. He puts a special emphasis on the logic of self-reference, the paradoxes of reflexivity, and the challenge of the notion that autonomy implies the essential incompleteness of any human or social totality. Dupuy argues that it is impossible to conceive self-sufficiency in the human world. He contrasts structuralists like Lévi-Strauss and deconstructionists like Derrida. While Lévi-Strauss resorts to cybernetical metaphors to account for incompleteness, Derrida shows how structures fall prey to a kind of vicious self-referential logic referred to as the "logic of the supplement." Dupuy argues that, to start with, we should not use cybernetic metaphors. Instead, we should employ the theory of complex autonomous systems. This promises, according to Dupuy, to clear up at least some of the most famous paradoxes like the leader, panic in Freud's theory of the crowd, and the notion of self-transcendence in Hayek's theory of spontaneous social systems.

In his chapter, "Ultra-Darwinian explanation and the biology of social systems," Niles Eldredge contends that sociobiology is not weak only with reference to human behavior, but also with regard to nonhuman behavior. Its general weakness is derived directly from underlying difficulties in orthodox biological evolutionary theory which exclusively emphasizes reproduction (fitness) success. On the basis of a hierarchical approach, he equally emphasizes the economic (interaction) aspect of organismic behavior. Thus, the chapter raises the issue of context and hierarchy of organization. The hierarchy, according to Eldredge, arises from reproductive activities of local population (demes), themselves parts of the largest system in which reproductive adaptations are shared (species). In contrast, economic behavior leads directly to the formation of local interactive populations (avatars) which are parts of the ecosystem. While reproductive activities generate genealogical hierarchy, economic interactions constitute ecological hierarchy. According to Eldredge, the fault of orthodox Darwinism is the stress on the primacy of reproductive activity (via fitness maximization criterion) over economic interaction.

Contrary to common perceptions, in his chapter "The complexity of social and mental structures in nonhuman mammals," Hubert Hendrichs shows that each mammal has unique mental characteristics. Furthermore, it has psychological qualities which cannot be completely explained by genetic dispositions. The qualities develop while the animal is growing up in close contact with several conspecifics, exploring possible ways to act in a network of highly complex relations. Thus, the chapter complements Eldredge's discussion of "economic" interaction. Hendrichs describes the socialization of a mammal as learning the rules of behavior and how to handle conflicts. What is most amazing is that the rules vary across groups of the same species. This indicates that culture is not uniquely human.

Milan Zeleny in the chapter "On the social nature of autopoietic systems," challenges implicit and dormant assumptions. The question should not be whether human organization is similar to the organism, but rather whether biological organization resembles social organization. He appeals to Francisco Varela's approach, called autopoiesis (self-production), in order to substantiate his thesis that cells and organisms should be studied as societies. Zeleny's thesis has implications with regard to the metaphysical question of whether there is no radical divide between human and non-human organizations.

In his contribution, "Organization, function, and creativity in biological and social systems," Vilmos Csányi complements Zeleny's approach, and its metaphysical ramifications, by drawing attention to the systematic nature of the biological and social evolutionary systems. He argues that Darwinian theory just looks for the changes of the components (lineages of descent) as does the neo-Darwinian agenda with the genes. Similar to Eldredge's thesis, Csányi maintains that both lineages and genes are important actors in the evolutionary theater. However, they are components of a higher system which needs to be attended. For Csányi, we need to study the structure, the constraints, and the degrees of freedom of the system as a whole. Csányi is ultimately interested in accounting for creativity in biological and social systems. He summarizes and extends his replicative component systems model. He argues that the proposed replicative model is capable of accounting for genetic mutation and evolution.

In their chapter, "Human society as an emerging global superorganism: A biological perspective," Gregory B. Stock and John H. Campbell draw further similarities, along ontological lines, between social organization and biological organization. They argue that modern industrial society – with its machines, domesticated plants and animals, and physical infrastructure such as buildings and highways – is becoming a cohesive global entity that has a physiology with close analogs to the circulatory, nervous, and digestive systems of animals. According to them, the dynamics of modern society can no longer be adequately understood by viewing humanity merely as a highly social species embedded in an extended planetary ecosystem. Rather, it is becoming a superorganism. An outstanding aspect of the emerging global superorganism is its ability to evolve rapidly. This is the case because, first, it has internalized natural selection so that its component parts and systems can compete aggressively among themselves. Second, it has further honed the evolutionary process by developing the power to build abstract models and plans which compete vigorously for future implementation.

In "Neurological and social bases of dominance in human society," Henri Laborit provides a stern assessment of the modern predicament. He argues that in order to understand human behavior, it is important to know how the central nervous system operates. One of the principal functions of the brain is to effect relationships among humans. In this sense, he exposes the ontological role of context or interaction for neural functioning. One of the activities of the brain, according to Laborit, involves centralizing information on the normal or disturbed operation of the cellular ensemble of the organism as well as on the environment. In this manner, the organism learns through reinforcements. The property concept arises from reward learning and how, in the quest for dominance, this leads to competition among individuals and groups. In modern society, the symbols of dominance have become more abstract. The quest after such symbols engenders stress and its associated pathological disorders. Thus, as much as modern man eludes himself to be free, he is in fact a prisoner of fabricated hierarchical systems which push him further towards non-reflective conformity.

Robert E. Ulanowicz, in "The propensities of evolving systems," starts with Karl Popper's recent book, *A World of Propensities*. Popper lends his pen to the anti-Cartesian view that the world is not a deterministic clockwork. This calls for an extension of our concept of causality beyond the confines of efficient and material agencies. For Ulanowicz, this is an opportunity to show that ecosystems are chaotic, i.e., far from transforming along deterministic pathways. However, that does not mean they do not generate patterns. Ulanowicz offers a calculus which could quantify propensities and may lay out the ground for a theory of transformation towards greater ecological ascendency.

In "Synergetics as a bridge between the natural and social sciences," Hermann Haken articulates how synergetics is an inter-disciplinary field of research which deals with systems composed of many parts that may produce spatial, temporal, or functional structures spontaneously. That is, it is capable of self-ordering in dynamical and organizational senses. The general principles are illustrated by means of applications to physics (lasers), biology (human finger movements), computer sciences (parallel networks for pattern recognition), and, in particular, to sociology. He demonstrates how a great variety of phenomena may be described by means of general concepts such as stability and instability, order parameters, and the slaving principle. Given such common principles, he argues for the unity of the sciences.

Howard H. Pattee maintains in "The problem of observables in models of biological organizations," that physical theories have come to be the epitome of models for all levels of complexity, including living organizations. However, the observables are simpler and observer-independent in physical theories compared with biological and social theories. Also, while observables in physical theories could be separated from measurement devices, this is not the case in biological and social theories. Pattee discusses the inadequacy of the physical model paradigm for discovering the significant biological observables and for modeling human organizations that are complex enough themselves to be observers and modelers of their world. He explains why concurrent, distributed networks now used to model cognitive activity, could prove to be complementary for modeling strongly interconnected, observer-dependent living organizations. While Pattee sees a divide between physical and living sciences, he argues for a continuity between biological and social sciences.

1

SOCIAL THEORY AND NATURALISM
An introduction

Elias L. Khalil

In "The History of Astronomy," Adam Smith (1980, pp. 33–105) shows how the origin of theories lies in the mind's attempt to alleviate uneasiness or tension usually felt when unexpected events arise. Theories are the fruit of the imagination in its thrust to bring order, and hence beauty, to the phenomenal world. Such order is associated with a variety of sentiments. Smith begins the essay by explicating three types of sentiments: "Wonder, Surprise and Admiration." Admiration is excited by "what is great and beautiful." This is best illustrated by Newton's system which unites Galileo's laws of terrestial motion with Kepler's laws of celestial motion. For Smith, while Newton's theory of gravity might be proven in the future to be wrong, it commands admiration for its ability to weave the wonders of nature within one great "connecting principle."[1]

In this light, the main thrust behind scientific inquiry – which might be opposed to vocational training – is not the collection of facts. Of course, the collection of facts engages the faculties of most scientists most of the time. However, the glimmer which sustains the thrust for knowledge is the possibility of organizing the diverse facts according to the simplest possible theoretical account. The glimmer usually grows in intensity as scientists become capable of integrating more facts without too much backward bending of the branches of theory. Such a successful stretching of theory enhances its aesthetic quality.

In the aesthetic quest after empirical comprehensiveness and theoretical simplicity, too often fine, but crucial distinctions have become neglected. In the first section, the chapter maintains that the principle of naturalism should not be confused with crude naturalism. The second section delineates between two kinds of natural orders: the structure order of markets and ecosystems, on one hand, and the organization order of firms and organisms, on the other. Finally, the third section suggests that there are at least three distinct theoretical questions surrounding organization order.

Given the synthetic character of this survey, many theses are not adequately defended. They are rather presented as signposts for further

1

inquiry. One must take stock of the wide-ranging arena so that a detailed defense of one thesis does not take the wrong turn.

THE PROBLEM OF NATURALISM

Naturalism involves diverse meanings. However, broadly speaking, it denotes the notion of the unity of nature as including living entities as well as human purposeful action, cultural institutions, and social organizations. Etymologically, the terms *nascor* in Latin and its equivalent *physo* in Greek denote the verbs of spontaneous change (Kerford, 1981, ch. 10). So the term "nature" was originally not contrary to spontaneously appearing human phenomena, but rather opposed to artifacts like chairs which are consciously designed (Hayek, 1988, p. 143).

So anti-naturalism could be understood as the advocacy of the *discontinuity* of nature where certain phenomena – living forms for some theorists and human forms for others – are not seen as the outcome of natural spontaneity. In contrast, the naturalist viewpoint translates into the idea that "there is (or can be) an essential unity of method between the natural and the social sciences" (Bhaskar, 1979, p. 3) because there are no sudden introductions of extra-natural principles in order to account for life or human forms. As put by Arthur C. Danto:

> Naturalism, in recent usage, is a species of philosophical monism according to which whatever exists or happens is *natural* in the sense of being susceptible to explanation through methods which, although paradigmatically exemplified in the natural sciences, are continuous from domain to domain of objects and events. Hence, naturalism is polemically defined as repudiating the view that there exists or could exist any entities or events which lie, in principle, beyond the scope of scientific explanation.
>
> (Danto, 1967, p. 448)

Given such a broad definition, the naturalist perspective accommodates diverse and even rival philosophies ranging from the materialist philosophy of Marx to the idealist philosophy of Leibniz and modern analytical philosophy.

In order to provide a greater clarity, it is argued below that there are different kinds of naturalism. If this is true, it is possible for an economist – as is the case – to hold naturalist and anti-naturalist positions depending on the specific question at hand. In order to show the consistency of one's methodological orientation, it would be imperative to delineate the distinct kinds of naturalism.

But before showing this, there is a need to defend naturalism on the ground that it differs from its commonly perceived crude version. As a warning, the defense does not easily fit the strict confines of what most

2

social theorists come to expect from an exercise in "methodology." It also does not conform to the narrow specialization of philosophers who wrote, in one way or another, on naturalism. The exercise here should be seen as the exploration of the contested terrain which separates science from philosophy.

Naturalism vs crude naturalism

The aim of the contributors to this volume, given their diverse orientations, is to shake off the specter of modeling human behavior, organization, and culture in light of the different facets of the biological sciences. The contributors attempt to answer fundamental questions in a way which hopefully would assuage the fear harbored by many social scientists about the usefulness of naturalism as a foundation of social theory.

The way to dispel misgivings concerning the naturalist agenda is to learn from new modes of thinking advocated by a new breed of natural scientists. Such modes, as detailed below, perceive the organism as purposeful (or, what is taken to be the same thing, intentional) and whose action is context-sensitive. This should prove to be foreign to commonly held crude naturalist assumptions. As suggested by Milan Zeleny and Vilmos Csányi in this volume, we need to switch the table around on one fundamental question: The question should no longer be whether humans, human organizations, and human systems resemble, respectively, nonhuman animals, biological organizations, and ecosystems. Rather it should be whether or in what respects nonhuman animals, biological organizations, and ecosystems correspond, respectively, with humans, human organizations, and human systems. Thus, as much as there is a need to learn from the natural sciences, some maverick natural scientists, including the contributors to this volume, derive insights from the social sciences. These insights include the attention to intentionality, cooperation, context-sensitive action, deep customs, and cumulative causation.

Thus, the borrowing of metaphors, in a non-superficial sense, from the natural sciences should not necessarily entail the introduction of mechanistic, nominalist, and reductionist reasoning into the human sciences.[2] As the contributions below attest, it is possible to extend metaphors from the natural to the social sciences without falling into crude naturalist conceptions. If the attempt is successful, it should certainly undermine the anti-naturalist tendencies prevalent in much of the modern social sciences.

Obviously, the attitude which a social scientist takes *vis-à-vis* naturalism depends on his/her conception of what constitutes natural tendencies and natural entities. This certainly invites the "Beatrix Potter Syndrome" (Rose, 1987), i.e., the anthropomorphic proclivity to view natural tendencies and entities in terms suited for humans, and then to argue that such characteristics of nature confirm the appropriateness of naturalism as the foundation

3

of social theory. In order to avoid the Beatrix Potter Syndrome, we need to subject, as much as possible, any supposed human-like quality found in nature to a careful scrutiny. But equally, we should not shun any parallelism among the human and nonhuman domains on the basis of some historically deposited, presupposed divide between the natural and the social.

Historically speaking, there are two fair reasons for maintaining the great divide between the social and the natural. First, most of the scientists who crossed the divide at the start of the twentieth century have used the insights derived from biology to promote social Darwinism at home and to justify Euro-ethnocentricism or, in some cases, racism abroad (see Degler, 1991). While crude social and political agendas are not totally gone, they no longer occupy the high water in the social sciences. However, their legacy, as detailed in the contributions in general, still lingers in crude naturalist modes of conception.

Second, most who crossed the divide misplaced the use of metaphors in the same way as the extravagances of Herbert Spencer's (1967) sociology. Spencer's major mistake or "identificational slip," consists of likening the evolution of organism and superorganism (society), on one hand, to the transformation of the galaxies, on the other.[3] In order to avoid such a slip, one should be careful with the use of metaphors.

Metaphors and identificational slips

Most identificational slips consist of connecting disparate phenomena as the result of superficial resemblance or of conflating distinct contextual arrangements. For example, as Philip Mirowski (1989) records, economists in the past century have been eager, in their quest for legitimacy, to borrow the conservation of energy metaphor from physics in order to discuss the maximization of the utility function. However, a careful distinction among different kinds of metaphors may help us avoid identificational slips and encourage us to disregard the well-entrenched divide between the social and the natural.

There are at least four kinds of metaphors (see Khalil, 1992c, pp. 29–30), viz., the superficial, heterologous (or analogous), homologous, and unificational. The four kinds are distinguished by the criterion of the *kind* of resemblance which a metatheoretical statement is supposed to inform. Given that researchers differ greatly with regard to metatheory or foundational issues, the invoking of specific metaphors engenders great controversies. Such controversies are not only the outcome of metatheoretical differences, but also the result in many cases of misunderstandings. That is, problems arise when users of metaphors are not careful in identifying in what sense they are employing the metaphor.

The first type of metaphor acts like similes which show superficial resemblance. It includes statements such as "the French Revolution swept

Europe like a hurricane," "the coconut is shaped after the cat's head," "the car speeded as fast as tropical wind," or "his face is rounded like a full moon." The observed similarities of shape or movement are not meant to indicate any functional likeness (in the biological sense), taxonomic or schematic (what biologists call "structural") similarity, or manifestation of the *same* law. Rather, the similarity is merely a nominal category, i.e., the product of impressions concocted by the human mind. Of course, researchers may debate whether a particular similarity is nominal or real. But such a debate is empirical and, hence, must assume that there are superficial metaphors.

For instance, while the same mathematical formula expresses the speed of the wind and the speed of the car, it does not mean they have anything else in common. Likewise, the law of entropy and Claude E. Shannon and Warren Weaver's theory of information, which have identical mathematical formulas, possess superficial resemblance. Among other things, the law of entropy is fundamentally based on the distinction between micro- and macro-states, while this is not the case with information theory (Wicken, 1987, ch. 1).

With regard to the second and third types of metaphor, the biological distinction between heterologous (i.e., homoplastic similarity) and homologous (i.e., homophylic similarity) traits is used as a metaphor to shed some light. Heterologous likeness denotes a similarity arising from the resemblance of *analytical functions*, while the respective contexts are different. In contrast, homologous likeness designates a similarity emanating from the resemblance of *contexts* even when, although it is not usually the case, the analytical functions are different.

To elaborate, when a metaphor highlights a feature in one phenomenon by alluding to a functionally similar feature in a phenomenon with a totally different setting – in terms of context, underpinning framework, or what biologists call "structure" – it highlights heterologous likeness. For example, the wings of a butterfly and the wings of a bat are heterologous: They perform the same analytical function of flying, but they emanate from different organizational context. That is, there is no common descent between the limbs of the butterfly and the limbs of the bat. Likewise, the driving of an automobile to work and the driving even of the same automobile by the same agent for pleasure express a heterologous similarity: Both activities perform the same analytical function of transportation, but they emanate from different purposes or contexts. That is, in the input–output production matrix, the driving to work is an input, while the driving for cruising is a final output. Likewise, one highlights a heterologous similarity when one likens the Algerian armed conflict in the 1950s with the quasi-armed conflict in the 1990s. In the earlier case it is a war of liberation from French colonialism. In the later case it is a Muslim revolutionary struggle against the nationalist secular regime.

In contrast, when a metaphor points out a characteristic in one phenomenon by referring to a corresponding phenomenon which has a similar scheme, context, or common origin, it usually shows homologous similarity. Biologists describe two organs in different species as homologous, as opposed to heterologous, when they are components of the same anatomy or scheme, i.e., emanate from a shared phylogenetic origin. In this light, the forelimbs of a mouse and the forelimbs of a bat are homologous: While both have different analytical functions (viz., in one case to help the animal run and in the other case to help the animal fly), the forelimbs emanate from the same organizational context or underpinning scheme.[4] Of course, the forelimbs of a mouse and the forelimbs of a dog are obviously homologous – a case where they do not only share the context or underpinning scheme, but also the analytical function.

One might be using, like Alfred Marshall (1920, pp. 200–201) who was greatly influenced by Herbert Spencer (see Hodgson, 1993), the homologous metaphor when one likens the division of labor within the firm to the differentiation of functions within the organism. Likewise, the autocrat of a chimpanzee troop, the leader of a hunting and gathering human band, and the modern state might be related in a homologous fashion. While they might perform different functions in detail, their activities are homologous in relation to the organization of work and the administration of political order (Masters, 1989). In addition, when one likens one's driving to work with one's neighbor's walking to work, one would be drawing a homologous analogy: While the two activities are physiologically different and are even performed by different agents for different companies, they share similar contexts. Similarly, one might be drawing a homologous metaphor when one likens the current revolutionary agitation in Algeria with the Iranian Revolution: Both aim at changing regimes, not to mention the common ideological inspiration.

Still, the homologous metaphor is different from the fourth type, the unificational metaphor. The unificational metaphor expresses similarities when they arise from the same law. For instance, Newton's law of gravitation established a unity between celestial motion and terrestrial acceleration of bodies as they fall downward. Both disparate events are regulated by the same law of gravity. Likewise, one would be using unificational metaphors when discussing the similarity of blood circulation of humans and chimpanzees as well as the likeness of energy expenditure in human production and the production activity of other organisms.

Given these different kinds of metaphors, it is easy to mismatch diverse phenomena. One would commit an identificational slip upon using a superficial metaphor to indicate a heterologous similarity, a heterologous metaphor to signify a homologous likeness, or a homologous metaphor to denote a unifictional homogeneity. Of course, it is a double or triple identificational slip to cross a greater partition and make greater mismatches. In order to be able to distinguish the different kinds of resemblances and avoid identificational slips, one needs some metatheoretical clarifications, as attempted below.

Naturalism, anti-foundationalism, and anthropologistic thinking

The defense of naturalism, even of the non-crude variety, does not generally jibe with the tide of anti-foundationalism which is in vogue in the current sophistical intellectual milieu. The tide is led by anthropologistic thinkers like Michel Foucault (1972, 1980), Richard Rorty (1979), Jacques Derrida (1973), and Mary Douglas (1986). Such thinkers seem to lump all searches for foundation under one umbrella. It is true that much of axiomatic theorizing is motivated by the obsessive desire to find solid grounds for policy issues, or to prove that there are direct, unambiguous policy implications of the offered theory.

However, the proposed naturalist foundation is by no means the Archimedean rock of certitude which was sought by, *inter alia*, René Descartes and, more recently, the logical positivists armed with the covering-law or the hypothetico-deductive model of explanation. That is, the proposed naturalism is not a rock which would alleviate what Richard Bernstein (1983, pp. 16–25) calls the "Cartesian anxiety." The Cartesian anxiety arises from limiting choices to *either* a theory which is based on a solid foundation *or* to no theory at all which would subject everything to relativism, mob psychology, and social convention.

The suggested naturalist foundationalism does not claim, or even attempt to establish, a certain one-to-one relation between fundamental principles and policy decisions. Rather, the approach advocated here presents a sponge-like foundation which could accommodate conflicting hypothetico-deductive models and their competing policy implications. For instance, in political science, a sponge-like foundation could simultaneously furnish a predictive, covering-law model showing how repression leads to political stability and another predictive model showing how it leads to greater revolutionary agitation. Likewise, in economics, a soft foundation should simultaneously entertain the hypothetico-deductive monetarist model of how the increase of money supply leads to inflationary pressure and another predictive one showing how greater money supply might tap new hidden potential for real output growth.

In this manner, the conflicting covering-law models are not pronounced useless. Rather, each is found to be suited for a different historical context. Thus, while maintaining a thrust for foundationalism, it is acknowledged that the proposed approach cannot offer comfortable or straightforward answers to immediate and pressing policy problems.

Soft foundationalism or the inability to provide solid, timeless policy recommendations should not be considered a shortcoming. On the contrary, it should be regarded as a sign of strength because it provides the hope that theoretical pursuits could account for the complexity of organization and conflicting historical processes. Furthermore, a soft naturalist foundationalism would avoid the famous "naturalist fallacy." The fallacy, stated tersely, is the deduction of what ought to be from what is conceived to be a matter of natural propensity or natural tendency. The lack of a solid naturalist rock makes such a presumed one-to-one correspondence unfeasible. On the other hand, in light of soft naturalism, the rejection of the naturalist fallacy would not lead to an unbridgeable and problematic divide between description and prescription.

In this light, the obsession of much of social theory, like the agenda undertaken by James Coleman (1990), with the grounding of policy proposals on supposedly solid foundations is justly criticized by the anti-foundationalists. In their criticism, however, the anti-foundationalists seem to throw out the baby with the bathwater. That is, they seem to deny the existence of any footing, even a sponge-like one. They generally regard conceptual apparatuses as, in the final analysis, arbitrarily constructed or designed sociocultural conventions. They normally distrust the attempt to make sense of nature, because such an attempt supposedly cannot escape, in the final analysis, from the culturally tainted impulse to justify social order.

Put differently, the movement considers the impetus to undertake theoretical investigations as quixotic because it ultimately arises from the need to legitimize culturally fabricated (i.e., non-natural) conventions. Such an anthropologistic thesis has influenced, in different ways, the perspective of certain economists (e.g., McCloskey, 1985; Mirowski, 1989; Milberg, 1988). Stated simply, the anthropologistic argument amounts to the thesis that institutions ultimately reflect a particular culture's image of itself. This entails that institutions do not emerge "naturally," but rather designed for diverse purposes including tribal or national self-gratification, ideological agendas, or the longing for any order.

It is true that the institution which defines what is a shameful transaction – like the selling of pigs in Islamic culture, cows in Hindu culture, drugs, political favors, and sex in modern western culture – is relative to environmental conditions. However, the relativity is about the particular form, not necessarily about some possible universal processes. It could be easily shown that the diverse forms of particular instances of what is shameful arise from common biological, psychological, and political imperatives at a deeper level. That is, there is a need to distinguish between the relative forms of what could be imperative, deep processes and arbitrary conventions like the standards of measure.

The failure to distinguish the relative from the arbitrary amounts to the argument that almost all institutions are arbitrary in the sense of being unrelated to the deeper biological realm. It is true that Philip Mirowski (1989, ch. 3), an advocate of the anthropologistic thesis, rejects such biological/social dichotomy thesis. This is so, however, because he, stated broadly, conceives the biological realm as the fabrication of sociocultural norms. Thus, he rejects the dichotomy only in order to deny the biological realm any role in social theory. In other words, his main interest is to discard the relevance of psychobiological, constitutive variables, or to object to the biological perspective in the social sciences. Mirowski would simply like to restrict the relevance of biology to medical schools. This inadvertently introduces, from the back window, the biological/social dichotomy because even if the biological domain is irrelevant for social theory, it is relevant for another sphere.[5]

Mirowski's socioculturalist or anthropologistic agenda, influenced by Mary Douglas, basically stipulates that all human conceptions of nature are anthropomorphic, i.e., cannot escape the Beatrix Potter Syndrome. Douglas relies mainly on the Durkheim–Mauss argument,[6] put forward in 1903, that the classification of plants and animals – i.e., determining similarity and dissimilarity – reflects specific organizational arrangement of human relations:

> [T]he most elementary logical idea . . . depends on social interaction. This is the idea of similarity or resemblance. When several things are recognized as members of the same class, what constitutes their sameness? It certainly seems circular to claim that similarity explains how things get classed together. It is naive to treat the quality of sameness, which characterizes members of a class, as if it were a quality inherent in things or as a power of recognition inherent in the mind.
>
> (Douglas, 1986, p. 58)

However, Brent Berlin (1992) and Scott Atran (1990) show that, put in a few words, there are widespread regularities in the way different cultures classify organisms.[7] Stated generally, folk taxonomy across cultures (but not across hunting and gathering vs small-scale agriculture societies) follows the taxonomy offered by professional sytematists for large vertebrates and well-known plants, but not as much for invertebrates and inconspicuous plants. This goes to undermine, according to Berlin and Atran, the anthropologistic thesis that the recognition of likeness and principles of classification are a function of potential utility or social symbolic importance. All languages keep the taxonomy of genuine classification separate from utilitarian and symbolic classification. That is, folk taxonomy of the joints of nature is not arbitrary.

The promoters of the Durkheim–Mauss thesis usually view the values and visions of human organization in muscular terms, i.e., capable of constructing the joints of nature according to culturally fabricated concepts. However, in order for the Durkheim–Mauss thesis to work, it must ironically assume some kind of a "proper" conception of nature in relation

9

to the social order. Such an assumption undermines, at a higher grade of reasoning, the Durkheim–Mauss thesis. That is, the Durkheim–Mauss thesis entails an image of reality grounded in metaphor-free reasoning, i.e., unfettered by negotiated standards and conventions.

Many critics have noted that such a circularity of reasoning besets the recent sociology of scientific knowledge. But such a circularity is no more reflexive than the Cretan liar paradox. Bertrand Russell (1956) attempted, with some success, to resolve the paradox through the theory of types. The paradox can be summed up in this statement: "Epimenides, a Cretan, said that all Cretans are liars, and all statements made by Cretans are certainly lies." If Epimenides' statement is a member of all statements made by Cretans, Epimenides would be lying and so Cretans, to wit, would be speaking the truth. However, if Cretans speak the truth, Epimenides' statement would be true as well, and hence Cretans would certainly be liars. The paintings of M. C. Escher are generally different forms of the Cretan liar paradox. Russell solved the paradox by simply distinguishing the set or type from its constitutive members: One should not treat the set (statement) as being on par with its elements. This solution goes to suggest that the circularity of reasoning problem is not the primary nail which seals the coffin of the Durkheim–Mauss thesis.

These issues cannot be explored further. For our purpose, in any case, there is no need to criticize the anthropologistic view of Douglas and Mirowski: Any critique would not be a specific defense of naturalism. Rather, it would amount to an epistemological defense of the possibility of approximating history-free theoretical and metatheoretical propositions *per se*.

Although the discussion here touches on epistemological issues at many points, they are generally avoided. Specifically, methodological questions concerning how human concepts related to sense-data are eschewed. This is an unusual strategy given that epistemology contaminates most of the contemporary investigations of metatheoretical issues. The strategy is justified on two grounds. First, it is not imperative to appeal to epistemology in order to justify every thesis about the joints of nature – a position which flies in the face of the anthropologistic view that the Beatrix Potter Syndrome is inescapable. The commencement with epistemology implies that the mind's relation to sense data is imperative to understanding the joints of nature. This entails an anthropocentric view of the nature of knowledge. Such a view does not start with the thesis that the human mind is a natural product of evolution and, hence, it is the subject of knowledge like other natural phenomena. Second, the obsession with epistemology, like many other intellectual movements, has started to experience decreasing returns as one could attest from the trite and repetitive debates in the past three decades between the followers of Karl Popper and of Thomas Kuhn in the social sciences.

10

Thus, the main focus of the volume is not on epistemology. The concern is rather with the enrichment of the social sciences in light of observations about the constitution, behavior, and evolution of nonhuman entities. The remainder of the chapter would like to make some distinctions which may help in the further defense of a non-crude naturalist approach.

NATURAL ORDER: ORGANIZATION VS STRUCTURE

It is important to distinguish between two kinds of natural order: organization and structure. They are natural because there is no agent who stands outside of them and manipulates them for his convenience – as is the case with the artificial order of a bird's nest or a table.

Examples of organization order include the division of labor at the levels of the state, the firm, the household, and even the organism and cell. It should not be confused with the coherent relation of, or capacity afforded by the set of institutions/traits scheme underpinning such different levels of organizations. It is called organization order because the order at a certain level is coordinated through some kind of organizing principles acting as a unifying or agreed set of goals shared by the members of the organization under focus. So, organization order is self-referential – the type which Dupuy (this volume) investigates.

In contrast, examples of structure order include – insofar as they are spontaneous or self-regulating by equilibrium forces – the business cycle, the polarization of a city into poor/rich neighborhoods (or, in general, regional discontinuities of core and periphery), the more-or-less orderly pedestrian traffic at a university campus, and even hurricane formation and ecosystem dynamics. The idea that "structure order" could arise from chaotic interaction seems to be an oxymoron. While units might have diverse ends, the intentionless order appears at the macro-level. Structure order characterizes systems which are open to energy/matter influx or even closed (i.e., open only to energy influx).[8] To note, structure order can be theorized in different ways: e.g., the deterministic chaos theory, Ilya Prigogine's irreversible thermodynamics, Poincaréan nonlinear dynamics, Eugen Yates's homeodynamics, Karl H. Pribram's holonomic order,[9] and so on. The term "structure order" is sufficiently neutral to admit diverse theories of explanation.

The task is simply to differentiate the phenomenon of structure order from the phenomenon of organization order. Their distinction does not mean they do not affect each other. In this volume, the contributors Karl H. Pribram, Niles Eldredge, Robert Ulanowicz, Hermann Haken, and Howard Pattee show, in different ways, how chaotic and recursive inter-actions, on one hand, affect organization order and, development of complexity on the other.

ELIAS L. KHALIL

Is the organization/structure dichotomy anti-naturalist?

It is fruitful, as a first step at least, to delineate organization and structure orders. To be clear at the outset, the organization/structure distinction is proposed to cut across the boundary between living and non-living matter. The distinction differs from many other approaches. It does not coincide, e.g., with Yates's (1993) trichotomy of mathematical, physical, and biological orders. It is plausible to argue, without being able to demonstrate here, the controversial thesis that mathematics is mostly a human created, fictional/nominal set of categories whose "order" is not natural. If this is true, mathematics could not stand on a par with the physical and biological orders. Also, Yates's distinction between the physical and biological realms might invite arguments for the autonomy of biology. Yates's physical/ biological dichotomy might even insinuate some anti-naturalist, vitalist principles. Such principles would raise questions about the origin of *vita* which supposedly distinguishes living from non-living, physical matter.

In fact, Yates and many others, like Francisco Varela (1979) and Friedrich Hayek (1967a, 1967b; Khalil, 1992a), confuse the definition of organization with one of its aspects, viz., the structure order or pattern arising from the dynamic interaction of pre-constituted, independent actors.[10] However, Joseph Schumpeter (1989, p. 62) made an implicit distinction between the two. He differentiated innovative activity carried out by entrepreneurs, which he called development, from adjustment activity carried out by optimizing agents who take advantage of price differentials created by external shocks to the system. While learning and innovation allow the economic organization to proceed along a developmental trajectory, the arbitrage-kind of activity permits the system to approach equilibrium states. The two temporal operations are not alternative. They are rather superimposed on each other – much as the business cycle is superimposed on the unidirectional process of the development of the organization.

It seems that chaotic or dynamic interaction, regulated by some equilibration forces, may fail to account for the most salient feature of complexity, viz., the extensive specialization of biological functions or, at the social level, division of labor. The autocatalytic chaotic dynamics, which typifies what is called elsewhere "natural system," is only one feature of organization order or, in general, "natural complex" (Khalil, 1990a).

If the proposed way of cutting the cake is a close approximation to the actual joints of nature, there are two radically different kinds of positive feedbacks, differentiated along the proposed divide between natural system and natural complex, which Yates and others (e.g., Barham, 1990, 1992; cf. Khalil, 1993b) neglect. First, there are the feedbacks which enhance learning through trial-and-error which may lead to punctuated evolutionary change – what biologists, psychologists, and economists generally call "development." Second, there are the feedbacks which are simply regulated by equilibrating mechanisms like storms, stock market fluctuations, eco-system dynamics, sleep pattern, heart beat, contraction of the uterus, and so on – what are commonly called "dynamics."

The proposed complex/system distinction of natural phenomena or, what is the same thing, the organization/structure dichotomy of orders seems consistent with the naturalist agenda. A natural complex could be a non-living entity like an atom. In contrast, a natural system – like the market or ecosystem – could be made up of living entities of people and other organisms, or – like the market and temperament rhythms – appear as an aspect of a living entity like the polity or organism.

To sharpen the suggested complex/system dichotomy, let us review first the ways Christine Skarda (1991) and Robert Rosen (1991; see also 1987) view the joints of nature. What their divergent approaches share with the proposed complex/system dichotomy is the suspicion of the appropriate-ness of the nonlinear dynamics heuristic, or the generic structure order metaphor, as the basis for understanding biological or organization order.

In particular, Skarda makes a radical distinction between systems like "storms, waves, clouds" and entities like "embryos, slime mold, and brains." According to her, while both exhibit nonlinearity, "nonlinearity does not itself help us grasp what invests matter with life. . . . Nonlinearity is necessary, but not sufficient to explain life" (Skarda, 1991, p. 222).

For Skarda, living matter like slime mold exhibits adaptive behavior in the sense of seeking survival in a biofunctional or teleonomic manner, while storms and waves are not adaptive. Moreover, Skarda maintains that only encephalic (brain characterized) organisms are purposive or what she calls "goal-directed."[11]

While she sees a radical rift in the joints of nature along the encephalic/anencephalic boundary, let us focus on her more important living/non-living divide. The divide certainly invites the charge of anti-naturalism and maybe even vitalism. That is, the thesis that the adaptive behavior of bacteria cannot be found in abiotic nature raises the question, from where did adaptive behavior arise? It must be pulled out of a hat either as an unprecedented emergent novelty or as an extra-natural vital force.

In contrast, Rosen provides a way of conception which accounts for purposive behavior without resorting to the encephalic/anencephalic divide or even the living/non-living distinction à la Skarda. He argues that the molecular level is where "one would expect physical theory to have its most immediate direct impact on biology" (Rosen, 1987, p. 316). In his analysis of the vehicle for carrying primary genetic information, he argues that the

relation of this sub-system of observables to the entire molecule in which it is embedded . . . is an example of a sub-system which is *not fractionable* from the molecule. That is, there is no physical procedure which can separate the molecule into two parts or sub-systems, one of which is the active site and the other of which is 'everything else.' We can describe the whole *molecule* in standard quantum-theoretic terms . . ., but we cannot recover the site from this description. . . . In a sense, the above considerations support . . . [the view that] enzyme is active site, not entire molecule, but the site is not fractionable from the molecule in which it is embedded.

(ibid., p. 317)

It is important for Rosen to reject the idea that subsystem is fractionable; it amounts to reductionism, which is common among biologists. The fractionalization of subsystems from the whole, and the consequent separation of "states" from "dynamical laws" could be traced to the Newtonian mode of conception:

At the moment, every mode of system description which we possess in physics, biology, human sciences, technology, or anywhere else, is at heart the same as the one which Newton propounded in the seventeenth century. However much these modes of system description differ technically among themselves, they all share a fundamental dualism, which can be thought of as a separation between *states* and *dynamical laws*. In some sense, the states represent what is intrinsic about a system, while the dynamical laws reflect the effects of what is outside or external.

(ibid., p. 324)

For Rosen, the separation of states and dynamical laws amount to the segregation of the Aristotelian four categories of causality, viz., the efficient, formal, material, and final. For instance, "writing the equations of motion the categories of formal and efficient cause are . . . fractionated from each other" (ibid.). Rosen argues that the class of material systems which could be described through the Newtonian fractioning is a limited class, which he calls "simple systems, or mechanisms." In contrast, his "complex systems" amounts to the non-segregation or interplaying of the four Aristotelian categories. As he puts it,

a simple system is one to which a notion of state can be assigned once and for all; or more generally, one in which the Aristotelian causal categories can be independently segregated from one another. Any system for which such a description cannot be provided I will call *complex*. Thus, in a complex system, the causal categories become intertwined, in such a way that no dualistic language of states plus dynamical laws can completely describe it. Complex systems must then process mathematical images different from, and irreducible to, the generalized dynamical systems which have been considered universal.

(ibid., p. 324)

14

For Rosen, biological organization is the epitome of "complex system" which cannot be reduced to a "simple system." Therefore, he argues repeatedly that biology is the universal science, where physics describes the special or limited cases of "complex system": "I will argue that it is physics, and not biology, which is special" (ibid., p. 315; see also Rosen, 1991). Thus, Rosen seems to maintain that the Newtonian method is valid only to physics "as the science of simple systems or mechanisms," while biology specializes in the study of "complex systems" which "allow a meaningful, scientifically sound category of final causation" (Rosen, 1987, p. 326).

As it turns out, Rosen's way of identifying the junctures of nature also ultimately fall onto the anti-naturalist divide between complex entities like organic molecules and some supposedly "simple systems." While the divide does not run along the living/non-living boundary as is the case with Skarda, it seems to run along organic matter which presupposes living matter, on one hand, and inorganic matter, on the other. It is an anti-naturalist divide because the simple/complex distinction is not about mental images of reality, but rather about reality itself:

> In simple systems, it is forbidden to refer ahead; one must not allow the future characteristics of a temporal sequence to affect what happens in the "present." In complex systems, where things cannot be generically mapped onto single temporal sequences, this difficulty disappears. Functionality appears of itself, without having to try to detour through "states" and state transitions.
>
> (Rosen, 1991, p. 220)

Rosen's simple/complex dichotomy is discussed at some length because it comes closest to recognizing teleonomic and even purposive activity, which typify organization order without appealing to either vitalism or to sophisticated nonlinear dynamics à la chaos theory, Prigogine's far-from-equilibrium thermodynamics, Poincaréan autocatalytics, or others. That is, Rosen's approach does not confuse organization order with structure order. However, his distinction between "complex system" and "simple system" seems to draw a metaphysical boundary between the organic and inorganic. This invites the problem of anti-naturalism – although in a milder form than others.

In comparison, the suggested category "natural complex" or "organization order" throws a wider net than Rosen's "complex system." The concept is Whiteheadian in the sense that it entails that atoms and simple molecules are complexes or organizations in the same ontological sense as cells (see Buchler, 1966). In contrast, as mentioned earlier, the suggested category "natural system" attempts to denote exclusively "structure order," which could be either a facet of the natural complex or the pattern which arises when separable natural complexes interact chaotically, i.e. without any organizing purpose.

To elaborate, while firms, tribes, states, organisms, or cells typify organization order, each one also manifests structure order or non-ergodic dynamics. However, the structures of storms, ecosystems, or stock markets typify *only* structure order. But such a structure order arises from the chaotic interaction of separate molecules, complexes, or organizations. That is, structure order is merely a macroscopic description of the association of organizations which are not cohesive enough to form a higher level organization.

Furthermore, one may object to the characterization of the stock market as equally chaotic as the ecosystem, noting that the stock market is regulated by informal and formal rules, some of which are geared to facilitate the pooling of capital funds. However, the goal intended by these rules makes sense only insofar as the stock market is embedded within a sociopolitical community. That is, the stock market in itself has no goal, but has a goal in reference to the wider sociopolitical community at large. Thus, as long as it is viewed from its level, one could safely say that the stock market, or any other market for that matter, expresses purely structure order.

In summary, structures are either facets of organizations or arise from the chaotic interaction of independent, lower level organizations. Thus, the organization/structure dichotomy or, more generally, the complex/system distinction is not based on drawing a demarcation line between two domains of nature like the living and nonliving or the organic and non-organic. Thus, the organization/structure dichotomy is not anti-naturalist.

Organization/structure dichotomy in terms of organism/ecosystem contrast?

The organization/structure or complex/system divide could be explored further in light of the organism/ecosystem contrast. For example, James Miller (1978) examines society mainly from the organismic standpoint, while Kenneth Boulding (1978) examines society mainly from the ecosystem aspect. In his examination of social organization, as detailed in the final chapter of his *magnum opus*, Miller locates nineteen fundamental functions which are paralleled at the levels of the organism, organ, and cell. In contrast, Boulding likens social dynamics to the self-feeding mechanisms found in ecosystems.[12]

In a reflection on his work, Boulding (1985–86, p. 3) subtly recognizes the difference between organization order and structure order. Boulding identifies Miller's *living systems* as the epitome of that branch of general systems research interested in physiology and organization, i.e., the organization order of "natural complex." In contrast, Boulding identifies his *ecodynamics* as representing the other branch of general system research

16

which is interested in ecological and market dynamics, i.e., the structure order of "natural system."

While at first glance the organism/ecosystem distinction seems self-evident, this is not, in some cases, made clear in theoretical ecology. We start with A. E. Emerson (1939), who argues that populations and their abiotic surroundings in the ecosystem form an interdependent web similar to the organism and, in fact, he calls it a "superorganism." More recently, Günther and Carl Folke (1993) identify nested hierarchy, called "holarcic," which differs from command, non-nested hierarchy characteristic of the army. The "holarcic" hierarchy consists of the levels of cells, organisms, ecosystems, ecosphere. In this manner, no conceptual distinction is made between cells and organisms, on one hand, and ecosystems and ecosphere, on the other. Likewise, James Lovelock (1979) likens the global ecosystem to a breathing superorganism which he calls "Gaia" after the Greek goddess of planet Earth. Even if such a likening is merely metaphoric, it signifies that Lovelock makes no distinction between the configuration of the organism and the configuration of the ecosystem.

Although achieved differently, the distinction between the organism and ecosystem is also obliterated by Jeffrey Wicken (1987) and Bruce Weber *et al.* (1989). They are part of a movement inspired by the "ecological Darwinism" of Alfred Lotka (Khalil, 1994, 1995e). Unlike Lovelock, who views the ecosystem as a superorganism, they conceive the organism as ultimately a miniature ecosystem. The main qualification is that the supposed miniature ecosystem is regulated by genetic information. The likening of the ecosystem and the organism entails that the interdependency of organisms within an ecosystem follows the same canons of organic co-operation observed within an organism.

Let us elucidate the postulated essential difference between firm and market, and concomitantly between organism and ecosystem, by elaborating on the difference between organic interaction, on one hand, and stochastic interaction, on the other. Stochastic interaction involves the pursuit of self-interest without regard to any common purpose. In contrast, organic interaction involves the pursuit of self-interest which is harnessed as part of a common goal of the organization. The conjectured common goal explains why command and authority within organizations are, generally speaking, accepted by the members. Of course, such authority could also be explained in terms of contracts (e.g., Alchian and Demsetz, 1972). However, such an explanation is weak in light of the fact that most contracts are incomplete (i.e., tacit); members seem to accept new directives not anticipated by the explicit contracts. Even when authority is questioned by members, what is at dispute is not usually the function of authority *per se*. Rather, what is challenged is either the content of the directives or the manner in which they are commanded. The acceptance of authority does not appear to be merely the outcome of socialization or

17

enculturation processes: No one has discovered a society without the asymmetrical distribution of power.

It is true that chaotic interaction in a market, which as a whole has no purpose, could be solidified by relations of trust underpinning incomplete contracts. But such trustful relations or incomplete contracts usually concern the strengthening of contingent arrangements of mutual interests on more dependable grounds; i.e., relations based on trust do not necessarily imply a common goal. Even associations like industrial cartels or a league of sovereign states, that could be founded on some relations of trust, are not typified with organic interaction and, hence, they do not form organization order. The binding force of cartels and associations is the coincidence of interests rather than loyalty or commitment to a common goal. The market, hence, resembles in a homologous sense the ecosystem since neither is imbued by a common purpose.

In this light, structure order arises from the coincidence of interests. The interests do not even need to be mutual as in the case of the food web in the ecosystem. Structure order simply expresses the interdependency among diverse actors within a region or even over a period of time. In contrast, organization order expresses cooperation insofar as it is based on the interpenetration of goals as each agent undertakes a specialized task within the whole organization of labor. This does not necessarily imply that the member makes "sacrifices" in order to advance the interest of the family or the firm. Rather, the member could be acting according to a set of tastes which includes the commitment to organizational goals. Thus, the most salient consequence of the proposed organization/structure dichotomy is the distinction between cooperation which arises from mutual interests (market structure) and cooperation which is embedded within common goals (organization).

Ramifications of the organization/structure dichotomy

The transaction cost approach of new institutional economics (Coase, 1937; Williamson, 1985) projects the organization as ultimately a nexus of internalized market contracts. Of course, Oliver Williamson and other neo-classical economists recognize authority relations within the firm. However, the firm is basically conceived as a vehicle for the reconciliation of mutual interests which affords less transaction cost than inter-firm trade. Stated generally, while such a transaction cost theory of organization highlights valuable market aspects of the firm, it tends to neglect common goals which define organization order. The focus on the status of common goals might shed light on the internal processes of development of firms.

The conception of organization *qua* market is not limited to the firm. Orthodox economists tend to conceive the economic society at large exclusively in terms of structure order. Orthodox economists usually apply

Adam Smith's invisible hand metaphor to describe the economy as the interconnection of actors through the forces of supply and demand. In contrast, one cannot understand Adam Smith's usage of the invisible hand metaphor without an appreciation of his natural theology (see Murakoshi, 1988). In such a theology, the deity is portrayed as an "absentee" Lord who is assured of public well-being because actors are equipped with elementary self-interest and sympathetic feelings. While neoclassical equilibrium or structure order of the market could occur in abject poverty, the organization order of Adam Smith must engender prosperity. Put broadly, the question of equilibrating supply and demand concerns the natural-system facet of the economy, while the issues of the rate of investment, innovation, and prosperity, involve the natural-complex aspect of the economy.

To provide further illustration, but without attempting anything close to a thorough review, let us contrast the proposed organization/structure distinction with a famous one with which most sociologists are familiar. Let us start with the dichotomy articulated so extensively by Ferdinand Tönnies (1957). He draws a non-erasable, thick line between rational will (*Kürwille*) and natural or essential will (*Wesenwille*). He employs the two wills to distinguish two types of social organizations which could be traced to, *inter alios*, Plato, Aristotle, and Ibn Khaldun. He calls families, friendships, and religious sects "*Gemeinschaft*" (community) because they are characterized by a spontaneous natural will and pursued for their own sake. In contrast, he calls bureaucracies, enterprises, markets, and states "*Gesellschaft*" (society) because they are characterized by calculative rational will interested in entering contractual arrangements as a means to an end.

In a few places, Tönnies's community/society dichotomy is presented as two facets of human organization in general. Insofar as it is presented as such, the suggested complex/system dichotomy is very close to Tönnies's community/society distinction. However, Tönnies uses his distinction as two *exclusive* human experiences of distinct kinds of human epochs.[13]

If the proposed interpretation is correct, Tönnies's dichotomy is no different from many others which litter the history of social theory. For example, Emile Durkheim (1933) represents the progress towards modernity (and especially socialism) as the emergence of "organic solidarity," ordained by free will, in place of "mechanical solidarity," dictated by traditional roles. This somewhat resembles Max Weber's distinction, notwithstanding his many strained qualifications (e.g., Weber, 1958, pp. 13–31), between modern occidental rationality and the rationality of "distant people," in terms of place and time, from modern Western Europe. We encounter the same typology of societies in anthropology as early as in the work of Sir Henry James Summer Maine, who makes a radical distinction between contract – characterizing modern societies – and status – typifying non-modern societies. This is reflected in one major theme in the sociology of Herbert Spencer (1967) who distinguishes between two types of society: the military, which is based on status, and the industrial, which is based on contract.

In contrast, the advocated organization/structure or complex/system distinction is not about two types of social formations – where one is characterized by solidarity/status and the other by non-sentimental/mechanical contracts. Rather, any human formation, as well as biological entities, seems to exhibit simultaneously system- and complex-like behavior. This does not mean that the discourses about the two facets of a phenomenon should be merged. It would be more fruitful if we approach the phenomenon by two distinct discourses.

With respect to economics, the two discourses would amount to the distinction between the formation of prices in relation to price controls and regulations imposed by the government, on one hand, and the degree of public prosperity with respect to entrepreneurship (including the state as entrepreneur), on the other. While price controls attempt to regulate the outcomes of structure order, the action of the state as an entrepreneur attempts to inform organization order.

The distinction between organization order and structure order or, more generally, natural complex and natural system certainly needs further defense (Khalil, 1990a). It should prove to be useful as an entry point to the identification of the Janus-like character of natural order. In the rest of the chapter I focus only on problems which arise from studying organization order through the naturalist window, ignoring structure order.[14]

ORGANIZATION ORDER: THREE PROBLEMS

I raise only three distinct problems pertaining to organization order (Khalil, 1997). They are usually confused in many theoretical debates. To keep them separate, let us dub them the "metaphysical," "phenomenist," and "ontological" problems:

(1) Metaphysical question: Do humans differ from the class of nonhuman organisms lumped together? Or does human behavior basically lack intentionally (or purposefulness) – i.e., subjected exclusively to efficient causality – as is supposedly the case with nonhuman behavior?[15]

(2) Phenomenist question: Does the scheme of traits (which could be particular habits of an individual or general habits shared with other individuals in the form of culture in the sense of institutions/customs) express a deep essence? Or is the scheme – as neoclassical economists and adaptationist biologists put it – the outcome of optimization and, hence, easily malleable?

(3) Ontological question: Is the behavior of organizational complexity fully explainable by the behavior of lower-level, constitutive individuals? Or

are social phenomena reducible to the pre-constituted strategy of its members, whose behavior could (but not necessarily) be further reduced to the pre-constituted strategy of genes?

The three problems are not an exhaustive list of the issues surrounding organization order. Specifically, although related, I disregard naturalist epistemology, as opposed to the anti-naturalist kinds such as objectivist and relativist epistemologies (see Bernstein, 1983).[16] Although germane, I also neglect naturalist ethics, as opposed to the anti-naturalist kinds like absolutist/prescriptive and relativist/descriptive ethics.[17] All these issues attend to the broad definition of naturalism. Naturalism advocates the conception of human purposes, institutions, organization, epistemology, and ethics as part of nature in the sense that there is no need to appeal to extra-natural principles or separate qualities (like scientific reason, intentionally, or spirituality) to account for the human phenomenon. Naturalism simply completes the Copernican dethroning of man from any meta-natural position.[18]

The metaphysical problem

The metaphysical problem deals with the issue of whether humans possess intentionality in a way which defies the deterministic, covering-law model of explanation (Khalil, 1996a). This issue seems to be the exclusive axis according to which Roy Bhasker (1979) classifies the anti-naturalist tradition, stretching from Vico and Dilthey to Weber and late Wittgenstein, against the naturalist tradition, which includes positivist philosophy of science. There is definitely an epistemological aspect to the question, viz., whether social and natural phenomena could be explained through the same methodology, which is ignored here. The focus is rather on the teleological aspect – and even then only a limited sense of "teleology." In light of Ernst Mayr's (1992) clarification, the term "teleology" has at least four meanings.[19]

As employed here, the term "teleology" is limited to the sense of purposeful or intentional action understood as entrepreneurial. The concept "purpose" or "intention" has proven to be profoundly enigmatic. Purpose could be defined formally as involving outcomes with a probability distribution which is somewhat conditional on the actor's estimate of ability.[20] This means that the future could, to some extent, determine the present since the future is partially undetermined at the theoretical level.

The concept of purposeful action has been the subject of discussion and development by G. L. S. Shackle (1952, 1970) and Austrian economists. These economists advance a perspective, sometimes called subjectivist economics (O'Driscoll and Rizzo, 1985; Buchanan and Vanberg, 1991), which stresses the role of entrepreneurial activity or creativity in creating

21

new economic opportunities. It is true that John Maynard Keynes (1937) and many post-Keynesians like Hyman Minsky (1975, 1982; see also Sethi, 1992) attend to the role of expectations and money in setting off economic instability and even depressions. But the Keynesian notion of expectation differs from the Austrian one in one important regard, namely, the Keynesian project is interested in studying how speculative financial markets could derail real economic variables, i.e., how the tail wags the dog. This might be appropriate for the study of the business cycle and other economic structures; in contrast, the Austrian project focuses on how expectations form the real world ranging from the organization of division of labor to the process of evolution. The idea of purpose employed here is closer to the Austrian project in the sense of relating entrepreneurial action to the tempo of economic development.

Such a sense of action (which does not mean all actions are purposeful) is contrary to the adaptationist agenda of neo-Darwinism. According to the adaptationist approach, any useful trait is not the result of directed mutation and creativity on the part of the organism (Khalil, 1993a). Rather, it is the outcome of nature not favoring successful differential reproduction of individuals that have less favorable traits.[21]

With respect to the metaphysical issue, the crude naturalist position in the human sciences, as best epitomized in B. F. Skinner's (1971) behaviorism, postulates that, similar to the neo-Darwinian agenda, humans are basically selected to act favorably to stimuli. In this fashion, intentionality is not introduced by humans from nowhere; there is no supranatural phenomenon emerging with the appearance of humans. With regard to the metaphysical sense of naturalism, crude naturalism amounts to the proposition of the continuity of purposeless mechanisms.

In comparison, the anti-naturalist position, as best expressed in the later work of Ludwig Wittgenstein, maintains that humans have "kicked" the naturalist, evolutionary ladder once they have emerged. So that humans, unlike all animals and plants, behave according to intention and purpose. Such a position certainly introduces a discontinuity in nature insofar as the metaphysical question is concerned.

Interestingly, the crude naturalist and anti-naturalist stands assume that nature has no room for purposeful behavior. That is, they presume, without empirical evidence, that nonhuman organisms lack intentionality. Such an assumption is problematic on two grounds. First, it is based on a dubious opposition between humans and nonhuman organisms. A non-crude naturalist position would maintain that the category "nonhuman organisms" is anthropocentric at best. It amounts to the lumping of bacteria, pine trees, slugs, honey bees, and chimpanzees around a nominal criterion. It is nominal because it could only be made valid with reference to the human observer: Since humans cannot tell if birds and bees act purposefully, they must not act purposefully. But human ignorance cannot justify any positive assertion.

Second, there are enormous new findings, suggested by some of the contributors here, that organisms do not act according to efficient causality only (Khalil, 1996a). Organisms behave differently according to opportunities in the environment. Thus, they must process the information and make judgments about the best strategy of behavior. This might not suggest creativity, but their behavior is not restricted to reacting to the given environment. They act purposefully when they create their own environments. Organisms in general do not take the environment as given. The amount of nutrients in the environment is a function also of the way in which they define them in light of their potential capability. The creativity encompasses the collection of food, selection of mating partners, and protection of the self. If such behavior suggests anything, it at least means that there is no sudden fault dividing the categories "humans" and "nonhumans." Insofar as one is ready to admit that humans deliberate over the best action and create new circumstances, one should not a priori reject the same features in the other category.

A non-crude naturalist position would be ready to entertain the idea of continuity of action across species, without a priori denying that such action may involve intentionality. One might want to specify differences among species in the way their respective organisms make judgments and make use of their potential, but these differences cannot be a priori posed as about radical jumps in nature. They may turn out to be differences in emphasis and gradation, rather than in kind.

The phenomenist problem

The phenomenist question deals with whether traits, taxonomic and institutional schemes of behavior, and surface appearances are regulated by deep essences or universals (Khalil, 1996b). To simplify, the crude naturalist position – which is unrelated to the position stated with respect to intentionality – maintains that the shared scheme of traits among individuals, or the particularized scheme of traits (i.e., habits), is the outcome of a Plato-like deep essence.[22] The old institutional school à la Thorstein Veblen and even constitutional economics à la Friedrich Hayek view the set of group norms or spontaneous cultural rules as a deep regulating essence. Some recent philosophers of economics have been critical of positivist views of the subject matter of economics and instead have been arguing for "realism," the idea of essence underlying sense data (see Lawson, 1989, 1994; Mäki, 1990; Smith, 1990; Foss, 1994).[23]

In contrast, the anti-naturalist perspective, usually advanced by neoclassical economists and behaviorist psychologists, dismisses the notion of deep, underlying nature as non-scientific at best. They rather stress that

23

traits are superficial features used for convenience (efficiency) reasons. Thus, as circumstances change, they are dispensable insofar as not obstructed by relatively high transaction costs.

The phenomenist question is not, as is the case with the ontological problem concerning reductionism, whether a behavior or a preference at the level of the firm could be reduced to the preferences of the members. The question is rather whether a trait or a habitual institution is real in the sense of being "natural" (i.e., immovable) as universalists in the Platonic tradition maintain. Or is it nominal in the sense of being superficial and the product of optimality calculation or convention as anti-essentialists (i.e., anti-naturalists) usually postulate?[24] The phenomenist question persists even if we take a hypothetical non-complex agent, i.e., consisting only of one level of organization. To recast the phenomenist question, is a habitual institution or taxonomic trait a part of the "identity" or "nature" of the agent, or is it a convenient rule or trait which could be disposed of, if transaction costs are low enough, in case of new circumstances?

The Platonic, crude naturalist perspective views the trait as deeply embedded in the identity of the agent. This is taken to the point of making the agent oblivious to new circumstances which necessitate the revision of the trait or institution. This view is propagated in economics by the followers of Thorstein Veblen (e.g., Hodgson, 1989, 1994). It is also advanced in evolutionary biology by the followers of D'Arcy Thompson who stress the persistence of the taxonomic scheme which they call "structure" (e.g., Gould and Lewontin, 1979).

The anti-naturalist approach with regard to the phenomenist question is deeply distrustful of ideas about deep essences. The nominalist, anti-naturalist viewpoint emphasizes that traits and institutions are the product of optimization calculation either made by agents or made for them by the Darwinian natural selection mechanism. But how can one explain the persistence of inefficient traits or institutions? The nominalist view maintains that it must be high transaction costs which hinder agents from changing the inefficient schemes. Such a view informs much of what is currently dubbed as neoclassical or new institutional economics (Hodgson, 1989).

A non-crude naturalist stand would make a distinction between origin and existence (Khalil, 1996b). With respect to origin, it might be true that some taxonomic and institutional schemes have arisen because they afford greater efficiency measured in terms of maximizing output per unit of effort. However, with regard to existence, many schemes persist because they have become, through time, part of the identity of the agent. They become so because they do not only afford efficiency, but also inform the agent on how to perceive the environment and divide it into resources and opportunities. As part of identity, it might be easier for the agent to perish and an organization to become extinct than to change its identity in order to adapt to new circumstances.

24

The origin/existence distinction, however, entails that the simple neo-classical thesis of global optimization has to be given up. New schemes which afford greater efficiency could only be adopted by taking older and deeper grades as given. The agent always takes a certain grade of identity as inflexible when he reviews more recent grades. Even when agents go further and re-examine deeper schemes, they would still do so by standing on much deeper taxonomic/institutional schemes. The agent cannot simply step outside millions of years of evolution and maximize.

Given the origin/existence distinction, old institutionalists such as Veblen and new institutionalists such as neoclassical economists need not be alternative to each other. A non-crude naturalist position would maintain that deeper essences are not "natural" to the extent that they could not have risen from optimization. But the fact that they have originated from optimization does not mean they cannot persist beyond what is justified by transaction costs.

The ontological problem

The ontological question deals with whether a trait at a higher level of individuality – like nation, tribe, firm, or troop of organisms – could be traced, almost exhaustively, to the traits of the constitutive components (Khalil, 1995f). If so, such a reductionist practice or ontological individualist approach should not be confused with methodological individualism. As Steven Lukes (1973, p. 118) argues, methodological individualism "advances a range of different claims in accordance with how much of 'society' is built into the supposedly explanatory 'individuals'."

In this sense, the use of the term "individual" raises the methodological or epistemological search for the best strategy of explanation: Should we start with the whole or should we commence with the part in order to explain the specified macro-phenomenon? The starting point may not be packed with a theoretical proposition about the origin or determination of the preferences, capabilities, and traits of the individuals. Thus, methodo-logical individualism may not present a position on how to conceive the phenomenon under focus.

In contrast, the ontological question, as differentiated here, deals with the more substantive issue of reductionist vs functional-holist perspectives of the phenomenon at hand: Are social organizations like households, firms, tribes, and nations constructed structures by preconstituted indi-viduals – like the construction of marked networks and industrial cartels by agents? Or are such organizations naturally engendered individuals, i.e., with self-determined autonomy very much like their constitutive, lower level individual agents?

Such an ontological question is certainly the most debated subject in metatheoretical discussions in social and biological sciences. In diverse approaches, the contributions in this volume by Hubert Hendrichs,

25

Jean-Pierre Dupuy, Henri Laborit, and Gregory Stock and John Campbell emphasize the role of context and higher level processes, without ditching the naturalist stress on lower-level units.

To be clear, the ontological question about the context-sensitivity of organization is independent of the previous issue of the universalism vs the nominalism of the scheme of traits and institutions. The two are commonly confused in the theory of the firm and large-scale social organizations like the state (Khalil, 1995c). Assuming that a scheme of traits/institutions of an individual like the firm is deep (i.e., the scheme is sustained by habits or Herbert Simon's rules of thumb, rather than by current optimization), the question remains whether the organization which is underpinned by the scheme could be exhaustively explained (i.e., reduced) in terms of the preferences of the members of the organization. If it could be explained, the firm would, in fact, be a structure order, rather than an individual in the sense of being indivisible without the loss of goals.

With regard to the ontological problem, the crude naturalist position would like to explain the behavior of the firm as the result of the behavior of members at the lower level of organization. In comparison, the anti-naturalist position presents the firm as a hegemonic individual, i.e., capable of greatly shaping the behavior of the lower-level individuals.

A naturalist approach would be critical of the functional-holist thesis which makes the members' strategies a function of the organization's goals, where the organization is viewed as a hegemonic or muscular individual (Khalil, 1995d). However, this should not lead us to a crude naturalism which reduces the objective of the organization to the separate goals of the members. If one adopts the view that individuality is a complex hierarchy of levels (Pribram in this volume; Khalil, 1995f), it would be possible to show how higher level group individuality could be entertained without denying that the lower level, constitutive components are also individuals. The contributors to this volume show, in diverse and concrete ways, how naturalist viewpoints could avoid the pitfalls of crude naturalism without appealing to anti-naturalist arguments.

Ramifications of the three-way distinction

The distinctions among the three problem areas pose a challenge as well as an opportunity to decipher any complex theoretical tradition – such as Marxian theory, neoclassical economics, institutional economics, behaviorism, structuralism, functionalist sociological theory, neo-Darwinism, and so on – according to these diverse issues. To return to Skinner, for instance, he would be considered a "crude" naturalist with regard to the first problem area: He advocates the human/nonhuman continuity thesis on the ground that humans, like animals, most likely do not possess intentionality or do not act purposefully.

However, in light of the essay by the neurologist Karl H. Pribram (in this volume), Skinner would be considered an anti-naturalist with respect to the third question (on which many of the contributors focus): Skinner does not explain behavior by reducing it to lower level neurological and genetic predispositions. As Pribram states, Skinner regarded the identification of behavioral and brain sciences as if the two objects of study belong to the same level of complexity, to be a "cardinal sin." If we regard the first and third questions as distinct, there would be no contradiction in Skinner's position.

With respect to the second question, orthodox neoclassical economists (and orthodox neo-Darwinists as well) should be viewed, in general, as anti-naturalists: They broadly conceive individual differences not as deviations from some Platonic essence or common nature; rather, the differences are seen as stochastic variations which express the uniqueness of the individual. That is, individuals are presumably not connected by some common nature. Such a position is anti-naturalist because it denies that there is an underpinning reality behind the phenomena.

With regard to the third question, however, neoclassical economists (and orthodox neo-Darwinists also) should be judged as crude naturalists: They see the firm (or organism) as merely a structure or a vehicle for the pursuit of the pre-given interests of the constitutive members. That is, firms (or organisms) are supposedly social associations which could be ultimately reduced to lower level entities. Such a position is crude naturalist because it does not recognize higher level or social organization as an individual in its own right.

If we consider the second and third questions as distinct, the orthodox orientation towards them (as anti-naturalist and crude naturalist, respectively) should not be considered inconsistent. In general, the distinctions among the three problem areas make it easier to understand different touching points among diverse traditions. Also, they shed light on why it is not inconsistent for a social theory (as well as a biological theory) to adopt a naturalist position with regard to one question, but an anti-naturalist attitude towards the other two.

CONCLUSION

To summarize, the first section tried to strike a wedge between crude naturalism and non-crude naturalism. The second section attempted to differentiate structure order and organization order. With respect to organization order, the third section tried to draw distinctions, on one hand, between the metaphysical and phenomenist questions and, on the other, between the phenomenist and ontological areas of research. The contrasts are proposed on the basis that the advocacy of the continuity of nature and the unity of science would not otherwise be specified sufficiently.

There are many ways to cut the cake and present the complexity of the joints of nature. Each way might turn out to be fruitful once the investigator's question is identified. However, if the purpose is to encompass greater numbers of phenomena within the simplest explanatory apparatus, the naturalist approach seems to be a fertile field to plant the seeds. While the contributors to follow have diverse orientations, and certainly come from disparate specializations, they share the same vision: Namely, we would attain a better understanding of our affairs and behavior if we situate humans within the creative, habitual, and context-sensitive world of the naturals.

NOTES

I appreciate the comments of Ernst Mayr, Mary Douglas, Roger Masters, Charles Tilly, Michael Ghiselin, David Hull, Karl H. Pribram, Timothy Shanahan, Glenn Hartz, Victor Burke, A. W. (Bob) Coats, and especially Martin O'Connor and James Murphy. I also acknowledge the technical help of Carole Brown and Patricia Markley. But they should not be blamed for any remaining errors.

1 While Adam Smith recognizes the prevalent psychological longing for simplicity and beauty as the motivation behind theory construction, he does not dismiss, as is the case with the deconstructive agenda discussed shortly, the search for truth (Khalil, 1989).
2 In his discussion of the concepts of "organism" and "evolution" in the history of twentieth-century economics, Martin O'Connor (1988; see also Murphy, 1993) emphasizes also that a naturalist perspective need not be reductionist and mechanistic.
3 To be fair, Spencer should be credited for coining the term "superorganic" for what is referred to in anthropology as "culture." For Spencer, society is composed of what biologists refer to as "structures" and "functions" which are subject to evolutionary forces. Thus, he also should be recognized for not upholding the pseudo opposition between evolutionary thought and what came to be called later structural–functional analysis (Levy, 1968). The evolutionary/functionalist opposition was assumed in much of the debate surrounding the merits of structural–functional analysis in twentieth-century sociology and anthropology.
4 To be precise, whether a likeness is homologous or heterologous depends on, first, how specific the focus is and, second, on whether we are interested in what biologists name "patristic" as opposed to "cladistic" comparison. With regard to the first issue, it is proper to say that "the forelimbs of a bird and the forelimbs of a bat are homologous" since they emanate from a common scheme. But it is incorrect to state that "the wings of a bird and the wings of a bat are homologous." This is not a question of linguistic maneuvers or socially constructed criteria. Rather, when one specifies the taxon trait, rather than the relatively generic term "limbs" to the more differentiated term "wings," one changes the context. While there is a common scheme for the forelimbs of bats and birds, there is no common scheme (or what biologists call "structure" given by the common origin) for the specified wings of a bird and wings of a bat. In fact, once the employed taxon trait is narrowed, biologists regard the wings of a bird and the wings of a bat as heterologous. Another example, the hindlegs of a kangaroo (a marsupial mammal) and the hindlegs of a rat kangaroo (a placental mammal) are homologous. However, once the employed scheme or trait is

narrowed to the hopping hindlegs of the two mammals, the similarity is heterologous: The hopping trait in both animals is merely the result of convergent evolution (homoplasy). That is, the hopping features in both animals do not emanate from a common scheme; they have evolved independently.

With regard to the second issue, all the examples mentioned so far involve cladistic comparison, i.e., cross-comparison of features in separate organisms in relation to whether they were present in a common ancestor. However, we employ patristic comparison when we invoke temporal contrast between a feature in an animal with an antecedent feature in a supposed ancestor.

These are intricate issues. The point is to show that metaphors could give rise to misunderstandings as much as to illuminations. (I owe the detailing to Mark Ronan.)

5 To complete the argument, if Mirowski is to follow the steps of neoclassical economics and reduce the tastes and goals of groups to the members' psychobiologically based (or whatever) utility functions, he would still be adhering to the biological/social dichotomy. That is, the mere denial of a realm (the social or the biological) by one approach or another does not mean necessarily the denial of the dichotomy.

6 See David Bloor (1982) for a modern defense the Durkheim–Mauss postulate drawn from the study of the history of physics and especially corpuscular philosophy.

7 I owe the reference to Scott Atran's work to David Hull.

8 Thus, for isolated systems, i.e., which are neither infused with energy nor with matter, equilibrium is attained because there are no exogenous forces which would give origin to the spontaneous rise of structure order. For instance, a hurricane forms a structure order with a center, but an isolated chamber of gas has no such pattern. What we have in isolated systems instead is static order. Static order typifies phenomena like a crystal of salt which is more statically orderly than liquid salt; similarly, ice is more statically orderly than liquid water, which is, in turn, more statically orderly than vapor. Static order is ignored here. It is mentioned only in order to clarify that it is a subspecies of structure order.

9 It is worth noting that Pribram's terminology "holonomy" comes closest to denoting the proposed structure order since he distinguishes it from organization order which he calls "structure" (Pribram, 1991).

10 With regard to Hayek, his position is more intricate because his most fundamental entry point is the distinction between natural order and artificial order – not the two kinds of natural order (organization and structure) as proposed here. Hayek classifies any kind of organization within the realm of artificial order – while it is proposed here that organization order is one kind of natural order.

This interpretation of Hayek needs some defense. Hayek draws a radical distinction between two kinds of order (which in actual phenomena could overlap somewhat): spontaneous order of *cosmos* and organization or *taxis*:

[T]he first important difference between a spontaneous order or *cosmos* and an organisation (arrangement) or *taxis* is that, not having been deliberately made by men, a *cosmos* has no purpose. . . .

A *cosmos* will result from regularities of the behaviour of the elements which it comprises. It is in this sense endogenous, intrinsic or, as the cyberneticians say, a "self-regulating" or "self-organising" system. A *taxis*, on the other hand, is determined by an agency which stands outside the order and is in the same sense exogenous or imposed.

(Hayek, 1978, pp. 73–74)

For Hayek, each kind of order is regulated by a different kind of canon (which he confusingly calls "rule"). The purposeless *cosmos* is underpinned by institution called "*nomos.*" *Nomos* is a rule of just conduct applying to any agent who falls under the stated circumstances irrespective of results. Thus, *nomos* is an end-independent kind of canon:

> By *nomos* we shall describe a universal rule of just conduct applying to an unknown number of future instances and equally to all persons in the objective circumstances described by the rule, irrespective of the effects which observance of the rule will produce in a particular situation. . . . Such rules are generally described as "abstract" and are independent of individual ends. They lead to the formation of an equally abstract and end-independent spontaneous order or *cosmos.*

(Hayek, 1978, p. 77)

In comparison, the purposeful *taxis* operates according to a goal "*thesis,*" a different kind of rule. *Thesis* is a canon concerning a particular task applying to specific persons. Thus, *thesis* is an end-dependent kind of rule:

> In contrast, we shall use *thesis* to mean any rule which is applicable only to particular people or in the service of the ends of rulers. Though such rules may still be general to various degrees and refer to a multiplicity of particular instances, they will shade imperceptibly from rules in the usual sense to particular commands. They are the necessary instrument of running an organisation or *taxis.*

(Hayek, 1978, p. 77)

Hayek is very clear that organization order like the firm (*taxis*), as quoted above, "is determined by an agency which stands outside the order." Therefore, the firm's order is an artifact, not different from the arrangement of furniture in the house or the making of a chair. In these cases, the actor is not part of the designed orchestration. Likewise, for Hayek, the firm's end expresses only the "unitary hierarchy of ends" of the organizer when the utilization of limited resources through the firm is more effective than leaving it to spontaneous, interfirm exchange:

> Where it is a question of using limited resources known to the organiser in the service of a unitary hierarchy of ends, an arrangement or organisation (*taxis*) will be the more effective method. But where the task involves using knowledge dispersed among and accessible only to thousands or millions of separate individuals, the use of spontaneous ordering forces (*cosmos*) will be superior.

(Hayek, 1978, p. 76)

So, for Hayek, the goal which the organization is commanded to pursue is not a common purpose consented to by the members of the organization – much as the furniture which is arranged cannot consent to the goal of the arranger. Hayek simply confuses the intentional manipulation of things to attain a goal like building a chair with the intentional deliberation among members to sustain a purpose like an organization. While both differ from the intentionless market order, they are not equal. Hayek's equation of the two amounts to the view of the organization as an artifact which lacks autonomy and, hence, cannot present the firm as a natural entity to begin with.

11 Almost all multicellular species of animals are encephalic.

12 Earlier, Boulding (1934) modelled capital goods as non-fungible organisms with certain life-spans – where the birth and death rates determine the growth rate of capital accumulation.

13 Tönnies states:

> In the most general way, one could speak of a Gemeinschaft comprising the whole of mankind, such as the Church wishes to be regarded. But human Gesellschaft is conceived as mere coexistence of people independent of each other.
>
> (Tönnies, 1957, p. 34)

> [T]he theory of Gemeinschaft starts from the assumption of perfect unity of human wills as an original or natural condition which is preserved in spite of actual separation. This natural condition is found in manifold forms because of dependence on the nature of the relationship between individuals who are differently conditioned.
>
> (ibid., p. 37)

> The theory of the Gesellschaft deals with the artificial construction of an aggregate of human beings which superficially resembles the Gemeinschaft in so far as the individuals live and dwell together peacefully. However, in the Gemeinschaft they remain essentially united in spite of all separating factors, whereas in the Gesellschaft they are essentially separated in spite of all uniting factors. In the Gesellschaft, as contrasted with the Gemeinschaft, we find no actions that can be derived from an a priori and necessarily existing unity; no actions, therefore, which manifest the will and the spirit of the unity even if performed by the individual; no actions which, in so far as they are performed by the individual, take place on behalf of those united with him. In the Gesellschaft such actions do not exist. On the contrary, here everybody is by himself and isolated, and there exists a condition of tension against all others.
>
> (ibid., pp. 64–65)

14 Structure order invokes issues like the merits of atomism, which is the basis of the Boltzmann law of gases, as opposed to collectivism, which characterizes the Clausius statement of the same law (Atkins, 1984, p. 25). The question of atomism versus collectivism appears most strikingly in the structure ordering of electron spins which is behind the magnetism phenomenon. Philip Anderson (in Anderson et al., 1988, pp. 265–273) argues that such ordering might inform the modeling of feedbacks and chaotic patterns which characterize human markets.

15 The term "efficiency" is used in the Aristotelian sense to signify when the cause is antecedent to the event. It is one type of causality which juxtaposes with, but not necessarily in placement of, final causality, i.e., purposive or teleological behavior. The term "efficient causality" seems preferable over "mechanistic causality" because the latter is more restrictive. The term "mechanism" usually entails efficient causality plus the operation of such a causality in a linear, non-recursive fashion which rules out autocatalytic feedbacks. That is, the word "efficient" could denote both mechanistic modeling as well as recursive, autocatalytic reasoning.

16 A prime example of naturalist epistemology is Alfred North Whitehead's

(1933, pp. 13–16) universalist classification of all ideas into two camps: the senseless drive away from inherited modes of order and the formulated beliefs of aspirations towards the refashioning of order. A less crude naturalist epistemology, which expresses the development process of thought, could be found in Adam Smith's (1980; Khalil, 1989) essay on astronomy.

In contrast, examples of objectivist epistemology include the Vienna circle of logical positivism, Karl Popper's falsificationism, and axiomatic foundational theories of justification in general. The categorization of objectivist epistemology as anti-naturalist is certainly strange given its advocacy of the unity of scientific methodology across the social and natural sciences. However, it is anti-naturalist in the sense of devising non-natural axioms of justification.

Meanwhile, examples of relativist epistemology embrace as diverse works as those of Richard Rorty, Paul Feyerband, (somewhat) Thomas Kuhn, and Darwinian evolutionary epistemologists (Khalil, 1995b). The classification of relativist epistemology, especially the Darwinian variant, as anti-naturalist is certainly curious (Khalil, 1992c, pp. 41–42). It seems that Darwinian evolutionary epistemology is basically relativist because it regards paradigms as different adaptations to peculiar and changing environments; i.e., paradigms lack any developmental or intrinsic link. As put by Donald Campbell (1974, 1990; see *passim* Shimony and Nails, 1987), its most articulate exponent, paradigms arise from the mechanism of blind variation and selective retention. In this manner, Darwinian epistemology provides, in the final analysis, a relativist description of the rise of cognitive and scientific theories.

Thus, it would be confusing to call Darwinian evolutionary epistemology "naturalist." But such a name seems to have been used in the sense that it is a descriptive (which means relativist) rather than a prescriptive. That is, it is a philosophy of science which is informed by the findings of cognitive and neural sciences. As Philip Kitcher's (1992) survey shows and the interviews in Werner Callebaut's (1993) volume record, such epistemological naturalism has been experiencing a revival lately. However, the tendency towards description, relativism, and anti-foundationalism is not the sense in which the term "naturalism" is used here.

17 Roger Masters lays out a lucid taxonomy with respect to the origin of justice in Western thought (which differs from the question of whether passion or reason is the source of knowledge of the just):

> Broadly speaking, there have been three main approaches to the question of justice in Western legal thought and philosophy: *relativism* or *nominalism* (the view that because justice is a convention or cultural opinion, the sense of justice is an unnatural rule or standard created by humans and varying from one place to another), *absolutism* or doctrinal orthodoxy (the view that justice is established by divine will or historical necessity and beyond dispute among the true believers or full members of the community), and *naturalism* (the understanding of justice as a feeling, intuition, or rational principle based on nature but taking different forms in specific circumstances).
>
> (Masters in Masters and Gruter, 1992, p. 68;
> see also Masters, 1989, 1991)

The relativist view of justice as non-natural corresponds to descriptive stories. This should not be confused with the neoclassical view. The view treats moral tastes as natural in the sense as not arising from a ground different from the more familiar tastes. Such a view is naturalist, although a crude account of the self. It presents the self as a plane which lacks complexity, composed of a unidimensional utility function. In this light, the absolutist perspective of justice somewhat corresponds to the multiple-self view advanced by Amartya Sen (1980/1981) and Amitai Etzioni (1986). They appeal to some non-natural grounds unrelated to the more familiar pleasure utility in order to account for the moral self and obligatory commitments (Khalil, 1995a). In contrast, the naturalist account of justice could be found in Adam Smith's (1976) *The Theory of Moral Sentiments*. While Smith does not reduce justice to sympathy, which would have been no different from the neoclassical account, he does not appeal to a non-natural ground (Khalil, 1990b).

18 Defined in that sense, naturalism should not be confused with other issues. To mention two of them, first, the term "naturalism," instead of "ecologicalism" has been unfortunately used in the literature (e.g., Davis, 1995) as about the limits posed by nature which Karl Marx vehemently rejected (Khalil, 1992b). The Malthusian idea views human production, or even nonhuman production à la Darwin, as propelled to grow (with population growth) beyond what can be sustained by the diminishing returns in agriculture. This Ricardian idea has been adopted, with some modifications to include all natural resources, by modern ecological economists (Christensen, 1989; Judson, 1989; cf. Khalil, 1995e). But this is not about naturalism, but rather the interface of the agent and environmental resources. Second, naturalism has nothing to do with political arguments that a certain form of authority or income distribution represents a natural order and, hence, should not be questioned. The use of the metaphor "nature" in support of the status quo is meaningless since it assumes the issue it tries to advance. What is *natural* about a particular organization order to start with?

19 To reconstruct his many presentations, Mayr (e.g., 1992) clarifies that *telos* has been used in the senses of "endpoint," "goal," "final goal," and "purpose." First, teleology as "endpoint" is illustrated by changes, which he calls "teleomatic," like rivers flowing to an endpoint, storms moving towards calm, ecosystems reaching a balance, markets arriving at equilibrium between supply and demand, and hot teapots reaching room temperature. Second, teleology as "goal" is represented by changes, which he calls "teleonomic," like a chick developing from an egg, an animal escaping from a predator, and an eyelid closing in reflex. Third, which Mayr understandably dismisses, teleology as "final goal" is exemplified by presumed orthogenesis; i.e., evolution, as a result of cosmic laws, moves the subject towards a higher purpose, freedom, material comfort, justice, spirit, reason, or God. Fourth, teleology as "purpose" or "intention" is represented as in the cases of stating that birds acquired wings in order to fly, some primates attained the thumb in order to grasp, mammals gained hair to preserve temperature, and humans developed language, money, property rights, and airplanes in order to make life more convenient. Concerning the sense of teleology as purpose, the concern here, Mayr repudiates it in general – but is ready to restrict it to human action. He repudiates teleology as purpose on the ground that the neo-Darwinian agenda provides an explanation for wings and thumbs, viz., adaptation as a result of natural selection, without resorting to purpose.

20 The estimation of self-ability is far from a subjective issue, where an incorrect estimation is corrected by experience. The agent could always dismiss actual experiences as more the product of intervening external "bad luck" than true revelations of ability. In this manner, a tenacious entrepreneur does not give up easily his faith in his capability. So, experience cannot present a clear, unambiguous test upon which the agent can solidly change his faith in his ability.

21 While biologists use language suggesting organisms acting purposefully, such language is just for shorthand. As Stephen Jay Gould maintains, such shorthand is meant to say that natural selection has favored adapted traits behind the back of the unit of selection:

> When he [Richard Dawkins] says that genes strive to make more copies of themselves, he means: "selection has operated to favor genes that, by chance, varied in such a way that more copies survived in subsequent generations."
>
> (Gould in Sober, 1984, p. 122)

Likewise, Mayr states that, in light of neo-Darwinian natural selection theory, useful features are "adapted" in the sense that it is the environment which selects what is useful, not the organism. In fact, this implies that the organism is passive and whatever is useful appears as *post hoc*:

> To be sure, natural selection is an optimization process, but it has no definite goal, and considering the number of constraints and the frequency of chance events, it would be most misleading to call it teleological. Nor is any improvement in adaptation a teleological process, since it is strictly a *post hoc* decision whether a given evolutionary change qualifies as a contribution to adaptedness.
>
> (Mayr, 1992, p. 132)

Along the same line, Robert Brandon (1981) argues that adaptationist language should replace the teleological terms (in the sense of intentionality) used casually by biologists. Such a proposal expresses the crux of the neo-Darwinian agenda: The dismissal of the idea of directed mutation in the sense that organisms, in light of severe environmental stresses, could act in a purposive manner.

22 Although such a position is a caricature of Plato's ideas, this is not the place for textual exegesis. At first approximation, Platonian naturalism is understood here as the advocacy of the primacy of some eternal forms.

23 As Tony Lawson (1994, p. 220) clarifies, the recent interest in realism in economics is mostly concerned with "scientific realism," i.e., the idea that objects of scientific knowledge exist independently of the probing scientist. This is related but somewhat different from the idea of the reality of universals or, what Roy Bhasker (1978) calls, "predicative realism."

24 The opposite terms "universalism" and "nominalism" are employed in the same sense by the economist Karl Pribram (1983, ch. 1) (not to be confused with his nephew, Karl H. Pribram, the neurologist and one of the contributors to this volume).

REFERENCES

Alchian, Armen A. and Demsetz, Harold (1972) "Production, information costs, and economic organization," *American Economic Review,* December, 62(5): 777–795.

Anderson, Philip W., Arrow, K. J. and Pines, David (eds) (1988) *The Economy as an Evolving Complex System,* Redwood City, CA: Addison-Wesley.

Atkins, P. W. (1984) *The Second Law,* New York: Scientific American Library.

Atran, Scott (1990) *Cognitive Foundations of Natural History: Toward an Anthropology of Science,* Cambridge: Cambridge University Press.

Barham, James (1990) "A Poincaréan approach to evolutionary epistemology," *Journal of Social and Biological Structures*, August, 13(3): 193–258.

—— (1992) "From enzymes to E = mc^2: A reply to critics," *Journal of Social and Evolutionary Systems*, August, 15(3): 249–306.

Berlin, Brent (1992) *Ethnobiological Classification: Principles of Categorization of Plants and Animals in Traditional Societies*, Princeton, NJ: Princeton University Press.

Bernstein, Richard J. (1983) *Beyond Objectivism and Relativism: Science, Hermeneutics and Praxis*, Philadelphia: University of Pennsylvania Press.

Bhaskar, Roy (1978) *A Realist Theory of Science*, Atlantic Highlands, NJ: Humanities Press.

—— (1979) *The Possibility of Naturalism: A Philosophic Critique of the Contemporary Human Sciences*, Brighton: Harvester.

Bloor, David (1982) "Durkheim and Mauss revisited: Classification and the sociology of knowledge," *Studies in History and Philosophy of Science*, December, 13(4): 267–297.

Boulding, Kenneth E. (1934) "The application of the pure theory of population change to the theory of capital," *Quarterly Journal of Economics*, August, 48(4): 645–666.

—— (1978) *Ecodynamics*, Beverly Hills, CA: Sage.

—— (1985–86) "The next thirty years in general systems," *General Systems Yearbook*, 29, 3–5.

Brandon, Robert N. (1981) "Biological teleology: Question and explanations," *Studies in the History and Philosophy of Science*, 12: 91–105.

Buchanan, James and Vanberg, Viktor J. (1991) "The market as a creative process," *Economics and Philosophy*, October, 7(2): 167–186.

Buchler, Justus (1966) *Metaphysics of Natural Complexes*, New York: Columbia University Press.

Callebaut, Werner (ed.) (1993) *Taking the Naturalistic Turn: Or How Real Philosophy of Science is Done*, Chicago: University of Chicago Press.

Campbell, Donald T. (1974) "Evolutionary epistemology," in Paul Arthur Schilpp (ed.) *The Philosophy of Karl Popper*, part I, La Salle, IL: Open Court, 413–463.

—— (1990) "Epistemological roles for selection theory," in Nicholas Rescher (ed.) *Evolution, Cognition, and Realism: Studies in Evolutionary Epistemology*, Lanham, MD: University Press of America.

Christensen, Paul P. (1989) "Historical roots for ecological economics – biophysical versus allocative approaches," *Ecological Economics*, February, 1(1): 17–36.

Coase, Ronald H. (1937) "The nature of the firm," *Economica*, New Series, November, 4: 386–405. (Reprinted in G. J. Stigler and K. E. Boulding (eds) (1952), *Readings in Price Theory*, Homewood, IL: Irwin, 331–351.)

Coleman, James (1990) *Foundations of Social Theory*, Cambridge, MA: Harvard University Press.

Danto, Arthur C. (1967) "Naturalism," in Paul Edwards (ed.) *The Encyclopedia of Philosophy*, vol. 5. New York: Macmillan, 448–450.

Davis, John (1995) "Femminis and Salanti on Ricardo and philosophical naturalism: Rejoinder," *History of Political Economy*, Spring, 27(1): 101–106.

Degler, C. N. (1991) *In Search of Human Nature: The Decline and Revival of Darwinism in American Social Thought*, New York: Oxford University Press.

Derrida, Jacques (ed.) (1973) *Speech and Phenomena, and Other Essays on Husserl's Theory of Signs*, Evanston, IL: Northwestern University Press (1968).

Douglas, Mary (1986) *How Institutions Think*, Syracuse, NY: Syracuse University Press.

Durkheim, Emile (1933) *The Division of Labor in Society*, trans. George Simpson, New York: Free Press.

Emerson, A. E. (1939) "Social coordination and the superorganism," *American Midland Naturalist*, 21: 182–209.

Etzioni, Amitai (1986) "The case for a multiple-utility conception," *Economics and Philosophy*, October, 2(2): 159–183.

Folke, Günther and Folke, Carl (1993) "Characteristics of nested living systems," *Journal of Biological Systems*, 1(3): 257–274.

Foss, Nicolai Juul (1994) "Realism and evolutionary economics," *Journal of Social and Evolutionary Systems*, February, 17(1): 21–40.

Foucault, Michel (1972) *The Archaeology of Knowledge and The Discourse on Language*, trans. A. M. Sheridan Smith, New York: Harper & Row.

——(1980) *Power/Knowledge: Selected Interviews and Other Writings, 1972–1977*, ed. Colin Gordon, trans. Colin Gordon, Leo Marshall, John Mepham and Kate Soper, New York: Pantheon.

Gould, Stephen Jay and Lewontin, Richard C. (1979) "The spandrels of San Marco and the panglossian paradigm: A critique of the adaptionist programme," *Proceedings of the Royal Society of London*, 205: 581–598.

Hayek, Friedrich A. (1967a) "The theory of complex phenomena," in *Studies in Philosophy, Politics and Economics*, Chicago: University of Chicago Press, 22–42.

——(1967b) "Notes on the evolution of systems of rules of conduct: (the interplay between rules of individual conduct and the social order of actions)," in *Studies in Philosophy, Politics and Economics*, Chicago: University of Chicago Press, 66–81.

——(1978) "The confusion of language in political thought," in *New Studies in Philosophy, Politics, Economics and the History of Ideas*, London: Routledge & Kegan Paul, 71–97.

——(1988) *The Fatal Conceit: The Errors of Socialism*, ed. W. W. Bartley, III, London: Routledge.

Hodgson, Geoffrey M. (1989) "Institutional economic theory: The old versus the new," *Review of Political Economy*, November, 1(3): 249–269.

——(1993) "The Mecca of Alfred Marshall," *Economic Journal*, March, 103(417): 406–415.

——(1994) "Evolution and optimality," in Geoffrey M. Hodgson, Warren J. Samuels, and Marc R. Tool (eds) *The Elgar Companion to Institutional and Evolutionary Economics*, A–K. Aldershot, UK: Edward Elgar, 207–212.

——(ed.) (1995) *Economics and Biology*, Aldershot, UK: Edward Elgar.

Judson, D. H. (1989) "The convergence of neo-Ricardian and embodied energy theories of value and price," *Ecological Economics*, August, 1(3): 261–281.

Kerferd, G. B. (1981) *The Sophistic Movement*, Cambridge: Cambridge University Press.

Keynes, John Maynard (1937) "The general theory of employment," *Quarterly Journal of Economics*, February, 52(1): 209–223.

Khalil, Elias L. (1989) "Adam Smith and Albert Einstein: The aesthetic principle of truth," *History of Economics Society Bulletin*, Fall, 11(2): 222–237.

——(1990a) "Natural complex vs. natural system," *Journal of Social and Biological Structures*, February, 13(1): 11–31.

——(1990b) "Beyond self-interest and altruism: A reconstruction of Adam Smith's theory of human conduct," *Economics and Philosophy*, October, 6(2): 255–273. (Reprinted in Steven Zamagni (ed.) (1995) *The Economics of Altruism*, Aldershot, UK: Edward Elgar.)

—— (1992a) "Hayek's spontaneous order and Varela's autopoiesis: A comment," *Human Systems Management*, 11(2): 101–105.

—— (1992b) "Nature and abstract labor in Marx," *Social Concept*, June, 6(2): 91–117.

—— (1992c) "Economics and biology: Eight areas of research," *Methodus*, December, 4(2): 29–45. (Reprinted in Hodgson, 1995.)

—— (1993a) "Neo-classical economics and neo-Darwinism: Clearing the way for historical thinking," in Ron Blackwell, Jaspal Chatha, and Edward J. Nell (eds) *Economics as Worldly Philosophy*, London: Macmillan, 22–72. (Reprinted in Hodgson, 1995.)

—— (1993b) "Is Poincaréan nonlinear dynamics an alternative to the selection theory of evolution?" *Journal of Social and Evolutionary Systems*, November, 16(4): 489–500.

—— (1994) "Entropy and economics," in Geoffrey M. Hodgson, Warren J. Samuels, and Marc R. Tool (eds) *The Elgar Companion to Institutional and Evolutionary Economics*, A–K. Aldershot, UK: Edward Elgar, 186–193.

—— (1995a) "On the scope of economics: What is the question?" *Finnish Economic Papers*, Spring, 8(1): 38–53.

—— (1995b) "Has economics progressed? Rectilinear, historicist, universalist, and evolutionary historiographies," *History of Political Economy*, Spring, 27(1): 43–87.

—— (1995c) "Organizations versus institutions," *Journal of Institutional and Theoretical Economics*, September, 151(3): 445–566.

—— (1995d) "The socioculturalist agenda in economics: Critical remarks of Thorstein Veblen's legacy," *Journal of Socio-Economics*, Winter, 24(4): 545–569.

—— (1995e) "Ecological economics and ecological Darwinism," *Journal of Biological Systems*, December, 3(4): 1211–1244.

—— (1995f) "Organization, naturalism and complexity," *Review of Social Economy*, Fall, 53(3): 393–419.

—— (1996a) "Economic action, naturalism and purposefulness," *Research in the History of Economic Thought and Methodology*, 14.

—— (1996b) "Institutions, naturalism and evolution," unpublished paper.

—— (1997) "Economics, biology, and naturalism: Three problems concerning the question of individuality," *Biology and Philosophy*, 12, in press.

Kitcher, Philip (1992) "The naturalists return," *Philosophical Review*, January, 101(1): 53–114.

Lawson, Tony (1989) "Abstraction, tendencies and stylised facts: A realist approach to economic analysis," *Cambridge Journal of Economics*, March, 13(1): 59–78.

—— (1994) "Realism, philosophical," in Geoffrey M. Hodgson, Warren J. Samuels, and Marc R. Tool (eds) *The Elgar Companion to Institutional and Evolutionary Economics*, L–Z, Aldershot, UK: Edward Elgar, 219–225.

Levy, Marion J., Jr. (1968) "Structural–functional analysis," in David L. Sills (ed.) *International Encyclopedia of the Social Sciences*, vol. 6. New York: Macmillan and Free Press.

Lovelock, James E. (1979) *Gaia: A New Look at Life on Earth*, Oxford: Oxford University Press.

Lukes, Steven (1973) *Individualism*, Oxford: Basil Blackwell.

McCloskey, Donald N. (1985) *The Rhetoric of Economics*, Madison: University of Wisconsin Press.

Mäki, Uskali (1990) "Mengerian economics in realist perspective," in Bruce J. Caldwell (ed.) *Carl Menger and his Legacy in Economics, Annual Supplement to Volume 22, History of Political Economy*, Durham, NC: Duke University Press, 289–310.

Marshall, Alfred (1920) *Principles of Economics*, London: Macmillan.

Masters, Roger D. (1989) *The Nature of Politics*, New Haven, CT: Yale University Press.

—— (1991) "Naturalistic approaches to the concept of justice," *American Behavioral Scientist*, January/February, 34(3): 289–313.

—— and Margaret Gruter (eds) (1992) *The Sense of Justice: Biological Foundations of Law*, Newbury Park, CA: Sage.

Mayr, Ernst (1992) "The idea of teleology," *Journal of the History of Ideas*, 53: 117–135.

Milberg, William (1988) "The language of economics: Deconstructing the neo-classical text," *Social Concept*, June, 4(2): 33–57.

Miller, James Grier (1978) *Living Systems*, New York: McGraw-Hill.

Minsky, Hyman P. (1975) *John Maynard Keynes*, New York: Columbia University Press.

—— (1982) *Can "It" Happen Again: Essays on Instability and Finance*, Armonk, NY: M. E. Sharpe.

Mirowski, Philip (1989) *More Heat Than Light: Economics as Social Physics, Physics as Nature's Economics*, New York: Cambridge University Press.

Murakoshi, Yoshio (1988) "Adam Smith's natural theology and the framework of economics," Ph.D. dissertation, Notre Dame, IN: Department of Economics, University of Notre Dame.

Murphy, James (1993) *The Moral Economy of Labor: Aristotelian Themes in Economic Theory*, New Haven, CT: Yale University Press.

O'Connor, Martin (1988) "Convolution and involution: The career of the biological organism in economic discourse," *Social Concept*, December, 5(1): 3–40.

O'Driscoll, Gerald P. and Rizzo, Mario J. (1985) *The Economics of Time and Ignorance*, Oxford: Basil Blackwell.

Pribram, Karl (1983) *A History of Economic Reasoning*, Baltimore: The Johns Hopkins University Press.

Pribram, Karl H. (1991) *Brain and Perception: Holonomy and Structure in Figural Processing*, appendices in collaboration with Kunio Yasue and Mari Jibu, Hillsdale, NJ: Lawrence Erlbaum.

Rorty, Richard (1979) *Philosophy and the Mirror of Nature*, Princeton, NJ: Princeton University Press.

Rose, S. (1987) *Molecules and Minds: Essays on Biology and the Social Order*, Milton Keynes, UK: Open University Press.

Rosen, Robert (1987) "Some epistemological issues in physics and biology," in B. J. Hiley and F. David Peat (eds) *Quantum Implications: Essays in Honour of David Bohm*, London and New York: Routledge & Kegan Paul, 314–327.

—— (1991) "Beyond dynamical systems," *Journal of Social and Biological Structures*, May, 14(2): 217–220.

Russell, Bertrand (1956) "Mathematical logic as based on the theory of types," in *Logic and Knowledge: Essays 1901–1950*, ed. Robert Charles Marsh, London: George Allen & Unwin, 59–102. (Originally published in the *American Journal of Mathematics*, 1908.)

Schumpeter, Joseph A. (1989) *The Theory of Economic Development: An Inquiry into Profits, Capital, Credit, Interest, and the Business Cycle*, trans. Redvers Opie, with a new intro. by John E. Elliott, New Brunswick, NJ: Transaction Publishers (1912). (A reprint of the 1949 book published by Harvard University Press.)

Sen, Amartya K. (1980/1981) "Plural utility," *Proceedings of the Aristotelian Society*, 80: 193–215.

Sethi, Rajiv (1992) "Dynamics of learning and the financial instability hypothesis," *Journal of Economics*, 56(1): 39–70.

Shackle, G. L. S. (1952) *Expectations in Economics*, Cambridge: Cambridge University Press.

—— (1970) *Expectations, Enterprise and Profit*, London: George Allen & Unwin.

Shimony, A. and Nails, D. (1987) *Naturalistic Epistemology: A Symposium of Two Decades*, Dordrecht, Holland: Reidel.

Skarda, Christine A. (1991) "The biology of life and learning," *Journal of Social and Biological Structures*, May, 14(2): 221–228.

Skinner, B. F. (1971) *Beyond Freedom and Dignity*, New York: Knopf.

Smith, Adam (1976) *The Theory of Moral Sentiments*, ed. D. D. Raphael and A. L. Macfie, Oxford: Clarendon Press.

—— (1980) *Essays on Philosophical Subjects*, ed. W. P. D. Wightman, J. C. Bryce, and I. S. Ross, general editors D. D. Raphael and A. S. Skinner, Oxford: Clarendon Press.

Smith, Barry (1990) "Aristotle, Menger, Mises: An essay in the metaphysics of economics," in Bruce J. Caldwell (ed.) *Carl Menger and his Legacy in Economics, Annual Supplement to Volume 22, History of Political Economy*, Durham, NC: Duke University Press, 263–288.

Sober, Elliott (ed.) (1984) *Conceptual Issues in Evolutionary Biology: An Anthology*, Cambridge, MA: MIT Press.

Spencer, Herbert (1967) *The Principle of Sociology*, ed. Robert L. Carneiro, Chicago: University of Chicago Press (1877–1896).

Tönnies, Ferdinand (1957) *Community and Society (Gemeinschaft und Gesellschaft)*, trans. and ed. Charles P. Loomis, New York: Harper & Row.

Varela, Francisco J. (1979) *Principles of Biological Autonomy*, New York: Elsevier North-Holland.

Weber, Bruce H., Depew, David J., Dyke, C., Salthe, Stanley N., Schneider, Eric D., Ulanowicz, Robert E. and Wicken, Jeffrey S. (1989) "Evolution in thermodynamic perspective: An ecological approach," *Biology and Philosophy*, October, 4(4): 373–405.

Weber, Max (1958) *The Protestant Ethic and the Spirit of Capitalism*, trans. Talcott Parsons and intro. by Anthony Giddens, New York: Charles Scribner's Sons.

Whitehead, Alfred North (1933) *Adventures of Ideas*, New York: Macmillan.

Wicken, Jeffrey S. (1987) *Evolution, Thermodynamics, and Information: Extending the Darwinian Program*, New York: Oxford University Press.

Williamson, Oliver E. (1985) *The Economic Institutions of Capitalism: Firms, Markets, Relational Contracting*, New York: Free Press.

Yates, F. Eugene (1993) "Order and complexity in dynamical systems: Homeodynamics as a generalized mechanics for biology," in D. Mikulecky and M. Witten (eds) *Dynamics and Thermodynamics of Complex Systems*, New York: Pergamon.

2

INTERFACING COMPLEXITY AT A BOUNDARY BETWEEN THE NATURAL AND SOCIAL SCIENCES

Karl H. Pribram

When I asked leading Berkeley astronomer and Nobel Laureate Charles Townes, "Which is more complex, the 100 billion stars in our galaxy or the 100 billion nerve cells in the 3-pound mass within our heads?" he answered without hesitation, "The brain. . . . For, after all, it is only the brain that can interpret our galaxy." And it is only the brain that can interpret its own cognizance.

Marian Cleeves Diamond, 1990

Science has only two ways of proceeding: it is either reductionist or structuralist. It is reductionist when it is possible to find out that very complex phenomena on one level can be reduced to simpler phenomena on other levels. For instance, there is a lot in life which can be reduced to physicochemical processes, which explain a part but not all. And when we are confronted with phenomena too complex to be reduced to phenomena of a lower order, then we can only approach them by looking to their relationships, that is, by trying to understand what kind of original system they make up.

Claude Lévi-Strauss, 1978, pp. 9 and 10

THE PARADOX OF COMPLEXITY

As noted in the quotation above, the brain has repeatedly been heralded as the most complex piece of matter in the universe. There are probably at least as many synapses, connections between nerve cells, as there are suns in the galaxies.

In the same vein, human social systems are the most complex on earth. There are also at least as many social connections as there are suns in the heavens. But human societies are made up of humans each blessed (or cursed) with a human brain. Which then is the more complex: The social system or the neural?

For years it seemed to me that the concept of "complexity" was untenable because self-similarity at different levels as in the case of fractals, defied simple categorizing (see Pribram, 1985). Nonetheless, as the title to this volume attests, serious scholars continue to find the concept useful and therefore try to define it (see e.g., review by Seth Lloyd, 1990). Each definition appears to grasp part of the puzzle – but the answer to the puzzle: "Which is more complex – the brain, or the social system, or the universe?" continues to be elusive.

I have now come to a new view. There is a reason for the current failure of definition: Modern analytical logic fails to cope with complexity. Not until we come to realize that the concept is paradoxical, can we begin to understand it. The dictionary definition of complexity already hints at paradox: complex, (1) from the Latin *co* (together) *plectere* (weave, braid): entwined; intricate; (2) from the Latin *complexus* (embracing, surrounding): anything formed by the union of interconnected parts; an assemblage; a system. Note that definition (1) emphasizes the intricacy of internal structure while definition (2) embraces the "system" as a whole.

Complexity is thus shown to encompass two levels or scales – a multiform interior or micro-level and a macro-level whole. Complexity, therefore, is a cross-scale, cross-level concept, and it must be measured accordingly. The paradox: an intricate diverse micro-level embraced within a simpler macro-level entity – unity in diversity.

In the brain/behavioral science interface, this paradoxical aspect of complexity has interesting consequences. Levels must be clearly discerned by an embracing relationship. A level or scale can be defined as a presentation, a description of an *entity* that is simpler than if it were made in terms of the collection of constituents of that scale or level. Thus the entity at each level can be characterized by a description that is a presentation. Components are described in some different fashion from the entity as a whole. Furthermore, there would be no need for a presentation of the entity as a whole were it not in some basic sense, simpler – that is, more efficient to process than that available to the components. For example, bytes are more efficient in use than the equivalent description in bits. A presentation of a program in Fortran is much more efficient than a presentation of the successive switch settings that form the hardware equivalent of the program. The question for us is whether psychological processes can, in the same manner, be considered to be simpler, more efficient, representations of functions of the brain.

In the sense of hierarchical levels of presentation, the analogy between computer software (programs) and hardware serves well. The psychological, mental level is described in presentations that are analogous to presentations at the program level. The "wetware" of the brain can be thought of as analogous to the hardware of the computer (Miller, Galanter, and Pribram, 1960; Pribram, 1986a). There is an equivalence between program and successive hardware switch settings. Can we say, therefore, that in some real sense the switch settings are represented in the program? If this is so, then in the same sense, psychological processes represent brain function.

This leads to a most tantalizing question: To what extent are the represented entities configured in a fashion similar to the entities they represent? In other words, to what extent are presentation and "representation" isomorphic to one another? The answer to this question obviously depends on reaching some consensus on the definition of isomorphic. Processes that map into each other in such a way as to preserve structure can be said to be either geometrically or algebraically isomorphic. For instance, although the Gestalt psychologists thought that the electrical fields of the brain have geometric *shape* resembling that of perceived objects, evidence shows that perspective transformations display algebraic (i.e., secondary), not geometric isomorphism (Shepard and Chipman, 1970).

By contrast, the computer program–hardware analogy suggests that significant *transformations* can occur between levels of presentation – indeed that the utility of representations is derived from these transformations. The analogy helped make understandable the results of neuropsychological research which showed that the search for "pictures" in the brain was misplaced (see Pribram, 1971, Chapter 6 for review). Understanding comes when the neuropsychologist searches for algebraic algorithms, such as computable *transforms* of sensory input. This emphasis on transformation is the key to resolving the larger issue of how to deal with the paradox of complexity: Same-level science by itself is ineffective. The resolution to issues comes when transformations across interfaces are taken into account.

PSYCHOLOGY AS A SAME-LEVEL AND AS A CROSS-LEVEL SCIENCE

In *The American Psychologist*, January 1989, p. 18, Skinner wrote: "There are two unavoidable gaps in any behavioral account: one between the stimulating action of the environment and the response of the organism and one between consequences and the resulting change in behavior. *Only brain science can fill those gaps.* In doing so it completes the account; it does not give a different account of the same thing." [Italics mine.]

At no time in my long association with Skinner did he ever disparage the utility of the brain sciences for an understanding of behavior. What he decried was the practice (as e.g., by Pavlov and Hebb) of neurologizing concepts derived exclusively from the experimental analysis of behavior. He was convinced that putting in neurological language what should properly be behavioral constructs gave such constructs unearned validity which often proved ephemeral.

Why then the empty organism approach? Skinner (1976) was clear on this point: We first need a behavioral science that can stand on its feet without recourse to biology. Once established, behavioral science can again turn to biology for filling "the unavoidable gaps" in the behavioral account. In short, with respect to the brain sciences, Skinner's philosophy abhorred the identity stance. The behavioral and the brain sciences were at different levels of inquiry; each had its place in explanation, and to mix levels operationally was a cardinal sin.

Much of science has initially proceeded in this fashion. In their early stages, physics was physics and chemistry was chemistry. But at a somewhat later epoch, an explanation of the periodic table of chemical elements was found to come from atomic physics and even, in the case of radioactive elements, from quantum physics. Today the boundary areas among the natural sciences form sciences in their own right: physical chemistry, thermodynamics, biochemistry, for example.

AFFORDANCES AND CONSEQUENCES

The brain/behavioral science interface is also spawning its own set of boundary sciences: Neuropsychology, psychobiology, cognitive neuroscience, etc. The question that needs to be answered is whether the gaps in the behavioral account can be filled by the brain sciences working solely at the biological-brain level of inquiry, or whether gap-filling is the province of these boundary sciences.

To answer this question, let us look in detail at the two gaps in the behavioral account. The first is between "the stimulating action of the environment and the response of the organism." Gibson has given the issues concerning this gap a name. He calls them "affordances": Certain aspects of the environment allow the organism to perceive what it perceives (Gibson, 1979). Originally, the concept was established the other way around: Certain characteristics of organisms afford the selection of aspects of the environment in order to perceive them (Gibson, personal communication). The change was made in order to facilitate an experimental program designed to find out just which environmental configurations, in fact, afforded particular perceptions. This program, called ecological psychology, has been successfully engaged by Turvey, Shaw, and Kugler (see e.g., Kugler, Shaw, Vincente, and Kinsella-Shaw, 1990; Shaw and Kinsella-Shaw, 1988; Turvey, Shaw, Reed, and Mace, 1981).

However, the earlier definition of affordances has merit as well. What are the characteristics of organisms that select just those aspects of the environment uncovered by ecological psychologists? In one set of experiments performed in my laboratory, we found that single neurons in the visual and auditory brain systems show their selective orientation and frequency responses (as determined by presenting a range of specific orientations and frequencies) even when the environmental stimulus consists of visual

43

or auditory white noise. (For a review of these and other experimental results bearing on the question of brain organization in perception, see Pribram, 1991.)

In such experiments, both brain variables and those describing the stimulating action of the environment were taken into account. Affordances are constituted by *both* their biological and their environmental determinants. With regard to affordances, therefore, my answer is that the gap in the behavioral account between the stimulating action of the environment and the resulting behavior cannot be filled by studies restricted to the brain level alone, any more that it can be filled at the environmental level alone. Answers are provided by boundary science inquiries which extend the ecological stance into the organism and do not stop short at the receptor surface (Pribram, 1982).

Next, let us examine the gap between consequences and the resulting change in behavior. The easy answer here might tempt one to conclude that consequences leave traces in the brain, and that the problem to be addressed is neuronal plasticity and "memory" storage. These are fascinating biological problems in their own right. But solving how plasticity leads to storage in the brain will not by itself fill the gap between consequences and the resulting change in the *organization* of behavior.

What we need to know is how behavioral organizations produce storage in such a way that they can configure changes in response. At a simpler level, how do brain processes configure at all? The problem is to account for figural equivalence in response as well as for figural change.

For Skinner, the figured consequences of behavior are the environmental resultants of that behavior. By his own statement, these consequences are the "cumulative records" he took home to analyze. According to his view, when I write in a notebook or type onto a word processor, the consequences of my behavior are in the environmental record. Storage is in my files, and once published, in bookcases of my colleagues. I hope these environmental storage consequences of my behavior will influence (change) my future behavior and that of my colleagues. Bruner is correct; much of what configures and influences my behavior is stored in an ever-evolving culture (Bruner, 1990).

But the question remains as to how such cultural configurations are produced? Production does not rest on the particulars of the movements that produce them; a document can be constructed on a keyboard, with a right or left hand, or even on sand or blackboard with toes or teeth in an emergency. Further, the mode of expression does not unduly alter what one wants to express. There must be some brain process that directly codes what is expressed, what is written (the cumulative record).

I have elsewhere reviewed in detail (Pribram, 1971, 1991; Pribram, Sharafat, and Beekman, 1984) experiments by Bernstein and his collaborators (Bernstein, 1967), by Brooks (1986), by Evarts (1967) and those performed in my laboratory that show how and where such a brain process occurs. Bernstein introduces the issue as follows:

> There is considerable reason to suppose that in the higher motor centers of the brain (it is very probable that these are in the cortical hemispheres) the localization pattern is none other than some form of projection of external space in the form present for the subject in the motor field. This projection, from all that has been said above, must be congruent with external space, but only topologically and in no sense metrically. All danger of considering the possibility of compensation for the inversion of projection at the retina . . . and many other possibilites of the same sort are completely avoided by these considerations. It seems to me that although it is not now possible to specify the ways in which such a topological representation of space in the central nervous system may be achieved, this is only a question of time for physiology. It is only necessary to reiterate that the topological properties of the projection of space in the C.N.S. may prove to be very strange and unexpected; we must not expect to find in the cortex some sort of photographic space, even an extremely deformed one. Still, the hypothesis that there exist in the higher levels of the C.N.S. projections of space, and not projections of joints and muscles, seems to me to be at present more probable than any other.
>
> (Bernstein, 1967, p. 109)

With these insights Bernstein set the problem which neurophysiologists must address if they are to relate the anatomical configuration of the central motor process to the configuration of the consequence of behavior. Neuroanatomists have demonstrated a somatotopic representation of muscles onto the cerebral cortex. But as Bernstein points out it is the topological representation of external space not of projections of joints and muscles, that is needed if patterns of behavioral *acts*, the consequence of movements, and not just patterns of movements *per se* are to be explained. Bernstein, in his experiments, used Fourier analysis to specify the topology of such behavioral actions and his specifications were sufficiently accurate to allow prediction of the patterns of continuing action.

Experiments were undertaken in my laboratory to test the hypothesis that the Fourier approach might also be as useful in analyzing the physiology of single neurons in the motor regions of the brain as it was for analyzing patterns of behavioral actions. Support for such an approach came from its success when applied to the analyses of the functions of the sensory systems. These analyses are reviewed here in some detail in order to provide a background of expectations and of problems faced when we attempt to relate the configuration of a neural process to the configuration of a behaviorally produced environmental consequence.

45

THE FOURIER APPROACH TO THE SENSORY SYSTEMS

The first suggestion that brain processing might involve a Fourier analysis was made over a century ago for the auditory system by Ohm (1843), the same Ohm who formulated Ohm's Law of Electricity. This suggestion was adopted by Herman von Helmholtz (1863) who performed a series of experiments which led to the place theory of hearing – essentially a view of the cochlea as a piano keyboard, whose keys, when struck by acoustic waves, would initiate nerve impulses to the brain where resonant neurons were activated. This view was modified in this century by George V. Bekesy (1959). His experiments showed the cochlea and peripheral neurosensory mechanism to operate more like a stringed instrument which is sensitive to the superposition of acoustic wave forms. This work led to the discovery that the initial stages of auditory processing can be described in terms of a Fourier transform of the acoustic input (Evans, 1974).

Bekesy went on to make a large-scale model of the cochlea composed of a row of five vibrators (1959). When the model was placed on the forearm and the phase of the vibrators adjusted manually, the phenomenal perception was that of a point source of stimulation which could be moved up and down the arm. When two such model "cochleas" were applied, one to each forearm, the point source appeared at first to jump alternately from one forearm to the other, and then suddenly to stabilize in the space between the two arms. The stimulus was "projected" away from the stimulating source and the receptive surface into the external world, much as sound is projected into the environment away from the source in audio speakers of a high fidelity stereophonic system.

Both macro- and micro-electrode studies performed in my laboratory have shown that multiple simultaneous vibratory stimulations of the skin also evoke only unitary responses in cortex (Dewson, 1964; Lynch, 1981). Just as in perception, the cortical electrical response does not reflect the actual physical dimensions of the stimulus. Bekesy noted that sensory inhibition, due to lateral inhibition in dendritic networks, might be the responsible agent in the transformations.

Evidence is therefore at hand to indicate that the input to the ear and skin becomes transformed into neural patterns that can be described by sets of convolutional integrals of the type that Gabor (1969) has suggested as stages in achieving a fully developed Fourier holographic-like process.

The manner in which such a stepwise process occurs is best worked out for the visual system. Recordings from units in the optic nerve (Rodieck, 1965) demonstrated that the moving retina decomposes the image produced by the lens of the eye into a "Mexican hat" organization which can be described as convolving retinal organization with sensory input. A second step in the process occurs at the lateral geniculate nucleus where each geniculate cell acts as a peephole "viewing" a part of the retinal

46

mosaic. This is because each geniculate cell has converging upon it some 10,000 optic nerve fibers originating in the ganglion cells of the retina. The receptive field of the geniculate neuron is composed of a center surrounded by concentric rings of receptivity, each consecutive ring of sharply diminishing intensity and of a sign opposite to that of its neighbors (Hammond, 1972; Pribram, personal observation).

At the cortex the transformation into the Fourier domain becomes complete. Beginning with the work of Campbell and Robson (1968), Pollen, Lee, and Taylor (1971), Maffei and Fiorentini (1973), and Glezer, Ivanoff, and Tscherback (1973), investigators using gratings as stimuli (e.g., Schiller, Finlay, and Volman, 1976; DeValois, Albrecht, and Thorall, 1978; Movshon, Thompson, and Tolhurst, 1978; Pribram, Lassonde, and Ptito, 1981) have repeatedly confirmed that the cells in visual cortex are selectively tuned to a limited band width of spatial frequency of approximately an octave ($\frac{1}{2}$ to $1\frac{1}{2}$ octaves). Ordinarily the term frequency implies a temporal dimension, but the spatial frequency (or wave number) of a grating reflects the width and spacings of the bars making up the grating. When such widths and spacing are narrow the spatial frequency is high; when widths and spacing are broad the spatial frequency is low.[1]

The findings do not, however, mean that the visual system performs a global Fourier transform on the input to the retina (see also Julesz and Caelli, 1979). The spread function, as such transformations are called, does not encompass the entire retina: Rather it is limited to the receptive field of a retinal ganglion cell. Similarly at the cortex encoding is restricted to the receptive field of the cortical neuron.

This patchy organization of the Fourier domain (Robson, 1975) does not impair its functional characteristics. The technique of patching or stripping together Fourier transformed images has been utilized in radioastronomy by Bracewell (1965) to cover expanses which cannot be viewed with any single telescopic exposure. The technique has been further developed by Ross (see Leith, 1976) to produce a hologram by which three-dimensional *moving* images are constructed when the inverse transform is effected. Movement is produced when spatially adjacent Fourier encoded strips, which capture slightly different images are scanned (temporally) as, for instance, when frames of a motion picture are used as the image base for the Fourier transformation.

Such framed Fourier patches have come to be called Gabor elementary functions. Gabor (1946) noted that the Fourier transform relates the spectral domain to spacetime in an either/or fashion. For the purpose of determining the maximum efficiency of telephone communication across the Atlantic Cable, Gabor quantified Hartley's Law (1928) which dealt with the trade off between spectrum (frequency) and spacetime. Gabor therefore developed a phase (Hilbert) space in which both spectrum and spacetime were simultaneously represented and thus were correlated (to describe the density of information transmission). Gabor used the same mathematics as had Heisenberg to develop the definition of a quantum in microphysics. Gabor therefore called his elementary function "a quantum of information". More on this presently.

NEURAL ENCODING OF THE CONSEQUENCES OF BEHAVIOR

In my laboratory (Spinelli and Pribram, 1967; Pribram, Lassonde, and Ptito, 1981) we showed that the Gabor function could be altered to reflect either the spacetime or the spectral dimension – i.e., the Gabor function could be "pushed" to its either/or Fourier origins. This was accomplished by electrically stimulating the posterior cerebral convexity (to produce the spacetime configuration) or the frontolimbic forebrain (to produce a spectral, holographic-like domain).

For motor function the Fourier (and Gabor) principles of organization were found to hold. Experiments were undertaken to find out whether there are cells in the motor system which respond selectively to a band width of frequencies of a cyclic up–down passive movement of a forelimb. The results of the experiment showed that a 20 per cent portion of a total of 306 cells sampled were tuned (i.e., increase or decrease their activity at least 25 per cent over baseline spontaneous activity) to a narrow ($\frac{1}{2}$ octave) band of the frequency spectrum.

Tuning could be due to a spurious convergence of factors relating to the basic properties of muscle: Metric displacement and tonicity or stiffness. An examination was therefore undertaken of variables related to these basic properties, variables such as velocity, change in velocity (acceleration), as well as tension, and change in tension. These factors in isolation were found not to account for the frequency selective effects. This does not mean that other cells in the motor system are not selectively sensitive to velocity and changes in tension. But it does mean that the frequency selectivity of the cells described is dependent on some higher order computation of the metric and tonic resultants imposed on the foreleg musculature by the external load.

In addition to controlling for selectivity to velocity and acceleration, position in the cycle of movement was investigated. Position was found to be encoded by cortical cells (but not by caudate nucleus cells), but only at the site of phase shift and specific to a particular frequency. This result supports the hypothesis that the cortical cells are in fact frequency selective in that any sensitivity to phase shift presupposes an encoding of phase and therefore of frequency. Furthermore, the fact that the cortical cells respond to position suggests that they are directly involved in the computation of the vector space coordinates within which actions are achieved.

There is thus no question that an approach to analysis of the functions of the motor system in frequency terms has proven useful not only in studying the overall behavior of the organism as initiated by Bernstein but also in studying the neural motor process. That some such an approach is required is amply documented in a review of the field, initiated by R. B. Stein in an article entitled "What muscle variable(s) does the nervous system control in limb movements?" which became available in the December issue (1982, 5 (4)) of *The Behavioral and Brain Sciences.*

PSYCHOLOGY: THE INTERFACE BETWEEN BIOLOGY AND THE SOCIAL SCIENCES

With respect to consequences, therefore, the gap in the behavioral account is filled by a process that reciprocally transforms, i.e., correlatively codes configured brain with environmental events including such cultural artifacts as writing. Thus, the data that describe this process are not obtained solely at the biological-brain level of inquiry. As in the case of affordances, both environmental and brain variables are critical to understanding. With respect to consequences in a human setting, the environmental variables are, to a large extent, cultural. The gaps in the behavioral account that are due to the processes that determine affordances and consequences are therefore filled by boundary, not by same-level science.

This analysis calls into question a program of research which aims to make psychology a purely same-level behavioral science devoid of its biological and social relations. I do not question the immense contribution technical behaviorism has made to our understanding of psychological processes. However, the yield in understanding harvested by this same-level science in psychology has been disappointing in one respect to many of us. Psychological science has been unable to put its house in order. Instead, a welter of languages has developed to address identical issues (e.g., in attention and in short-term memory research) and many issues go unexplored (e.g., learning through imitation) due to a failure to find applicable same-level science tools.

Biology did not come of age until boundary sciences were established. Genera and species were identified by recourse not only to anatomical morphology (analogy) but also to functional changes in morphology (homology). Classification led ultimately to the theory of selective evolution (as in horticulture and animal breeding) and to molecular genetics, all the results of explorations in interface sciences.

Psychology, the science of mental processes, may well depend for its maturity on the development of its interfaces with the social and biological sciences. As I have indicated, studying plasticity in the brain is not enough. To know the resultants of plasticity in the brain is not enough. The resultants of plasticity are configured by environments – in the case of humans largely by culture. But studying culture alone is equally barren;

culture is constructed by behaving humans whose brains generate the multiforms encoded as cultures. Behavior is central, but behavior, whether verbal or instrumental, is only an expression of mind – the generative psychological process.

TRANSCENDING THE MIND/BRAIN DUALITY

The considerations lead directly to the perennial question: Can such disparate entities as the material brain and our ineffable, private mental experiences be related by crass neuropsychological cross-scale endeavors? Whether we ought or not, the fact is that clinical neuropsychology is successfully pursuing just such a program, not only in enhancing knowledge, but also in the practical matters of alleviating suffering. How has this come about? Again some defining concepts are in order. In *Languages of the Brain* (1971), I stated the matter as follows:

Over the past half century subjective experience has rarely been admitted as a legitimate field for scientific inquiry. Instead, the focus of study has been instrumental or verbal behavior *per se*. This approach has been generally successful in quantitatively delineating environmental variables that influence behavior, but somewhat less than successful when variables within the organism codetermine what happens. In such circumstances the data make considerably more sense when physiological as well as environmental variables are monitored. It is important to emphasize that the behavioral approach cannot, however, be dispensed with: many clinical neurologists and brain physiologists have neglected specification of relevant environmental circumstance, uncritically asserting an identity between what they observe physiologically and some psychological function. Thus the study of psychological processes had become polarized, with behaviorists at one extreme and physiologists at the other. On the one hand, most early behaviorists declared that operations defining subjective statements were impossible and that scientific psychological language should, therefore, entirely exclude mental terms; meanwhile, medically trained scientists would loosely refer to psychological functions such as voluntary action, affective feeling, or imagination on the basis of uncontrolled subjective reports without specifying the defining operation of their language, thus making it difficult for other scientists to know what was being talked about.

During the 1960s behavioral psychology came to appreciate the dictum of Gestalt psychology that subjective awareness is an integral part of the biological and social universe and is too central to these operations to be ignored. Thus "respectable" psychologists began to work on problems such as cognition, thought, and attention. By the end of the decade even Imaging, our present subject, could be discussed openly at psychological meetings without undue risk.

This broadening of the base of psychological inquiry came about, of course, by a rigorous attempt to detail the defining operations that make possible scientific communication about subjective processes. My own procedure is to start with nonbehavioral means to describe categories of organismic and environmental circumstances. I then use behavior as a dependent variable to study interactions between the categories (which constitute the independent variables of the experiment). From data obtained in such experiments I *infer* psychological functions and examine their similarities and dissimilarities to verbal reports of subjective experience. When the fit appears right, I use mental language (Pribram, 1962; 1970).

This recourse to mental terms is not capricious. For one thing, much of clinical neurological analysis is based on the verbal reports of subjective experience when the brain is damaged or electrically stimulated. Further, I found the behaviorist jargon (with which I had been doing my thinking) replete with inconsistencies that couldn't be clarified until I admitted the relevance of the subjective mode. In other words, I had to come to terms with Gilbert Ryle's (1949) famous "Ghosts in the Machine". Images and feeling are ghosts – but they are ghosts that inhabit my own and my patients' subjective worlds. They are our constant companions and I want to explain them.

(Pribram, 1971, pp. 99–101)

Interest in the relationship between psychological function (mind) and brain has become further invigorated by the surge of activity in the neurosciences over the past two decades and in what has become called "cognitive science." The surge of interest in mind/brain issues has come in various guises. Cognitive scientists have argued whether "representations" or "computations" characterize the relationship (see e.g., Gardner, 1985; "Special issue" in *The Behavioral and Brain Sciences*, 1980). A philosopher and a neuroscientist have banded together only to find themselves maintaining an interactive separateness of mind and brain (Popper and Eccles, 1977). Further, a neuroscientist (Sperry, 1952, 1969, 1976, 1980), as well as a philosopher (Searle, 1979) have declared themselves solidly on the side of mind. Meanwhile, a psychologist (Skinner, 1971, 1976) has given up hope that a "science of mental life" as William James (1901), and more recently George Miller (1962), have dubbed it, is possible at all. Skinner bases his view on the premise that such a science would depend on verbal communications, which are notoriously ambiguous.

It is this variety in the attempts to deal with mind/brain relations that called forth my reevaluation. The time was therefore ripe to take a new look at this fascinating interface from the standpoint of the scientist as well

KARL H. PRIBRAM

as from that of the philosopher (see Pribram, 1986a). I know most of the protagonists personally and have high regard for all of them, as I have for much of the philosophical discourse that bears on the issues. It seemed to me that these intelligent scholars cannot all be wrong despite the fact that their respective contributions are at variance with one another. Could it then be that they are all correct, in some nontrivial sense? If so, how?

My suggestion was that each of these espoused philosophical positions has captured a part of the domain of issues, and that what is necessary is to determine the database on which the position rests. The failure of philosophy to resolve the issues comes when a position is maintained beyond the confines of its relevant database to a point where another position is more appropriate.

The danger of such an eclectic approach is that one may end up with an "any worlds" or at least with a "many worlds" relativist viewpoint, which is fine if one wishes to show merely that there are many different answers to the questions posed. But I am not satisfied with such a result. I was able to show that the several databased theoretical frames fit different epistemological agendas in philosophy, but that a unified ontological view can be constructed out of the diversity of theories.

A proposal made by Eccles provides a good starting point to explore this relationship between the different epistemological agendas and a unified ontological view. Eccles (1986) discerns elementary aggregates of dendro-synaptic structures he calls dendrons; being a dualist, he suggests corresponding mental entities, psychons. But what might a psychon be? Behavioral scientists have only rarely concerned themselves with "the unit entities of behavior," and when they have, they usually invoke the reflex (see Miller, Galanter, and Pribram, 1960). There is no conceivable correspondence between a reflex and a dendron.

The computer/program metaphor suggests that a search for a psychological "machine language" – Fodor (1980) has called it "mentalese" – might be fruitful. If so, its code must correspond to the neural code described in terms of dendrons. Holonomic brain processing theory, developed from the holographic metaphor, addresses this issue. The theory is based on the finding that the elementary dendritic process, a receptive field property of visual and auditory cortex neurons, is best described in terms of Gabor elementary functions (Gabor, 1946; see above and review by Pribram, 1991, Lecture 2). Instead of the binary code which described Shannon's measure of information, information processing in the dendritic microstructure of the brain proceeds in terms of *quanta* of information. As described earlier, Gabor developed this measure to assess limits on the efficiency, or the minimum uncertainty with which human communication across the Atlantic cable can proceed. This limit was found to be defined by the same mathematics that Heisenberg had used to define quanta in microphysics. The quanta of informa-

52

tion, the Gabor elementary functions, are thus measures that apply equally to microphysics, the operations of the material wetware of the brain in terms of the operations of dendrons, and the operations of mental communication in terms of the operations of psychons among human actors.

Just as in classical programming hierarchies, brain/mind processing structures at each level are transformed into those at the next level. For instance, the Gabor quanta responsible for image processing are assembled into group structures that are involved in object perception, and these, in turn, become organized into neural systems that categorize objects (see Pribram, 1991, for details). Still, something remains invariant across these transformations, or the process would fail to work. There is, therefore, a difference between surface structures which become *trans*-formed and the deeper identity which *in*-forms the transformation. Transformations are necessary to material and mental realizations – Plato's particular appearances – of the ideal in-forms. The instantiation of Beethoven's 9th Symphony is transformed from composition (a mental operation), to score (a material embodiment), to performance (more mental than material), to recording on compact disc (more material than mental), to the sensory and brain processes (material) that make for appreciative listening (mental). But the symphony as symphony remains recognizable, "identical" to Beethoven's creative composition over the centuries of performances, recordings, and listenings.

Instantiations depend on transformations among orders. What remains invariant across all instantiations is "in-formation," the form within. Surprisingly, according to this analysis, it is a Platonic "idealism" that motivates the information revolution (e.g., "information processing" approaches in cognitive and neural science) and distinguishes it from the materialism of the industrial revolution. Further, as information is neither material nor mental, idealism displaces not only materialism but also mentalism and dualism as the center of concern. Alternatively, a new tension is developed between Platonic idealism and Aristotelian realism perhaps in the guise of a Pythagorean-like structural pragmatism (see Khalil, 1990; Lévi-Strauss, 1978; Pribram, 1965) which investigates the relations among levels of inquiry by specifying the transformations that characterize the differences among their forms.

Along these lines, an ontological origin neutral to the mind/brain for information was shown (Pribram, 1986a) to resolve the apparent paradox of (a) invariance in ideal informational structure and (b) a plurality of instantiations. It was shown that to identify invariance solely as mental leads to awkward interpretations such as those that would endow computers with "minds" and "feelings." Instead, a plausible case was made that what remains invariant across transformations is neutral to the mind/brain, mental–material duality and is captured by physicists' definitions of energy and the amount of its structure – entropy (and its converse, negentropy) and information. Information can be instantiated mentally as well as materially, an idea captured by the aphorism that, on occasion, the pen can be mightier than the sword.

Central to the view expressed above are measures of process, i.e. change. The efficiency with which the change proceeds is ordinarily measured in terms of entropy. The relation between measures of efficiency and measures of information (i.e., entropy and negentropy) has been discussed at length by Shannon (Shannon and Weaver, 1949), Brillouin (1962), and Mackay (1969). However, these authors came to somewhat different conclusions: Shannon equated the amount of information with the amount of entropy, Mackay and Brillouin with the amount of negentropy. A conciliation of these views comes from a modification which results in a definition of entropy as potential information. The reasoning is similar to that which motivated Shannon, who called the structure within which information processing occurs "uncertainty." Recall here that Gabor's quantum of information is a measure of the *minimum* uncertainty, that is the maximum amount of potential information that can be processed at any moment.

In addition, Shannon (Shannon and Weaver, 1949) and Lila Gatlin (1972) have noted that the efficiency of information processing depends on the presence of redundancy and, by virtue of pattern matching, on actively structuring redundancies. George Miller (1956) called attention to the importance of such structuring, which he called "chunking." Elsewhere (Pribram, 1991, Lectures 8 and 9), I have reviewed the evidence that the frontolimbic portions of the forebrain are critically involved in structuring redundancy and by this means enhancing the efficiency of information processing. Thus, initial conditions, measured as an amount of uncertainty, and a controlling context, measured in terms of chunking, constrain the efficiency with which information is processed.

CODA: THE PARADOX OF CHOICE

Einstein in his famous aphorism, "I don't believe God is playing dice with the universe," voiced his concern as to whether measured change in physics could remain determinate in the face of quantum probability. Monod (1971), in his book *Chance and Necessity*, posed this same concern as a paradox that faces biological scientists. Are biological processes determined, or are they subject to the vagaries of the unpredictable? In the brain/behavioral sciences, the issue of free will has filled volumes of discourse.

In keeping with the theme of this chapter, I maintain that we need not make an either/or choice between freedom and determinism. By accepting the paradox as such, we simply specify the constraints under which freedom is displayed. When this is done, the full measuring of the paradox unfolds. Freedom of an action path is dependent upon the presence of a determinate structure.

It is the determinate structure of Einstein's dice that makes possible the probabilistic path initiated by a throw. It is the determinate structure of orbits that allows the probabilistic path of placement of electrons in quantum mechanics. And, in biology, though it is the genetic given in strands of DNA that determines the development of every part of the body, every tissue, every organ, development also depends on a path dictated by operations of inductors, derepressors of the DNA's potential.

The path of process is ordinarily quasi-predictable: "degrees of freedom" are specified by the constraining structures. For the most part, degrees of freedom can be determined, and thus the determinist will claim that, though the boundaries of determinism may be more fuzzy than had been anticipated, in principle determinism remains intact. But this view is placed in jeopardy when the boundaries become stretched sufficiently to constitute a paradigm shift. For the cross-level endeavors that must relate the natural to the social sciences, such a shift has provided important insights.

Much of natural science has flourished by modeling processes under an umbrella of determinate linear invertible equations. The paths described by a variety of least action principles are examples. The three-body problem is, however, a counter-example. In the social sciences, models so conceived are more often inadequate. If this were not so, more of us could quickly become wealthy by playing the stock market; wars would not be so frequently undertaken through miscalculation; setting up a business would entail considerably less risk.

The recent emergence and popularity of nonlinear dynamics attests to how a chaotic state can result from a deterministic path of a process. The danger accompanying any enthusiasm is that it overreaches the bounds of applicability and becomes "the answer" to everything, and therefore risks becoming an answer to nothing. Much of established knowledge, even in the social sciences, does deal with the predictable and the quasi-predictably probable. Predictions through polls are an example. Controlling constraints are often present that keep a process from becoming completely unmanageable. At the same time, interactions among people are, as Toynbee (1972) noted, challenges, not causes (see also Khalil, 1990). There is as yet no plausible science that can predict the results of a challenge.

For me, the most important observation that has come from the study of nonlinear processes is the observation made by Prigogine (1980) that stabilities can be formed far from equilibrium. I very much want to know whether such stabilities can form as a result of processes hitherto modelled in terms of least action paths. If, in fact, entropy can be thought of as potential information, the path to minimum entropy – that is to maximum information – should be strewn with stabilities far from equilibrium. Such stabilities should be formed by way of the coaction of ensembles of quanta of information when these ensembles are cooperatively engaged within a controlling context.

To use the language of behavioral psychology, stabilities far from equilibrium ought to characterize the reinforcement process. Reinforcement is defined as a process that enhances the likelihood of recurrence of a response. In turn, a response is defined as an environmental outcome, an environmental event, produced by the organism. In order for the event (dictionary definition: 1. ex-venire; outcome) to have the effect of enhancing the likelihood of recurrence of a similar (or identical) event, a stability must be engendered in the brain process that controls the behavior. During discrimination learning, such temporary stabilities are displayed as plateaus in the acquisition curve as each element composing the discrimination is attended (see review by Pribram, 1986b).

Learning, in primates at least, is thus seen to be a process of self-organization. The ordinary view that a reinforcer produces its effect by way of drive reduction or drive induction is readily abandoned when one is conversant with testing monkeys (or educating children). A monkey rewarded for making a correct choice will put the reinforcing peanut in his cheek pouch. When, however, he next makes an error, he pops the peanut out of his pouch and chews and swallows it with obvious relish. Should the occasion demand, I have seen monkeys work for hundreds of trials to solve a problem when the "reward machine" was broken. Self-organization, not self-indulgence, is the overarching motive in learning.

Computational and mathematical models of the learning process in these terms are well within our reach. Given such models, we might begin to understand the constraints necessary to control cooperative processes among ensembles of quanta of information – the cross-scale processes that engender the paradox of complexity.

NOTES

I have gained much from listening to "tutorials" presented by Peter Kugler on the topics of cross-scale science and nonlinear dynamics. Thanks also are due to Debbie Akers, without whose assistance this chapter would not have been accomplished.

1 The temporal dimension can be evoked by successively scanning across the grating (as, for instance, by walking across the path of illumination of a projection of a slide of such a grating). Conversion to the temporal dimension is, however, not necessary. The grating is a filter whose characteristics can be understood either as a spatial or a temporal modulation of a spectral frequency.

56

REFERENCES

Bekesy, G. V. (1959) "Synchronism of neural discharges and their demultiplication in pitch perception on the skin and in hearing," *Journal of Acoustical Society of America* 31: 333–349.

Bernstein, N. (1967) *The Co-ordination and Regulation of Movements*, New York: Pergamon Press.

Bracewell, R. N. (1965) *The Fourier Transform and its Applications*, New York: McGraw-Hill.

Brillouin, L. (1962) *Science and Information Theory*, New York: Academic Press.

Brooks, V. B. (1986) "How does the limbic system assist motor learning? A limbic comparator hypothesis," *Brain and Behavior Evolution* 29: 29–53.

Bruner, J. (1990) *Acts of Meaning*, Cambridge, MA: Harvard University Press.

Campbell, F. W. and Robson, J. G. (1968) "Application of Fourier analysis to the visibility of gratings," *Journal of Physiology* 197: 551–565.

DeValois, R. L., Albrecht, D. G., and Thorall, L. G. (1978) "Cortical cells: Bar and edge detectors, or spatial frequency filters?" in S. J. Cool and E. L. Smith (eds), *Frontiers of Visual Science*, New York: Springer-Verlag.

Dewson, J. H., III (1964) "Cortical responses to patterns of two-point cutaneous stimulation," *Journal of Comparative and Physiological Psychology* 58: 387–389.

Diamond, M. C. (1990) "Morphological cortical changes as a consequence of learning and experience," in A. B. Scheibel and A. F. Wechsler (eds), *Neurobiology of Higher Cognitive Function*, New York: The Guilford Press, pp. 1–12.

Eccles, J. C. (1986) "Do mental events cause neural events analogously to the probability fields of quantum mechanics?" *Proceedings of the Royal Society of London* 277: 411–428.

Evans, E. F. (1974) "Neural processes for the detection of acoustic patterns and for sound localization," in F. O. Schmitt and F. G. Worden (eds), *The Neurosciences: Third Study Program*, Cambridge, MA: MIT Press.

Evarts, E. V. (1967) "Representation of movements and muscles by pyramidal tract neurons of the precentral motor cortex," in M. D. Yahr and D. P. Purpura (eds), *Neurophysiological Basis of Normal and Abnormal Motor Activities*, Hewlet, NY: Raven, pp. 215–254.

Fodor, J. A. (1980) "Methodological solipsism as a research strategy for cognitive psychology," *Behavioral and Brain Sciences* 3: 63–110.

Gabor, D. (1946) "Theory of communication," *Journal of the Institute of Electrical Engineers* 93: 429–441.

—— (1969) "Information processing with coherent light," *Optica Acta* 16: 519–533.

Gardner, H. (1985) *The Mind's New Science*, New York: Basic Books.

Gatlin, L. (1972) *Information Theory and the Living System*, New York: Columbia University Press.

Gibson, J. J. (1979) *The Ecological Approach to Visual Perception*, Boston: Houghton Mifflin.

Glezer, V. D., Ivanoff, V. D., and Tscherbach, T. A. (1973) "Investigation of complex and hypercomplex receptive fields of visual cortex of the cat as spatial filters," *Vision Research* 13: 1875–1904.

Hammond, P. (1972) "Spatial organization of receptive fields of LGN neurons," *Journal of Physiology* 222: 53–54.

Hartley, R. V. L. (1928) "Transmission of information," *Bell System Technical Journal* 7: 535.

Helmholtz, H. von (1863) *Lehre von den tonempfindungen*, Braunschweig: Vieweg.

57

James, W. (1901) *Principles of Psychology*, London: Macmillan.

Julesz, B. and Caelli, T. (1979) "On the limits of Fourier decomposition in visual texture perception," *Perception* 8: 69–73.

Khalil, E. L. (1990) "Natural complex vs. natural system," *Journal of Social and Biological Structures* 13(1): 11–31.

Kugler, P. N., Shaw, R. E., Vincente, K. J., and Kinsella-Shaw, J. (1990) "Inquiry into intentional systems. I: Issues in ecological physics," *Psychological Research* 52: 98–121.

Leith, E. N. (1976) "White-light holograms," *Scientific American* 235(4): 80.

Lévi-Strauss, C. (1978) *Myth and Meaning*, Toronto, Canada: University of Toronto Press.

Lloyd, S. (1990) "The calculus of intricacy," *The Sciences*, 30: 38–44.

Lynch, J. C. (1981) "A single unit analysis of contour enhancement in the somesthetic system of the cat," Ph.D. dissertation, Neurological Sciences, Stanford University, CA.

Mackay, D. M. (1969) *Information Mechanism and Meaning*, Cambridge, MA: MIT Press.

Maffei, L. and Fiorentini, A. (1973) "The visual cortex as a spatial frequency analyzer," *Vision Research* 13: 1255–1267.

Miller, G. A. (1956) "The magical number seven, plus or minus two, or some limits on our capacity for processing information," *Psychological Review* 63: 81–97.

—— (1962) *Psychology: The science of mental life*, New York: Harper & Row.

Miller, G. A., Galanter, E. H., and Pribram, K. H. (1960) *Plans and the Structure of Behavior*, New York: Holt, Rinehart & Winston.

Monod, J. (1971) *Chance and Necessity: An essay on the natural philosophy of modern biology*, New York: Knopf. (Translation by Austryn Wainhouse.)

Movshon, J. A., Thompson, I. D., and Tolhurst, D. J. (1978) "Receptive field organization of complex cells in the cat's striate cortex," *Journal of Physiology* 283: 79.

Ohm, G. S. (1843) "Über die Definition des Tones, nebst daran geknüpfter Theorie der Sirene und ähnlicher tonbildener Vorrichtungen," *Ann. Physik. Chem.* 59: 513–565.

Pollen, D. A., Lee, J. R., and Taylor, J. H. (1971) "How does the striate cortex begin the reconstruction of the visual world," *Science* 137: 74–77.

Popper, K. R., and Eccles, J. C. (1977) *The Self and its Brain*, Berlin: Springer-Verlag.

Pribram, K. H. (1962) "Interrelations of psychology and the neurological disciplines," in S. Koch (ed.), *Psychology: A Study of a Science*, Vol. 4, *Biologically Oriented Fields: Their place in psychology and in biological sciences*, New York: McGraw-Hill, 119–157.

—— (1965) "Proposal for a structural pragmatism: Some neuropsychological considerations of problems in philosophy," in B. Wolman and E. Nagle (eds), *Scientific Psychology: Principles and approaches*, New York: Basic Books, 426–459.

—— (1970) "The biology of mind: Neurobehavioral foundations," in A. Gilgen (ed.), *Scientific Psychology: Some perspectives*, New York: Academic Press, pp. 45–70.

—— (1971) *"Languages of the Brain: Experimental paradoxes and principles in neuropsychology*, Englewood Cliffs, NJ: Prentice-Hall.

—— (1972) Review of *Chance and Necessity* by J. Monod, in *Perspectives in Biology and Medicine* 16.

—— (1982) "Brain and ecology of mind," in W. S. Weimer and D. S. Palermo (eds), *Cognition and the Symbolic Process*, Hillsdale, NJ: Lawrence Erlbaum Associates, 361–381.

—— (1985) "Complexity and causality," *The Science and Praxis of Complexity*, The United Nations University, pp. 119–132.

—— (1986a) "The cognitive revolution and mind/brain issues," *American Psychologist* 41: 507–520.

—— (1986b) "The role of cortico-cortical connections," in F. Lepore, M. Ptito, and H. Jasper (eds), *Two Hemispheres – One Brain: Functions of the corpus callosum*, New York: Alan R. Liss, Inc.

—— (1991) *Brain and Perception: Holonomy and structure in figural processing*, Hillsdale, NJ: Lawrence Erlbaum Associates.

Pribram, K. H., Lassonde, M. C., and Ptito, M. (1981) "Intracerebral influences on the microstructure of receptive fields of cat visual cortex," *Experimental Brain Research* 43: 131–144.

Pribram, K. H., Sharafat, A., and Beekman, G. J. (1984) "Frequency encoding in motor systems," in H. T. A. Whiting (ed.), *Human Motor Actions – Bernstein Reassessed*, North Holland: Elsevier, 121–156.

Prigogine, I. (1980) *From Being to Becoming – Time and Complexity in the Physical Sciences*, San Francisco, CA: Freeman.

Robson, J. G. (1975) "Receptive fields, neural representation of the spatial and intensive attributes of the visual image," in E. C. Carterette (ed.), *Handbook of Perception*, Vol. V: *Seeing*, New York: Academic Press.

Rodieck, R. W. (1965) "Quantitative analysis of cat retinal ganglion cell response to visual stimuli," *Vision Research* 5: 581–601.

Ryle, G. (1949) *The Concept of Mind*, New York: Barnes & Noble.

Schiller, P. H., Finlay, B. L., and Volman, S. F. (1976) "Quantitative studies of single-cell properties in monkey striate cortex," *Journal of Neurophysiology* 39: 1320–1374.

Schmidt, R. A. (1980) "Past and future issues in motor programming," *Research Quarterly for Exercise and Sports* 51: 122–140.

Searle, J. R. (1979) *Expression and Meaning*, London: Cambridge University Press.

Shannon, C. E. and Weaver, W. (1949) *The Mathematical Theory of Communications*, Urbana, IL: University of Illinois Press.

Shaw, R. E. and Kinsella-Shaw, J. M. (1988) "Ecological mechanics: A physical geometry for intentional constraints," *Human Movement Science* 7: 155–200.

Shepard, R. N., and Chipman, S. (1970) "Second-order isomorphism of internal representations: Shapes of states," *Cognitive Psychology* 1: 1–17.

Skinner, B. F. (1971) *Beyond Freedom and Dignity*, New York: Knopf.

—— (1976) *About Behaviorism*, New York: Vintage.

—— (1989) "The origins of cognitive thought," *American Psychologist* 44(1): 13–18.

[Special issue on the foundations of cognitive science.] (1980) *The Behavioral and Brain Sciences* 3(1).

Sperry, R. W. (1952) "Neurology and the mind–brain problem," *American Scientist* 40: 291–312.

—— (1969) "A modified concept of consciousness," *Psychological Review* 76: 532–636.

—— (1976) "Mental phenomena as causal determinants in brain functions," in G. G. Globus, G. Maxwell, and I. Savodnick (eds), *Consciousness and the Brain*, New York: Plenum Press, 163–177.

—— (1980) "Mind/brain interaction – Mentalism, yes – Dualism, no," *Neuroscience* 2: 195–206.

Spinelli, D. N. and Pribram, K. H. (1967) "Changes in visual recovery function and unit activity produced by frontal cortex stimulation," *Electroencephalography and Clinical Neurophysiology* 22: 143–149.

Stein, R. B. (1982) "What muscle variable(s) does the nervous system control in limb movements?" *The Behavioral and Brain Sciences* 5(4): 535–577.

Toynbee, A. (1972) *A Study of History*, Oxford: Oxford University Press.

Turvey, M. T., Shaw, R. E., Reed, E. S., and Mace, W. M. (1981) "Ecological laws of perceiving and acting: In reply to Fodor and Pylyshyn," *Cognition* 9: 237–304.

3

THE AUTONOMY OF SOCIAL REALITY

On the contribution of systems theory to the theory of society[1]

Jean-Pierre Dupuy

TOWARD A CONCEPT OF AUTONOMY

This chapter pursues an interdisciplinary approach, for it seeks to apply two different intellectual traditions to the solution of a specific problem. These two traditions have largely remained ignorant of each other, since they stand on opposite sides of the abyss separating the "two cultures," the sciences and the humanities. On the one hand there is social theory, which has developed within the various humanistic disciplines and social sciences, as well as in political and social philosophy; on the other, there is systems theory, at times called "systemics," a meta-discipline born within the "hard sciences" and situated at the crossroads of the sciences of nature, life, and complex artifacts.

There have already been several attempts to "apply" systems theory to social science, such as the classic studies by Talcott Parsons, David Easton, Karl Deutsch, and so on. Yet to import the concepts and models of one discipline into another is a risky undertaking, and the limitations and dangers of this kind of approach have been the object of an abundant secondary literature. My approach is quite different. Both fields which I consider have had to confront a similar type of problem concerning the logic of organization, the relation between the many and the one, processes of totalization, etc. In both fields there has been debate over a variety of conflicting positions. I suggest that it may be worthwhile for both fields to compare these separate debates. In any case, we will find that some such comparisons have already been made to some degree and that the two fields have already influenced each other. Accordingly, the first stage of an interdisciplinary approach such as the one I am pursuing here must discover the conditions under which these exchanges took place, while the second should consider whether they could have been more successful. The present study will in fact combine these stages.

The question of autonomy forms the basis of this discussion. Elevated to the level of a concept by Kantian philosophy, the notion of autonomy first concerns man and the human world. Autonomy is the capacity to establish laws for oneself and obey them, and this obedience to one's own laws is not an obstacle to liberty, but rather its condition. Whether posited as actual or as a regulative ideal, autonomy informs the (western) metaphysical conception of subjectivity, which holds that a human being is a subject who is conscious of himself, present to himself, and capable of acting. In short he is capable of initiating processes in the system of human relations which do not result from natural determinism. The irony of the intellectual history of the twentieth century is that philosophy and the social sciences have set out to destroy the notion of autonomy at the very moment that it is beginning to influence the hard sciences such as physics, biology, and the cognitive sciences.

On the one hand, there has been a spectacular development of theories concerning "self-organizing systems" in diverse scientific disciplines: in physics, disorderly systems, such as spin glasses and percolation; in chemistry, the thermodynamics of irreversible processes and states far from equilibrium (the so-called theory of dissipative structures); in biology, the theory of autonomous or autopoietic systems; in cognitive science, the study of the properties of neural networks and connectionist machines. In each domain it has been shown that matter, without at all escaping from the determinism of natural laws, is capable of producing new patterns of organization. Matter evolves, becomes more complex, has a history, and exhibits the characteristics which have always been attributed to the mind. The philosophical impact of these remarkable scientific discoveries has been double and partially contradictory. First, they have comforted an intransigent materialist monism, which sometimes goes as far as denying all reality to the mind, liberty, and so on. But these discoveries have also nourished a somewhat vague idealistic oecumenism, which heralds the near reconciliation of the natural and human sciences.

Yet at the same time, the human sciences have participated in a somewhat comical exchange of places by starting to proclaim the "death of man," i.e. the end of the metaphysical conception of the autonomous human subject, endowed with consciousness and free will. Issued from the philosophy of Martin Heidegger, this current of thought initially exerted little influence in North America, where the social sciences and philosophy (analytic) remain fundamentally individualist. The "deconstruction of the metaphysics of subjectivity" actually blossomed in the 1950s with French structuralism in its varied forms: the anthropology of Claude Lévi-Strauss, the psychoanalysis of Jacques Lacan, the Marxism of Louis Althusser, and the historiography of Michel Foucault. The poststructuralism of Jacques Derrida finally appeared. The new historical irony was that as these ideas began to wane in their country of origin, they found fertile ground in the United States, and the role played by deconstruction in the literature departments of American universities is only too well known. One of the objects of this article is to attempt to put a little order into the misadventures surrounding the notion of autonomy.

I shall begin by indicating how these issues were identified within social theory. Later I will investigate how these same issues were addressed in systems theory.

Modernity strives to conceive of the self-sufficiency of the human world but never really manages to do so. Modernity also tries to bring about a practical realization of this ideal but has never succeeded in achieving that goal either. Many thinkers, and indeed whole schools of thought, have measured themselves against the challenge presented by the notion of autonomy, either by accepting it boldly, or, more recently, by declaring simply that it cannot be met. According to this latter tendency, mankind's project of attaining mastery over his own universe is logically doomed to incompleteness. The nature of this incompleteness, or lack, and its precise theorization are subjects of great divergence, but the major thinkers of this tendency nonetheless agree on its irreducible necessity. Their writings exhibit a preponderance of metaphors, often drawn from geometry, and various topological or visual tropes are employed to designate the impossibility of autonomy. These paradoxical figures leave us puzzled, however, for how are we to grasp such notions as "society's exteriority in relation to itself," the "opacity of the self to itself," the idea of an "unconscious reflexivity," and so on?

In fact, the general schema behind such figures of speech is no real mystery at this point. The broad strokes are as follows. The members of primitive and traditional societies, whose mode of organization was religious, believed that all order and meaning came from a will that was both superior and external to men. In contrast, modernity rests upon the knowledge that men owe the laws of the city entirely to themselves. The historical appearance of societies having a centralized state marks the beginning of a long process during which the exteriority of the social is internalized. Formerly characteristic of the logic of the sacred, the division of society from an external point of reference is imported within the boundaries of society. Society is divided from itself. It was long hoped that this internalization of the rift between society and its Other would logically and necessarily bring about a *total* reappropriation of the collective being by itself. Yet the history of democratic societies, the growing awareness of their inherent fragility, and reflection on the phenomenon of totalitarianism would seem to show that this ideal is not only unrealistic, but extremely dangerous. It would seem that the attempt to realize the absolute sovereignty of the people over itself paradoxically leads to the exact opposite: a total alienation of sovereignty in the form of an arbitrary and unlimited concentration of power in a site that is radically cut off from the rest of society. A political body can be its own subject only upon the condition that the instruments used to realize this sovereignty actually deprive it to a certain degree of this very sovereignty. According to Marcel Gauchet, this occurs with the administrative and bureaucratic state, and with the institutionalization of conflict in the context of a democratic society. Both render manifest the fact that although the social bond – the meaning and direction of collective life – is a purely human reality, no one can take possession of it. Here we encounter the logic of the *entre soi* (a notion roughly translated as the "in between"). Thus Gauchet writes of the state:

> Everything that happens, happens among men, and the omnipresence of the state exists in order to give a tangible form to the full embodiment of the "in between" (*l'entre soi*). Yet at the same time, everything happens in such a way that there can be no appropriation by the social agents of the final meaning and direction of the "being-together." Such an appropriation is impossible, at any time and in any form, be it individual and dictatorial or collective and self-managed, for then the social bond would not be *in between* the social agents, but *in* them.
> (Gauchet, 1985, p. 290)

Although Gauchet's formulations differ significantly from those of other contemporary thinkers (particularly on the role of the state), his central points are wholly representative of the most vital tendency within contemporary French political philosophy. It should be noted that the most rigorous of these thinkers do not believe that the irreducible opacity of the collective being necessarily entails the impossibility of autonomy. The undeniable conclusion is rather that autonomy cannot be properly conceived of as a form of mastery or self-mastery (Castoriadis, 1975; Gauchet, 1985).

Here I shall briefly present some of the many variations concerning the themes of lack, incompleteness, exteriority, and the unconscious, all obstacles encountered by theories addressing the notion of autonomy in the human sphere. I have chosen these particular examples because they are at the center of contemporary debates within the human and social sciences, but also because we will encounter them once more when we turn to the analysis of systems theory.

Individualism versus holism For an anthropologist such as Louis Dumont, the most basic truth of sociology is that every society is essentially holistic and hierarchical, even when it tries to negate these principles in its ideas and values – as is the case in modern society. Yet these very principles nonetheless continue to shape the societies which seek to negate them. Holism, then, asserts the logical and ontological anteriority of the social totality to its constitutive parts. The hierarchical relation, which is the "logical formula" of this holism, relates the totality, seen as a set, to the elements within that set (Dumont, 1983).

In contrast, individualistic social sciences take as their starting point individuals who are thought to be separate, independent, and autonomous – individuals who therefore are not always already social. Given this basis, these social sciences would then proceed to reconstitute the social totality. What was taken away at the start will be rediscovered in the end, but in the form of a lack, and all sorts of theoretical acrobatics are needed in order for the diverse systems of political philosophy to fill this lack. It may seem in the end as if the whole is greater than the sum of the parts, but according to Dumont, this is no surprise because these social sciences deprive the parts of what they owe to the whole. Yet we should note that the theoretical metaphor of the set which he utilizes is inadequate here. The very paradox which had to be neutralized in order to construct a coherent set theory has been reintroduced: the set has been posited as a totality, the members of which can only be defined by presupposing the existence of the totality as such.

The reconstitution of the social whole on the basis of separate individuals has taken two major forms within modern political thought. The first, that of the social contract, is essentially unstable. It combines a traditional vision of the social as a "fact of consciousness" expressly willed by the members of society, with the modern tendency toward individualism and artificialism. It is all too easy to establish that the various models of the social contract reproduce the very figure of exteriority that they were meant to abolish. In the case of Hobbes, the Leviathan stands above the laws and does not even take part in the contract. Rousseau's general will, and the law that is supposed to be its expression, are supposed to have the inflexibility characteristic of natural laws. Rousseau wants the laws of the city to be *above* men, yet men are the authors of these same laws and they know it. Rousseau himself compares this problem to the squaring of a circle.

The social contract has been supplanted by a second model, that of the marketplace. Yet exteriority remains equally important in this approach because the social bond is fashioned independently of the consciousness and will of mankind. Exteriority is the effect of a pure automatism in which everyone has a part, but which no one fabricates or preconceives. The gap between the individual and collective levels is filled by an "invisible hand." For Dumont, this amounts to a degradation of the social bond into a "fact of physical nature" (Dumont, 1977). Yet in this regard, Marcel Gauchet's criticism of Dumont is quite interesting. Gauchet asks whether the fiction of individualism was not, quite paradoxically, the necessary condition of man's becoming aware of the *autonomy* of the social in relation to his own consciousness and will. The very idea of a social science springs from the discovery of the self-organizing properties of the social – that is, the fact that the social is neither the product of an external program (the will of a radically different Other) nor that of an internal program (such as a general will, social contract, or the activity of a State). Such a discovery could not be made within a social order thought to be consciously willed and known, one where an "unknown" is inconceivable (Gauchet, 1979). Thus the autonomy of the social amounts to its objectivity, whereby it resists man's efforts to fashion it and is governed by its own specific laws. Gauchet is the first to recognize that we have no convincing metaphors to describe the strange process in which the result of our very own actions is transformed into an object.

"Methodological individualism" in sociology encounters the same problems. Its reduction of social phenomena to the sum of individual actions only appears plausible through the playing out of "perverse," "counter-intuitive," and "unintentional" effects (Boudon, 1977). Yet this actually means that collective phenomena are not immediately deducible from the properties of the individuals who participate in them. The question of exteriority is displaced but not eradicated. Although the counter-intuitive effects may very well surpass the intuitive knowledge of the agents, they do not escape from the wisdom of the putatively "external" observer who is the sociologist. Yet what, indeed, is the basis of this observer's external status? Is it necessary, then, to sweep away these (false?) mysteries by putting the essentialism of a "methodological holism" in the place of this nominalism? This would amount to positing from the outset the exteriority and the anteriority of the social totality in relation to its own elements. In order to grasp the identity of a society do we have to remain confined to the old Leibnizian categories of the monad and the aggregate, the former having a "substantive unity," while the unity of the latter is purely accidental? Are no more recent – or more appropriate – conceptual tools available to us?

The systems of suspicion Benefiting from a certain perspective, we understand better today the genealogy of those trends in the French "human sciences" that were so very influential during the 1960s and 1970s (Ferry and Renaut, 1985). Inspired by the modern masters of "suspicion," Marx, Freud, and Nietzsche, these currents competed with each other in their zealous desire to deepen (or pervert) Heidegger's critique of the metaphysics of subjectivity. These thinkers sought in their respective ways to show that man is not the master of his own house. In other words, the consciousness he may have of his own affairs is necessarily limited, for it is exteriorly limited or determined by some sort of unconscious. Ferry and Renaut classify these systems into two major types (pp. 32–33):

(a) The rationalist variety employs the motifs of the "ruse of reason" and the "ruse of history." Althusser's "subjectless historical process" is a perfect example of this trend. According to this conception, men are not the subjects of their own history. They merely recite a text they neither composed nor understand. There is, however, a site – that of absolute knowledge – where this understanding is possible, but this site is found at the level of the System, not the elements. Thus the System is granted all the attributes of subjectivity. The "liberal" version of this model is most interesting in our context, for it is clear that there are profound affinities between the ruse of reason and the invisible hand of the marketplace.

(b) The "Nietzschean–Heideggerian" variety rejects the possibility of any exogenous fixed point, as we shall elaborate below. Thinkers situated within this trend mercilessly attack any pursuit which vaguely resembles a reassuring quest for a transcendental signified. According to this dogma, there are only signifiers, which signify one another in an infinite hermeneutic chain of interpretations. This perpetual drifting of the sign has neither origin nor end (reality, being, truth).

Structuralism and post-structuralism clearly indicate where the exaggerations of this tendency may lead. The reflections of Jacques Derrida, who interrogates the "rupture" that structuralism is supposed to have introduced into the secular concept of structure, may be situated at an advanced stage along this path. Previously, structure, "although it has always been at work, has always been neutralized or reduced, and this by a process of giving it a center or of referring it to a point of presence, a fixed origin." But this center, which organizes the "play" of the elements in the structure, is also the place where this play is "prohibited." In this center:

> the substitution of contents, elements, and terms is no longer possible. . . . Thus it has always been thought that the center, which is by definition unique, constituted that very thing within a structure, which, while governing the structure, escapes structurality. This is why classical thought concerning structure could say that the center is, paradoxically, *within* the structure and *outside it.* The center is at the center of the totality, and yet, since it does not belong to the totality (is not part of the totality), the totality *has its center elsewhere.* . . . The concept of centered structure . . . is contradictorily coherent.

According to Derrida, the contemporary human sciences, and especially the ethnology of Lévi-Strauss, have eliminated this conception of the centered structure, much in keeping with the deconstructions already undertaken by Freud, Nietzsche, and Heidegger. But what has replaced this center? Here is where the mystery begins, and the terms used by the proponents of this tendency are consistently marked by the obscurity of sacred language. Thus in the place of the center, there is not just nothing, but a "non-center." It is the substitute for a "lack" (*suppléance d'un manque*), or a hole in the structure, "a kind of non-place in which the infinite substitutions of the sign are played out" (p. 411). Thus a finite structure can be the frame for a limitless play, like the "empty square" which allows the other pieces in the puzzle to move about (Deleuze, 1979). This lack and the impossibility of filling it reflect the impossibility of escaping from the structure in order to survey it from the higher level of a metalanguage.

Before proceeding to examine what systems theory has to say about our subject, it may be useful to underscore a few points often forgotten. It is crucial to remember that cybernetics played a key role in the elaboration of these various theoretical trends by providing numerous metaphors which enabled them to distinguish themselves from other currents. Yet the same didn't occur with systems theory. One should keep in mind that though systems theory was born of cybernetics, both differ on a number of essential points.

Let us begin by recalling that cybernetics was a key reference even for thinkers whose work is rarely associated with the movement. As is well known, the French structuralists began to proclaim the death of the human subject in the 1950s. They strove to show that man does not master language, but is mastered by it. The "symbolic order" is irreducible to human experience, so that when man thinks that he is speaking, it is actually language which speaks. Students of modern French thought are all familiar with these arguments, but they are rarely aware of the extent to which information theory and the automata of cybernetics were employed as illustrations. The case of Jacques Lacan is most typical, for his entire seminar of 1954–55 was placed under the rubric of cybernetics. The summit occurred with his reading of Poe's "The Purloined Letter," a reading couched in terms of automata theory (Lacan, 1966, 1978). Four years earlier, Claude Lévi-Strauss had published his "Introduction to the Work of Marcel Mauss," a text considered by many as the manifesto of French structuralism. Herein Lévi-Strauss places great hope in the general theory of communication developed in the work of Norbert Wiener and John von Neumann (Lévi-Strauss, 1973).

It is easy to guess why these unholy alliances frequently go unmentioned today. As Ferry and Renaut rightly point out, the anti-humanist tendencies of the French human sciences have their main source in Heidegger. Heidegger's hatred of cybernetics, which he termed "the metaphysics of the atomic age," is still a major influence on many philosophers. Heidegger believed cybernetics to be an extreme form of what is known as the "philosophy of the *cogito*," for it seeks to realize the metaphysical project in which man makes himself the master and owner of all things including himself. As the climax of the will to power, cybernetics would make us miss "the essence of technology." Accordingly, it is hard to see how cybernetics could be the theoretical ally of schools of thought which expressly label themselves as the continuation of Heidegger's deconstruction of western metaphysics. Vincent Descombes, for example, considers it totally incoherent for structuralism to pretend to fight against "the philosophy of consciousness" while borrowing its concepts from "the thought of engineers" (1979, pp. 123–124).

Yet such opinions rest upon a very basic misunderstanding of what the cybernetic project was all about. Here I will limit myself to recalling that cybernetics began in 1943 with the independent publication of two seminal articles, "Behavior, purpose, and teleology" by Arturo Rosenblueth, Norbert Wiener, and Julian Bigelow, and "A Logical Calculus of the Ideas Immanent in Nervous Activity" by Warren McCulloch and Walter Pitts.[2] The former aims to show that the will amounts to a mechanism, while the latter makes a like claim for perception, thought, memory, and consciousness. Pitts and McCulloch sought to establish a neurology of mind by discovering a purely neuroanatomical and neurophysiological foundation for synthetic a priori judgments. Thus they are the initiators of "Kantianism without the transcendental subject." Thanks to these two articles, it was henceforth possible to provide rigorous representations of thought or behavior processes without a subject.

The cybernetic project is indeed marked by the ambivalence Heidegger referred to concerning the "essence of technology." This is evident in the two possible interpretations of research on automata. The most frequent and popular rendering is anthropomorphic: human properties are attributed to machines (they think, act, etc.). Also plausible is the opposite interpretation, which reveals the mechanization of humans and unveils what is nonhuman in them. The "French Heideggereans" were most sensitive to this second aspect and could thus coherently make reference to cybernetics in order to make their own points. I shall later return to this issue at some length in regard to Lacan.

The other approach to the "social unconscious," that of the "ruse of reason," has also frequently employed cybernetic and later systems metaphors to project a cutting-edge aspect. Here one must cite the work of Friedrich von Hayek, who is anything but a stranger to the systems theories to be discussed. It is remarkable to note how both major strains of theory we have identified adopted the same set of concepts from the hard sciences in order to contemplate mankind's lack of self-mastery.

A brief digression on the case of Régis Debray will serve to illustrate the fascination that twentieth-century mechanistic philosophies have exerted on thinkers who hold human autonomy to be impossible. In his *Critique de la raison politique* (1981), Debray asserts that the "secret of our collective misfortune . . . takes the form of a logical law" (p. 256). He adds that this "secret" of human reality is not to be sought in the social sciences, "for the simple reason that this secret is inhuman, and thus theological" (p. 263). Logic is at the origin of religiosity, which is the principle of all exteriority. In particular, it lies at the origin of all religiosity in politics, which is the source of all collective irrationality. This logic is said to impress itself absolutely and "transcendentally" on the consciousness of mankind. Thus logic is ultimately the "pure form" of the social and political unconscious of mankind. Debray certainly could have given a human form to this social unconscious by following Durkheim, who posits society as the source of our logical categories: "the origin of the very special authority that is inherent in reason" is "the authority of society" (Durkheim, 1968, p. 24). But this is precisely what Debray wishes to rule out. Instead, he insists that logic is inhuman, like a natural fact.

What is it, then, that this logic requires? Debray's answer is clear: "There is no organized system without closure, and no system can be closed solely by means of the elements internal to the system. The closing of a field can only take place in a contradictory manner through its opening onto an element external to the field" (p. 256). This "law of incompleteness" is set forth by Debray as being "a generalization of Gödel's theorem." Debray's argument here can be added to the list of the many errors that have been made by thinkers who have become fascinated by Gödel's theorem but are unfamiliar with the discipline and rigor of work in logic. As often occurs, a result obtained within the specific framework of formal systems and in regard to specific hypotheses is suddenly extended to all sorts of systems. It can easily be shown that some very simple systems violate the "generalization" postulated by Debray. But some complex systems do this as well: this is one of the major contributions of the theory of autonomous systems that I shall take up in a moment.[3]

Applied to the political sphere, Debray's postulate produces the following results: "The relation of a whole to itself cannot be direct. It necessarily adopts the figure of a Mediator, who serves as its touchstone and most sensitive point, which cannot be touched without threatening the vital integrity of the whole" (p. 262). Every human collectivity therefore owes its unity and truth to the operation of an external element, which is transcendent in relation to it. It would seem to follow that "the government of a collectivity by itself – *verbi gracia*, 'of the people by the people' – would be a logically contradictory operation" (p. 264). Given Debray's conclusions, the only political freedom that remains to men would be to choose from among the diverse types of exteriority: sacred kingship, constitutional monarchy, democratically-elected president of the republic, etc.

Now, if we look closely at the embryonic justifications Debray advances in support of his thesis, we find that the argument is not ultimately based on Gödel's incompleteness theorem. Rather, we discover a "cybernetic theorem." This theorem may be less venerable than Gödel's but has in fact played a major role in the history of the ideas I am discussing. More specifically, we encounter the so-called Ashby theorem of the impossibility of self-organization (Ashby, 1962), which challenges us to make sense of the expression, "a program that programs itself." We can of course imagine a program capable of modifying part of its own rules of operation, but this ability would itself have to be programmed and must consequently surpass the program's self-mastery. Thus such mastery can never be complete.

If a system is programmed, its elements can never depart from the program in order to modify the program itself. The program will always remain external to the elements and hence out of their reach. Despite all of Pirandello's talent, we know very well that his characters have "always already" had an author and that they never had the ability to choose him or create him. Yet this merely proves that if we wish to conceive of the autonomy of a system, we must not think in terms of a program. By taking their metaphors from cybernetics, the structuralists made their work easy for themselves. From the beginning they made it impossible to conceive of the very thing they proclaimed to be impossible: autonomy.

Even if systems thought was born within cybernetics or closely related fields, contemporary systems theory developed in reaction to the basic postulates of cybernetics. This reaction was rooted precisely in the desire to make autonomy conceivable.

All the organized totalities which cyberneticians studied – from ecosystems to human societies, from mechanical animals to ant colonies, from neural networks to living organisms – were treated according to a single model. This model is an artificial totality in which the parts are anterior to the whole. These nominal totalities are made complete only when a third term, an organizing consciousness, perceives and conceives of them. Yet from the beginning cybernetics encountered another, richer conception of organized totalities, a conception which was aimed directly against it. These criticisms arose from within gestalt psychology (W. Köhler) and neurophysiology (K. S. Lashley), but above all, they were formulated by the embryologist Paul Weiss. Weiss's ideas play a central role in the history of systems theory (Weiss, 1968; Dupuy, 1985; Stengers, 1985). He draws a very sharp distinction between "machines" and "systems." The latter are natural and nonnominal totalities. However, these are not monads and their recognition does not amount to holist philosophy, which treats wholes as substances. The appropriate method for the study of systems avoids essentialism as well as reductionism; it is neither "top-down" (a subordination of elements and their relations to the totality), nor "bottom-up" (a deduction of the properties of the totality from those of fully specified elements). This necessitates a third approach, which is more complex because it rejects the easy answers provided when the scientist posits an ultimate level of explanation. Weiss admits that every system is hierarchical, which means that it is made up of different interlocking levels of integration. Yet he claims that an adequate conception of the unity of such a system – that is, of its *autonomy* – demands the formulation of the principle of a *circular causality* connecting the levels. In a material system (an organism), the laws of physics leave a large degree of freedom to the individual elements. This basic indeterminacy is reduced by the constraints exercised by the whole,

71

constraints which are themselves the result of the composition of elementary activities. The whole and its parts are mutually determined, and this co-determination explains the complexity of living beings.

The Hixon Symposium of 1948 was a key moment in the debate between Weiss and the cyberneticians (Dupuy, 1985). Ironically, Weiss's ideas would be rediscovered and developed much later by the theoreticians of autonomous systems (also known as self-organizing systems), who were largely biologists influenced by cybernetic concepts (Maturana and Varela, 1980; Varela, 1979; Atlan, 1979). These thinkers realized that the cybernetic metaphor of the program upon which molecular biology had been based rendered a conception of the autonomy of the living being impossible. Consequently, these thinkers were led to invent a new cybernetics, one more suited to the organizations mankind discovers in nature – organizations he has not himself invented. Is it possible that this new cybernetics could also account for social forms of organization? This topic has remained an object of debate among the theoreticians of self-organization (Dumouchel and Dupuy, 1983; Dupuy, 1982).

The notion of system elaborated here is a very restrictive one, and its definition seeks to be exclusive and distinguishing rather than inclusive. Systems, then, are only those organizations which are "informationally and operationally closed." This implies that the system – or the *automaton*, in the primary meaning of the term – itself engenders the organization that defines it as a unit. This organization is not the result of the execution of an external program, nor is it the product of an internal one. The autonomous system is *not* a cybernetic machine, classically defined as a black box which transforms inputs into outputs (the behaviorist's stimulus-response schema). It is not a machine that receives instructions and processes information according to a pre-established schema. To represent an organization as a system is to postulate that is has neither a cause nor an effect outside itself. It constitutes its own frame of meaning and existence. Two comments may help to make this notion of closure more precise and thereby avoid misunderstandings.

(1) As a result of the widespread popularizing of biological notions, everyone knows that the living organization is an "open" system. This does not contradict our notion of closure, for the openness concerns the flow of matter and energy.

(2) The organizational and informational closure obviously is not meant to imply that the system has no interactions with its environment. Yet these interactions should not be thought of as instructions received from the environment. Rather, they are perturbations in the system's modalities of closure. The system knows the world surrounding it through and by means of its own organizational closure. The model of the autonomous system therefore entails a criticism of the *repre-*

sentationalist paradigm which dominates the cognitive sciences. According to this paradigm, there exists a homomorphism between the state of the environment and a living being's knowledge of it. In the new paradigm, however, to know is not to recognize, but to bring forth a world according to the forms that are allowed by one's own internal organization.

Difficult questions are raised in response to this new paradigm. For example, what are the capabilities of a systemic totality? What behavior can it display, and what knowledge of its environment can it possess? How can we represent or model an organization which is closed upon itself?

I cannot enter into the details here but will deal with the most basic points in the case studies which follow. Two preliminary remarks are, however, in order. As a matter of definition, the operationally closed system violates the universal law of incompleteness set forth by Debray: such a system owes its coherence, identity and meaning entirely to itself. The fact that such systems are conceivable indicates that the limits assigned to formal systems by Gödel's theorem cannot be generalized to all kinds of systems. Thus, Soto-Andrade and Varela have recently formulated the necessary and sufficient conditions for reflexivity in a mathematical structure, in the sense that there exists an isomorphism between the level of the elements and the level of the operations on these elements (Soto-Andrade and Varela, 1984). In certain situations, it is possible to master self-reference without succumbing to insurmountable paradoxes. We can speak of an operator which operates on itself and of a function which is its own argument. (It is clear that if such structures exist, Ashby's argument collapses: thus the theory of autonomous systems stands *against* Ashby's "theorem".)

The completeness of an autonomous system does not, however, imply that it is wholly the *master* of its own meaning. Unlike a program, nevertheless, it does not receive its meaning from an external and transcendent "meta-level." This overly simple figure of exteriority is replaced by a less comprehensible notion, that of *complexity*. It is here, on a formal level, that systems theory joins political thought's considerations on the difficulty (but not the impossibility) of conceptualizing the self-sufficiency of the human and social world. The notion of complexity gives a precise and rigorous form to the notions of "the lack" and of "the opacity of self to self."

FIXED POINTS, COMPLEXITY, AND SELF-TRANSCENDENCE

Exogenous and endogenous fixed points

The most fundamental concept in the theory of autonomous systems is the emergence of behavior proper to the system (*eigenbehaviors*). Organizational closure, the looping together of the elements and their relations, results in the emergence of new properties at the level of the whole. These new properties cannot be foreseen in an examination of the parts alone. These phenomena of emergence at the level of the whole are also referred to as "systemic effects." Within the class of behavior proper to the system, the notion of a *fixed point* is isolated. This concept must not be confused with the one which Michel Serres once said was at the heart of science during the classical period (Serres, 1968). The emergent fixed point, which I also refer to as an "endogenous" fixed point, is not a unifying principle by which the totality is organized. Instead, this point is a singularity of the totality that results from its closure upon itself. It is an effect, not a cause.

In order to illustrate this distinction, I will examine the theory of the crowd and the social phenomenon of panic Freud proposes in "Group psychology and the analysis of the ego" (Freud, 1985; original edition 1921). Freud begins with a theory of the crowd which is constructivist or "structuralist." In his own words, the phenomenon of panic seems to be a paradox. Yet it can be shown that this phenomenon is in no way a logical problem once we adopt a systemic perspective on crowd phenomena.

Briefly, Freud characterizes the crowd by means of three traits:

(1) Its principle of cohesion: the *libido*. For a collection of individuals to form a crowd, selfishness or narcissism, the antisocial force par excellence, must be overcome. Only a "libidinal bond to others," Freud claims, can subdue selfish interests.

(2) The focal point of these libidinal bonds, namely, the *leader*. Freud of course follows Le Bon and Tarde in recognizing the existence of leaderless crowds, spontaneous and ephemeral gatherings, but the real models for his theory of the crowd are the army and the church. These "artificial" crowds are *constructed* by and around their leader. The leader is the operator of the collectivity's totalization, its *fixed point*.

(3) The phenomenon characteristic of the crowd: *contagion*. Contagion leads to imitation, or a kind of resonating effect propagated through the affective bonds which link the members of the crowd together.

Yet this topology has a double singularity. The first is the figure of the leader, the navel of the crowd. Everyone but the leader has abandoned his self-love, and everyone loves the leader. The leader loves only himself and has no need for the others. This very independence is what makes him the chosen individual and guarantees his power. Paradoxically, the founding block of society (the crowd) is an antisocial individual. Here we rediscover the aporia of the centered structure which was denounced by Derrida: the center is both inside and outside the structure, it governs the structure while escaping from structurality.

The second singularity is the notion of panic. What happens, then, when

74

the crowd loses its fixed point, the leader, when the centered structure loses its center? Freud's answer is unequivocal: the affective bonds which had maintained the cohesion of the crowd to its leader are broken, and "disintegration" soon follows. Narcissism and selfish interests return in full force.

Yet Freud recognizes that at the precise moment when two of the three structural features of the crowd have vanished – the leader and the affective bonds – the crowd seems most like a crowd to us. Thus we arrive at the *"paradoxical* position that this collective mind does away with itself at the very moment at which it manifests its most characteristic properties. It dissolves by the very means of this manifestation" (my italics; Freud, 1985, p. 127). Freud notes this paradox but makes nothing of it. Yet there is something even more unsettling in his analysis. Once the affective bonds are destroyed, in principle there is no longer a pathway for the phenomenon of contagion, which should disappear as a result. Yet we know that the opposite occurs, which Freud recognizes. How does the fluid travel during the panic?

My own contention is that a systemic approach to crowds resolves these various paradoxes (Dupuy, 1983). The sharp distinction between artificial and spontaneous crowds must be abandoned, and we should reject Freud's quick dichotomy between anarchical groups and those constructed around a leader. These distinctions remain trapped in the paradigm of the *exogenous fixed point*, which is at once the program and producer of the crowd. In order to leave this paradigm, we need to conceive of an *endogenous fixed point*, the "emergent eigenbehavior" or "systemic effect." This endogenous fixed point is *produced by the crowd although the crowd believes itself to have been produced by it*. Such a tangling of different levels is, we have said, a distinguishing feature of autonomous systems.

To construe the leader as an endogenous fixed point is to note that he does not gain his central position because of any intrinsic features, such as his supposed narcissism or charisma. Rather, this position emerges when the autonomous system of the crowd loops back upon itself. The leader gives the impression of not needing the others' affection, but this is only an illusion. We believe he could do without this affection only because he has already acquired it. Should he lose it (which is inevitable given the unstable and arbitrary nature of all endogenous fixed points), he will be willing to go to great lengths to regain his former status. Self-love is only possible to the extent that the love of others is possessed. Narcissism is an illusion, since only pseudo-narcissism is real (Girard, 1961). The leader's singular nature is not the result of his individual characteristics, but is a systemic effect.

To say that the leader (or power) is an endogenous fixed point is to claim that the human group in fact uses an element within the group as its external point of reference. The selection of this point results from the interdependent actions of its members. The same mechanism of externalization is at

work in the phenomenon of panic. Only from the artificialist perspective of
Freud is the crowd set in opposition to the panic. In a systems perspective,
the transformation of the crowd during a situation of panic raises no logical
problems since it simply consists of substituting one endogenous fixed
point for another. Although the leader has disappeared in the panic, another
fixed point representing the collectivity takes his place and appears to
transcend the members. This fixed point is nothing other than the movement of the group itself, a movement that acquires distance and autonomy
in relation to the individual movements. Yet this movement is merely the
result of individual actions and reactions. As Durkheim well noted, in these
moments of "effervescence" the social totality assumes all the features men
attribute to the divine: exteriority, transcendence, unpredictability, and
inaccessibility. Elias Canetti points out that the "crowd needs a direction," a goal which would be given *from outside* each individual," and be
"identical for all." The nature of this goal is unimportant as long as it is
"not yet attained" (Canetti, 1966). In the flight of panic, this result is
achieved precisely by the very process of totalization.

The form of panic is typically systemic, for it consists of communication
between the elements of a totality through the intermediary of the totality
itself. This totality is considered transcendent, although it is actually an
emergent phenomenon. It is possible that this figure is the key to all forms
of social division. Here we find the most complex and strange morpho-
genetic principle of social forms: the exteriorizing of the self in relation to
the self. This is what some systems theoreticians call "bootstrapping," a
term adopted from quantum mechanics. It is also referred to sometimes as
"self-transcendence." It is advantageous to substitute this metaphor for
that of exteriority. The concept of an endogenous fixed point also gives a
precise and rigorous form to the wilfully obscure Derridian notion of the
"non-center" of the structure.

Hayek's system: self-transcendence and the
complexity of the social

Reference to Hayek's work is necessary in the present context for several
reasons. Hayek brings the tradition of the invisible hand to its culmination
point, by revitalizing it in a deep and far-reaching system. But most
importantly, Hayek understands society as a system that is organizationally
closed in the sense understood by systems theory. This is no accident given
that Hayek has long been acquainted with cybernetics and the theory of
autonomous systems, for he was invited by Heinz von Foerster to one of
the three major conferences on self-organization held in the 1960s. Moreover, Hayek participated with von Bertalanffy, Paul Weiss and C. H.
Waddington in the Alpbach Symposium of 1969, "Beyond Reductionism," which was organized by Arthur Koestler. This conference was a

great moment in the history of systems thinking. Rosenblatt has acknow-ledged that Hayek influenced him in his conception of the famous "perceptron," one of the first sketches of an "autonomous machine." In today's interdisciplinary colloquia, Hayek's "spontaneous social orders" have become the frequent companions of the "autopoietic" systems of Maturana and Varela, as well as the "dissipative structures" of Prigogine (Zeleny, 1980). It is precisely this aspect of Hayek's work which concerns us here. The fact that Hayek reaches conclusions which reject the well-anchored certainties of progressive thinking should not be allowed to obscure the philosophical importance of his work.

For Hayek, the social order is organized around points of reference which arise from within it but are nonetheless "external" to the individuals who make up that order. These points are external in the sense that the individuals in the group do not master them and are often unaware of their existence. To situate this in the terms of my previous discussion, I would say that the social totality plays the role of an endogenous fixed point. Hayek is no holist, and yet it is true that for him there is more in the whole than the sum of the parts. His position is original and must not be identified with either holism or individualism; if anything, it corresponds to the third path defined by Paul Weiss in his critique of cybernetics.

Liberals (in the European sense) such as Hayek must confront the theoretical problem of the articulation of two forms of autonomy – first of all, the autonomy of the individual who is freed from the traditional bonds of subordination, such as those which formerly linked the individual to the sacred or to the state. The second form of autonomy is social. It implies not that men master society, but the opposite: society eludes their grasp and appears to have a life of its own. This life is foreign to humans, although they are part of it. In relation to individuals, this form of autonomy has traditionally been known as heteronomy. Here we see the striking contrast with the artificialism or constructivism characteristic of other traditions, liberal or not.

Humans make their own society – this is the first type of autonomy. But they do not know what they are making, nor how they do it – and that is the second type of autonomy. Herein resides the paradox. Both forms are "autonomies" in the ordinary sense of independence, and the two forms are reconciled in light of the technical sense the word acquires within the theory of autonomous systems. It is clear that the paradox is the same as the one which consists of *making an automaton*, that is to say of making an entity that by definition contains the principle of its movement within itself. It is the paradox of being the cause of an entity that is the unconditioned cause of itself.

That Hayek knew von Neumann's solution to this paradox is apparent in his remarks made during discussions at the "Beyond Reductionism" symposium (Koestler and Smythies, 1969, pp. 331–332). Von Neumann set forth his argument at the Hixon Symposium in 1948, where he confronted Warren McCulloch and criticized the constructivist approach of cybernetics. In the ordinary case of simple machines, it is easier to describe what a machine can do than to give a diagram of its wiring. Von Neumann proceeded to conjecture that beyond a certain threshold of complexity, the opposite would be the case: it would be simpler, indeed infinitely simpler, to construct the automaton than to describe its behavior. This conjecture was based on the results of Gödel and Turing, who had revolutionized mechanist philosophy in the 1930s. The set of the productions of the universal computer, or Turing machine, is infinitely more complex than the machine itself, since the machine is incapable of making a complete survey of everything it is able to produce. The matrix is infinitely surpassed by its own offspring. This prodigious result gives a rigorous meaning to the figurative expressions of bootstrapping and self-transcendence, for it appears that the output somehow becomes "autonomous" in relation to its own generative principle.

For Hayek, society is a *complex* automaton in von Neumann's sense. Thus he echoes Durkheim's claim that reason, the categories of human thought, the system of social rules, etc., are irreducible to individual experience and cannot be recapitulated by any form of consciousness (Durkheim, 1968, p. 23). Yet at the same time, Hayek can consequentially reject the notion of "collective representations" and the correlative idea that the social totality is anterior to its constitutive parts. Durkheim had written in 1912 that "it is impossible to deduce society from the individual, the whole from the part, the complex from the simple" (Durkheim, 1968, p. 22). He did not suspect that twenty years later it would be discovered that a mechanical operation of deduction can effectively produce novelty and complexity. Hayek, on the other hand, experienced the shock of this discovery, and his social theory was affected by it. Given this concept of complexity, Hayek can conceptualize the autonomy of the human world without doing so in terms of mastery and transparency.

Hayek's liberalism sees two types of progress in recognizing society's misrecognition of itself. There is progress in knowledge as well as in freedom. The disappearance of the "synoptic delusion" marks progress in knowledge. Following this delusion, the fact that individuals possess a considerable amount of knowledge in their totality should make it possible to gather this knowledge together in a single point. But in an autonomous system (unlike a program that obeys the logic of the exogenous fixed point), a localizable operator of totalization or integration does not exist. Any such operator coincides with the system as a whole. Men therefore increase their capacities for action if they recognize that there are spontaneous social orders which are the "result of human action but not of human design" (Hayek, 1973, p. 20). In other words, they must recognize that there are emergent orders and systemic effects. Men also increase their capacities for action by relying upon the diverse knowledge these orders mobilize, which nevertheless cannot be individually appropriated. This knowledge takes the form of rules and institutions resulting from habit, tradition and culture. The abstract rules of the spontaneous order allow us to orient ourselves in a world comprised of particular facts that are too complex to be mastered by constructive reason. Thus the "knowledge" in question here is the opposite of the kind of knowledge Descartes tried to define. It is implicit and non-conscious, incorporated within the mind but not produced by it: "The mind does not so much make rules as consist of rules of action" (Hayek, 1973, p. 18). Hayek claims that "we can make use of so much experience, not because we possess that experience, but because, without our knowing it, it has become incorporated in the schemata of thought which guide us" (1973, pp. 30–31). Hayek pointed out at the "Beyond Reductionism" symposium that the system of rules which constitutes the mind in unconscious, not because it is located at an excessively low level, as in the case of the Freudian unconscious. Rather it is situated at too high a level: "these processes are not 'sub-conscious' but 'super-conscious.' They govern the conscious processes without appearing at their level" (Koestler and Smythies, 1969, p. 319).

In regard to human freedom, this valorizing of non-mastery and of the opacity of the social is justified by Hayek in the following way: considerable freedom results from knowing that one need not worry constantly about social cohesion, and one need not make manifest one's subordination to the collective order with all of one's will and consciousness. In addition, by keeping the seat of power empty, the market provides an obstacle to the delirious dreams of omnipotence which have resulted from the various social "constructivisms."

Hayek's theory of knowledge can also be considered a kind of Kantianism without a transcendental subject. The only subject is at the level of the whole system of humanity and history. The spontaneous order is not part of the natural order, nor of the artificial order, but belongs to an order of a third sort, that of cultural evolution. Culture is memory, or the sum of abstract rules the human group has selected because they have proven beneficial over time. This selection occurs in an anonymous process whose logic is in many respects identical to that of natural selection. Whence the original nature of Hayek's theory of law. He obviously refuses juridical positivism's equating of justice and legality. Justice as well as law is anterior to legislation, providing norms and standards that permit it to be judged. At the same time Hayek rejects all reference to natural law taken as some kind of eternal and transcendent norm. Justice may not be what mankind wants it to be, but it does not arise from a transcendent nature either. In this sense, Hayek is neither an ancient nor a modern historicist who would identify what is with what ought to be. The norm is provided by "opinion" and tradition, which allows itself to be criticized according to the norm. The apparent paradox is quite simply that of bootstrapping or self-transcendence:

> It may at first seem puzzling that something which is the product of tradition should be capable of both being the object and the standard of criticism. But we do not maintain that all tradition as such is sacred and exempt from criticism, but merely that the basis of criticism of any one product of tradition must always be other products of tradition which we either cannot or do not want to question; in other words, particular aspects of a culture can be critically examined only within the context of that culture. . . . Thus we can always examine a part of the whole only in terms of that whole which we cannot entirely reconstruct and the greater part of which we must accept unexamined.
>
> (Hayck, 1976, p. 25)

Hayek's system, of which I have presented a few aspects, can and must be criticized. Here I shall limit myself to two comments which reveal that Hayek's error results from too little systems thinking, not too much. Hayek thinks that only a personal action can be considered just or unjust. To say that a spontaneous order is unjust is to fall back into the anthropomorphism or animism of primitive thought, which attributes all social morphogenesis to the voluntary and conscious efforts of an identifiable agent. This is to look for "scapegoats." It follows that the very expression, "social justice," has no meaning (Hayek, 1976). But this argument can be turned as easily as we turn a glove inside out. If modernity amounts to progress over primitive thought in knowledge, it is precisely because we have learned that injustice, and evil in general, are most often *systemic effects*.

Moreover, even if Hayek's logic of the cultural system consists largely of autonomous systems having endogenous fixed points, it remains true nonetheless that this logic is ultimately governed by an exogenous fixed point. In other words, there remains a seat of absolute knowledge, which is why Hayek's system continues to exhibit figures of the ruse of reason. It is indeed in the name of such a knowledge that Hayek can state that the processes of cultural selection lead, with more or less hesitation and difficulty, to the *best* rules, those of liberalism. If Hayek had followed the theory of autonomous systems to the end, he would have understood that this theory cannot accept the vicious circularities of neo-Darwinism's selection of the fittest (Maturana and Varela, 1984). In this way Hayek could have avoided the contradictory trap in which his system hopelessly entangles him: in fact it is the bureaucratic state and not liberal society that has been "selected" by history. Thus we must admit either that the former is the best, or that evolution does not have the optimizing virtues attributed to it by Hayek.

THE HOLE IN THE STRUCTURE

In their struggle against anything bearing the slightest resemblance to an exogenous fixed point (the transcendental signified, truth understood metaphysically as adequation, or *homoiosis* in relation to a referent, etc.), structuralism and post-structuralism have engaged in various successive forms of "deconstruction." Clarity is not the greatest virtue in the writing style characteristic of these schools. For such thinkers, it is not sufficient to designate some locus of the unconscious which can be said to govern our action and thoughts behind our backs. Instead, this locus must remain "unthought" (*impensé*), for it must not become an object of knowledge. It is not sufficient to replace the center of the structure by a non-center, a lack, or a vacuum, which could still function as some kind of inverted or disguised version of the fixed point. In spite of their seeming negativity, all of these notions would still block the infinite play of the substitutions of the sign. It is not enough simply to maim or disable the classical discourse of representation: there must be no chance of reappropriation, return, or "re-adequation." If a hole in the structure is what is wanted, it must not have a specific place or delimitation. We must conceive a hole which is "disseminated."

Jacques Lacan's "Seminar on *The Purloined Letter*" (1966, 1978) and Derrida's subsequent critique (1980) figure among the high points of the French debate over the deconstruction of western metaphysics. My interest here concerns the predominance of the cybernetic metaphors informing these texts, and a comparison of them to autonomous systems will allow us to reveal the blind spot shared by Lacan and Derrida.

The truth of the purloined letter

Lacan's most basic thesis asserted that the human subject is constituted by the "symbolic order," and he thought that decisive arguments in support of this thesis could be found in game theory. It would seem that he was not entirely mistaken. We may recall that mathematical game theory was formalized by von Neumann and that it was one of the earliest ingredients of cybernetics. Such a theory schematizes conflicts between fully rational subjects, whose rational conduct requires them to identify with the perspective of the adversary. This combination of rationality and identification with the Other also fascinated Edgar Allan Poe, as is evidenced in many of his writings, especially *The Purloined Letter*. Game theory demonstrates that when free and rational individuals interact, they constitute a system governed by universal laws, which are in a sense "external" to the players and determine them without their knowledge. Thus mathematical game theory would seem to support Lacan's thesis.

In the published seminar on *The Purloined Letter*, Lacan's demonstration

81

proceeds on two levels. First there is the story, and then the story within the story, namely, the passage on the game of odd and even: "This game is simple, and is played with marbles. One player holds in his hand a number of these toys, and demands of another whether that number is even or odd. If the guess is right, the guesser wins one; if wrong, he loses one" (Poe, 1982, p. 215). Lacan attempts to convince the reader that the strategy recommended by Dupin – "an identification of the reasoner's intellect with that of his opponent" – is a trap. In fact such a strategy is doomed to failure. In applying it one discovers that there is no way to decide between the simple-minded playing of the idiot, who simply changes from even to odd or vice versa with each move, and the meta-ruse of the super-clever player who, anticipating that his opponent expects a trick at the first level, consisting in *not* moving from even to odd, makes the same move as the idiot. On the other hand, no matter how the players try to trick their opponents, they are unaware that they produce a series of moves governed by necessary and universal laws. Lacan shows this by drawing upon some elementary ideas from the theory of automata. Here Lacan recognizes what he calls the *Grand Autre* ("Big (br)Other") – the discourse of the symbolic order and the unconscious.

Lacan elaborates a similar demonstration on the level of the story. He contends that traditional interpretations of the tale all fail to *differentiate* the fiction. They remain captivated by what Poe places in the foreground, namely, the play of mirrors, identification, and doubling – in short, the *imaginary*. Critics point out that the brilliant and supposedly impartial detective Dupin is himself drawn into the mimetic vortex, since he ends up by avenging himself cruelly against the Minister D., who is his rival and enemy twin. Critics also point out, along with the narrator, that if D. has the upper hand because he holds the letter, this fact depends "upon the robber's knowledge of the loser's knowledge of the robber" – a typical figure in mirror games and financial speculation. Lacan contends, however, that if the story's lesson amounted to nothing more than these truisms, it would not be terribly interesting. He concludes that the real lesson is as follows: "the displacement of the signifier determines the subjects in their actions, destiny, refusals, blindness, success, and outcome . . ." (Lacan, 1966, p. 30). The actors in the drama suffer from a compulsion to repetition (Freud's *Wiederholungszwang*). Their behavior is dictated by the place they occupy in relation to the *letter*, the symbolic element of the structure which, like the unconscious, is "structured like a language." The *symbolic* order differentiates the structure in specific places that determine the actions of those who occupy them in turn. The *imaginary*, on the other hand, reflects, identifies, indifferentiates, and assimilates – but this is only a matter of "surface effects that hide the far more subtle differential mechanisms of symbolic thought" (Deleuze, 1979, p. 310). The symbolic is presented as something that remains hidden from sight, acting upon people from the depths of an invisible underground; or again, it is depicted as an equally inaccessible transcendence. In either case, it is clear that the symbolic governs the imaginary and is in no way affected by it.

This hierarchical relation is what the hard-core deconstructionists cannot bear. It smells of incense and the sacred, of the onto-theology they are out to destroy. Since the symbolic would seem to be a vestige of transcendence, its desacralization is necessary. Lacan was right in seeing the ultimate limitations of the position of the cleverest party, first occupied by the thief and then the detective. From this position one sees that the others do not see, or that they see that others do not see. Far from immunizing one against the infinite play of intestine rivalry, this position inevitably precipitates one into the whirlwind of conflict. Yet Lacan incorrectly left a true form of exteriority in place, a position from which the truth of the system could be perceived. Even though the ultimate signified is presented as a hole, lack, or absence (castration understood as the symbolic lack of an imaginary object, the phallus), this lack has a fixed place and a univocal, literal meaning (Derrida, 1980). Derrida wants to carry the demystification begun by Lacan to the extreme. Nothing can be allowed to escape from this demystification, and thus in Derrida's reading the putative "law of the signifier" is broken, fragmented, and "disseminated." The differentiating power of the symbolic turns out to be an illusion. Derrida's reading leads us back to the *undifferentiation* of the traditional interpretation: there is only "a labyrinth of doubles without originals, of facsimile without an authentic, an indivisible letter, of casual counterfeits (*contrefaçons sans façon*), imprinting the purloined letter with an incorrigible indirection" (Derrida, 1980, pp. 109–110). Such a statement on the part of the thinker of *différance* could seem surprising, but it really should not be. A moment's reflection reveals that a pure difference, lacking any frame of reference or point of orientation, cannot be distinguished from sheer chaos.

Derrida's deconstruction ends up by dissolving the symbolic within the imaginary. Its advantage from our perspective is that it demystifies the false exteriority the symbolic enjoyed in relation to the imaginary within Lacan's theory. But in the absence of the necessary conceptual tools, this deconstruction can only leave us with formlessness and obscurity. Thus I suggest that we replace the figure of exteriority with the notion of bootstrapping or self-transcendence. This procedure contains two requirements: (1) against Derrida, we would maintain a distinction between the symbolic and the imaginary; (2) against Lacan and structuralism in general, we would have the symbolic emerge from the imaginary as a systemic effect or endogenous fixed point. The symbolic order does in fact enable a certain orientation and control of mimetic conflicts and identifications, but it is anything but inaccessible to them. Rather the symbolic has its origin in these conflicts, and can at any time be swallowed up by them (Girard, 1972).

The subject of "common knowledge"

Faithful to my method, I will now attempt to justify my claims from within the framework of systems thinking. An article written by a Lacanian mathematician, Jean-Michel Lasry, entitled "Common Knowledge" (1984) serves as a point of reference. Lasry conjectures that he has proved the existence, if not of God, then of the "Other." Although his proof is rather remarkable, I think that he has actually demonstrated something else entirely.

The theory of "common knowledge," upon which the argument is based, emerged within the philosophy of language as a response to the question: should language be deemed a convention (Lewis, 1969)? The concept was later mathematized by the game theoretician R. J. Aumann, and its many developments today concern a broad range of disciplines, including political philosophy, economics, logic, and the cognitive sciences. Lasry's goal was to use this concept to consider "intersubjective communication" as it is understood by Lacan.

The proof is based on a specular game not entirely unlike the game of odd and even. More precisely, the game is a simplified version of the game of the three prisoners, which Lacan discussed in "Le temps logique et l'assertion de certitude anticipée" (Lacan, 1966, p. 197). Two players are needed. A third party gives each of them a card with a positive integer on it, such as 1, 2, 3, etc. The two numbers given to the players are consecutive, and the players know it (if one of them has a 4, he knows the other party has to have either 3 or 5). The object of the game is to determine by means of logical reasoning the number the other person is holding. The third party asks each of the players in turn if he knows the answer.

Although it may not seem so initially, the game is in fact decidable. Let us consider a simple case. Suppose Peter gets 2 and John 3. The judge asks John: "Do you know what number Peter has?" John says that he does not know. Next the third party asks Peter the same question. His answer is "Yes, John has 3. Since I have 2, John either has 1 or 3. If he had 1, he would know that I have 2, since there is no 0 in the game. But since he said that he didn't know, he must not have 1, and therefore has 3."

The game has a solution because at some point, one of the players will be able to reason in this manner. Bringing into play a *finite* regress of nested calculations, he can base himself on the case where one of the players has 1 and knows that the other one must have 2. The following theorem can be formulated: "If I have n (for example, 35), and after $n - 1$ questions (in this case, 34), neither of us has said 'I know' yet (and if the third party began by asking the person holding an odd number), then I know that my opponent has the number $n + 1$ (here, 36)."

Yet a formidable problem remains. One other hypothesis must be confirmed for the theory of this game to be true. It is necessary for

84

both players to know the theory, but that is not enough, for each player must also know that the other player knows it too. Each must also know that the other one knows that he knows it, and so on, to infinity. Thus the theory's existence is presupposed by the theory. Lasry recognizes here a form of bootstrapping. In other words, the theory of this game is an autonomous system.

The game is really quite simple. But it raises a question which, although it too is simple, is nonetheless quite odd ("simple and odd," as Dupin is in the habit of saying). Let us imagine that John has 3 and Peter 4. Questioned first, John answers "I don't know." Peter already knows that this will be John's answer. Peter knows that John either has 3 or 5, and in either case, it is not possible for John to guess at the outset the number that Peter has. So when John answers "I don't know" he does not teach Peter anything. And John obviously cannot teach himself anything either. Yet the negative response is necessary to the game's progress, as we see when we trace the steps of the reasoning that leads to the solution. So here is our odd and simple question: To whom does John give information when he answers, "I don't know"? "To the Big Other," replies Lasry as he utilizes the theory of common knowledge. His argument can be expressed rigorously only in the language of one form of modal logic, called "epistemic logic," so I will only be able to present a few elements in the present context. We introduce into the calculus of propositions a knowledge operator, "K," which can be used to form a new proposition, KP, from any proposition P. This operator satisfies the following four axioms:

(1) $KP \rightarrow P$
(2) $KP \rightarrow KKP$
(3) $K(P \wedge Q) \rightarrow KP \wedge KQ$
(4) $\text{Neg } KP \rightarrow K (\text{Neg } KP)$

Thus a syntax is provided, and we can assign it a semantics: a knowing subject is associated with every operator, K, that satisfies the axioms. Given k, the subject associated to K, KP reads as follows: k knows the proposition P is true. The first axiom, then, is interpreted to mean that if k knows that P is true, then P is true; the second means that given the same premise, we deduce that k knows that it is true that k knows that P is true; the third means that if k knows that P and Q is the case, then he knows that P is true and he knows that Q is true; the fourth means that if k does not know that P is the case, then he knows that he does not know.

Now, given two subjects, a and b (John and Peter, for example), associated with epistemic operators A and B, we say that the proposition P is "common knowledge" to a and b if *all* of the following propositions are true: P, AP, BP, ABP, BAP, ABAP, BABP, etc. In other words: a knows P and b knows P, and a knows that b knows P, and b knows that a knows P, etc., "all the way down." Common knowledge consists of more than simply everyone knowing some true proposition about the world. This definition would not rule out what some theoreticians of totalitarianism have called a "public secret," an instance where a fact is known by everyone but no one knows whether the others know it. It does not, however, satisfy the definition of a *public space*. An example of the latter would be the space defined by a contract, whereby parties formally engage themselves *vis-à-vis* each other to respect its clauses. In order for such a public space to be established, "common knowledge" must exist (Rawls, 1971, p. 133).

At this point we may introduce the operator of "common knowledge," O, which appears as follows in the notation introduced above: OP = (P and AP and BP and ABP and BAP and . . .). The central theorem of the theory establishes that the operator O verifies the four axioms which define a knowledge operator. If the semantics which has been adopted is coherent, there must be a subject who corresponds to the operator. But who is this subject?

The subject of common knowledge clearly does not coincide with any of the individual subjects who have helped to constitute it. Thus it must be a third party, an Other who exists only in order to maintain the coherence of our semantics. When John answers "I don't know," he is addressing himself to this subject, who is "external" to both John and Peter. The bit of information "John does not know" is already known separately by both John and Peter, but it is not common knowledge until it has been *spoken between them* in the contractual space of their communication. Each one knows but does not know that the Other knows, and so forth. Or we might say that each one of them knows, but the Other does not know.

Lasry conjectures that this knowing third party is the Lacanian Big Other, defined as the "common site of intersubjective communication." He foresees the unavoidable objection provoked by this assimilation of concepts: far from having *always already* been there, the subject of common knowledge is an emergent phenomenon, an endogenous fixed point produced by the specular play between subjects when this play is pushed to infinity. The public space has a subject, but this subject can say: "Only when you are together will I be among you." The social pact has a subject, but far from being external or transcendent in relation to its parties, this subject is the product of their pact. Once again, the figure of exteriority must be replaced by self-transcendence.

Contrary to the cybernetic theory advanced by Régis Debray and many others, a human collectivity can constitute an autonomous totality. Certainly, in order to see this autonomy, one must take into account the operational closure between the totality deprived of its principle of integration and the organizational principle itself. Indeed deconstructionists of the metaphysics of autonomy are correct in underscoring that totality always presents itself as suffering from a lack. Yet they are mistaken in concluding that autonomy is impossible, for they fail to realize that it is the system itself which produces this lack. According to a process of self-externalization, it projects its principle of integration outside the totality. Once we renounce thinking in terms of self-mastery, autonomy once again becomes a key category for understanding the human world.

NOTES

1 This research was funded by the CNRS program, "The Sciences of Communication."
2 The history of cybernetics is in general poorly known. Here I am relying upon research undertaken by the CREA of the Ecole Polytechnique, the results of which were published in the *Cahiers du CREA*, 7 and 8 (November, 1985). See also my *Aux origines des sciences cognitives* (1994).
3 On the history of the theories, concepts, and models relative to "autonomous," "autopoietic" and "self-organizing" systems, and their relation to cybernetics, see the above-cited *Cahiers du CREA*.

REFERENCES

Ashby, Ross (1962) "Principles of self-organizing systems," in *Principles of Self-Organization*, H. von Foerster and G. W. Zopf (eds), New York: Pergamon.

Atlan, Henri (1979) *Entre le cristal et la fumée*, Paris: Seuil.

Boudon, Raymond (1977) *Effets pervers et ordre social*, Paris: PUF.

Canetti, Elias (1966) *Masse et puissance*, Paris: Gallimard.

Castoriadis, Cornelius (1975) *L'Institution imaginaire de la société*, Paris: Seuil.

Debray, Régis (1981) *Critique de la raison politique*, Paris: Gallimard.

Deleuze Gilles (1979) "A quoi reconnaît-on le structuralisme?", in *La Philosophie au XXe siècle*, Vol. 4, ed. François Chatelet, Verviers: Marabout.

Derrida, Jacques (1967) "La structure, le signe et le jeu dans le discours des sciences humaines," in *L'Ecriture et la différence*, Paris: Seuil.

—— (1973) *Writing and Difference*, tr. Alan Bass, Chicago: University of Chicago Press.

—— (1980) "Le facteur de la vérité," in *La Carte postale*, Paris: Flammarion. (Tr. "The purveyor of truth," Willis Domingo, James Hulbert, Moshe Ron and M.-R. L. (1975) *Yale French Studies* 52.)

Descombes, Vincent (1979) *Le Même et l'autre*, Paris: Minuit.

Dumont, Louis (1977) *Homo Aequalis*, Paris: Gallimard.

—— (1983) *Essais sur l'individualisme*, Paris: Seuil.

Dumouchel, Paul and Dupuy, Jean-Pierre (eds) (1983) *L'Auto-organisation*, Paris: Seuil.

Dupuy, Jean-Pierre (1982) *Ordres et désordres*, Paris: Seuil.

—— (1983) "De l'économie considérée comme théorie de la foule," *Stanford French Review* 7: 245–263.

—— (1985) "L'Essor de la première cybernétique (1943–1953)," *Cahiers du CREA* 7: 7–139.

—— (1994) *Aux origines des sciences cognitives*, Paris: La Découverte. (English tr. forthcoming, Princeton University Press.)

Durkheim, Emile (1968) *Les Formes élémentaires de la vie religieuse*, Paris: PUF.

Ferry, Luc and Renaut, Alain (1985) *La Pensée 68*, Paris: Gallimard.

Freud, Sigmund (1985) "Group psychology and the analysis of the ego," in

Civilization, Society and Religion, Vol. 12 of *The Pelican Freud,* Harmondsworth: Penguin.

Gauchet, Marcel (1979) "De l'avènement de l'individu à la découverte de la société," *Annales* 3: 451–463.

—— (1985) *Le Désenchantement du monde,* Paris: Gallimard.

Girard, René (1961) *Mensonge romantique et vérité romanesque,* Paris: Grasset.

—— (1972) "Système du délire," *Critique* 28: 957–996 tr. P. Livingston and T. Siebers (1978), "Delirium as system," in *"To Double Business Bound": Essays on Literature, Mimesis, and Anthropology,* Baltimore: The Johns Hopkins University Press, 84–120.

Hayek, Friedrich (1973) *Rules and Order,* Vol. 1 of *Law, Legislation, and Liberty,* London: Routledge & Kegan Paul.

—— (1976) *The Mirage of Social Justice,* Vol. 2 of *Law, Legislation, and Liberty,* London: Routledge & Kegan Paul.

Koestler, Arthur and Smythies, J. R. (eds) (1969) *Beyond Reductionism,* London: Hutchinson.

Lacan, Jacques (1966) *Ecrits,* Paris: Seuil.

—— (1978) *Le Séminaire II,* Paris: Seuil.

Lasry, Jean-Michel (1984) "Le common knowledge," *Ornicar* 30: 75–93.

Lévi-Strauss, Claude (1973) "Introduction à l'oeuvre de Marcel Mauss," in Marcel Mauss, *Sociologie et anthropologie,* Paris: PUF.

Lewis, David (1969) *Convention,* Cambridge, Mass.: Harvard University Press.

Maturana, Humberto and Varela, Francisco (1980) *Autopoiesis and Cognition,* Boston: D. Reidel.

—— (1984) *El Arbol del Conocimiento,* Santiago du Chili: Editorial Universitaria.

Poe, Edgar Allan (1982) *The Complete Tales and Poems of Edgar Allan Poe,* Harmondsworth: Penguin.

Rawls, John (1971) *A Theory of Justice,* Cambridge, Mass.: Harvard University Press.

Serres, Michel (1968) *Le Système de Leibniz et ses modèles mathématiques,* 2 Vols, Paris: PUF.

Soto-Andrade, Jorge and Varela, Francisco (1984) "Self-reference and fixed points: A discussion and extension of Lawvere's theorem," *Acta Applic. Mathem.* 2: 1–19.

Stengers, Isabelle (1985) "Généalogies de l'auto-organisation," in *Cahiers du CREA* 8: 7–104.

Varela, Francisco (1979) *Principles of Biological Autonomy,* New York: Elsevier–North-Holland.

Varela, Francisco and Dupuy, Jean-Pierre (eds) (1992) *Understanding Origins,* Kluwer: Boston Studies in the Philosophy of Science.

Weiss, Paul (1968) *Dynamics of Development: Experiments and Inferences,* New York: Academic Press.

Zeleny, Milan (ed.) (1980) *Autopoiesis, Dissipative Structures and Spontaneous Social Order,* Boulder, Colorado: Westview.

4

ULTRA-DARWINIAN EXPLANATION AND THE BIOLOGY OF SOCIAL SYSTEMS

Niles Eldredge

REDUCTIONISM AND HIERARCHY IN EVOLUTIONARY BIOLOGY

Two competing themes vie for center stage in contemporary evolutionary theory. One, which I have termed *ultra-Darwinism*, adopts a profoundly reductionist stance.[1] Building on the neo-Darwinian view of evolution as predominantly a matter of change in gene content and frequency within a population, ultra-Darwinians view organisms (or even their very genes – cf. Dawkins, 1976) as in constant and active competition for reproductive success. Ultra-Darwinians have transformed the concept of natural selection from its original postulate as a passive accumulator of "what-worked-better-than-what" in the previous generation, to an active process of open competition for reproduction success. Crucial to this transformation is the ultra-Darwinian view that economic[2] behavior is pursued solely in service of reproduction. Economic behavior is interpreted solely in the context of its implications for reproductive competition: to an ultra-Darwinian, an organism lives to reproduce.

Further, ultra-Darwinians view large-scale biological structures (e.g. species, ecosystems, social systems) as ephiphenomena of the competitive organismic quest for reproductive success. Such a view contrasts strongly with the second, *hierarchic* (or *naturalistic*) theme that has emerged in evolutionary biology during the past two decades (see especially Eldredge and Salthe, 1984; Eldredge, 1985, 1986, 1989; Salthe, 1985, for general accounts). Within this general paradigm, large-scale systems are seen as real, spatiotemporally bounded entities with their own properties, internal structures and behaviors. Though the self-organization of such entities springs in large measure from both the reproductive and economic behaviors of organisms, by no means can ecosystems, social systems or even species be "reduced" either in terms of their histories or their organizing functional properties to mere within-population competition for reproductive success.

I shall focus particularly on social systems. I will argue that, as a rule, large-scale biological systems are either economic *or* genealogical in nature; e.g., ecosystems are purely economic systems, while species are purely genealogical entities. In that context, I take social systems to constitute an exceptional class of large-scale biological system in which economic and reproductive elements are fused. In contrast to this interpretation, the application of ultra-Darwinism to social systems has yielded sociobiology – which, true to its intellectual roots, seeks to reduce social structure to competition for reproductive success. Sociobiology sees economic behavior in social systems strictly in terms of its implications for the paramount issue of reproductive success, and generally ignores the existence of social systems *per se* as spatiotemporally bounded, real historical entities. In my view, the hierarchical approach to social systems yields a more accurate description of the nature of such systems than that provided by ultra-Darwinian-inspired sociobiology.

ULTRA-DARWINIAN DESCRIPTION OF SOCIAL SYSTEMS

It is well known that Hamilton's (1964a, b) development of the notion of kin selection, and the related concept of "inclusive fitness," constitutes one of the cornerstones of sociobiology. In one blow, an answer to a paradox known to Darwin – that organisms will seemingly sacrifice their own direct reproductive activities to support the reproductive activities of others – was explained. The altruism of cooperative breeding arises as an alternative strategy of seeing one's genes vicariously passed along to the next generation by close relatives that share a certain (specifiable) percentage of alleles. This extension of the evolutionary concept of "fitness" brought the analytic description of social systems fully into the sphere of contemporary evolutionary biology.

No one (ever since Darwin) has doubted that social systems, like all other biological systems, have had (evolutionary) histories. Yet sociobiology, though rooted in evolutionary biology, has been concerned far more with the analytic description of the very structure of social systems than with the evolutionary history *per se* of such systems (but cf. Wilson, 1985, for one of a number of conspicuous exceptions to this statement). Such description arises from evolutionary theory, specifically the core postulate that the central dynamic within social systems is the maximization of reproductive success. The vector of causality in the concept of natural selection is from the economic to the reproductive: Differential economic success begets differential reproductive success. In applying evolutionary principles to the analytic description of the structure and function of social systems, economic activity has come to be seen as pursued primarily for its effects on reproduction.

Social systems are conventionally defined in the following way: They all have overlapping generations, parental care, and the existence of "more or less non-reproductive workers or helpers" (Andersson, 1984, p. 165). The organization of social systems revolves completely around aspects of reproduction: who is and is not reproducing, who takes care of offspring, and so forth. And, though there can be no doubt that reproductive patterns are important in the description of the actual structure of social systems, reproductive considerations have been given prime consideration in socio-biology to the virtual exclusion of other vital aspects of social organization – specifically, economic themes. And economic activity, when it is discussed, is interpreted almost solely in terms of its reproductive implications.

Florida scrub jay sociality

I turn now to a concrete example of a social system analyzed in purely reproductive terms – the classic analysis of Florida scrub jays (birds) by Woolfenden and Fitzpatrick (1984). Their study contains the telltale ingredient that sees economic survival as not only underlying, but basically geared for, reproduction. Economic activity is interpreted fundamentally in reproductive terms. The example is biased in favor of a straightforward ultra-Darwinian interpretation, simply because the item of social behavior to be explained in this example is manifestly reproductive in nature. Yet I will endeavor to show that, if the system is viewed purely in reproductive terms, the consequent description of sociality is distorted and incomplete.

Even when reproductive behavior is on the face of it at the center of some aspect of social organization, exclusion of economic considerations leads readily to conceptual problems. According to Woolfenden and Fitz-patrick (1984, sole source of this example of scrub jay sociality) offspring often remain within their natal territory, helping (in various ways, mostly through foraging and territorial defense) to raise additional broods of their parents rather than setting off immediately the next year to establish their own territories to mate and breed. Early in the history of sociobiological discourse, Florida scrub jays were seized upon as a prime example of altruistic behavior; and kin selection was adjudged to have been at work, favoring the helping behavior and thus adding to the helpers' inclusive fitness.

Florida scrub jays constitute a relict aggregation, separated by some 1,600 km from the main concentration of the species in western North America. Significantly, western scrub jays do not engage in cooperative breeding. Florida scrub jays are restricted to scrub oak habitat, which has an exceedingly patchy distribution. Woolfenden and Fitzpatrick (1984) conclude that the dense populations of scrub jays wherever suitable habitat is developed reflect a level at or near the maximum carrying capacity of the environment. They note, further, that distributions are sharply limited by the unavailability of marginal habitat: Blue jays quickly replace scrub jays in all but pure scrub oak habitat.

Florida scrub jays form permanently monogamous pair bonds that usually terminate only upon the death of one of the mates. Woolfenden and Fitzpatrick document a "divorce" rate of only 5 per cent. The signal element of scrub jay social behavior is the phenomenon of delayed breeding: Rather than leaving the nest within a year to establish territories, pair and mate (as, for example, occurs in western scrub jay populations), Florida scrub jay offspring typically become "helpers" through "site tenacity": Offspring tend to remain within parental territory.

According to Woolfenden and Fitzpatrick (1984), Florida scrub jay helpers are most often offspring of the mating pair whose reproductive efforts they are aiding. Over 90 per cent of helpers are the offspring of at least one of the mating pair. Yet helping continues when the parents are replaced by another pair bond: 10 per cent of helpers are aiding the reproductive efforts of non-relatives.

Helpers cooperate in all phases of reproductive effort save (of course), mating and egg laying, nest construction and incubation. Helpers' activities include foraging and feeding nestlings and young fledglings and territorial defense. According to Woolfenden and Fitzpatrick (1984, p. 83), "all foraging, resting, roosting, territorial, and antipredator behavior (i.e. of helpers) qualitatively resembles that of the breeders. Group members spend much of the day in close proximity to one another, and helpers often participate in sentinel activity while the rest of the group forages." Only 50 per cent of breeding pairs during any one breeding season have helpers.

Crucial to a consideration of the biological basis of scrub jay sociality is the fact that these birds "*always* reside in territories with well-defined boundaries defended *year round by all group members*" (Woolfenden and Fitzpatrick, 1984, p. 101; all italics mine). These territories are very stable, remaining essentially "the same piece of ground for many years." Most critical of all, "ownership of territories is passed on through sequential mate replacements *or through inheritance by helpers*" (Woolfenden and Fitzpatrick, 1984, p. 101). Woolfenden and Fitzpatrick (1984, p. 101) conclude that "*the territory represents a land bank, the defense of which is vital to ongoing reproduction by the breeders, and to survival and later reproduction by the helpers.*"

Helpers become breeders in several ways, most of which involve obtaining territory in one way or another by inheritance. Sometimes they replace mates outside their parents' territory, or (rarely) they may establish new territories between pre-existing ones; but, more usually, they inherit all or a subdivided portion of the territory in which they were helpers (i.e. usually, but not invariably, their "natal" territory). (Most females disperse to new

92

territories; Woolfenden and Fitzpatrick (1984) report that roughly 56 per cent of breeding males inherit territory.)

Crucial to the interpretation of the purely *reproductive* significance of Florida scrub jay behavior is the observation that "pairs with helpers fledge 1.5 times more young than do pairs without helpers." Moreover, the data suggest that territory quality is less important that the presence of helpers in fledgling production. Helpers, moreover, tend to produce more offspring of their own (i.e. once they become breeders) than non-helpers – but the longer they act as helpers, the lower are their survival rates once they become breeders (for unknown reasons). Woolfenden and Fitzpatrick (1984, ch. 8) conclude that a young jay's inclusive fitness is increased more by breeding than by acting as a helper.

Thus Woolfenden and Fitzpatrick (1984) conclude that the helper behavior of Florida scrub jays represents a delaying tactic until such time as a "breeding vacancy" can be located outside the territory, or created within it. Unlike the situation in western North America, where there are many habitats suitable for scrub jays, available habitat for Florida scrub jays is severely limited. They point out that biologists have often failed to look additively at total numbers of successfully produced offspring over an organism's entire reproductive lifetime, which can reflect the input of a number of different variables. They conclude (Woolfenden and Fitzpatrick, 1984, ch. 10) that the cooperative breeder behavior of Florida scrub jays reflects far more a strategy for maximizing fitness through the actual reproductive efforts of helpers-turned-breeders than it reflects the action of kin selection, where helper jays are hypothesized to be contributing to their inclusive fitness by helping to rear (at least predominantly) younger sibs. It is the territory they are after, so that they can spread their own genes, not simply those they share with their sibs.

The example as I have presented it so far involves a levels-of-selection dispute; earlier discussions invoked kin selection, whereas Woolfenden and Fitzpatrick maintain that their data are better explained by normal, organism-level competition to maximize reproductive success in the time-honored way: The *real* strategy is to obtain a territory to maximize one's own reproductive success. But whichever explanation is accepted, both center around strategies to contribute heavily to the next (Florida scrub jay) generation – as seems only logical as the very behavior being described is reproductive.

Yet, surely, there is a more straightforward and value-free interpretation of these data. It is certain that the acquisition of territory (a precious commodity in very short supply in the restricted Florida scrub jay habitiat) lies at the heart of scrub jay sociality. Why do scrub jays "need" a territory? Well, those without territories of their own do not reproduce, so reproduction clearly hinges on territory possession. As Woolfenden and Fitzpatrick put it (1984, p. 101) "the territory represents a land bank, the defense of which is vital to ongoing reproduction by the breeders, and survival and later reproduction by the helpers." True, economic activity is a requisite for reproduction: you must stay alive, and expend energy, to reproduce. Thus survival is explicitly mentioned in conjunction with the *helpers* as they bide their time waiting to reproduce. The whole *purpose*, once again, of this entire behavioral syndrome (especially defending territory the year round) is to hang onto the site to reproduce again next year, or to inherit the territory as one's own at some future time.

But territory is fundamentally about energy resources and protection from predation. Such concerns, of course, have reproductive implications. But the jays, in vigorously defending their territories, are first and foremost ensuring that they will have an adequate slice of the economic pie. Telltale in all this is Woolfenden and Fitzpatrick's mention of survival only for the helpers (who are hanging around to get a shot at reproduction); yet, clearly, the mated, reproducing pair that "own" the territory at any given moment are also faced with the necessity of existing. Why is it necessary to claim that their continued existence is simply to get them to the next breeding season?

Most organisms, most of the time, are engaged purely in economic activities. Even most thorough sociobiological treatises (e.g. Oster and Wilson, 1978) devote the greater percentage of their space to economics ("ergonomics" of Oster and Wilson), reflecting simply the vastly greater percentage of energy outlay on such activities over the purely reproductive. At the very least, neutral description of the "functional anatomy" of any biological system ought to reflect what actually goes on. And imputation of ulterior motives – as when frankly economic behavior is seen only for its relative effects on reproductive success – can profitably be dropped in favor of the simple realization that organisms engage in both economic and reproductive activities. Florida scrub jay territorial behavior is thus both economic and reproductive, and, consequently, fraught with both economic and reproductive implications.

ORGANISMS, ECONOMICS AND REPRODUCTION: SELF-ORGANIZING BIOLOGICAL SYSTEMS

If we simply look at what organisms *do* (adopting, for the moment, a purely functional perspective), we quickly see that there are but two classes of activity: those pertaining to matter–energy transfer processes, and those pertaining to reproduction. The same distinction applies to anatomical features and to behaviors in addition to physiological functions. Aspects of the phenotype generally are devoted to one or the other class of functions. To the extent that phenotypic features represent adaptations shaped through selection, these two categories correspond to natural (economic) and sexual (reproductive) selection – as originally defined by Darwin (1859 and 1871, respectively).

All organisms *must* obtain energy at some time during their lifetimes; most seek renewed energy sources throughout their lifetimes. Most organisms, save especially members of some castes in (especially non-vertebrate) colonial and social systems, belong as well to the reproductive pool at some point during their lives. Most organisms, in other words, at least attempt reproduction during their lifetimes.

Matter–energy transfer processes, and reproduction, are the fundamental elements of many different sorts of biological systems. It is appropriate at this juncture to consider precisely which sorts of systems share elements of both matter–energy transfer processes ("economic" activities) and reproductive processes ("genealogic" activities). Clearly, organisms themselves represent such a combined system. It soon becomes apparent in any such survey, however, that, above the organism level, most specifiable biological systems are based *either* on the economic *or* the reproductive activities of organisms – and that imputation of economic attributes to genealogical systems, or vice versa, represents deep ontological confusion in the history of biology (Eldredge, 1985, 1986). The most compelling counter-example to the generalization that most biotic systems are either economic or genealogic in basic character is social systems – which represent, in my view, an integration of the economic and reproductive organismic activities in local populations of conspecifics (i.e. local members of a single species).

Indeed, the nature of biotic systems (i.e. biological systems composed of more than one organism) generally flows from one or both classes of organismic activity. Both the genealogic and economic hierarchies are held to form as a natural consequence of simple pursuit of one or the other class of organismic activity (e.g. Eldredge and Salthe, 1984; Eldredge, 1985, 1986, 1989; Eldredge and Grene, 1992; Salthe, 1985). The nature of social systems as biotic entities is best seen after a brief characterization of these two hierarchical systems.

The genealogic and economic hierarchies

Table 4.1 summarizes in outline form my preferred version of the twofold hierarchical system of organization of large-scale biotic entities. Details of these hierarchical arrays – and alternative viewpoints on the composition and structure of the economic and genealogical hierarchies – are available in the above-cited literature and references cited therein.

I stress here only a few general points about the two hierarchies. Organisms find themselves, simultaneously, as parts of two distinct systems as a simple consequence, respectively, of their economic and reproductive behaviors. In the economic hierarchy, the interactive, economic behavior of organisms is carried out in the context of a local population of

Table 4.1 The genealogical and economic hierarchies

Genealogical hierarchy	Economic hierarchy
Monophyletic taxa	Biosphere
Species	Ecosystems
Demes	Avatars
Organisms	Organisms

conspecifics. That local population (often termed an "avatar") interacts with other such avatars to form local biological communities – the biotic components of local ecosystems. The interaction is purely economic, involving, at base, matter–energy transfer. Ecosystems are patently cross-genealogical. Thus a focal population – say, the population of Carolina gray squirrels in New York's Central Park – interacts with predators, disease-causing microbes, competitors and food sources (local populations of various plant species).

Such systems are self-organizing: economic interaction among squirrels in effect creates the avatar. Ecosystems are formed from, and bound together by, the interactions of all local avatars. Moreover, local ecosystems are bound together by networks of energy flow that interlink them into regional systems – and eventually into the entire interactive biosphere.

But organisms also reproduce, and sexual reproduction both requires and produces a local breeding population (often called "demes" to distinguish them from the economic "avatars"). At this point, the genealogical system departs radically from the economic – as the reproductive population of squirrels in Central Park is connected (by occasional reproductive contact), not with local populations of other species, but with members of the same squirrel species living in adjacent regions in New York City and beyond. It is ongoing reproduction that creates and sustains demes, and demes are parts of species – which in turn are the entire array of demes in which organisms share a common mating system. Species give rise to descendant species in the evolutionary process – creating skeins of species termed "monophyletic taxa."

Thus it is the process of reproduction – of "more-making" – that serves as the self-organizing factor of each of the entities of the genealogical hierarchy. It is matter–energy transfer that performs the equivalent role in the economic hierarchy. Note, further, that each category term within both hierarchical systems stands for a class of individualized, real spatiotemporally bounded entities, composed of individual subunits – and themselves forming parts of larger individual entities. Thus every lion is a member of a local deme, which in turn is part of the species *Felis leo*. The species *Felis leo* is itself part of a nested array of higher taxa. But each individual lion is also a member of a local avatar of lions, which is integrated into a specific local ecosystem which differs in its details – sometimes quite profoundly – from other ecosystems in which other avatars of lions are found.

This dual system of hierarchical arrays corresponding (but not simply reducible) to the two general classes of organismic activity provides an accurate, albeit general, description of the organization of biotic nature at and above the level of individual organisms. For most organisms, the dichotomy between their reproductive and economic lives is quite distinct (but see, e.g., Eldredge and Grene, 1992, for detailed discussion of the necessary connections between economics and reproduction in all organisms).

But what, then, do we make of a *pride* of lions? Clearly, lion prides combine economic with reproductive themes: a pride is neither an avatar, nor a deme, but something in between, combining elements of both. In the context of the dual hierarchy description of biotic nature, social systems are clearly a bridge, a sort of hybrid category, at the deme/avatar level, that brings the separate biotic worlds of economics and reproduction together. It should be noted as well that social systems are every bit as much individualized entities as are avatars and demes, ecosystems and species (Eldredge, 1988). Lion prides and beehives play concerted roles in both the local economy of nature (local ecosystem) and in the reproductive dynamics of their respective species. I turn now to the complex interplay between economic and reproductive behavior that lies at the very heart of all social systems.

ECONOMICS, REPRODUCTION AND SOCIAL SYSTEMS

Sociobiology, it is fair to say, originated with the application of ultra-Darwinian theory to insect social systems. Wilson (1975) speaks of four basic "pinnacles" of social evolution: Marine invertebrate colonies, insect societies, vertebrate social systems, and human sociality. Eldredge and Grene (1992) have argued, however, that insect social systems display far greater similarity to marine invertebrate colonial systems than to any vertebrate system, including human, and excepting, of course, naked mole rats – the insects of the vertebrate world. Social insects (hymenopterans and termites) resemble colonial invertebrates in two fundamental respects: (1) the characteristic fashion in which reproductive and economic labors are subdivided among members of the system, and (2) the pattern, and degree, of genetic relatedness among members of the system.

My goal in this section is twofold: to stress that social systems indeed arise from a complex commingling of reproductive and economic organismic activity – which reflect, of course, historical adaptations; but to stress, as well, that because reproduction is indeed a crucial biological component of social organization (save in some, but by no means all, elements of human social organization), the importance of economic behavior *per se* in understanding social structure and internal function has been downgraded. Social systems are simply not all about reproduction, nor is economic behavior in social systems really all about reproduction. As discussed earlier, even in aspects of social behavior where the central element directly concerns reproductive behavior, absence of an economic perspective can distort the actual description of the system itself.

Invertebrate colonial systems, such as those developed in several groups of cnidarians (corals, "jellyfish" and related forms) and ectoproct bryozoans, are typically clonal: All component individual organisms share the same genotype. As has been appreciated by many biologists, there really are two levels of "individuality" within any such system: The component organisms, and the colony itself. Division of labor in the more complex of such systems typically involves (a) reproductive individuals, plus (b) one or (often) more types of economic individuals: Polyps, or zooids, as the case may be. These perform a proscribed range of economic activities such as feeding, cleaning, or defense. The division of labor is, first, between reproduction and economics, and then among various subsets of economic tasks – as is the case in eukaryote cells, with discrete nuclei and a number of cytoplasmic organelles dedicated to particular economic tasks. Wilson (1985) has discussed caste structure of social insects, pointing to instances where, as an individual cycles through life, workers typically proceed through a variety of different economic tasks. Such tasks are never literally reproductive (though they may well include care of the young – a frank application of economic behavior towards group reproductive goals).

In such invertebrate systems, it really is a matter of one for all and all for one. Especially in situations where genetically identical individuals bud asexually from one another and reproductive and various economic tasks are parcelled out among them, of course there is no (within-colony) competition for reproductive success. But just because Darwin's dilemma (i.e., how could some organisms dedicate themselves to rearing another's young in violation of the universal principle of natural selection?) is resolved when the genetic structures of such systems became apparent does not mean that such invertebrate colonial/social systems should be understood strictly in reproductive terms. Indeed, as already noted, such excellent sociobiological works as Oster and Wilson's (1978) *Caste and Ecology in the Social Insects* devote the bulk of the actual descriptive pages on insect societies to the economic activities of various social castes. Apparent altruism, a true intellectual puzzle, has been resolved in such systems.

But solution of the altruism puzzle does not mean that reproduction is all that social systems are about. Slobodchikoff (1984, p. 246) has argued that "in evolutionary terms, social behavior has developed in response to the distribution and abundance of resources." All members of any given social system require energy resources, protection, and so forth. Those busy

98

reproducing depend upon others for such energetic resources; those performing the economic roles owe their existence to the reproductive activities of present and past reproducers. Selection maintains and modifies such systems according to how well the economic system supports the reproductive activities. Selection has obviously built ever more complex such systems (without necessary extinction of still viable, simpler, systems).

But it is not therefore true that all moment-by-moment activity in the colony is to be construed to be *about* reproduction. It is the successful integration of economics and reproductive behavior that is being selected, nothing more: A colony or a beehive is not just an efficient reproducing machine; it is also an equally efficient economic machine. It is no more about reproduction than it is about economics; nor is the economic activity there to support the reproductive any more than the reproductive behavior exists solely to make more organisms to serve purely economic ends.

Vertebrates are different. Again, with the exception of naked mole rats, there is no division into economic and reproductive castes in vertebrates. And no vertebrate totally surrenders its stand-alone economic role, though behaviors such as pack hunting belie some division of labor. Humans, of course, construct such elaborate economic systems that the vast majority in a society may have nothing to do (directly, that is) with the production of food or any save one small facet of the variety of economic activities in which humans may be involved. (I am using "economics" for humans in the same general, matter–energy transfer sense that I use it for organisms generally.)

In addition to there being no reproductive/economic dichotomy along caste lines in vertebrate social sytems, it is also true that males and females both play reproductive and economic roles, however different, complementary or even identical these roles might be. With few exceptions, organisms in vertebrate social systems lead both economic and (potentially, at least – and in the main apparently fulfilled) reproductive existences.

Nor are vertebrate social systems organized around a particular pattern of genetic relatedness – with the conspicuous exception, of course, of families and the extended kinship groups found in a variety of species, especially among primates, and most especially among ourselves. Application of kin selection and the notion of inclusive fitness has always been dubious for vertebrates. It is simply more difficult, on the face of it, to claim that vertebrate social systems are organized around the reproductive imperative, than it is in the case of invertebrate colonial and insect social systems.

But in all such systems, there are reproductive implications of economic behavior – implications which are recorded as biases in transmission of genetic material: natural selection. And there are economic consequences of reproductive behavior. Nowhere is this more vividly clear than in human social systems. According to Kevles (1985), eugenicists have long been bedeviled by the propensity of the economically more prosperous classes to produce fewer children per family per generation than less advantaged classes. Darwinian expectations (as seen by members of the very same advantaged classes, at any rate) are simply not met in such situations. What is missing, of course, from the equation is the realization that children are frequently thought of as a source of labor – a source of economic wealth – by people in precisely those socioeconomic classes that happen to produce more children per family per generation. As in biotic nature generally, it is true in all vertebrate social systems that reproduction provides the players for the economic arena. In terms of social systems *per se*, reproduction at the very least keeps group size up beyond the minimum lower limits necessary to maintain the group – and up to the maximum size, where the negative effect of still larger numbers levels off the size of the system.

Thus there are purely economic effects of reproduction, just as there are the more usually considered reproductive effects of economic behavior. It is no exaggeration to say that the sociobiological literature vastly emphasizes the latter over the former: Economics, when it is considered at all, is examined only in the light of its effects on reproductive success. The economic implications of reproductive behavior are seldom considered, simply because to do so would be to admit the possibility that economic behaviors are pursued to their own ends. And that is a proposition lying outside the Darwinian canon, especially as formulated in "ultra-Darwinian" terms since the mid-1960s, and particularly as viewed from Richard Dawkin's perspective of the selfish gene.

SOME FINAL THOUGHTS

Reproductive behavior is a vital element in the description of the structure and function of several different sorts of biological systems: Organisms, certainly, but also especially demes and species. (The latter two I, at least, construe as purely genealogical, i.e. "reproductive," entities: Eldredge, 1985.) Social systems, representing complex fusions of organismic economic and reproductive adaptations, also require accurate descriptions of reproductive behaviour as part of their complete description. But what has happened in the twenty-odd years since the advent of sociobiology has been the emphasis of reproductive over economic concerns as the central dynamic of social systems generally. Nor is this phenomenon restricted to sociobiology *per se*. The recent, much-vaunted wedding of evolutionary biology with ecology has also represented much more a reinterpretation of the classical postulates of ecology in terms of differential reproductive success (fitness) than an incorporation of traditional ecological concerns with biological economic processes into evolutionary theory.

The net effect has been the construction of a conceptual edifice that sees the propagation of the assembly instructions of a system as the very process that drives the system itself: The instructions somehow emerge as of greater significance than the system itself. In downplaying the importance of organisms in biology, the "selfish gene" notion utterly ignores the simple, direct, yet powerful effects that the two classes of organismic functional behavior have on the very organization, hence existence, of biotic systems.

Put another way, natural selection has come to be seen as a dynamic process, one that not only shapes the frequencies of properties of component parts of a system, but which, as well, is manifested through the daily behaviors of the system's components – interpreting even economic behavior as, ultimately, competitively reproductive in purpose.

It is time, I believe, to reconsider the more neutral proposition that natural selection is simply an effect, a fallout that represents what worked better than what in the previous generation as organisms in that previous generation grappled with a world of finite economic and reproductive resources. That is powerful enough: It is certainly adequate to explain why organismic properties change, or remain the same, from generation to generation – the original and still the core phenomenon to be explained by evolution. It is adequate, for example, to frame a powerful explanation of how Florida scrub jay sociality originated and continues to be maintained in its present form – and why such sociality is missing in the disjunct western populations of scrub jays.

Above all, we should avoid the pitfall of thinking that, just because differential economic success engenders differential reproductive success (natural selection), therefore economic behavior is only pursued as part of a competitive race among local conspecifics to leave as many copies of their genes to the next generation. After all, organismic selection is a generation-by-generation phenomenon. We should reserve its formidable explanatory power for such situations, i.e. for *historical* explanation – and not make the mistake of attributing moment-by-moment organismic behaviors as inspired by their roles in the selective process. To do so is to impute future effect as a goal of present-day activity – a teleological construct that all good biologists should strive to avoid.

Sociobiology has had a profound effect on several disciplines in the social sciences. There are indeed implications for the social sciences potentially to be found in biology. But *caveat emptor*: The hyper-reductive stance of ultra-Darwinian evolutionary biology lurks just behind the sociobiological façade. The less assumption-laden hierarchical approach restores economics to co-equal status alongside reproduction as the organizing principle of complex biological systems. This approach should be familiar (and perhaps more acceptable) to social scientists already well versed in the relevance of economic processes to social organization. Everyone approaching complex systems – whether in physics, chemistry, biology or the social sciences – needs beware the simplicities and distortions of reductive analytic description and the insistence that all structure devolves from a single, simple process. Complexity no longer yields so readily to such simplistic paradigms.

NOTES

This paper draws heavily on the arguments set forth, in greater detail, in *Interactions: The Biological Context of Social Systems*, cowritten with Dr Marjorie Grene. I thank her for the privilege of having worked with her to produce that book.

1 See Eldredge and Grene (1992) and Eldredge (1993) for a more complete characterization of the ultra-Darwinian perspective. Prominent post-1959 (Darwinian centennial) contributors to ultra-Darwinian theory include George Williams, John Maynard Smith, and Richard Dawkins, as well as authors cited in my discussion of the application of ultra-Darwinism to social systems – i.e. sociobiology.

2 As used in this paper, "economics" refers to the general class of matter–energy transfer processes involved in the growth, differentiation and maintenance of an organism's soma ("body") – and to matter–energy transfer processes indentifiable in various other biotic systems (e.g. energy flow within ecosystems). It is thus a more general usage – even when applied expressly to humans – than usually understood within social science disciplines.

REFERENCES

Andersson, M. (1984) "The evolution of eusociality," *Annual Review of Ecology and Systematics* 15: 165–189.

Darwin, C. (1859) *On the Origin of Species*, John Murray: London.

—— (1871) *The Descent of Man, and Selection in Relation to Sex*, John Murray: London.

Dawkins, R. (1976) *The Selfish Gene*, Oxford University Press: Oxford.

Eldredge, N. (1985) *Unfinished Synthesis. Biological Hierarchies and Modern Evolutionary Thought*, Oxford University Press: New York.

—— (1986) "Information, economics and evolution," *Annual Review of Ecology and Systematics* 17: 351–369.

—— (1988) "The evolutionary context of social behavior," in G. Greenberg and E. Tobach (eds), *Evolution of Social Systems and Integrative Levels*, Lawrence Erlbaum Associates: Hillsdale, New Jersey, 19–30.

—— (1989) *Macroevolutionary Dynamics. Species, Niches and Adaptive Peaks*, McGraw-Hill: New York.

—— (1993) "History, function and evolutionary biology," in M. K. Hecht *et al.* (eds), *Evolutionary Biology*, New York: Plenum Press, ch. 7, pp. 33–50.

Eldredge, N. and Grene, M. (1992) *Interactions: The Biological Context of Social Systems*, Columbia University Press: New York.

Eldredge, N. and Salthe, S. N. (1984) "Hierarchy and evolution," *Oxford Surveys in Evolutionary Biology* 1: 182–206.

Hamilton, W. D. (1964a) "The genetical theory of social behavior. I," *Journal of Theoretical Biology* 7: 1–16.

—— (1964b) "The genetical theory of social behavior. II," *Journal of Theoretical Biology* 7: 17–32.

Kevles, D. J. (1985) *In the Name of Eugenics*, Knopf: New York.

Oster, G. F. and Wilson, E. O. (1978) *Caste and Ecology in the Social Insects*, Princeton University Press: Princeton.

Salthe, S. N. (1985) *Evolving Hierarchical Systems*, Columbia University Press: New York.

Slobodchikoff, C. N. (1984) "Resources and the evolution of social behavior," in P. W. Price, C. N. Slobodchikoff and W. S. Gaud (eds), *A New Ecology. Novel Approaches to Interactive Systems*, John Wiley and Sons: New York, 227–251.

Wilson, E. O. (1975) *Sociobiology: The New Synthesis*, Belknap Press of Harvard University Press: Cambridge.

—— (1985) "The sociogenesis of insect colonies," *Science* 228: 1489–1495.

Woolfenden, G. E. and Fitzpatrick, J. W. (1984) *The Florida Scrub Jay. Demography of a Cooperative-breeding Bird*, Princeton University Press: Princeton.

5

THE COMPLEXITY OF SOCIAL
AND MENTAL STRUCTURES IN
NONHUMAN MAMMALS

Hubert Hendrichs

INTRODUCTION

For several thousand years our ancestors lived in close contact with other mammals, and they developed a thorough knowledge of their specific behavior and ways of handling them effectively. During recent decades, remarkable advances have been achieved in the scientific exploration of animal behavior, sociology, and ecology. Thus it seems astonishing that we are still so far away from a satisfactory understanding of mammalian psychosocial qualities, structures, and reactions. This is all the more astonishing as such a knowledge is, or would be, essential for several important but so far poorly completed tasks. These include the following:

(a) to categorize the observable behavior in such a way that the recorded frequencies can be correlated with physiological data from reacting systems;

(b) to judge the well-being of an individual mammal in its specific situation with its specific frustrations and possible compensations;

(c) to discover qualities in mammals from which human qualities, like consciousness and moral orientation, might have developed, or which became included in such developments.

My contact with mammals – free-living and domestic – has continued for more than fifty years now, and for the past thirty years I have been engaged in the scientific exploration of mammalian behavior. Our main field of research is psychosocial structures in larger terrestrial, non-primate mammals: Marsupials, caviomorph rodents, ungulates, and carnivores. The animals are studied both in the field and in the laboratory. The method is a detailed observation of individually known animals in their social environment. In addition, in some cases physiological data are recorded: Temperature, heartbeat, hormone concentrations, and activity of the immune system; but our main area of competence is a detailed knowledge of the psychosocial reactions of the observed individuals. The research strategy can be described as follows:

(a) to develop a solid experience of the species and the individual animals observed;
(b) to assess and to document in the observed groups the established social structures and the specific strategies of the individual animals, living in their specific social situations with specific types of social stress and specific possibilities for coping;
(c) to model the psychosocial processes resulting in these structures, performances, and achievements.[1]

Struggling with the task to assess adequately the performances of the observed animals with regard to their orientations and coping reactions, it became increasingly clear in the course of the years that it is of fundamental importance to consider the individuality of each animal. And it also became clear to us how difficult a task this is. In the following I will try to point to some of the problems encountered, both epistemological and ontological.

THE COMPLEXITY OF PSYCHOSOCIAL PROCESSES IN MAMMALS AS A PROBLEM FOR THE OBSERVER

The complexity of psychosocial structures in higher mammals cannot be studied without realizing the problem faced by the observer in trying to recognize the relevant phenomena and the contexts of their occurrence.

Most physical and chemical scientists tend to consider biology a discipline of less scientific rigor than their own, and many biologists tend to consider ethology to be a subdiscipline with still less rigorous standards. Some ethologists agree with this judgment and, employing new and more formalized methodological procedures, aim at higher scientific standards. Some ethologists exploring psychosocial dynamics in groups of mammals hope to increase the accuracy of their investigations by a more precise definition of specific observable and countable elements of behavior. Increasing a specific precision of their recording, they at the same time strongly orient their attention toward the "visible" surface dynamics of the processes to be explored. They thus move away from the animals' structural qualities, as well as from the social context in which the animals live, and in relation to which their behavior is generated. This, in my view, is a serious problem in modern ethology.[2]

The structures and rules established in its social environment are of the greatest importance for the dynamics of a mammal; its behavior cannot be interpreted nor explained without knowledge of, and reference to, these structures and rules. The problem for the observer is that structures, rules, and the specific context of an animal's action cannot be recorded as countable units of behavior, but have to be recognized and identified on the basis of actual and previous actions of the observed animals. The context cannot be recognized without recording behavior, yet on the other hand behavior cannot be recorded without reference to the context of its occurrence. It cannot be defined by its form alone: An identical movement can be performed with different motivations, "seriously" or in play, in an agonistic or a sexual context. Without reference to this context, the movement cannot be counted to be used in a quantitative analysis.

The context can usually be diagnosed reliably by an experienced observer well acquainted with the possibilities of the species. For his judgment, he does not rely only on the actual behavior of the animals present, but also on his extensive past experience with these individuals and other individuals and groups of this species. Drawing on this experience, he recognizes situations, contexts, structures, and rules. This cognitive process of diagnostic judgment – though of great importance in any scientific exploration – is often neglected in methodological considerations.

The observer's judgments can be intersubjectively confirmed by other experienced observers and be tested with the aid of additional data, or by an explanation or the prognosis of a recordable development. But the observer is often unable to state clearly the foundations of his reliable and valid diagnostic categorization.[3] Some ethologists, therefore, are inclined to dismiss these judgments as being not up to scientific standards. This seems unreasonable as diagnostic decisions are required in categorizing (a) the observed animals – as to their species, sex, age, and social and emotional state – and (b) the context of their action – feeding, fighting, playing. They cannot be avoided in any data collecting, nor can they be avoided in establishing adequate information. Definition of recordable events obviously is an important tool of scientific investigation, but it tends to move from "what cannot be defined precisely, should not be included in scientific analysis" over "one had better not aim at qualities that are not clearly definable" to "such qualities are of no importance" or even "not existent." Definition tends to isolate units and levels of organization; diagnosis combines levels of organization and dimensions of perception and orientation. Diagnosis may be less precise than formal definition, but it is the only way leading to adequate information, indispensable for recognition, analysis, and evaluation of empirical data.

The animal itself is in a comparable situation with regard to the structures and rules of its social environment: It has to learn them without being able to perceive or understand them. A young mammal of a group-living species, such as red deer, horse, lion, wolf, or baboon, is born into a social unit of several animals living permanently together – a unit with specific social structures and specific rules for behaving in relation to these structures which the young animal has to learn while growing up and being "socialized." The rules concern the established ways of behaving within the given structures, maintaining and documenting them, and handling conflicts and states of escalating arousal. The mammal has partly inherited and, during socialization, partly has to develop the ability to adapt to these structures and rules of its social environment. These can be quite specific in different populations and in different groups of the same species.

A basic structure of any group is formed by the dominance relations among its members. The animals have generally established clear dominance relations, which they can maintain and display by agonistic behavior – threat, evasion, retreat, submission. The dominance position of an animal, however, does not always show clearly in these interactions: A dominant animal may, in a number of situations, not threaten the other away, but let it continue with its action and even withdraw and keep out of its way. This does not occur only in play but also in "serious" enterprises, even involving access to food; although the access to a female in estrus may be a different matter. To maintain a dominant position in a group does not necessarily require a physical strength superior to that of others. An older individual past its physical prime can still retain its dominance and remain a focus of attention for the other animals, a source of reassurance, and a center of their orientation. It can thus generate important decisions regarding actions to be taken by the group.

An inexperienced observer is often unable to recognize the stable dominance relations in a group. All the behavioral elements recorded quantitatively by him still do not provide any orientation: Each of the observed animals gives way at times to others, and many individuals displace others. Thus, the recorded frequencies do not make sense and cannot be interpreted.[4] An experienced observer, on the other hand, is able to recognize the context in which the observable behavior occurs, and from the context-specific frequencies, he can clearly read the dominance relations. He can recognize the situation quickly, but without being able immediately to present the basis of his judgment in formal argumentation. Such judgments are regularly required of the ethologist concerning species, sex, age class, arousal state of the individuals observed, and concerning the motivational and structural contexts of their actions. Are the animals feeding, caring for young, fighting, or playing? Are they socially interacting with group members, neighbors, or strangers?

Another complication easily recognized by an experienced observer is the following: In some groups, the dominant male will not tolerate any display, especially courtship behavior, of subdominant males. In other groups of the same species, the dominant male will "generously" tolerate such behavior. In some groups, this tolerance can indicate a "strong" dominant male in an undisputed position. In other groups of the same species, such a tolerance can indicate a "weak" dominant male, possibly in a "disputed" position. For a subdominant male, it obviously makes a great difference in which one of these four situations he is living. The animals know the rules in their group and the possible consequences of their behavior.

Other important types of structures in mammalian societies are the so-called "bonds" established by the various individuals: Specific attachments to specific places and to conspecifics. Such bonds can develop like processes of imprinting: being formed during a short phase but nevertheless lasting long and not reversing easily. The individuals becoming attached in that way often show astonishing changes: Moving differently, showing orientations and abilities different from before. Nevertheless the state of being attached is difficult to assess quantitatively by recording spatial distances or frequencies of contact behavior. Individuals strongly attached to each other, which live together harmoniously, and are strongly oriented toward each other, may rarely show contact behavior and move quite apart from each other. While pairs, on the other hand, that are less strongly attached, and live together less harmoniously, may show contact behavior – possibly with agonistic components – more frequently and move in greater proximity to each other.

One more complication: the context in which an animal acts can switch very quickly – sometimes in seconds, such as when a predator appears near animals feeding or courting. The animal itself can even switch its motivation and thereby the context of its action, thus changing the qualities of the elements and structures of its social environment. It can, in a critical agonistic situation, activate its state of arousal and start to play, or even "invent" or "hallucinate" predators.

The individual relations of all animals are relevant to each animal in the group and are represented in each animal in different ways. The individual animal can make use of its "knowledge" in a specific way. For example, a subdominant animal may learn to use the proximity to an individual of high dominance as protection against the pestering of a less dominant one. It may learn the areas of social security like places with warm sunshine or those affording protection from the burning sun. Such performances, while requiring "mappings" of the physical and social space, do not require intentionality or awareness. They can, in varying degrees, be accompanied by these qualities.[5]

The learning required does not primarily result from the animal's observing and imitating the behavior of other individuals, but from realizing, sensing, and developing its own possibilities when involved in agonistic and cooperative interactions with experienced animals, responding to the established structures and rules. The mammal can develop individual ways of orientation and of handling specific situations and get used to its own specific "inventions." It can in analogy to the observer learn to improve its performance and thereby its "knowledge," without intending to do so and without understanding it.[6]

These acts of social learning in mammals are possibly not dominated by digital, symbol-transporting information processing, but rather result from the dynamics of non-symbolic network processing. The same may even hold true for some intentional acts of mammals. The recognizing of structures, processes, and goals, as well as the internalizing of rules and constructing "images" in mammals, does not necessarily rely on a transportation of symbols, but may use different types of representation and information transformation. There are several oscillating conditions and states which, in mutual contact through processes of resonance, compensation, and harmonization, can generate "decisions" in a field containing several possible ways that lead to distinct, clearly "recognizable" structures. This could possibly be a very basic and very general quality of living as well as of psychosocial processes. The connectionist "neural" network model is discussed widely as a new concept that competes with the more "classical" symbol-manipulating concept in the struggle for understanding processes of information transmission and of cognition and learning. The new development may be just an extension of classical artificial intelligence (AI), or a sophisticated branch of classical cybernetics, and it may be completely inadequate to simulate higher neural processes. I am not competent to answer these questions. The model nevertheless appears to provide a stimulating challenge to look for new solutions to some important unsolved problems, and it may open new possibilities to conceptualize the processes of orientation, learning, and psychosocial organization in mammals.

In the following, after characterizing some of the different levels of complexity in the social organization of mammals I will try to sketch some aspects of mammalian individuality and intentionality that have to be taken into account when investigating the behavior of mammals and which are indispensable for an adequate understanding of their psychosocial reactions.

COMPLEXITY OF SOCIAL STRUCTURE VERSUS COMPLEXITY OF COGNITION AND OF AWARENESS

The populations of free-living mammals are organized spatially and socially in very different ways. The individuals of some species live on their own with only passing contacts with conspecifics, while the individuals of other species live permanently together in closely knit groups of conspecifics with division of labor and highly differentiated social relations. In a number of cases closely related species show very different social organizations.[7] Basic elementary mechanisms in all types of organizations are the spatial and social attachments of individual animals.[8] The ontogenetic development of these individual attachments is connected with changes in orientation and in the potential for arousal, control, and coping. The fundamental and only attachment of the newborn mammal is that to its mother. The growing mammal differentiates between parents, siblings, other conspecifics, and also places, objects, and habits. In relation to the changes in attachment the attention of the young mammal also changes, the "meanings" of social and of nonsocial occurrences change. Adult mammals have developed stable spatial, social, and mental attachments. They exhibit considerable individual variability, but also a large measure of species-specific universality, which points to inherited dispositions.

The primary attachment of the young to its mother is fundamental because it enables it to realize the species-specific potential in the development of its mental qualities. This development promotes the independence of the young, leading finally to the termination of its attachment to the mother. The attachments of adult animals to conspecifics, places, and habits can be of a transient – passing, seasonal – nature, requiring only reversible mental adaptations; or they can be permanent, with more irreversible mental adaptations: Species-specific possibilities in imprinting-like processes are realized and become fixed. Examples of transient attachments are seasonal mating relations, dominance relations, and seasonal territories. Examples of permanent attachments are found in monogamous pairs, permanent territories, and permanent social units. It is still an open question to what extent mechanisms of the mother–young bond are still operative in permanently bonded relations, and to what extent different mechanisms become involved. In most cases the bonds between adult animals are established when the mother–young bond has terminated. In one type of organization the permanent social attachment of the adult animal develops as a continuation of the mother–young bond: In many species there is a tendency to continue the close mother–daughter relation to the adult age of the daughter, and in some species the daughters remain with their mothers and grandmothers and form permanent "matrilinear" units – forming new separate groups only when the number of individuals becomes too high. Such "matrilinear" units can live in close relation to one or more males, or without permanent relations to specific males.[9]

The size and the cohesion of groups are often taken as an indicator of the complexity of social organization. The evolutionary development of group life is considered as an increase in social complexity, and the question arises as to what extent social complexity is a necessary condition for the development of mental complexity, of cognition, and awareness. In what way is the complexity of mental processes in mammals related to the complexity of social processes? To investigate this question a first essential step is to establish criteria to distinguish between levels of complexity (a) in social organization, and (b) in mental capacity and performance.

A closely knit group of permanently attached – bonded – individuals can be organized in such a way that, in their orientation and behavior the younger and the less dominant animals are strongly influenced by the older and more dominant ones. The attention of the subdominant individuals is mainly directed to the dominant individuals of their group. Their contact with the "outer" environment is therefore largely mediated by the behavior of the dominant individuals. This leaves them only limited opportunities to develop their own knowledge of the "world" outside their own group, social and nonsocial. The decisions regarding the activities of the group are generated by the dominant animals. But a closely bonded group can also be organized such that, in their environmental perception, the subdominant individuals are less restricted by the dominant animals. In such groups subdominant individuals too, with increasing age, can develop their own environmental experience and their own orientation in space and time. These older, experienced individuals can contribute considerably to the decisions generated in their group.

The bonding of several individuals into one tightly knit, permanent social unit obviously has to be seen as an increase in the complexity of social structure and a differentiation of social mechanisms. The conspecifics become divided up into in-group and out-group members of the population. The bonding of individuals can be achieved by simple inborn mechanisms. But with an increasing number of individuals the mechanisms providing for a smooth cooperation require an increasing complexity of the means of social cognition and communication. It is a complex task to integrate several competing adult individuals of the same sex into one cooperative unit. In a number of species, this has been efficiently achieved by restricting reproduction to only one of the males and one of the females in the group, by complex behavioral and physiological mechanisms preventing the reproduction of the subdominant animals.[10] In many species it has been achieved that more than one of the group's females can breed regularly. Only in very few species has it been achieved by complex social mechanisms that more than one of the group's males breed regularly. This can be considered the most complex organization of permanently bonded groups in mammals. The few species in which such groups occur show quite different levels of cognitive complexity. On the other hand, some species, closely related to these, exhibit a distinctly less complex social organization, but nevertheless show the same cognitive level as the related species living in groups with an organization of the highest complexity.[11]

A complex social structure is thus neither a sufficient nor a necessary condition for the development of a complex cognitive ability. The same social structure can be found in species with modest cognitive abilities, and in others with high cognitive capacities. The same social structure in one species can be maintained without, and in another with, complex mental performances. A social structure can be maintained and used with both low and high cognitive differentiation. The mechanisms involved in efficient performances can be of simple or high complexity. Structures and rules may be perceived or not, intended or not.

The (evolutionary) development of increasing complexity of the mechanisms maintaining and using a complex social structure can be seen as one important thread in the differentiation of perception and orientation in a differentiating environment with widening spatial and temporal horizons. But the differentiation of social structures has to be considered separately from the differentiation of the mechanisms used to establish and maintain the structures. And the differentiation of these mechanisms has, in turn, to be considered separately from the differentiation of the perceptual and cognitive processes involved. The differentiation of these perceptual and cognitive performances has then to be considered separately from the differentiation of the awareness accompanying the processes.

The differentiation of social and nonsocial environments brings new ways of being stressed and new possibilities to cope with stress. Changing phases of "hot" and "cold" stress, each followed by phases of specific forms of relaxation, provide ample opportunities for mental development, for a differentiation of representations and cognitive abilities. Individual mental representations, as developed in complex socially transmitted environments, can imply individual causes of fear and of reassurance, individual ways of being stressed and individual ways of coping with stress.[12] With the differentiation of perception and cognition, and with an increasing differentiation of mental representations, an increasing demand can be assumed for mechanisms generating and stabilizing decisions in situations with several possible alternatives for effective action, and for mechanisms evaluating alternatives in regard to possible goals. The demand is for the differentiation of the possibilities of communication, both inside the individual – planning, "thinking" – and between individuals – "language." And it is also a demand for the development and stabilization of identity, a self that has to, and can, retain its original decisions against changing actual impulses, that can persistently adhere to a goal against actual difficulties, i.e. an intentional self.

A high and phylogenetically late achievement of mammals is the psycho-social reaction of group members to the quality of role performance of individuals. The term "role performance" refers to acting in a cooperative system with division of labor in such a way that the functional achievement can be realized in a number of specific ways. Individual qualities of the acting animal can shape the specific performance in a way that influences the behavior of the other animals, their physiological reactions, and their motivations. The role-performing individual – in leading the way or ending a quarrel – not only combines various reactions to various stimuli in one response, but also shapes this response in a specific way, using specific attitudes and displays, exhibiting more or less tension and more or less arousal. The ease with which a function is achieved by the performing individual does influence group processes. In higher mammals the differences can be perceived by the animals of the group. In some species, this can be attributed to the performing individual, affecting the social status of this animal.

112

INDIVIDUAL PSYCHOSOCIAL STRUCTURES

Even in the insects, the nervous sytems develop neurons that interact with specific anatomical environments. The results of these developments, therefore, are not completely genetically determined. Similarly, social structures in groups of vertebrates are established and, in interacting with these, the psychosocial structures of individuals. There is an important difference, though: while the media in which the insect nervous systems develop are largely controlled by genetic programs, the environment of psychosocial development in mammals is not. The structures and qualities of this environment are formed in an area only partly controlled by genetic programs. The physiological reactions occurring in a state of fear are inherited, while the causes of fear may be learned. Behavioral elements, the forms of motor actions may be inherited, while the activations of such actions are learned. Information can be transmitted by inherited mechanisms, inherited channels, and processed by inherited mechanisms, while its evaluation, its meaning, the way it can be used have to be learned. The terms "homology" and "analogy" are used in biology as referring to qualities – traits, abilities, tendencies – that are transmitted genetically from one generation to the next. They therefore cannot be used in this sense to refer to qualities that are transmitted socially or culturally. In these socially and/or culturally transmitted qualities, it is still much more difficult than in genetically transmitted ones to distinguish between components of common ancestry and those of functional adaptation. The term "common origin" in this context can refer to a common biological origin – inherited – as well as to a common cultural origin – acquired through the same cultural tradition.

Concerning individual qualities developed in areas not genetically determined, the following distinction is important: Are they accidental, acquired by the organism during ontogeny without essentially contributing to species-specific functions, or do these individual qualities of an organism contribute to the perfection of the animal, to the terminal state of its ontogenetical development? This is a difficult, but also an important question discussed by philosophers for some thousand years. It is essential for understanding organismic dynamics. The answer obviously depends on the type of quality and the type of organism considered. In organisms whose development is largely determined genetically, the individual qualities not resulting from genetic dispositions are predominantly accidental, while in organisms whose psychosocial individuality is developed and structured in an area left open by genetic programs, these individual qualities are not merely accidental, but of fundamental importance for the functional performance of these organisms.[13] This is especially the case in humans, but the boundary between accidental and structural acquired individuality is not one between animal and man. In both animal

113

and man, inherited and acquired, and accidental and structural acquired individual qualities are found in various combinations.[14]

The mammalian psychosocial individuality does get constructed in an area left open by genetic dispositions. It is not focussed here on individually developed traits, preferences, and aversions of the mammal, but on the connecting composition of these acquired traits in one relatively stable structure. Specific qualities, preferences and aversions, attachments and relations, developed by the animal in interacting with its specific social environment, and essential for the control of its motivational and arousal states, become connected in a specific way, providing the animal with an individual structure which is of paramount importance for the integration of its functional subsystems as well as for its environmental orientations. In accordance with the philosophical tradition such a structure can be called an "eidetic" structure. Various developments end and stabilize as they settle in a specific relation of their qualities, an imprinting type of settling in a specific state of connectedness. The term "eidetic" is used here to point to this important non-accidental structural component of individuality in mammals. It is not meant to refer to an "idea" incorporated into the mammalian organism.

In two packs of wolves or wild dogs, prey preference can be different; and, in addition, with the same preference, the coordination of predation can be achieved in different ways: In some packs the animals assemble for the hunt with a lot of agonistic behavior: Growling, snarling, snapping at each other, and they show a similar behavior after the hunt, at the prey – not during the hunt, which is without visible agonistics and efficiently carried through. In other packs there is no growling or snarling before or after the hunt; the animals remain friendly towards each other in all phases. Imagine if it would be possible to take some cubs from one to the other pack and let them develop prey preference and become "snarlers" or "non-snarlers," different from the behavior of their original pack. They would have to develop an individual structure quite different from that of their original litter mates, and they would not lose this individual structure any more, even when brought back to their original pack.

INDIVIDUALLY ORIENTED INTENTIONALITY

What are the qualities and origin of the intentionality[15] of an organism with such an "eidetic" individual psychosocial structure? This structure was produced while the animal was ontogenetically developing in an environment influenced by socioculturally transmitted qualities. It was produced in a type of organism whose steering control had phylogenetically developed away from the domain controlled by genetic dispositions. Regarding the control of directed processes, we can distinguish three types in agreement with the biologist Ernst Mayr: Teleomatic, teleonomic, and teleological directedness.[16] Teleomatic processes come to end at a state of balance according to their mechanico-chemical properties, like an apple falling off a tree and rolling down a slope until the mechanical properties of the process reach a state of balance, possibly in a tuft of grass. Processes of self-organization and homeostatic processes are teleomatic as long as they result from mechanico-chemical properties and are not controlled by additional programs. By contrast, teleonomic processes are directed toward a goal by specific programs, developed either phylogenetically by natural selection or ontogenetically by experience or social tradition. They do not, in the biologist's view, require consciousness or a knowledge of the goal by the acting animal. These two are different from teleological processes, which are usually understood as requiring a more or less conscious intentionality of a subject, and are therefore generally considered to be of little importance for the biology of nonhuman organisms.[17]

Teleomatic processes are controlled by physico-chemical mechanisms between the elements involved and their environments. Teleonomic processes are controlled, in addition, by programs providing dispositions and specific reactions and intentions. Teleological processes are controlled in addition to mechanisms and programs, by conscious individual decisions in relation to individually developed orientations. Mental processes in higher mammals can be combinations of two or three of these types. Such processes can occur without any awareness, or they can be accompanied partly or fully by different forms of awareness.

In mammals an important type of sociomental process occurs that possibly has to be seen as an intermediate form between the teleonomical and the teleological types. It is neither controlled by specific programs nor by conscious intentionality. Such processes occur in situations of environmental or motivational changes, when new decisions have to be generated in relation to possible goals or possible orientations concerning the actual behavior at a particular moment and its possible implications for achieving possible aims. Such decisions efficiently interrelating situation, orientation, and goal achievement can be produced in some cases unguided by programs and do not require consciousness. As these inventive decisions require a specific orientation of the animal, which is more stable than the situation and the possible goals, one could call these processes "goal-directed in an orientation" or "oriented intentionally". They may, as a successful invention, become memorized and incorporated in the program of the animal, closing some small part of the area left open by its programs, but at the same time may open it for further, new inventions. The "opening" in the steering of intentionality in higher mammals generally does not become fully closed in ontogeny; it may even be widened considerably in the direction of an elementary form of consciousness.

Consider the case of three female wolves of the same litter, living together with clear dominance relations in a relatively small enclosure in a zoo. When the two dominant animals are active, the movements of the lower ranking female are mostly restricted to a specific part of the enclosure; when the two dominant animals are resting, this female sometimes moves into the area which she usually may not use; she does this very cautiously, alert and tense, always keeping her attention on the two dominant animals. If one of them only raises her head, she at once, with two or three big leaps, withdraws to "her" area. But when the two others do not show any offense, she may move on, intensely attentive, approach a bone with some residue of meat, sniff at it from a small distance, but not touching it, move on to a marking place of the two dominant animals, sniffing it without marking it herself, always remaining attentive toward the resting dominant animals. When the two dominant females still have not shown any offense, she relaxes and to some extent begins to show some signs of well-being, but still keeps her attention on the two resting animals. She finally returns to her area and then shows behavior distinctly indicating well-being – this is one of the relatively few ways in which this individual, strongly constrained in its actions by the other animals, can generate a feeling of well-being. This regular performance has been described in a simplifying manner. The details always vary and the evaluation of events by the wolf appear to change by the hour, motivation and attention changing with specific occurrences of the day. The dominant wolves recognize this behaviour and are generally not disturbed by it. Yet on some days, they are and do not allow it.

What are the motivations and intentions of this animal during its excursion into "forbidden territory"? What is driving it? Which are the goals of its actions? How did this behavior develop? To what extent is it inherited and to what extent learned? Such questions are very difficult to investigate. But with experience and patience this can be done, and the questions then sometimes can partly be answered. The main goal of the behavior described is not for the wolf to reach the bone with its residue of meat, or to inspect the marking place of the dominant animals, or to explore the rarely used space, or to prevent the dominant animals from getting up. All these constitute goals and points of orientation for the low-ranking female wolf, but they are not the basic motivation of her action. Her main aim comprises the following tendencies: To explore the boundaries of her social existence, to build up the intensity required for that kind of enterprise, to make use of a natural potential, the activation of which includes physiological and emotional reactions resulting in a state of well-being. This low-ranking female wolf uses inherited qualities in a specific connection developed by her exploring the possibilities of her specific situation and aiming at the fullest possible realization of well-being. The strategy as such was not provided by her program. Its development required a number of decisions in the area left open by genetic programs. Its becoming part of the animal's program did not require any form of conscious intentionality. The actual carrying out of the described behavior does not require consciousness, but decisions unguided by any program.

INTENTIONALITY AND AWARENESS

Social actions of mammals, although they often look very similar to the observer, even among different species, can to various degrees be intentional and non-intentional, and to various degrees can be accompanied by different states of awareness. These differences can change the quality of the control of the behavioral patterns involved and of their functional significance. Examples of such actions are a low-ranking individual seeking the proximity and protection of a dominant individual, thereby escaping the threat or aggression of a less dominant animal than the one approached, or the intervention of a dominant individual ending a quarrel or fight between two subdominant ones. Such behavior may "just happen," without any intention and without any awareness on the part of the animals involved, or it can be learned and intentionally employed by one or both of the interacting animals. It can even by recognized and "understood" by other individuals "observing" the event. This can sometimes by read from the consequent actions of these animals, including their intentional movements, which can enable the observer to follow the processes of orientation and decision in the observed individuals.

Seeking proximity and protection of older and of more dominant animals does occur in most mammalian taxa, including the marsupials. In lower mammals, such behavior rarely includes learned intentional components and is probably not combined with states of awareness. In higher ungulate-type mammals, such as the various species of pigs, cattle, and horses, learned intentional components and elementary forms of awareness do occasionally occur and can be documented. In higher carnivores, elephants, and higher primates, they regularly occur and, to varying extents, can become part of the control system integrating the motivational components of the organism.

The attention of a mammal is only very rarely restricted to one specific object or to one functional or motivational context. Its attention generally, in various stages of intensity, covers several areas simultaneously. It is thus able to choose several impulses out of many, and to respond to the combination of these selected impulses in a way fitting its program. It can, in such a case, sometimes choose its action, while possibly not the form in which it is carried out. A mammal even can "load" specific structures and events in its environment with specific significance and meaning, attributing to them specific qualities that make them a source of security or fear, of excitement and tension. In attributing such qualities to specific parts of its environment the mammal can show some kind of what, in humans, would be called imagination, invention, and creativity.

In the steering of an organism various domains or areas of different dimensions have to be combined and integrated: Physiological, emotional, cognitive, and social processes. These operate with different mechanisms in different environments; they are differently organized and controlled. A fright reaction can change an animal at all the levels influencing its control: Physiologically, motivationally, mentally, and socially. It is therefore misleading to conceive of a mammal as mainly controlled by its cortex. The older brain structures play an important role, and the rest of the nervous system including its autonomous parts are also involved. Physiological, emotional, motivational, cognitive, and psychosocial conflicts and tensions have to be solved by the acting animal. Decisions concerning possible and optimal regulations have to be taken and, in the process of acting, maintained with some independence from the further development of the original situation with its specific constellation of incentives. Both the resulting behavior and the process leading to its realization can be inherited or acquired. In many cases the behavior shown is inherited, while the program for its implementation is not. The maintenance of such a process can be achieved by tenaciously adhering to the decisions taken entering the process, such as an attack or a chase, warding off all further influences, or by an intentional maintenance in a specific orientation balancing influences from various domains.

The tendencies of a mammal leading to intentional, goal-directed actions and enterprises can primarily result from its effort to master the integration of various competing and interacting motivations into one distinct action, and to accomplish this integration effectively. In this process, a number of "decisions" become necessary in relation to the actual possibilities of a successful integration in a common orientation. To carry through and thereby achieve an effective action, specific states of arousal and states of "aggressive" determination are often required to keep the various decisions combined in a specific goal-orientation. In situations of conflict, processes of intentionality and awareness reinforcing each other, higher mammals are for brief moments possibly able to generate states approaching consciousness.

QUALITIES POSSIBLY CONTRIBUTING TO HUMAN CULTURE

There is a further important unanswered question: To what extent does the intentionality of an organism result from inherited and learned motivations, behavior patterns, or abilities, and to what extent from impulses of its sociocultural environment evoking these qualities? Put differently, to what extent is the intentionality driven or pushed from within, and to what extent attracted or pulled out from without? The answer to this question changes with the level of sociocultural organization the organism in view has

118

reached. In higher mammals, the orientation of the individual in its social environment has gained central importance for the control of its dynamics, overruling at times regulating impulses from other domains. Important parameters are the spatial and temporal distance covered by the orientation, the "farsightedness" of the orienting, steering, and deciding organism.

Structures and qualities that develop in spaces influenced, but not determined, by genetic dispositions are also present in humans, but in a different way. In nonhuman mammals, these qualities are realized in close connection with qualities dependent on genetic dispositions, while in humans such qualities can be developed in relation to qualities already independent of genetic dispositions. In higher nonhuman mammals, the domain of oriented decisions is only marginally involved, and only occasionally gains control, while in humans it is generally available, and, in addition, can itself be controlled in turn by new domains. Prehuman qualities in humans become integrated by influences from new domains of orientation not present in nonhuman mammals, such as that of conscious cognitive evaluation and that of conscious moral evaluation.

Among the qualities present already in non-primate mammals, which can be regarded as material requirements for the realization of human culture, the following possibly deserve special attention:

(a) structural patterns that are generated in a domain not controlled by genetic dispositions, at a considerable distance from genetic constraints (the functional relations of such patterns being different from those generated by genetic dispositions interacting with environmental constraints);

(b) the individual psychosocial or mental structure built in that domain, allowing the integration of organismic subsystems in an individual orientation, and, in addition, making possible and requiring individual decisions in an area left open by the individual's programs, inherited or acquired;

(c) an intentionality which develops in this domain at a long distance from genetic control, in a domain of self-organizing patterns more "pulled" by possibilities of the social and cultural environment than "pushed" by endogenous drives.

Mammals live and develop in socially transmitted environments and during their ontogeny develop a mental individual structure, important for their own organization and a necessary foundation for a number of qualities contributing to human culture. This "eidetic" mental individual structure of mammals contributes at least to the following requirements for cultural developments:

(a) programs that remain structurally open;

(b) knowledge that can be continuously enlarged, with qualities of experience enabling contact with new environmental dimensions;

(c) the realizing of new levels of abstraction, awareness, and reflexion, gaining distance from actual activities and from the actual environment;
(d) oriented intentionality, with the orientation shifting from close to distant events and horizons.

This again points to the fundamental importance of structural individuality in mammals. For the scientific analysis of mammalian behavior, stress reaction, and well-being, it is necessary to consider the individual mental structures of the animals studied. In addition, it appears important to take these structures into account when trying to discover qualities contributing to the development of human culture.

NOTES

For critical and encouraging comments on earlier drafts of this paper I am grateful to K. E. Boulding, P. M. Hejl, Ursula Hendrichs, E. L. Khalil, Sandra D. Mitchell, and M. Wolff.

1 Publications include: Sachser, N. (1986) "Different forms of social organization at high and low population densities in guinea pigs," *Behavior* 97: 235–272; Stahnke, A. and Hendrichs, H. (1986) "Social variability in male guinea pigs: Different dominance quality resulting from early social experience," *Zoologische Beiträge Neue Folge* 29: 413–435; Stefanski, V., Hendrichs, H. and Ruppel, H. G. (1989) "Social stress and activity of the immune system in guinea pigs," *Naturwissenschaften* 76: 225–226; Thyen, Y. and Hendrichs, H. (1990) "Differences in behavior and social organization of female guinea pigs as a function of the presence of a male," *Ethology* 85: 25–34; Schwede, G., Hölzenbein, S. and Hendrichs, H. (1990) "Sparring in white-tailed deer (Odocoileus virginianus)," *Zeitschrift für Säugetierkunde* 55: 331–339; Dressen, W., Gruen, H. and Hendrichs, H. (1990) "Radio telemetry of heart-rate in male tammar wallabies (Marsupialia: Macropodidae): Temporal variations and behavioral correlates," *Australian Journal of Zoology* 38: 89–103; Korz, V. (1991) "Social relations and individual coping reactions in a captive group of Central American agoutis (Dasyprocta punctata)," *Zeitschrift für Säugetierkunde* 56: 207–218; Schwede, G., Hendrichs, H. and Wemmer, C. (1992) "Activity and movement patterns of young white-tailed deer fawns," in Brown, R. D., ed., *The Biology of Deer*, Springer: New York–Berlin–Heidelberg; Dressen, W. and Hendrichs, H. (1992) "Social behavior and heart rate in tammar wallabies (Macropodidae: Macropus eugenii)," *Journal of Zoology* 227: 299–317; Schwede, G., Hendrichs, H. and McShea, W. (1993) "Social and spatial organization of female white-tailed deer, Odocoileus virginianus, during the fawning season," *Animal Behavior* 45: 1007–1017.
2 Some other ethologists, trying to increase scientific standards, test trained animals in specific artificial environments and situations. They conclude from the results of these experiments on specific qualities of the performing animals. In such cases, often highly speculative assumptions have to be made concerning the intentionality of these animals and their central orientations.
3 Polanyi especially pointed to this "tacit" component of knowledge, cf. Polanyi, M. (1966) *The Tacit Dimension*, New York: Doubleday.
4 This becomes especially obvious when sex and age of the observed animals have not been recorded, or are not considered in the analysis of frequencies.

5 Ryle's distinction between "knowing how" and "knowing that" points to an important difference (Ryle, G. (1949) *The Concept of Mind*, New York: Barnes and Noble). Possibly "knowing" can and should be differentiated still further.

6 Boulding has presented a very general concept for the "know how" of living systems in their world: The "image" as an internal structure related to the system's external environment (Boulding, K. E. (1956) *The Image*, Ann Arbor: Michigan University Press). This structure gains different extensions at the different levels of complexity reached in evolution. Only at the highest levels it becomes accompanied by awareness and includes value systems. As image of its own identity it contributes to the system's organization and integration (cf. Boulding, K. E. (1978) *Ecodynamics*, Beverly Hills, London: Sage Publications).

7 Cf. Hendrichs, H. (1978) "Die soziale Organisation von Säugetierpopulationen," *Säugetierkundliche Mitteilungen* 26: 81–116.

8 Bowlby, J. (1958) "The nature of the child's tie to his mother," *International Journal of Psycho-Analysis* 39: 350–373. Bowlby, J. (1975) *Bindung. Eine Analyse der Mutter-Kind-Beziehung*, Kindler: Munich; Wickler, W. (1976) "The ethological analysis of attachment," *Zeitschrift für Tierpsychologie* 31: 163–170; Bischof, N. (1985) *Das Rätsel Ödipus. Die biologischen Wurzeln des Urkonfliktes von Intimität und Autonomie*, Piper: Munich.

9 Well-documented social organizations in which cohesive units of several permanently attached breeding females live without permanent contact to specific breeding males are those of the European red deer (*Cervus elaphus*), the African elephant (*Loxodonta africana*), and the sperm whale (*Physeter macrocephalus*). Prolonged mother–daughter relations occur in many species and have been documented from marsupials to apes.

10 Examples for such groups are the marmosets and tamarins (*Callitrichidae*, e.g. *Callithrix jacchus*, *Saguinus oedipus*), the wolf (*Canis lupus*), the dwarf mongoose (*Helogale parvula*), and the naked mole rat (*Heterocephalus glaber*).

11 Closely related species of similar cognitive abilities, but with social organizations of different structural complexity are slender mongoose (*Herpestes sanguineus*) and dwarf mongoose (*Helogale parvula*), tiger (*Panthera tigris*) and lion (*Panthera leo*), orang-utan (*Pongo pygmaeus*), and gorilla (*Gorilla gorilla*). The species named first is that with the less complex social organization.

12 Cf. Hendrichs, H. (1992) "On social stress in mammals," *Bielefelder Ökologische Beiträge* 6: 105–110.

13 The game-theoretical cost–benefit calculations widely used at present in "sociobiology" are not designed to be applied to individualized populations. They therefore should be applied to mammals only with caution.

14 Duns Scotus (1270–1308) in the first years of the fourteenth century conceptualized non-accidental individuality and coined the term "*haecceitas*" for this quality of individual beings, cf. Reportata Parisiensia, Liber II, Distinctio XII, in Duns Scotus, J. (1969) *Opera omnia* (Lyon 1639), Bd. XI, Olms, Hildesheim.

15 The term "intentional" is used here in a wide sense, not restricted to conscious intentionality, but including unconscious efforts to reach a goal.

16 Mayr, E. (1974) "Teleological and teleonomic: A new analysis," *Boston Studies in the Philosophy of Science* 14: 91–117.

17 As exception cf. Griffin, D. R. (1981) *The Question of Animal Awareness*, New York: Rockefeller University Press.

6

ON THE SOCIAL NATURE OF AUTOPOIETIC SYSTEMS

Milan Zeleny

INTRODUCTION

Every organism, even if temporarily isolated, can emerge, survive, and reproduce only as part of a larger societal network of organisms. Similarly, each cell, organelle, or neuron can exist only as part of a group or society of cells, organelles, or neurons. Each component of an autopoietic (Varela *et al.*, 1974; Zeleny, 1980) system can emerge, persist, and reproduce only within the complex of relationships that constitute the network of interconnected components and component-producing processes.[1]

Before any organism can reproduce, it must first be produced (or self-produced), and it must survive. Autopoiesis therefore precedes, and in fact creates, the conditions for a subsequent reproduction.

Survival activities of individual organisms (economic and ecological) directly form and re-form local societies of interactive populations which are further concatenated into regional networks and full ecosystems. Reproductive organismic activities can take place only within such preformed networks and thus assure their own (networks') reinforcement and self-production. In fact, autopoietic systems can, and many do, adapt and evolve without their own reproduction; only their components may reproduce.

Eldredge (this volume) concludes that a gene-centered view of such systems is unnecessary, and that social networks are demonstrably biotic systems. The entire human society is such an autopoietic superorganism (Stock and Campbell, this volume) embedded in another autopoietic superorganism, Gaia – as is often propounded by L. Margulis (Mann, 1991).

The so-called "Gaia hypothesis" is, of course, not new in the history of science; A. A. Bogdanov formulated it quite early, clearly, autopoietically and with much elegance:

> The entire realm of life on earth can be considered as a single system of divergence, based on the rotation of carbon dioxide. This rotation forms a basis for complementary correlations between life as a whole – the "biosphere" – and the gaseous cover of the Earth – the

"atmosphere." The stability of atmospheric content is sustained in the biosphere, which draws from the atmosphere the material for assimilation.

(Zeleny, 1988a)

Bogdanov, the father of tectology (the precursor of modern autopoiesis), has thus conceptually coupled biosphere, atmosphere, hydrosphere, and lithosphere into a single holistic[2] system of mutually co-evolving influences.

Margulis has also targeted neo-Darwinism[3] and its inability to answer important questions or explain fundamental phenomena – for example, there is not a single case of a new species created by building up of chance mutations. She has embraced the so-called "autopoietic Gaia" (Mann, 1991).

Organisms cannot be separated (except through artificial cleavage) from their economic, ecological, or social environments which they themselves co-produce. Only a temporarily disembodied human mind can venture to remove itself, also temporarily, from its social surroundings – from its life base.

AUTOPOIESIS

If Nature possesses a universal psyche, it is one far above the common and most impelling feelings of the human psyche. She certainly has never wept in sympathy, nor stretched a hand protectively over even the most beautiful or innocent of her creatures.

(Eugène Marais, 1970)

Among the physical, biological, and social systems, the most complex and the most interesting ones are those which are autopoietic, i.e., autonomous and self-producing. The definition of these systems has been introduced by Varela, Maturana, and Uribe (1974). Also Haken (this volume), defining synergetics, refers to systems composed of many individual parts which, by their cooperation, can form organizations and structures – i.e., he refers to social systems.

An autopoietic system has been defined as a system that is generated through a closed organization of production processes such that the same organization of processes is regenerated through the interactions of its own products (components), and a boundary emerges as a result of the same constitutive processes.

Varela et al. (1974) have conceived autopoetic organization as an autonomous unity of a network of productions of components, which participate recursively in the same network of productions of components, which produced these components, and which realize such a network of productions as a unity in the space in which the components exist.

Such organization of components and component-producing processes remains essentially invariant through the interaction and turnover of com-

123

ponents. The invariance follows from the definition: If the organization (the relations between system processes) changes substantially, there would be a change in the system's categorization in its identity class. What changes is the system's structure (its particular manifestation in the given environment) and its parts. The nature of the components and their spatiotemporal relations are secondary to their organization and thus refer only to the structure of the system.

System's boundary is a structural manifestation of the system's underlying organization. The boundary is a structural realization of the system in a particular environment of components. In physical environments this could take the form of a topological boundary. Both organization and structure are mutually interdependent.

The concepts of the autopoietic nature of a system were developed by Varela *et al.* (1974) based on a living (biological) system as a model of self-production. Yet self-production has the potential to mean and be interpreted in many different ways by a variety of observers. "Autopoiesis" has been coined (not translated from Greek) as a label for a clearly defined interpretation of "self-production." This phenomenon of self-production can be observed in living systems. A cell, a system that renews its macro-molecular components thousands of times during its lifetime, maintains its identity, cohesiveness, relative autonomy, and distinctiveness despite such turnover of matter. This persisting unity and its holism is called "autopoiesis."

Zeleny (1981) presents an overview of autopoiesis as a theory for the living organization. Varela *et al.* (1974) have developed a six-point key that provides the criteria for determining whether or not a system is autopoietically organized. These criteria, as they are applied to biological (living) systems, can also be applied to other systems that are currently not considered "living." This is a simple exercise with very important implications; yet it has not been carried out even by the "fathers" of autopoiesis. We have found (Zeleny and Hufford 1991, 1992) that not only are spontaneous social systems autopoietic, but also that the relationship is much stronger. Although all living systems are autopoietic, not all autopoietic systems are living. For example, inorganic osmotic growths (Zeleny *et al.*, 1989) are often autopoietic.

All autopoietic systems must be social systems. In other words, all autopoietic, and therefore all biological (living) systems, are social systems. Also, the topological boundary, that has been necessary to describe an autopoietic system within a favorable environment of physical components (such as those within and around a cell), may not necessarily take a physical form in other types of systems, e.g., in social systems.

In social systems, dynamic networks of productions are being continually renewed without changing their organization, while their components are being replaced; perishing or exiting individuals are substituted by the birth or entry of new members. Individual experiences are also renewed; ideas, concepts and their labels evolve and serve as the most important organizing factor in human societies. The organizing core for the implementation of ideas must be the emergent society as an autopoietic entity.

Autopoietic systems can persist in their autopoiesis for many decades (humans, trees), for many days (cells) or for mere flashes of hours, minutes, seconds, or milliseconds (osmotic growths). The time-measured "lifespan" of autopoiesis in no way enters (or should enter) into its definition. Also, autopoiesis is bound to exhibit gradation; it does not jump into being in a magic instant – it becomes. It gradually degrades itself; the processes of autopoiesis weaken and dim more or less rapidly (Zeleny, 1978).

There is a great modeling and explanatory potential, certainly on the rise in modern sciences, in treating autopoietic systems as social systems. At the same time, as a fringe benefit, it also disposes of the recently fashionable scholastic "discussions" as to whether social systems are or are not autopoietic.

SOCIAL SYSTEMS

Have you ever seen, in some wood, on a sunny quiet day, a cloud of flying midges – thousands of them – hovering, apparently motionless, in a sunbeam? . . . Yes? . . . Well, did you ever see the whole flight – each mite apparently preserving its distance from all others – suddenly move, say three feet, to one side or the other? Well, what made them do that? A breeze? I said a quiet day. But try to recall – did you ever see them move directly back in the same unison? Well, what made them do that? Great human mass movements are slower of inception but much more effective.

(Bernard M. Baruch, Foreword to Mackay (1849))

It is time to define social systems and to elucidate the meaning of "social" for the purposes of this chapter.

Social systems, in spite of all their rich metaphoric and anthropomorphic meanings and intuitions, are networks characterized by inner coordination of individual action achieved through communication among temporary agents. The key words are coordination, communication, and limited individual lifespan.[4]

Coordinated behavior includes both cooperation and competition, in all their shades and degrees. Actions of predation, altruism, and self-interest are simple examples of different and interdependent modes of coordination. Communication could be physically, chemically, visually, linguistically, or symbolically induced deformation (or in-formation) of the environment and consequently of individual action taking place in that environment.

So I, as an individual, can coordinate my own actions in the environment only if I coordinate it with the actions of other participants in the network.

In order to achieve this, I have to in-form (change) the environment so that the actions of others are suitably modified; I have to communicate. As all other individuals are attempting to do the same a social network of coordination emerges, and, if successful, it is "selected" and persists. Such a network improves my ability to coordinate my own actions within the environment effectively. Cooperation, competition, altruism, and self-interest are therefore inseparable.

Social systems cannot be limited to human systems. Human systems simply in-form a special meaning on the universal acts of coordination, communication, and birth–death processes in general social systems.

A group of fish thrown together by a tide wave is a passive aggregation, not a social system. A swarm of moths lured to a porch light is an active aggregation, but not a social system. A flag-pattern of athletes constructed through bullhorn-shouted commands from a center is a purposeful hetero-poietic aggregation, not a social system. All of these can transform into social systems as soon as internal communication patterns become established; they should then temporarily persist (become autonomous), even after removing the external impetus.

Mere externally induced interaction of components does not suffice; billiard balls interact and so do wind-blown grains of sand – nobody would call them social systems. Schools of fish, swarms of bees, flocks of birds, packs of animals, and even Barcelona wave-patterns of Olympic Games spectators are, however, no matter how ephemerally shortlived, exquisitely social systems.

Any social system, in order to adapt and persist in its environment, must be capable of reshaping itself, controlling its growth, and checking the proliferation of individuals. In other words, the long-term persistence of a social system is critically dependent on harmoniously balanced birth and death processes. There can be no life without death.

A proliferation of individuals without death processes and without death-inducing communication is "cancer" – a shortlived, environmentally destructive outburst of life-like processes, but not the life itself. A dominant death process, without a sufficient birth-process complement, takes any social system towards its extinction. Life of a social system, and thus life itself, is based on a dynamic and autopoietic harmony between birth and death processes. Life is necessarily a social phenomenon; the life of an individual cannot take place outside of a social network, and individual life itself must be socially embodied at the level of its components.

This view is quite different from the deterministic and essentially non-biological dogma that (somehow) the growth of an organ is genetically (symbolically) programmed into the cells which are then guided (read-only memory) by this "geneprogram" through an exquisitely precise and predetermined series of events. But no communication and no death implies no life.

AUTOPOIESIS – THE SIX-POINT KEY

To determine whether a system is or is not autopoietic in its organization, Varela *et al.* (1974) have developed six key points or criteria that should be applied to a system. Their criteria can be stated as follows:

(1) Determine, through interactions, if the unity has identifiable boundaries. If the boundaries can be determined, proceed to (2). If not, the entity is indescribable and we can say nothing.

(2) Determine if there are constitutive elements of the unity, that is, components of the unity. If these components can be described, proceed to (3). If not, the unity is an unanalyzable whole and therefore not an autopoietic system.

(3) Determine if the unity is a mechanistic system, that is, the component properties are capable of satisfying certain relations that determine in the unity the interactions and transformations of these components. If this is the case proceed to (4). If not, the unity is not an autopoietic system.

(4) Determine if the components that constitute the boundaries of the unity constitute these boundaries through preferential neighborhood relations and interactions between themselves, as determined by their properties in the space of their interactions. If this is not the case, you do not have an autopoietic unity because you are determining its boundaries, not the unity itself. If (4) is the case, however, proceed to (5).

(5) Determine if the components of the boundaries of the unity are produced by the interactions of the components of the unity, either by transformation of previously produced components, or by transformations and/or coupling of non-component elements that enter the unity through its boundaries. If not, you do not have an autopoietic unity; if yes, proceed to (6).

(6) If all the other components of the unity are also produced by the interactions of its components as in (5), and if those which are not produced by the interactions of other components participate as necessary permanent constitutive components in the production of other components, you have an autopoietic unity in the space in which its components exist. If this is not the case and there are components in the unity not produced by components of the unity as in (5), or if there are components of the unity which do not participate in the production of other components, you do not have an autopoietic unity.

Thus, the successful application of the six-point key to a system will determine if the system is or is not autopoietically organized.

SYSTEMS ANALYSIS USING THE SIX-POINT KEY

To illustrate the diversity of autopoiesis in its application to systems analysis, Zeleny and Hufford (1991, 1992) have analyzed three systems: A biological (living) system, a chemical system, and a spontaneous social system. Here we summarize only the conclusions.

The eukaryotic cell

The generalized non-plant eukaryotic cell may be described as having a plasma membrane which surrounds the cytoplasm and cytoplasmic components of the cell. The cytoplasm contains the nucleus, mitochondria, golgi apparatus, endoplasmic reticulum, various vesicles, lysosomes, vacuoles, cytoplasmic filaments and microtubules, centrioles, and other components of the cell.

After applying the six-point key to the generalized eukaryotic cell, it can be concluded that the cell is an autopoietic unity in the space in which its components exist.

L. Margulis (Mann, 1991) is one of the few biologists who viewed eukaryotic cells as autopoietic populations of components. "We are walking communities," she insisted. Yet, this understanding of the role of symbiotic factors in biological organisms has been rarely carried beyond eukaryotes, to its logical conclusions.

Osmotic growth

Stephane Leduc (1911) described an "osmotic growth," a membrane of precipitated inorganic salt, as having many processes, functions, and characteristic forms that appear to be analogous to those found in living systems. The osmotic experiments performed by Leduc have been also reproduced by Klir, Hufford, and Zeleny (1988).

Unlike typical experiments in simple precipitation, where two solutions are mixed and a cloudy solution of an insoluble salt results, osmotic growths precipitate and grow over a period of minutes to days and go from a thin transparent membranous state to an opaque state. An actual photographic sequence has been provided by Zeleny, Klir, and Hufford (1989).

After applying the six-point test, based on the evaluation of osmotic growths (specifically the calcium chloride/tribasic sodium phosphate system), it can be concluded that an osmotic growth is an autopoietic unity in the space in which its components exist.

At the macroscopic level, the osmotic precipitation membrane exhibits fluidity, elasticity, and resealability identical to the properties of the plasma membrane. As the internal osmotic pressure increases, an expansion occurs (not a rupture) allowing components from the internal and external spaces to flow through the membrane and "couple" within the membrane. The osmotic growth phenomenon occurs because the operational integrity of the precipitation membrane is maintained.

At the microscopic level, the membrane exhibits various degrees of permeability to water and small ions in a fashion analogous to the plasma membrane. These features are a consequence of preferential neighborhood relations and interactions of the membrane components.

Osmotic growths are, temporarily and often ephemerally, autopoietic. This implies that if we hold the current autopoietic theory to be correct and intact, then we must reassess our definition (redefine our criteria) of what it means to be "living." If we do not give up our current definitions of "living," then we must conclude that there is a fundamental problem within the existing theory of autopoiesis which needs to be addressed.

Kinship system: a spontaneous social system

As our third system, the kinship system is an example of a spontaneous social order that has a substantial impact and great significance in the life of social, economic, and political networks. A kinship system constitutes, prototypically, an autopoietic system that is produced and maintained through organizational rules (which are potentially codified) of a given society. No matter what the particular mix of its components (men, women, and children), the kinship system organizes its social domain and coordinates its social action in a spontaneous self-perpetuating fashion. It must also continually adapt, spontaneously, to the external challenges and interferences of the society, represented by social engineers (shamans) and reformers.

Social networks, embodying kinship systems, are not static and unchanging structures, but highly dynamic ones.

Cochran et al. (1990), in their study of kinship systems, established that the distribution of different types and roles of network participants (kin, friends, neighbors, formal ties) remains relatively stable, even though the names and faces of network members keep changing. In the language of autopoiesis: It is their organization that remains stable, while their structures and components continually change.

Social networks can therefore change in their structure or in the nature of their component relationships (organization). One can therefore study shifts in the network's structure, turnover among its members, and changes in the character of continuing network ties. For example (Cochran et al., 1990), in spite of frequent moving and changes of neighborhoods, American white children maintain the largest stable social networks (8 adults, 8 peers) while relatively immobile Swedish children maintained the smallest (4 adults, 4 peers).

Viewing families and kinship networks properly as autopoietic systems could lead to new and important understanding of the effects of residential mobility, divorce rates, death and disease disruptions, loss of employment, or state intervention on the structure, organization and durability of social bonds in important social and support networks – primary, functional, peripheral, and formal. Through social autopoiesis, one also can learn more about which social environments produce desirable social supports in transaction with parents. What is the role of friends and relatives? What is the role of parental self-confidence, and how can it be enhanced? What is the role of a parents' level of formal education? How do intervention programs interact with the spontaneous self-organizational nature of social autopoiesis? The research agenda of self-producing social systems is remarkable in its challenge and significance.

It was F. A. Hayek who integrated the concepts of self-production directly into the domain of social systems (1975). Hayek stated that:

> Although the overall order of actions arises in appropriate circumstances as the joint product of the actions of many individuals who are governed by certain rules, the production of the overall order is of course not the conscious aim of individual action since the individual will not have any knowledge of the overall order, so that it will not be an awareness of what is needed to preserve or restore the overall order in a particular moment but an abstract rule which will guide the actions of the individual.

Consequently, the individuals in a society spontaneously assume the sort of conduct which assures their existence within the whole. Of course this conduct must also be compatible with the preservation of the whole. Neither the society nor the individuals could exist if they did not behave in this manner. The overall order, preservation of the society, is not the "purpose" or the "plan" of the individuals. The individual actions are motivated by their own goals and purposes.

AMOEBA: BIOLOGICAL SOCIAL SYSTEMS

Howard Topoff (1981) asks:

> What do human beings, ants, and slime have in common? Despite their differences in structure, physiology and ecology, all three consist of individuals whose behavior is sufficiently coordinated for the group to be called a society.

The question is, is this "coordination" and the resulting society due to executing a preconceived plan of a social engineer, central planner, or a

130

great designer (like in heteropoietic systems), or is it due to the distributed and unintended self-coordination of goal-seeking and autonomously behaving individuals (like in autopoietic systems)?

Cellular slime mold (Garfinkel, 1987) is another good example of an autopoietic social system. The slime molds (Gymnomycota) are an example of a fungus-like protist. They are decidedly fungus-like at some stages and animal-like at others. Their life cycle includes an ameoboid stage and a sedentary stage in which a fruiting-body develops and produces spores.

In Dictyostelium discoideum, a well-documented strain, the vegetative cell is amoeboid. Amoebas are individual cells moving around in search for bacteria to feed on. They will grow and divide indefinitely. Often they digest so much and produce new amoebas so rapidly that their food supply has no chance to replenish itself. When the food supply has been exhausted, they move rapidly to a central point, collecting themselves into a well-differentiated spontaneous aggregation (center cells, boundary cells, etc.) – a pseudoplasmodium. The aggregation is triggered by the production of cyclic adenosine monophosphate (AMP) which attracts other amoebas in a chemotactic fashion.

The group then assumes the shape of a "slug" with a head, tail, and an apparent "purpose": searching collectively for a new, potential source of food. Around the outside is secreted a mucoid sheath (aggregate boundary). It migrates as a unit across the substratum as a result of the collective action of the amoebas. The changing of the roles of individual amoebas is prevalent; the original leaders who formed the center of attraction are dispersed throughout the "slug", and new leaders emerge, forming the "goal-seeking" head.

The head of the home-hunting "slug" are simply the fastest-moving amoebas. The "slug" is just a spontaneous temporary metaorganism, preserving each amoeba as a separate individual. The slug is positively phototactic (migrates toward light), and it usually migrates for a period of hours. Its behavioral responses are essential "to ensure" that the spores will be borne in the air and so can be effectively dispersed.

Fruiting body formation begins when the slug ceases to migrate and becomes vertically oriented. The amoebas change quickly from the first to the last. The head of the slug forms the base of a stalk which follower-amoebas continue to build (they secrete cellulose to provide rigidity) up into a mushroom-like metaorganism. At its top, hundreds of thousands of amoebas differentiate into spores that are embedded in slime and, after the mushroom "head" matures, it bursts. It disperses the spores to new and potentially nourishing environments. When they fall to earth, they change once again into the individual amoebas which reproduce by cell division. This ecological cycle is then repeated.

AMOEBA: HUMAN SOCIAL SYSTEMS

> To the naive mind that can conceive of order only as the product of deliberate action, it may seem absurd that in complex conditions order, and adaptation to the unknown, can be achieved more effectively by decentralising decisions, and that division of authority will actually extend the possibility of overall order.
>
> (F. A. Hayek, 1988)

After the undisputed failures and fatal conceit of large-scale social engineering and experimentation of the past (Hayek, 1975, 1988), the phenomena of spontaneity and emergence in social systems are being emphasized again. Of significance are the surviving and robust social institutions such as market, family, culture, money, language, economy, city, and myriads of other voluntary orders. They have spontaneously emerged as a result of the natural (nonhuman engineered) formation and organization of society. The biological amoeba metaphor has recently found its organizational embodiment in the well-known "amoeba system" at Kyocera Corporation (Hamada and Monden, 1989). This system is also reminiscent of the famous Bata-system of management in the 1920s and 1930s in Moravia (Bata, 1992; Zeleny, 1988c).

The "amoebas" here are independent, profit-sharing and self-responsible units of three to fifty employees. Each amoeba carries out its own statistical control, profit system, cost accounting and personnel management. They compete, subcontract, and cooperate among themselves on the basis of the intracompany market of transfer prices.

Depending on the demand and amount of work, amoebas can divide into smaller units, move from one section of the factory to another, or integrate with other amoebas or departments. All amoebas are continually on the lookout for a better buyer for their intermediate products. Many amoebas even produce the same or similar products. They are authorized, as in the Bata-system (Zeleny, 1988c), to trade intermediate products with outside companies; if the internal vendor is unreasonable, the buyer amoeba will search for a satisfactory supplier outside the company.

A most remarkable feature towards autonomy is the member trading. Heads of amoebas lend and borrow members and so eliminate losses caused by surplus labor. So, Kyocera's amoebas multiply, disband, and form new units in the spirit of autopoiesis (self-production) of the enterprise. Amoeba division and breakup are everyday occurrences and are based on the criteria of output and a worker's added value per hour. This concept of ultimate flexibility is best summed up by Kyocera's President Inamori: "Development is the continued repetition of construction and destruction" (Hamada and Monden, 1989), as if coming directly from the systems theories of autopoietic self-organization.

Neither age nor training are essential to become the head of an amoeba –

only the faculty for the job under the immediate circumstances. If unsuitable, amoeba heads are replaced immediately.

This system represents quite a revolutionary step beyond the traditional Toyota "just-in-time" system. At Kyocera, orders received by the sales department are passed directly to the amoeba of the final process. The rest of the amoebas in the preceding processes are then given free rein in entering into mutual contracts: the intracompany market takes over. Kyocera Corporation is one of the most profitable companies in Japan.

BOUNDARIES OF SOCIAL SYSTEMS

In kinship systems, boundaries are usually well defined. The distinction between family and non-family members is rarely ambiguous or subject to fuzzy interpretation. A definite family boundary can be established, although it is not necessarily topological. In the context of the family, the concept of boundary might be defined as the members included in a set. Family members are usually distinguished from their environment (from the "society") more sharply than any engineered or designed physical "membrane" can assure. Based on the six-point evaluation, the family is an autopoietic unity defined in the space of its own components.

All social systems, and thus all living systems, create, maintain, and degrade their own boundaries. These boundaries do not separate[5] but intimately connect the system with its environment. They do not have to be just physical or topological, but are primarily functional, behavioral, and communicational. They are not "perimeters" but functional constitutive components of a given system.[6]

Boundaries do not exist for the observer to see or identify, but for the system and its components to communicate with its environment. These boundaries range from phospholipid bilayers, globular proteins, osmotic precipitates, and electric potentials, through cell layers, tissues, skins, metabolic barriers, and peripheral neural synapses, to laterally or upwardly dispersed boundaries of territorial markers, lines of scrimmage, social castes, secret initiation rites, and possessions of information, power, or money.

A company can have a number of geographically separate offices or be entirely "in the air" of electronic communication. The USA includes Alaska and Hawaii. A doctor does not leave the social system of a hospital while "on call" or connected with a beeper. Many additional examples and details of non-topological social boundaries are discussed by Miller and Miller (1992).

Although social systems are necessarily physical because their components realize their dynamic network of productions in the physical domain (their components are cells, termites, lions, adult humans, etc.), many computer simulations (Zeleny, 1978) of autopoietic systems show that topological boundaries arise only if very minute rates of production processes are very finely adjusted and harmonized. In other words, the underlying organization of processes has to be "tuned into." If not, a human observer might not be able to "see" or recognize any "topological" boundary. Yet the organization remains functional and invariant; autopoiesis continues; we do not see any boundary, but the system remains autopoietic.

Thus, topological boundary cannot occupy any definitional or "divine" position; it is the entire system (the entire biological cell) that reveals the underlying autopoiesis of production processes, not just some of its components (e.g., the boundary, cell membrane).

It is often easier to climb or even destroy a Berlin Wall, or to escape from Sing-Sing, than to become a member of an elite club or cross the subtle boundaries of race, habit, and culture.

The fact that a human observer or scientist cannot identify, see or touch a topological boundary of a given system cannot prove anything about the system's autopoiesis – except perhaps the observer's lack of adequate tools, correct models, or requisite intelligence.

ALL AUTOPOIETIC SYSTEMS ARE SOCIAL SYSTEMS

Recent advances in the areas of artificial life (Langton, 1989), synthetic biology, and osmotic growths (Klir *et al.*, 1988; Leduc, 1911; Zeleny *et al.*, 1989) have established that at least some autopoietic systems are non-biological, i.e., self-producing in inorganic milieus.

Autopoiesis can take place only where there are separate and autonomously individual components interacting and communicating in a specific environment according to specific behavioral (including birth and death) rules of interaction. This is why autopoiesis (autopoietic organization) can be studied by postulating each component as a separate entity and tracing its behavior through cellular automata types of computer simulation.

Approaches which sacrifice this essential individuality of components, like the statistical systems of differential equations used in the traditional systems sciences, cannot model autopoiesis. This is because they are definitionally incapable of treating autopoietic systems as social systems. Components and participants in autopoiesis must follow rules, interact, and communicate – they must form a community of components, a society, a social system.

That the sciences of physics, chemistry, and biology are capable of treating their object systems as statistical masses, and not as social systems of communicating components, is bad enough. But that even the social systems proper (i.e., human systems) are also treated as differential mathematical equations, thus destroying their "social" quality, is inexplicable.

134

Even though all autopoietic systems are social systems, social systems themselves are not often treated as autopoietic systems.

As F. A. Hayek (1988) pointed out, social engineers assume that since people have been able to generate some systems of rules coordinating their efforts, they must also be able to design an even better and "improved" system. The traditional norms or reason guiding the imposition and subsequent restructuring of socialism embody a naive and uncritical theory of rationality, an obsolete and unscientific methodology which Hayek calls "constructivist rationalism" and which E. L. Khalil (1990) traced to Karl Marx's concept of social labor.

Although the family (and other spontaneous social orders (Zeleny, 1985, 1991b)) can easily produce and generate systems other than itself, its primary capability is that of producing (and reproducing) itself. Concentration camps and other "engineered" societies are capable of heteropoiesis (producing "else") but are not capable of autopoiesis (producing "self"), except through sustained external force or coercion. The removal of such external pressures and props is one of the safest tests of viability (i.e., autopoiesis) of social systems. If the coercive boundaries (physical or otherwise) dissolve, and the social system ceases to exist, it was not autopoietic; if it reasserts its social boundary and voluntarily increases the level of cohesiveness, then it is autopoietic and self-sustaining.

It is only in the sense of such centrally-imposed "command" systems that we present our hypothesis: All autopoietic (biological) systems are social systems, but they are not hierarchical systems of command. Social organization can be defined as a network of interactions, reactions, and processes involving, at least:

(1) Production (poiesis): the rules and regulations guiding the entry of new living components (such as emergence, birth, membership, acceptance).
(2) Bonding (linkage): the rules of guiding associations, functions, and positions of individuals during their tenure within the organization.
(3) Degradation (disintegration): the rules and processes associated with the termination of membership (death, separation, expulsion).

In Figure 6.1 we graphically represent the above three poietic processes and connect them into a cycle of self-production. Observe that all such circularly concatenated processes represent productions of components necessary for other processes, not only the one designated as "production." To emphasize this crucial point we speak of poiesis instead of production and autopoiesis instead of self-production. Although in reality hundreds of processes could be so interconnected, the above three-process model represents the minimum conditions necessary for autopoiesis to emerge.

From the vantage point of Figure 6.1, all biological (autopoietic) systems are social systems. They consist of production, linkage, and disintegration of

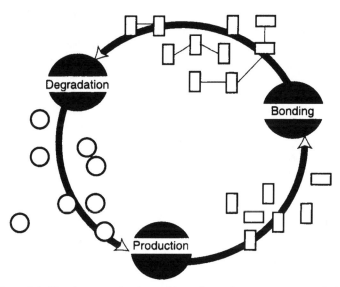

Figure 6.1 Circular organization of interdependent processes and their
"productions"

related components and component-producing processes. An organism or a
cell is, therefore, a social system. Without the understanding of the poiesis
of their components, we cannot even hope to understand them as wholes.

Australian TCG (Technical Computer Graphics) provides a good example of a self-producing network in a business-firm environment. There are
no coordinating divisions, "leading firms," or management superstructures
guiding TCG's twenty-four companies; the coherence, growth and maintenance of the network is produced, according to J. Mathews (1992), by a
set of network-producing rules:

(1) Mutual independence through bilateral commercial contracts.
(2) Mutual preference in the letting of contracts.
(3) Mutual non-competition among members.
(4) Mutual non-exploitation among members.
(5) Flexibility and business autonomy; no group approval needed.
(6) Network democracy without "central committee" or formal govern-
ance structure.
(7) Non-observance of rules leads to expulsion.
(8) All members equal access to the external open market.
(9) Entry: new members welcome, but not through drawing on group
resources.
(10) Exit: no impediments to departing firms.

TCG network grows through a "triangulation process" (TCG plus external company plus a customer) and through spinning-off new companies.

Marvin Minsky has titled his book *The Society of Mind* (1986), attempting to exploit the social metaphor in studying the mind as a society. According to Minsky, mind is neither a unified, homogeneous "black box" or entity, nor a collection of entities, but a heterogeneous system of networks of processes. Unfortunately, Minsky's view of "society" is the hierarchy of agents (or experts), based on extreme division of labor (Zeleny, 1988b), each of them doing "some simple things that needs no mind or thought at all." Minsky writes like a social engineer of command systems, with little awareness of spontaneous social orders (Zeleny, 1985):

". . . when *we* [italics M.Z.] join these agents in societies – in a certain and special way – this leads to true intelligence." The society has truly a very special meaning to Minsky (Minsky, 1986).

Minsky has made a very small step by calling mind, but not all biological systems, a society. He also revealed that by society he understands artificial hierarchies and heterarchies of specialized computeroid-agents. No self-organization and self-management of such agents emerges (Minsky, 1986). But a step has been taken; there is a benefit to be derived from studying complex biological systems as social systems.

G. M. Edelman improves upon Minsky by stating, as if responding directly and more eloquently than we ever could, to our query:

Any satisfactory developmental theory of higher brain function must remove the need for homunculi and electricians at any level and at the same time must account for object definition and generalization from a world whose events and "objects" are not prelabeled by any a priori scheme or top-down order.

(Edelman, 1988)

BIOLOGICAL ORGANISMS AS SOCIAL SYSTEMS

The body of a mammal with its many vital organs can be looked upon as a community with specialized individuals grouped into organs, the whole community forming the composite animal.

(Eugène Marais, 1970)

Although here we cannot analyze living systems in specialist's detail, let us explore the cellular organism, including the human organism, as a social system. Living organisms have often been studied as "black boxes," or as component-free machines, by mechanistic cybernetics. Therefore, no social-system view of life or the living could have emerged; no study of *inner* communication and birth–death processes was encouraged. Only a signal-feedback exploration of external responses of a uniform and homogeneous black box was proposed, with the obvious results.

Biological organisms are not component-free black boxes but communicating and birth–death process balancing social systems. Jim Michaelson of Harvard is one of the few biologists who is prepared to treat biological systems as social systems, positing the "competition" of cells, the selection and survival of the most "fit" during their embryonic development, as being dependent on the cell's ability to secrete enzymes, rate of proliferation, etc.

Communication

Whenever a living cell is unable to communicate with other cells, it does not die, but rather grows uncontrollably, multiplying into other non-communicating cells, forming a malignant tumor which is unable to survive in its life-sustaining environment because it destroys it.

All organismic cells are interconnected through tiny channels in cell membranes or gap junctions. Through these channels, all molecular, chemical, metabolic, and electric communication among cells takes place. These communicative junctions are made of proteins (connexins) that align all cells into one, continuous channel-network: a social system.

Malfunction in intercellular communication channels affects the intercellular social system and thus could "kill" the organism itself. If regulatory and inhibitory signals do not get through, the uncontrolled, deathless growth, and the voracious feeding on its own environment, would result.

Cancer, a variety of malignant tumors, can kill the entire social system of an organism via uncontrolled growth of small subsystems. Both lack of communication *per se* or good communication of wrong messages could lead to the breakdown in the social system of an organism. A good and clear communication system tends to suppress the spontaneous formation of tumors, but it could also help to proliferate wrong signals of malfunctioning components. The Catch-22: one abnormal cell could spell organismic doom if it is not held incommunicado, but if a normal cell becomes isolated, it could go abnormal quickly.

To study cancer processes without studying cellular gap junctions amounts to a case of professional neglect. Clogged channels block social-regulatory signals and allow cells to go awry; clear channels allow the propagation of deadly signals. Gap junctions themselves are selective self-regulatory; they tend to close and protect against chaotic signals and to open for and receive regulatory signals.

Even a fetus could not develop if particular groups of cells would not stop reproducing and growing "just-in-time," or more precisely, would not start dying. There would be no organ, no hand – just a cancerous, suicidal cellmass.

In order to treat cancers, one has either to re-establish communication channels and thus self-regulation or block communication channels in order to stop rampant proliferation, depending on the cancer source type. This is not a trivial mechanistic task, but it can only be mastered if we start viewing biological systems as social systems.

Social neighborhoods

As discussed in an American Association for the Advancement of Science (AAAS) symposium volume (Zeleny, 1980), cellular neighborhoods, rather than some inheritable genetic "programs," are the main determinants of cells' functions. Autopoietic systems are illustrated better by the American plan of development, where one's status and fate are determined by one's neighborhood, and not by the British plan, where one's status and fate are determined by one's ancestors.[7]

The neural network especially, i.e., the autonomous autopoietic system embedded in a larger complex of organismic networks, requires quick-response flexibility and adaptability which cannot wait for a mutations buildup or rely on requisite but cumbersome "genetic alterations." Neural networks develop as autopoietic societies; individual cells wander around, get exposed to differential signalings of different cellular neighborhoods, and ultimately settle down (or get captured) within these neighborhoods, becoming functioning neurons of the visual, hearing, or smell regions of the cerebral cortex. "Look, Ma, no genes!"

As H. Maturana insists in the above volume, "genes" and viral DNA are structural components of autopoiesis. Their distribution and mutation therefore affect structures and structural characteristics (inheritable shapes and adhesion properties of proteins), but they do not partake in organization; they do not organize matter, but are themselves organized and ordered by autopoiesis. If the neurons of the cortex are not prefixed and do not carry a "complete code" of how to behave, then they cannot provide the organizing principle of the brain and thus certainly not of the organism as a whole.

The greatest mistake biologists could make at this paradigmatic bifurcation point is searching for the seat of the master plan behind the body's gray matter. There is no master plan; spontaneous social systems (i.e., also biological systems) do not rely on their "Gorbachevs," and that is why they can persist. There are no black-box feedback loops within feedback loops; there is only a society in autopoiesis, organizing matter of different structural attributes and properties (including viral DNA), thus arriving at different, sometimes important, structural manifestations. Dr C. L. Cepko of Harvard Medical School puts it quite bluntly: "The mother cells do not impart specific information to their daughters about what to become."

139

Death process

In addition to communication, social systems are also characterized by limited lifespans of individual components, i.e., by death. If molecules would not break down, or cells, organisms, individuals and entire species would not die, there would be no social systems and thus no self-sustaining life on earth.

Death dominates development. The vestigial webbing between human fetus fingers must be dissolved before birth. About 80 per cent of the nerve cells of the baby's brain must perish within hours of their creation. No biologist can claim to be studying life without studying death. Caterpillar's crawling muscles must be sloughed off in order to have a butterfly; female genitalia must be whittled away in order to have a male.

Yet uncontrolled and massive death is non-redeeming; Alzheimer's, Parkinson's, and Lou Gehrig's degenerative disorders result. Uncontrolled and massive birth is equally unredeeming; cancerous cellmasses, killing their own environment (i.e., organism) result. Individuals must die in order to maintain their social system. So the species must die in order to maintain *theirs* – the Gaia. Why biologists study protein production and cell proliferation, while at the same time neglecting protein degradation and cell death amounts to one of the great mysteries of life. Is it the result of extreme specialization (Zeleny, 1988b), where some study only the "ins" and others only the "outs" of intellectual intercourse? Can such be a way towards understanding "conception"?

Death is not a chaotic, haphazard, or disorganized part of social system autopoiesis; it is a harmonized, choreographed, and often suicidal dance of the most exquisite complexity. The creation of autopoiesis is inconceivable without the trimming of apoptosis, and the study of apoptosis is crucial in biology: in fact, no true biology can exist without it.[8] Death is not the absence of life, but the crucial building block of life. Life is never "individual" life, but life of a social network of balanced and communicating birth–death processes. Death is not a passive default but an active system–creative response to intrasystemic, unity-maintaining signaling. A good example is the immune system. Millions of T and B cells are continually generated, each capable of assaulting foreign proteins, but unfortunately also the body's own proteins. Up to 98 per cent of them have to undergo immediate apoptosis in order to maintain the body's autopoiesis in a hostile environment.

Death is a productive process of the social system; it creates space, it generates production substrate, it brings in the innovation, and it allows trial-and-error adaptation to the environment. Individual cells are created in order to die, and thus their social system, i.e., living organism, can persist. The same principle is repeated at other levels, all the way to the Gaia and the Universe.

Evolution

> The idea that reason, itself created in the course of evolution, should now be in a position to determine its own future evolution is inherently contradictory, and can readily be refuted.
>
> (F. A. Hayek, 1988)

Social systems persist. They can persist as societies of agents only if their individual agents are born, communicate, and die in harmony with themselves and their environment. Because of the turnover of components, the social networks not only persist and are renewed, but they also evolve.

The unit of evolution (at any level) must be a network capable of a variety of self-organizing configurations. The entire social networks, including neuronal groups (Edelman, 1992) are being "selected," not their individual components. These evolving networks are interwoven and co-evolving with their environment; they do not only adapt to the environment, but also adapt the environment to themselves – through intimate structural coupling. Margolis (Mann, 1991) also insists that not the individual, but the symbiotic system, characterized primarily by autopoiesis, is the proper unit of biological study and symbiosis the major force behind evolution.

A bird must undoubtedly adapt to a mountain. A society (network) of birds can make the mountain adapt to them. By overconsuming particular berries, the new brush growth is controlled, the mountain's erosion enhanced, and the production of both berries and birds thus limited until a temporary balance or harmony is restored. Colors of flowers have co-evolved with the trichromatic vision of bees; shapes of flowers with the structural traits of insects and animals; modern breeders with the changing tastes and preferences of man. To quote R. Lewontin:

> The environment is not a structure imposed on living beings from the outside but is in fact a creation of those beings. The environment is not an autonomous process, but a reflection of the biology of the species. Just as there is no organism without an environment, so there is no environment without an organism.
>
> (Lewontin, 1983)

Varela et al. (1991), in their book *The Embodied Mind*,[9] conform to the view that living beings and their environments stand in relation to each other through mutual specification or codetermination: "The world is not a landing pad into which organisms parachute; nature and nurture stand in relation to each other as product and process."

This new view of evolution of social networks implies that there can be no intelligent distinction between inherited and acquired characteristics. What evolves is neither genetically encoded nor environmentally acquired, but is ecologically embedded in a social network. There is also

MILAN ZELENY

no one fixed or pre-given world (a universe), nor is its dynamics simply observed or viewed differentially from a variety of vantage points (a multiverse), but this world itself is continually re-shaped, and re-created by co-evolving social networks of organisms.

Linkage or pleiotropy of "genes" is the rule, not an exception. Organisms are integral and holistic societies, not mechanistic aggregations of separate traits. Therefore, neither DNA sequences, nor genes, organisms, or species, but their entire social networks, coupled and interwoven with their environments, can be the proper units of natural selection and evolution.

This kind of gentle and "velvet" *coup de grâce* to neo-Darwinism and modern synthesis, in all their forms and neoforms, is not to be immediately felt, registered, or even acknowledged. Like the "velvet revolutions" of Eastern Europe, it does not "draw blood," it does not cut off or disconnect "the communists," it does not degrade but firmly establishes new conditions for further growth and evolution. Yet, as Margulis has observed (Mann, 1991), the old *nomenklatura* of neo-Darwinians already hates and resists any autopoietic or Gaian worldview because "it threatens everything they do."

The evolution of paradigms is itself an autopoietic process, and thus inevitably we see how the aged "revolutionaries" are clinging to the old and suddenly ineffective ideas, how they themselves have become conservatives, and how they individually resist the new interpretations of their younger colleagues, often without realizing that their collective time has passed.

CONCLUSION

When I began my work I felt that I was nearly alone in working on the evolutionary formation of such highly complex self-maintaining orders. Meanwhile, researches on this kind of problem – under various names, such as autopoiesis, cybernetics, homeostasis, spontaneous order, self-organization, synergetics, systems theory, and so on – have become so numerous . . .

(F. A. Hayek, 1988)

Living systems, i.e., cells, organisms, groups, and species, are social systems. Their interaction forms the entire terrestrial biosphere or Gaia, a social system akin to the unified organism of a living cell, which itself is a social system of its constitutive organelles.

Connecting different species into a coherent, interactive, and self-organizing system cannot happen without death and dying – the fuel of environmental adaptation. The natural death of species does not signal maladaptability of the species, but harmony, adaptability, and systemic perseverance of the social network of species. Death is a cosmological event – the most exquisite assurance of life yet to be. At one point, individuals of all species receive, by waves on the shore, sound of the wind, or with radio telescopes, the exquisite, life-sustaining message: "Now, now it would be indecent not to die."

Harmony and fitness does not imply dominance or competitive advantage but intimate coupling with the environment through all-embracing communication. Nature, as a social system, is replete with communication channels of great variety and subtlety. All life on earth (and most likely interstellar too) is interconnected through internal and external harmonies, often unnoticed or ignored by linear science.

The connexins of cells, dances of bees, odors of fire ants, allochemicals of Douglas firs, and the language of humans are only the hints, only the shy peepholes into the veiled mysteries of life – the promises of science still to come.

NOTES

1 In this sense, talking about, e.g., "social insects" is inadequate as all insects – and also all other organisms – must be social by virtue of their existence.
2 Holistic here does not coincide with the popular "wholistic" as the opposite or the complement to reductionism or atomism. J. C. Smuts's holism (Smuts, 1926) is based on the essential circularity of autopoietic systems: A whole is a unity of parts that affects the interactions of those parts. There can be no parts apart from the whole, and the whole cannot be contemplated apart from its parts: the whole is the parts.
3 In fact a very old (since 1896) and mostly exhausted paradigm (or paradigmatic aberration), fatally unable to explain even the prevalence of stasis in the fossil record or how one species could evolve from another.
4 It is well appreciated that using mere words (especially those loaded with ancient meanings), to express holistic or self-organizational concepts is quite inadequate. This is why the new field of computer simulated patterns of artificial life (AL), if not quickly monopolized by elites of computer hackers, could become so important; it could create a new, wordless language of concepts of complexity.
5 This topological notion of "separation" still persists in some theories of systems, see, e.g., Jessie L. Miller and James Grier Miller (1992), "The Boundary" (*Behavioral Science* 37: 23–38): A living system's boundary is a region at its perimeter that separates the system from its environment.
6 The food moving through the mouth and the digestive tube is not necessarily "inside" the body, but remains "outside," in the "captured" or "enveloped" environment of the body torus. The same holds true for all other "boundary" organs; there is no inside or outside, and boundary does not separate anything, except in the human observer's mind.
7 This analogy was first suggested by the British geneticist Sydney Brenner.
8 A promising start could be made by learning to properly pronounce the term apoptosis, meaning "falling from the trees," coined by Andrew Wyllie of Edinburgh.
9 The index of this remarkable text does not contain any references to autopoiesis, Maturana, or artificial life (AL). Yet it refers quite profusely to Abhidharma, Madhyamika, Mahayana, and Sunyata. This constitutes a profound enigma: the book clearly builds upon or motivates the former, while being profoundly irrelevant to the latter.

REFERENCES

Bata, T. (1992) *Knowledge in Action: The Bata System of Management*, IOS Press: Amsterdam.

Cochran, M. *et al.* (eds) (1990) *Extending Families*, Cambridge University Press: Cambridge.

Edelman, G. M. (1988) *Topobiology*, Basic Books: New York.

—— (1992) *Bright Air, Brilliant Fire*, Basic Books: New York.

Eldredge, N. (this volume) "Ultra-Darwinian explanation and the biology of social systems."

Garfinkel, A. (1987) "The slime mold dictyostelium as a model of self-organization in social systems," in *Self-Organizing Systems: The Emergence of Order*, ed. F. Eugene Yates, Plenum Press: New York, 181–212.

Haken, H. (this volume) "Synergetics as a bridge between the natural and social sciences."

Hamada, K. and Monden, Y. (1989) "Profit management at Kyocera Corporation: The amoeba system," in Y. Monden and M. Sakurai (eds), *Japanese Management Accounting*, Productivity Press: Cambridge, MA, 197–210.

Hayek, F. A. (1975) "Kinds of order in society," *Studies in Social Theory* 5, Institute for Humane Studies: Menlo Park, California.

—— (1988) *The Fatal Conceit*, University of Chicago Press: Chicago.

Khalil, E. L. (1990) "Rationality and social labor in Marx," *Critical Review* 4(1–2): 239–265.

Klir, G. J., Hufford, K. D. and Zeleny, M. (1988) "Osmotic growths: A challenge to systems science," *International Journal of General Systems* 14(1): 5–9.

Langton, C. G. (1989) "Artificial life," in *Artificial Life: The Proceedings of an Interdisciplinary Workshop on the Synthesis and Simulation of Living Systems*, ed. C. Langton, Vol. VI, Santa Fe Institute Studies in the Sciences of Complexity Series: Addison-Wesley, 1–47.

Leduc, S. (1911) *The Mechanism of Life*, Rebman: London.

Lewontin, R. (1983) "The organism as the subject and object of evolution," *Scientia* 118: 63–82.

Mackay, C. (1849) *Memoirs of Extraordinary Popular Delusions*, Richard Bentley: London.

Mann, C. (1991) "Lynn Margulis: science's unruly earth mother," *Science* 252, 19 April: 378–381.

Marais, E. N. (1970) *The Soul of the White Ant*, Human & Rousseau: Pretoria.

Mathews, J. (1992) *TCG: Sustainable Economic Organisation Through Networking*, UNSW Studies in Organisational Analysis and Innovation, No. 7, July.

Miller, J. L. and Miller, J. G. (1992) "The boundary," *Behavioral Science* 37(1): 23–38.

Minsky, M. (1986) *The Society of Mind*, Simon & Schuster: New York.

Smuts, J. C. (1926) *Holism and Evolution*, Macmillan: New York.

Topoff, H. (ed.) (1981) *Animal Societies and Evolution*, W. H. Freeman & Co.: San Francisco, CA.

Varela, F. J., Maturana, H. R. and Uribe, R. (1974) "Autopoiesis: The organization of living systems, its characterization and a model," *Biosystems* 5: 187–196.

Varela, F. J., Thompson, E. and Rosch, E. (1991) *The Embodied Mind*, MIT Press: Cambridge, MA.

Zeleny, M. (1978) "APL-autopoiesis: Experiments in self-organization of complexity," *Progress in Cybernetics and Systems Research* 3: 65–84.

—— (ed.) (1980) *Autopoiesis, Dissipative Structures, and Spontaneous Social Orders*, Westview Press: Boulder, Colorado.

—— (ed.) (1981) *Autopoiesis: A Theory of Living Organization*, North-Holland: New York.

—— (1985) "Spontaneous social orders," in *The Science and Praxis of Complexity*, The United Nations University: Tokyo, 312–328; *General Systems* 11(2): 117–131; (1986) "Les ordres sociaux spontanés," in *Science et pratique de la complexité*, Actes du colloque de Montpellier, May 1984, IDATE/UNU, La Documentation Française: Paris, 357–378.

—— (1987) "Cybernetyka," *International Journal of General Systems* 13: 289–294. Also: (1990) "Trentowski's cybernetyka," in *Advances in Systems, Control and Information Engineering*, Pergamon Press: Elmsford, NY.

—— (1988a) "Tectology," *International Journal of General Systems* 14: 331–343.

—— (1988b) "La grande inversione: Corso e ricorso dei modi di vitaumani," in *Physis: abitare la terra*, ed M. Ceruti and E. Laszlo, Feltrinelli: Milan, 413–441.

—— (1988c) "The Bata-system of management: Managerial excellence found," *Human Systems Management* 7(3): 213–219.

—— (1991) "Spontaneous social orders," in *A Science of Goal Formulation: American and Soviet Discussions of Cybernetics and Systems Theory*, ed S. A. Umpleby and V. N. Sadovsky, Hemisphere Publishing Corp.: Washington, DC, 133–150.

Zeleny, M. and Hufford, K. D. (1991) "All autopoietic systems must be social systems," *Journal of Social and Biological Structures* 14(3): 311–332.

—— (1992) "The application of autopoiesis in systems analysis: Are autopoietic systems also social systems?" *International Journal of General Systems* (to appear).

Zeleny, M., Klir, G. J. and Hufford, K. D. (1989) "Precipitation membranes, osmotic growths and synthetic biology," in *Artificial Life: The Proceedings of an Interdisciplinary Workshop on the Synthesis and Simulation of Living Systems*, ed. C. Langton, Vol. VI, Santa Fe Institute Studies in the Sciences of Complexity Series: Addison-Wesley, 125–139.

7

ORGANIZATION, FUNCTION, AND CREATIVITY IN BIOLOGICAL AND SOCIAL SYSTEMS

Vilmos Csányi

INTRODUCTION

In this chapter I introduce a system-model worked out in a framework of the natural sciences for studying problems of the social sciences. What does vindicate the use of a natural scientific approach?

The main support for such a strategy might be the fact that an ever-quickening integration process could be observed in the various sciences during the last half of the century. During the early development of natural sciences, the main scientific branches (e.g., physics, chemistry, biology, psychology) were only concerned with their own specific problems; they described the observed phenomena and tried to explain them without considering the results of related scientific investigations. It was discovered afterwards that there are certain principles and laws valid in all natural sciences. A good example is the law of the conservation of energy. One of the main breakthroughs of the last five decades in biology was the realization that biological processes are always based on chemical reactions. This discovery led to the emergence of molecular biology.

To researchers exploring the world around us, it became evident that, though each organizational level of matter can be characterized by a special class of laws, final explanations on a given level can be formulated only when the mechanisms of the lower organizational levels are clarified; e.g., biology needs chemical knowledge, and the study of the origin of galaxies cannot be explained without nuclear physics. Nowadays a very efficient "superscience" is evolving, all parts of which are interconnected by common principles and a developing common language. This superscience can be characterized by three features: (a) double description, (b) homogeneity of logic, and (c) convertibility.

Double description means that explanations related to any group of phenomena have to be given on at least two organizational levels (Pattee, 1965). The description of the cell for example needs the "cellular level"

146

(on which reproduction, feeding, reactivity, intercellular relationships can be explained) as well as the "molecular level" (on which chemical reactions, catalytic phenomena, metabolism, the synthesis of macromolecules, etc., can be described). The explanation of animal behavior is based on both ethological descriptions (the level of the whole organism) and neurophysiological mechanisms (the level of the neural system).

The homogeneity of logic simply means that any two different phenomena of the integrated science can be linked up by a common chain of logic; e.g., diabetes is a biological phenomenon, while the atom is a term belonging to physics. The train of logic linking the two is the following: symptoms of diabetes occurring at organismic level can be explained by the malfunction of the pancreatic gland; the explanation involves blood glucose regulation, insulin, and its secretion; insulin is a polypeptide molecule made up of various atoms. Each part of this chain can be linked with the others by a satisfying causal explanation.

The third feature is *convertibility*. This is related to scientific language: it means that explanations given at different organizational levels demonstrating logical homogeneity are perfectly concordant and semantically equivalent. The description of cell division at the cellular level, for example, can be translated exactly to molecular processes.

Presently "superscience" includes only natural sciences – i.e., physics and related fields, chemistry, and to an increasing degree, biology – but the involvement of social sciences is also inevitable. This process necessarily demands the examination of psychological, sociologic, and economic problems by the tools of the natural sciences.

Actually the most important thing is to connect social and natural sciences. Similar to chemistry, which provides explanations for biologists, we expect biology to contribute mostly to the explanation of some social phenomena. Why do we prefer living in groups? How did human languages evolve? Why do we discriminate against people belonging to other groups? Why do we have politics? Why do we easily accept the concept of property? Why do we exchange our property continuously? All these are questions rarely discussed from a biological point of view. However, biological explanations are possible, though we must stress that these explanations exclusively concern biological aspects. They clarify the mechanisms acting on the lower organizational level; for the accurate understanding of the whole phenomena, explanations formed on the higher level (provided by traditional social sciences) are also indispensable.

NATURAL SCIENCES AND THE USE OF MODELS

Natural sciences use two basic methodologies in their everyday practices: first, experimentation and observation, and second, model constructions for explaining the facts obtained by experimentation and observation. Experiments in social sciences can seldom be performed, but the results of observations allow explanations, theories, and descriptions to be built up, which in themselves are models. A model is always a simpler system in which the components and the interactions of components are more or less *isomorphic* to the components and some interactions of a more complex system. The essential feature of modeling is that we arbitrarily choose the components of the complex system under examination, and we make an analogy between the components and their interactions of the modelled and model system. It is obvious that models can never be perfect, because they are always simpler than the modelled system. However, even a relatively simple model may suggest various hypotheses, the validity of which may be verified later in the real world, and the model can be improved based on the findings.

Any kind of scientific statement, concept, law, and any description of a phenomenon is a model construction which tries to reflect phenomena of the external world. Reality is extremely complex; it consists of strongly or more weakly related events. Science makes an attempt to separate and isolate different effects and phenomena. It seeks the simplest relationships by which examined phenomena can at least be described or demonstrated. It creates simplified models which only partially reflect reality, but which allow contemplation, and what is most important, pragmatic, even if sometimes modest, predictions. The laws of Newton, for example, did not explain anything about the nature of forces. Newton simply consistently interpreted some phenomena connected to the motion and interaction of bodies. He made a "model" and succeeded in predicting some events related to the motion of these bodies. We know that these predictions are more or less valid in a wide (but clearly not unlimited) range of phenomena; however, we still do not know what force is. The laws of Newton are not explanations in the true meaning of the word, but are models allowing predictions.

If we carefully examine the history of natural sciences, we realize that the internal construction of models is always accidental, and the relevance of a model is appreciated only on practical considerations. There is no philosophical or other system of criteria which would make possible the recognition of the relevance of a given model. As a consequence, we are not very loyal to our models. If we find a phenomenon which cannot be incorporated in the given model – in other words, the model cannot make the correct predictions – then we have to replace our model with a new one. The sole measure of pertinence of the new model will be its usefulness in making correct predictions in both the old and the new group of phenomena.

Kepler's laws regarding the period and orbit of planets are nowadays taught in high school physics. However, only a few people know that Kepler's main work *The Harmonice Mundi* includes ninety-eight similar laws. Kepler thought that the world's harmony can be found in mathematics formulae; consequently, he created ninety-eight such formulae. There is no sign that he considered the two taught in school to be anything special; however, the other ninety-six have since proved to be useless (Koestler, 1963). Hence the sole criterion of a good model is practice. Practice is the basis of the scientific method which always makes models based on phenomena, observations, and experiments. The operation of these models leads to predictions, which are verified by observation and experiment. From a philosophical point of view, the most important lesson is that sciences do not work on reality directly, but only on various representations of it. The form and internal structure of a model are not important in themselves; the value of the model is given by its predictive power.

Models in the animal and human brains

Modern natural science is based on the studying of models. Recent neurobiological concepts affirm that the use of models in science cannot be accidental, since the biological essence of human thinking is also a model-making process (Artigiani *et al.*, 1989). Moreover, the world is modelled not only by the human brain, but also by any animal nervous system (Mackay, 1951–52). The internal representation of the environment which is made by the brain of any animal can be considered as a neural construction, which in essence is a model (Craik, 1943), more precisely, a dynamic model of the environment (Csányi, 1987b, 1988a). Model-building in the brain therefore is always a kind of simplification and a special identification between two different systems, one of which is the model made up from the internal neuronal networks of the brain, and the other is the system being modelled "out there." So the most important biological function of the animal brain is the construction of this dynamic model of the environment, which includes the most important environmental factors and their interactions, the continuous maintenance and operation of this model, and the use of the obtained data for predictions in the interest of the survival and reproduction of the animal (Csányi, 1986, 1987b, 1993b).

According to neuro-ethological studies, the models of the animal brain are not only conceptual tools created by neurobiologists necessary to describe the brain's function, but actual physical entities, which can be verified experimentally (Collett, 1983).

Evolutionary emergence of the conceptual thought based on human language resulted in a fundamentally new way of model-making. Mental superstructures built up from linguistic concepts also reflect experiences, and therefore they can be regarded as models of the outer world. And their values are also dependent solely on their predictive and explanatory power (Csányi, 1992a, 1992b).

Evolutionary models

The concept of evolution first appeared in the social sciences. Herbert Spencer's intuitive definition of evolution is interesting even today: "Evolution is definable as a change from an incoherent homogeneity into a coherent heterogeneity, accompanying the dissipation of motion and integration of matter" (Spencer, 1862). In its first scientific formulation, evolution appears as a metaphor for changes; moreover, it was a metaphor for system-level transformation. This was a very important idea for the scholastic social sciences in those times.

Behavior of complex biological systems is also connected to systemic changes. As a consequence of Darwin's work (Darwin, 1859) the concept of a once-and-for-all created, unchangeable world was replaced in biology by the concept of evolution. Biology, being one of the natural sciences, was not satisfied by the use of a metaphor but made an attempt to replace it with particular mechanisms and models. To a certain degree, this was a step back from Spencer's concept; the biological model did not tackle the coherent change of the whole system, but the changes appeared in certain components of the system. More precisely, it dealt only with the transformation of species.

According to one of the contemporary evolutionary biologists:

> We shall regard as alive any population of entities which have the properties of multiplication, heredity and variation. The justification for this definition is as follows: any population of any entities with these properties will evolve by natural selection so as to become better adapted to its environment. Given time, any degree of adaptive complexity can be generated by natural selection.
>
> (Maynard-Smith, 1969)

This formulation also stresses that evolution is the property of the components.

However, in the last decades several integrative processes started in the biological sciences (Bertalanffy, 1968). Fields emerged which deal with biological problems on a systemic level such as ecology, cognitive science, etc. Thus, the possibility has risen that an evolutionary system theory can be formulated (Csányi, 1978, 1982, 1989a), which does not simply seek explanations for the temporal transformations of components (species), but reflects the changes of the whole system. Changes occur simultaneously at several organizational levels (Csányi, 1993a). The theory makes possible the formulation of truly general laws of evolution, which are valid not only in biological but also in social and abstract systems as well (Csányi, 1992d).

THE COMPONENT SYSTEM MODEL

The component system model has been worked out for studying organized natural systems (Csányi, 1980, 1981, 1982, 1985, 1987a, 1988b, 1988c,

1989a; Kampis, 1985, 1987a, 1987b, 1988, 1991; Csányi and Kampis, 1985, 1987; for a detailed description see Csányi, 1989a). All natural entities on earth which are organized in some way embody various components. A single-celled organism is built up from various molecules as components. A higher organism, such as a plant or an animal, consists of various cells. Ecosystems are composed of organisms of various species. Human societies also contain components such as humans, artifacts, and ideas. These entities can be characterized by their *components*, their *processes*, and their *organizations*. The most simple way to understand the component system model is to look at the origin of natural systems.

The origin of any natural system could be modelled by an autogenetic process starting from an appropriate *zero-system* (Csányi, 1978, 1980, 1982). A zero-system is defined as a physical entity which contains all those components, more exactly all those classes of components, which will constitute the emerging organized entity. It is characteristic of the zero-system that its components are assembled and disassembled continuously by the effect of the energy flux flowing through the system, which thermodynamically is an "open" system. The properties of such systems are well studied and characterized (Morowitz, 1968; Prigogine and Stengers, 1984; Csányi, 1989a). The components are built up from elementary building units. In the case of biological systems, in cells for example, the building units are the atoms of the chemical elements, and the components are the molecules. In a zero-system suitable for the emergence of cells, simple molecules containing carbon, hydrogen, oxygen, nitrogen, and some other elements were assembled, interacted, and broken down continuously because of the effect of the radiation of the sun. If we want to model the emergence of an ecosystem, then we postulate an ecological zero-system in which animals, plants, and micro-organisms as components are created continuously because of the effect of the energy flow going through the ecosystem. Individuals of higher species of animals and plants are themselves very complex systems, but if we want to study the nature and organization of even more complex systems created from them, then they must be regarded as components. If we consider the cells constituting the plants and animals as components, then we may study the formation of organisms as component systems.

The next assumption of the basic model is that the components, during their assembly, disassembly, and interaction processes, could *influence the probability of genesis and existence* (survival) of the other components. This important condition is usually fulfilled in the case of natural systems. In the zero-system of the origin of life from primeval soup, the various simple compounds already assembled have been interacting with each other and have influenced the probability of genesis of other more complex compounds. The same is true in the case of the ecological example. The presence of certain plants and animals influences the genesis and survival of others. The component system model can be applied only to those cases in which this condition is fulfilled. A simple example in which this condition is not fulfilled might be an artificial "system" of Lego building blocks in which higher structures are built continuously as components and disassembly processes are also acting. The assembled Lego structures are not able to influence the probability of genesis of other similar ones, so this "system" is not a proper zero-system.

It could be asserted that in a proper zero-system, higher, organized structures containing a set of components which increase the probability of genesis and survival of each other spontaneously emerge. The base of such organizations is always a self-maintaining cyclic process in which the components form, and by their own formation and further interactions, promote the formation of other component members of the cycle. The minimal set of the components that is able to replicate in a cyclic process in a given zero-system is called *system precursor* (Gray, 1975; Csányi, 1982). The spontaneous emergence of such system precursors can be validated in the processes of the origin of life and in the processes of the evolution of higher life structures (King, 1982; Csányi, 1989a). Further developments of a system precursor to an organized network of components, e.g., a component system, was termed *autogenesis* (Csányi, 1985).

An important feature of the autogenetic process is that the components of the self-maintaining cycle are not unchangeable during time. Certain components can "mutate" slightly; they can be closed out from, or new components can enter into, the cycle. These changes are "creative acts," but only those changes which do not interrupt the cycle or do not interfere with its self-maintenance can be maintained for a longer time. The creative autogenesis increases the complexity of the cycle, which slowly transforms into a self-maintaining network of the components. The end-phase of the autogenetic process is the emergence of a network of the components which produce exactly the same kind of components which constitute the network itself. Such a system exists in the state of continuous self-renewal, and its definition is exactly the same as an autopoietic system described by Varela *et al.* (1974) and others (Maturana, 1975; Zeleny, 1977; see also Zeleny in this volume). The relations and differences between the autopoietic and autogenetic systems are discussed in Csányi and Kampis (1985).

The main advantage of the autogenetic model over the autopoietic one is that it enables one to study not only the maintenance of such systems but also their origin and evolution, problems which are definitely excluded from the theory of autopoiesis. Autopoiesis is a model for a closed, unchanging, stable system, it is an important theoretical work, but unsuitable for modeling real systems.

The simplified discussion of the autogenetic model in this study serves only to show the emergence of organization, function, and organization levels and the source of creativity in such a class of systems.

The arrangement of interactions of components of a component system in space and time which contributes to its self-maintenance is called *organization*. Because of the components' involvement in all processes and interactions in the system, the organization defines how the system maintains itself in a closed network of processes. Description of the organization is an account of the assembly and disassembly of the components and also the relation of these processes to each other. Because self-maintenance is always a cyclic process, the organization of such systems is always "replicative." Since the organization of a cyclic network of processes is closed by definition, it is also replicative, because the running of a cycle provides the conditions for the next running. Replication is a self-copying process; a constructor (the whole network of the components in this case) produces a copy (a replica) of the network of the components. In this process, both the components and the whole system itself are replicated because of the organization. Two forms of replication are distinguished.

"Temporal replication" is defined as the system's continuous renewal in time by the sequential and functional renewal of the system components while the unity and identity of the system are maintained. In this process, the component or system to be copied itself contains the information needed for copying. It is obvious, however, that for the essentials of the process of replication, it does not matter at all whether the copy is that of a separated entity or the constructor itself, and it also does not matter whether the information necessary for the copying process appears separated in a special memory device (as is mostly the case with replication of proteins and nucleic acids) or whether the information is dispersed and is to be found distributed in the system. The fact of replication lies not in the special solution but in the functional operation (Kampis and Csányi, 1987a, 1987b, 1991).

Molecular components are constantly produced and broken down in a cell. The components appear in the same quality and quantity because of the replicative organization of the cell. Any particular component contributes to the organizational process; therefore, its presence is needed for its own production through its functional relation to the whole self-renewing network. This special relation is the essence of the replicative organization. Renewal of the components in time, temporal replication, is the maintenance process of the component systems. As the same kind of molecules are constantly assembled and disassembled in a cell, individuals of the same species of plants and animals are produced and pass through in an ecosystem. In the interactions of the everyday life, new generations of people come and old ones pass away; new artifacts are made for substituting the discarded ones, and during learning and teaching, ideas are also transferred from the present generation to the next in society. Production and decay of particular components do not change the self-renewing organization and the identity

153

of the system. Existence of individual components and the existence of the whole system are completely independent of each other.

Another form of replication is "spatial replication"; it is identical to reproduction. The system produces its own replica, which becomes separated from it in space. From one unit, two units are formed. This process is reproduction in biology.

Replication processes are never error free. Replication can thus be characterized by its "fidelity," which can be expressed by a value between zero and one. If fidelity is exactly one, it is called "identical replication." "Nonidentical replication" is characterized by fidelity below one. In the case of nonidentical replication, either the structure of the components or the system's component composition is different from the preceding state. Appearance of nonidentical copies of components is one of the main forces of evolution (Ho and Saunders, 1979).

The concept of "function" can be inferred from organization and can be formulated by means of either a general or a specific interpretation. In general interpretation, components of a replicative system are considered the entities which, during the course of their interactions, take part in the replication. Thus it is clear that components have a replicative function, for they promote the replication of both the system and themselves. That means their "general function" is to participate, as components, in the replication. On the other hand, if we observe the interactions between the components, we can identify them as special mechanisms to affect the probability of each other's genesis and existence. This is a manifestation of the "replicative function." An enzyme-splitting glucose in a cell contributes to the continuous maintenance of the cell's metabolic network; that is; it has replicative function. The special function of this enzyme is to catalyze glucose breakdown. The concept of the function also usually raises the question of teleology. In the model of the component systems, existence is the final "goal" and "cause." All functions, including the general replicative function, can be deducted from simple "being" of the particular system. The operation of the functions at the component levels is the consequence and evidence at once of the existence of a higher systemic organizational level; it does not need further explanation.

Creativity in the component systems

Although there is no accepted definition of a system's creativity, an intuitive approach could be given by using concepts of the biological evolution (Kampis and Csányi, 1988; Csányi, 1991). An enormous variety of forms, structures, and behavioral patterns emerged in the living world for solving a concrete problem or serving a concrete function during evolution. If we look at the forms of beaks of birds, which are tools for catching food, great variety can be observed. A beak could serve its function if the prey is a tiny insect, a slimy fish, or a well-armored creature of four legs. The functional variability represented here by the beak's structure is considered to be the result of the creativity of the evolutionary system. The living system has become more and more complex during evolution. Not only have new structures emerged for the same function, but variability of the functions themselves also increased continuously. Energy and material fluxes of the living world flow by the contribution of more and more species fulfilling more and more special functions, which are supplementing each other in the replicative web of the biosphere.

Hence, a system can be considered as creative if, during its existence, it is able to create new functions and new components to serve these new functions. Creativity of the living system during evolution is manifested, therefore, by "selected variability."

The number of the chemical elements, the elementary building units of the cell, is about one hundred, and most of these are not playing an important role in the cell. But the kinds of molecules which can be built from them are immense. The properties of the atoms are the same in every cell; therefore, the differences among the various cells are based upon the properties of the particular set of molecular components embodied by the particular cells. Only those sets of molecules which could build up a functionally closed replicative network became cells during evolution. Some cells make new components by genetic mutations in every generation. Only those cells from the ones containing new components survive and reflect the creativity of the evolutionary system, which is able to fulfill some new function which exists on the cellular level of organization. All other variants disappear. This is the process of natural selection.

Two generalizations can be made for the component systems: (1) Any differences in components' structure are regarded as variability. (2) Intuitive definition of creativity is the following: Creativity is the "variability adjusted to the organization" in a system. In other words, the measure of creativity is the extent of the functionally fit variability of the components, which might exist without altering the identity and survival of the system.

To summarize the findings above, creativity of the component systems has at least three main sources.

The first one is the replicative system itself. As soon as the most primitive organizing forces emerge in the form of a system precursor, further changes of the evolving system are strongly selected. Even the simplest organization behaves as a tremendously powerful selection screen. It only admits changes which do not alter the replicative nature of the organization of the system, and among them those which are able to join functionally to the system (Riedl, 1978). As the complexity of the system increases, it becomes a more and more specific screen, although parallel to the increase in complexity, the degree of freedom of changes also increases. This organizationally maintained kind of selection was termed "replicative selection" (Csányi, 1989a). Replicative selection's only negative effect is its elimination of changes that risk or inhibit replication – that is, division of cells or reproduction of higher organisms. Compared to this negative effect, its creativity has a much greater importance. Replicative selection permits every change that does not inhibit replication, and the conservative nature of replication helps to maintain and accumulate these changes in the course of evolution. There is an enormous variety and richness of the forms of organisms, and all these are capable of self-replication. The creative nature of replicative selection in evolutionary biology can be shown satisfactorily.

The second source of creativity is the environment, whose impact could alter the conditions for the replication of the system from one moment to another, and which also acts as a selective device through the Darwinian natural selection.

The third very important source of creativity is based upon the so-called "hidden properties" of the components (Csányi, 1992c). For every system, we could define the components that are to produce a list of their various properties depending on their function in the given organization. This list is finite. However, if we define properties of the components as independent entities, the list of their properties could never be exhaustive because generally we define properties from the known interactions, and these are necessarily finite and limited by our observations. In fact, the general list of properties of any kind of a component is infinite; this originates from the inherent nature of the interactions of matter, which are infinite and immeasurable (Bunge, 1963). Properties other than that are included in our description of the organization of the system we call hidden properties, and they play a rather important role in the evolution of the system. In a component system, only a small part of these properties is used to create organization, and therefore in cases of changes in one or some of the components, or introduction of new components to the system, some new properties of the components, some hidden information, will show up which will influence the organization of the component system in an absolutely unpredictable way.

A complex molecule has almost infinite possibilities to interact with other such molecules, but a given organization needs only a low number of interactions to carry out a particular component's function. All the other properties remain hidden. But if further creative acts bring new molecular components into the system, they might unexpectedly fit into a new organization based upon the hidden properties. Such creativity is not restricted to the molecular level. Frogs, for example, have webbed fingers which help them to swim more forcefully, but some species living on jungle trees in Brazil use them for gliding. Frogs, originating from water, evolved webbed fingers to solve problems of survival in water, but certain hidden properties of the webbed fingers allowed them to evolve into a gliding device when appropriate environmental conditions appeared.

The three sources of creativity mutually support and even amplify, the effects of each other. As a consequence, there is a very limited possibility of predicting the events of evolution. We can make some predictions within limits concerning the general direction of changes, but there is no way to predict the properties of the new entities created in creative acts and in the future evolutionary process.

Organizational levels

Autogenesis of component systems invariably leads to the emergence of new levels of organizations (Csányi, 1989a, 1989b). We again take the cell as an example.

The components of the zero-system from which the cells originated are the various molecules which have their own chemical dynamics, and their structural arrangement belongs to the "molecular level" of organization. With the formation of the initial system precursors, organizational constraints appear on the dynamics of the molecules they contain. Therefore, in the long run, only those sets of molecules prevailed which, in the form of the cyclic molecular networks, were able to replicate fairly exactly. As the organizational constraints evolved, the molecular networks transformed into almost closed physical and organizational compartments; step by step, new units of selection, the cells, were formed. The cell became an autonomous unity – an individual system which is able to replicate both in time and space. All these properties are based upon a few thousand highly organized chemical reactions and molecular components. Description of the original (molecular) zero-system could be given by the description of the components and their dynamics. With the appearance of the organizational constraints, the description of the emerging organized system needs two levels. Besides the components, a description of the constraints which characterize the existence of the compartments is also necessary (for the necessity of the double description see Pattee, 1965; Polanyi, 1968). To simplify the emergence of a new organizational level, we can state that among the sets of components of an appropriate zero-system, organizational relationships appear spontaneously, and those sets which are able to maintain themselves as dynamic unities, in the form of topological or organizational compartments, become new "components" of a higher level of organization.

The evolving cell compartments in many respects behave as a unit, and in this way, complex, entirely new components on the cellular level of organization appeared. The cells have their own dynamics, but by taking up and releasing molecules, they are able to exert "function" at the cellular level. They can influence the probability of survival and genesis of other cells; that is, the various cells are forming a new zero-system, small sets of cooperating cells are acting as a new system precursor in it, and a new level of organization can appear in the form of replicative multi-cellular networks which leads to the emergence of multi-cellular organisms.

The replicative organization of the biosphere with its multi-layered organization intuitively is very similar to a series of Benoit Mandelbrot's fractals (Mandelbrot, 1977). The same organizational patterns can be found on each organizational level of the biosphere. This makes the adaptation of the living systems so successful.

THE REPLICATIVE AUTOGENETIC MODEL AND THE SOCIOCULTURAL SYSTEMS

In order to use the replicative model for studying social systems, first we have to clarify whether such systems could be defined by their components and organization and whether their organization is replicative. In this part, I want to support the assumption that any society is an autogenetic replicative system, and its components are people, ideas, and artifacts (Csányi and Kampis, 1987). Moreover, not only the whole society as a closed system is assumed to have replicative organization but also its major components on their own levels.

The biological nature of man

The theoretical bases of the different social theories were elaborated a rather long time ago, during the early period of the development of the social sciences. This explains why social theories make little reference to an analysis of the biological characteristics of man. It is supposed in most cases that biological features influence social organization through nourishment, breathing, and similar physiological functions only, and that the structure of society evolves exclusively through the functioning of cultural factors. On the other hand, our knowledge of human biology, evolution, ethology, and evolutionary anthropology has developed dramatically during the last ten to twenty years, clearly demonstrating that human societies can be studied and understood on the basis of a combined analysis of both biological and cultural factors.

As this analysis is rather limited in extent, I will consider only a few major elements. A somewhat more detailed analysis was published recently (Csányi, 1989b).

Man is a member of the animal world, with his biochemical, physiological characteristics not leaving any doubt about this. What nevertheless sets him apart from the animals is his behavior, developed and constrained by both environmental and genetic factors and characteristic of the human race (Passingham, 1982).

If we examine different cultures, we find that human behavior shows wide variations, but we can also recognize certain general features (Csányi,

1992e). All human cultures are based on *language* and human languages, as different as they may be in their surface structure, represent a well-defined class of the possible biological communication mechanisms. Characteristic of all cultures is a hierarchical order of human relations including mechanism of structuring power which took the form in most of human history, of kinship systems. Although it is again clear that kinship systems, for example, show large variations across societies, all people living in a society reckon with relatives and classify them in some way, which suggests that the ability to develop a system of kinship is a biological trait of our race. A third characteristic of cultures is the use of *artifacts*. It is a biological feature of man that he has an affection for objects of all kinds, and it is hard to imagine an active human being without artifacts. Of course, there are substantial differences between cultures regarding the sophistication and abundance of artifacts produced and used. The fourth characteristic of human cultures is the existence of *ideas*, that is of abstract thoughts – thoughts that we are thinking, expressing verbally, performing, implementing, or expressing through the making of artifacts. Emergence of ideas presumes the existence of highly evolved language.

Ideas can be understood as organized thoughts which are built up from the simplest units that can be considered meaningful, hereinafter referred to as concepts, and which lead to the creation of some more complicated thing, artifact, or behavior including linguistic communications. Ideas may be simple habits, techniques, communicated tales, myths, values, and norms, but they may also appear in the form of artifacts as instruments, tools, or items of cults or arts.

Ideas and artifacts are characteristic of all cultures, and although differences may be great, all cultures are reflected in their ideas and artifacts, so that idea production and making of artifacts are specific biological features of man.

The above four defining characteristics of human cultures can be traced back to three purely biological features, namely "social affection," "fondness for objects," and the "ability to follow rules." Let us consider each of these features in turn and then look at the social phenomena arising from them.

Among mammals, man is the most social being, feeling extraordinary affection for his kin, and even being ready to sacrifice his life for the group (Eibl-Eibesfeldt, 1989). Whatever the culture in question, the life of the individual takes place within the framework of some kind of social group. Even the misanthrope hates *people*, not objects or animals, and his social affection is obvious.

It is not necessary to list special arguments to demonstrate this feature of ours to someone living in the modern world (Morris, 1962), while the spontaneous and irresistible desire in small children to collect pebbles as a first sign of our fancy for objects may be mentioned. Throughout our whole lives we are accompanied by a great many different artifacts. We deal with their preparation, acquisition, exchange, and use.

The ability to obey rules, however, may need a more detailed explanation. The ability of animals and man to learn has been much studied, and it has been revealed that a special form of this ability distinguishes man from the most intelligent animals (Eibl-Eibesfeldt, 1982). Although animals are capable of learning behavior patterns, signs, and time schedules, and they can readily associate signs with events, consequences, etc., only man is able to learn and respect complicated rules of behavior. The term "rule" is used here as an organization of conduct which is expressed and acquired in linguistic form. Our use of this term is the closest to Khalil's "formal" and "informal" rules (Khalil, 1994). Most of the "principles" in his formulation are excluded here because these are not acquired solely by learning the linguistic expressions.

In language-teaching experiments with anthropoid apes, it was found that a chimpanzee or a gorilla can easily learn a "set of words" of a few hundred signs, and will use them in the proper sense. But it will not be able to learn the rules concerning the order and connection of those words and signs (Sebeok and Umiker-Sebeok, 1980). This means that the animal mind is not able to learn and obey grammatical rules, for example. Rule-following behavior is a species-specific feature of man, and language is one of the most manifest forms of it. However, representing the rules is not limited to language. The kinship system is, in fact, social affection regulated in a defined way, with family relations being manifested in rules of behavior and in respecting the rules.

Making of artifacts also depends on following rules, activated by the fondness for objects. A tool-maker works the natural object in conformity with rules fixed in advance. Animals, too, are able to perform elementary shaping, but they are unable to learn a system of rules, no matter how simple the latter may be (Bonner, 1980). This rule following is also manifested in elaborating ideas. A habit or a technique may be character-ized by a description or through a fixed system of given rules, which means that the shaping of an idea in our mind, or in our behavior, or in any other way, is reflected just like the shaping of an object in the successive application of a set of rules.

Obeying the rules is the most essential biological feature of man. Our nearest relative, the chimpanzee, can be taught to do many things, and with a suitable amount of training, it may even be taught maneuvers and operations used by people living a simple country life. But if a few hundred chimpanzees were taught this way and placed in an empty village, a social life characteristic of human communities would never develop, as the colony of chimpanzees is unable to obey a complex system of rules. If hungry, the individuals will acquire food at any price, and they also satisfy their sexual desire immediately and forcefully. A human may enhance hunger rather than act in a disrespectful manner. That cannot happen with an animal. For man, obedience to the rules is more important than any other thing. However, if we do break the rules, we do so on the basis of another system of rules considered more important.

Human cultures, in their essence, display systems of rules that operate continuously by social affection and the fondness for artifacts. Systems of rules concerning human relations are understood within the cultural group, as well as the rules concerning the preparation, the use, the exchange, and the production of objects and rules relating to the genesis, the values, the functioning, and the history of the culture. Language is the general communication system which, once again, consists of a system of rules which intervenes in shaping and transmitting the various rules of the culture, and thus reflects the fullness of the given culture.

It has been shown before that one of the preconditions of autogenesis is the emergence of an autogenetic system precursor, which organizes the construction of special constraints on the dynamics of the components of the organizational level already in existence.

The emergence of cultural man is usually attributed to a single characteristic, for example language, or tool-using, or common hunting to mention just a few. Recent comparative evolutionary studies show that these simplifying explanations are inadequate, because all these traits depend on one another (Richards, 1987). Human proto-cultural groups were formed on the biological basis of sociability and the various behavior features of the proto-cultural man discussed above. The biological proto-cultural organization was the system precursor of cultural evolution, the organizer of the replicative autogenesis of human culture (Csányi, 1989c).

The behavior of the early Homo groups at the beginning of their cultural evolution can well be described through the replicative autogenetic model. The components of the group are the Homo sapiens and the few objects they are using, as well as the experiences the group has obtained during its functioning, about its environment. And this group is more and more able, by means of language, to transmit these to new generations. This system manifests the ability of replication in the course of time: It has the ability to continually renew its components without changing its organization. Perishing individuals are substituted by newborn ones, objects are renewed through copying, thoroughly taking care of their formal and functional similarities. Experiences of individuals are also renewed by means of the developing cultural inheritance mechanisms of teaching/learning. Such systems are very stable, as has been proven in the first two million years of the history of our race.

It was the autogenesis of the ideas in these proto-cultural groups that initiated cultural evolution, promoted co-evolutionary biological changes, and resulted in "group-societies." Group-societies are replicative units not only in their biological aspects, but also in their cultural aspects. To satisfy their basic needs, cultural complexes, including social and mental ideas, and objects were necessary. Social ideas shaped the organization of the group; mental ideas included useful knowledge and technics; and artifacts were made for cultic or practical purposes. The ideas of the group, its artifacts, and social connections were replicated from generation to generation within the limits of fidelity provided by linguistic communication.

The group-society is an organization controlled by cultural constraints and built upon the dynamics of the biological level of human existence. Its components represent a functional network, and they produce again the very same network during their operation. The group-society, as a system, has no inputs and outputs, creating only the conditions for its own existence, and it cannot produce a surplus, to be traded, exchanged, or unevenly distributed. It is organizationally closed, stable, and in equilibrium with its environment. Emergence of this organization took several million years of human evolution.

Linguistic concepts as replicative structures

As was mentioned on p. 149, experiments of neuro-ethology suggest that the main function of the brain of the higher animals is the modeling of the events of the animal's environment. Three-part functional structures can be regarded as units of the neuronal model. Percepts originated from the outer stimuli of the environment through animal perception play the part of a "key," which is the basic connection between the inner and the outer world. The stimuli are always followed by some action of the animal, sooner or later. Neural structures which organize animal "actions" form the third part of elementary units of the neuronal models. Nevertheless, there is no direct connection between percepts and actions. The same stimuli could activate different actions, depending on previous experience. But actions also depend on the actual internal state of the animal, on motivational systems, and primarily on mechanisms of memory. The functional elements that link percepts and actions are called "reference structures." The triadic "key-reference structure-action" units can be combined through the reference structures, and their complicated make-ups are the very models of the environment (Csányi, 1993b).

The three-part units of these models are called "concepts." A concept can be considered as a neural controller unit of a behavioral act or thought of the animal mind. The general capacity of the higher structures which can be built from the concepts is rather limited in the animal brain because each individual can form its models only from its own limited experiences. Each and every model made by animal brains is highly particular in this respect.

Animal communication conveys information about internal states and intentions of the animal, and less often about the environment. This communication, and the information povided by it, becomes an organic part of the structure of models in the animal's brain, but its influence is rather limited. Animals cannot communicate either the internal structure of the model, or their individual past experiences and future expectations. Animal communication is closed, and its code system is an analog type (Csányi and Kampis, 1988).

Evolution of the linguistic competence of man has changed the structure of the brain's models. By naming something, a key which has only a very loose connection with percepts and actions arises. The "word-referential structure-action" segmented units could be combined, not only through experiences, but also through grammatical rules, and this results in the very complicated superstructures of "conceptual thought." A linguistic concept can be regarded as an utterance or human thought. The linguistic concept also could activate actions, but primary experience is no more a prerequisite for these actions than it was in the case of animals. Human language, unlike in all other forms of animal communication, is open: it uses an abstract and digital code (Glaserfeld, 1976). Cognitive superstructures built up from concepts can be regarded as models of the environment so much so that it is certain that animal-type concepts and linguistic concepts combine together to create a world model in man (Csányi, 1992b).

The most important consequence of linguistic competence is the opening up of the closed inner world of the individual. By linguistic communication, individuals are able to exchange parts of their models in the form of linguistic concepts or even whole models of linguistic nature.

With the appearance of this language, it became possible to form *supermodels* in human groups. All individuals of the group have almost identical concept components, but they share only part of the set of components which belong to other individuals, and no individual has a complete set. Experiences and expectations of any individual become used collectively by the group. The predictive value of these models can be checked by any other group members, and with the death of individuals the experience does not vanish. Instead, independent of the individual, it has a history on the level of the collective memory of the group. This forms a new organizational level of model-building activity.

Although linguistic concepts are formed in individual brains, the supermodel contains only those which were communicated, and the very act of communication is a "replicative" process. Memory traces of linguistic concepts are copied by the communicating individuals; therefore, the whole language-based supermodel is a genuine replicative system.

The origin and organization of ideas

It is worthwhile to compare animal and linguistic concepts in an example. It is a well-known observation that in cooperative groups of certain higher mammals, like wolf, the individuals use hunting tactics in which they are

163

very attentive to each other's actions. Each pack member positions itself in such a way that the appearance of a fellow member in the right moment and right place is clearly supposed. This significant form of cooperation can exist because of the high similarity of the brain's models in each wolf. The individuals have the capacity to identify themselves with fellow members, and they can figure out the next actions of the latter. That is, they have appropriate models of the behavior of others. This kind of cooperation occurs without the exchange of plans, intentions, or thoughts. Wolves can communicate only certain parameters of their inner state, like the hunting or the aggressive mood. This kind of cooperation is based on an *action-plan* which, while it is very flexible, is based on the genes. The participants do not need explanations or reconciliation, there are no roles to assign, there is no need to set up schedules. All participants have internal drive for cooperation and everybody fulfills that role which is the consequence of its position in the rank order of the group and the particular instances of the actual situation. Therefore, the creativity of such animal groups is rather limited. The structure of the "action-plan" is simple and does not change too much during thousands of generations.

Animals living in these highly evolved social groups are cooperating but the result of their cooperation is immediate and the prey is a resource which can easily be distributed on the bases of the rank order. In principle everybody joins to the common action for their own self-interest. There is no "group-interest" above individuals' own; the groups are loosely organized. Individuals can leave the group and try another one occasionally. There is nothing, like an object, a possession or a common learned rite which lasts because of the cooperation. There is nothing which can be regarded as a *product* of the group. The participation therefore is completely based on individual interests.

The nature of cooperation was entirely different in the early Homo groups which already used tools and primitive language (Csányi, 1992a). Cooperation in human groups occurs on the base of an individual action-plan which is designed well before the action. The participants plan the forthcoming actions, they envisage the proceeding of the actions, ponder over the different favorable or unfavorable outcomes. There are temporary roles which are discussed and assigned. The basic difference to the animals is the *individuality* of the action-plan of cooperation, which is relatively independent of the genetical factors. Every cooperating animal group proceeds on the basis of a genetically determined plan, while the freely created individual plans are characteristic of the cooperating human groups. Each group designs its own individual action-plan on the basis of its learned culture.

Individuality plays an enormous role in evolution (Sterrer, 1992). Individual uniqueness of the organisms is the consequence of sexual reproduction, i.e., the fact that in a sexually reproducing population no two individuals (except identical twins) are identical in their genotypes and because of the ontogenic processes even less so in their phenotypes. The nervous system of the higher animals is able to modify the behavior of the individual through various learning mechanisms. In this way a neural type of individuality is also built up on the constrained genetical individuality, which enables the animals to react with an appropriate behavioral response to the finest environmental changes. Emerging individuality, let it be genetic or neural, was the *precondition* to the appearance of creativity in the living system, because only the variability of the enormous number of individuals provides the necessary base for selection to act in producing new life forms.

Nowadays it is rather clear why human evolution has been so fast. The individual, learned character of the human cooperation provided man with enormous advantages. The individual action-plan is such an entity, which in its most primitive form exists as memory traces of the participants and directs the proceedings of the cooperation. That is, the plan is not given genetically but it is formed by the group itself and its activity is bound to the very group in which it was formed. The abstract human language which is different from any form of animal communication (Csányi, 1992b, 1992c; Csányi and Kampis, 1988) has evolved just as a means to form this individual action-plan. The action-plan of the human groups is a linguistic structure. Although this action-plan exists in distributed form in the brains of the group members, nevertheless it can be regarded as an entity above the organization level of the group. This means that a new entity appeared in the evolutionary theater. In fact, if we are considering the important role of individuality in evolution it is clear that new classes of individual entities appeared whose mere existence started a new level of the evolutionary dynamics. These new entities are the "group-beings" or group-societies. Group individuality established by human culture made an enormous variability among the groups emerge. Structural selection among the variants was the source of creativity of cultural evolution.

There was a heated debate among the students of animal behavioral evolution some years ago, as to whether natural selection acts only on individuals as was assumed by the classic Darwinian theory, or whether selection can act among groups as well. In a "group-selection" process competition occurs among groups for survival and the replication of the group (Alexander and Borgia, 1978). This debate was very interesting because the group-selection mechanism makes evolution proceed faster than individual selection and if it really existed it must be accounted for in the theories of the evolution of animal social behavior. A large amount of data were published and some experiments were even performed, but after a while the general conclusion was that possibly group-selection mechanisms have not appeared in animals other than man. It is supposed that man is the only organism in which, besides individual selection, some role has been played by group-selection process and just this latter has accelerated human evolution. Among the conditions for group-selection to occur, one is isolation. If in an animal group new members immigrate in numbers exceeding 4–5 per cent of the number of individuals in the group during a generation, then group-selection mechanisms cease to act. Evolution of the early Homo species has been characterized by isolation of a high degree just because of language and culture. We assume that as the group-being mentioned above started to form, the degree of isolation grew accordingly, and evolution accelerated. That is, a system with a positive feedback emerged, and as far as it advanced the more possibility it acquired for further advance.

A linguistic structure is a simple action-plan but action-plans can acquire extreme complexity if they are further organized. The action-plans can be divided into small but still meaningful parts – concepts – and from these parts new action-plans can be structured. Using exact timing, action-plans could create very complex organizations.

In such a way, concepts existing in individual brains become parts of a higher collective structure, which then determines the aim and the exact path to its achievement. We define this higher structure of individual concepts as an "idea."

Concepts consisting of an idea are not selected at random; rather they form a *functionally organized set* which makes the performances purposeful and possible. It is not important for every member of the hunting group to know everything about the task or roles of the others. It is enough for the leader to know the main program; but even for him, it is unnecessary to learn about finer details. Ideas can be organized hierarchically, and the whole set is available only in the whole group whose activity is regulated by the ideas. The ideas belonging to a group, such as the care of parents, ownership, or freedom are ideas that can also be considered as fixed systems of rules – not as simple sets of rules, but as a complex system of organization of the set. The idea of parental care, for example, includes all the rules of behavior to be followed by parents in a given culture in interacting with their children. These are partly small techniques of taking care, partly rules of how to decide between conflicting interests. But the idea of parental care also includes rules which are commands regarding the relations of subordination between this and other ideas, such as when I may be allowed or obliged to sacrifice my child in the interest of the group or of the homeland, as in cases of infanticide for population control, or giving soldiers for the army.

An idea composed of rules for behavior may be considered to be working well if its organization is suitable, it does not imply contradictions, it (desirably) does not go against biological dispositions, and it allows clear-cut decisions in all situations. There are also ideas, of course, in which a purely cultural restriction of biological dispositions is expressed, for example in the case of ideas relating to sexual behavior. In such cases, the idea will be unstable to a certain extent. It will frequently be reevaluated, certain component rules will be left out, or new rules will be built in.

Individual concepts existing in the brains of the group members can be functionally combined only by a specific self-organization of the ideas. Only ideas that contain those, and only those, concepts which are suitable to achieve the given goal can act and accomplish something. This clearly shows the replicative and special functions of the concept components by which they influence the probability of genesis and existence of other components in the organized set of the idea.

Many different goals arise in the life of a group. Therefore very strong selection is exerted on the formation of ideas connected to these goals, and those concepts which are unsuitable for a given goal are selected out. Suitable concepts are memorized by the members of the group, and these are connected by strong functional bonds. Survival values of the ideas are much stronger than those of the concepts just because of the high organization of the ideas. The brain's model of the environment made from animal concepts also has a survival value if the individual has the appropriate experiences during its life and can make the right model. However, ideas built up from the linguistic concepts above the individual level are useful controlling agents which carry both the experiences of the acting and contributing individuals and the experiences of their ancestors too. Over the generations, the concepts which are unsuitable for realizing the given goal for some reason or other are selected out from the idea pool. Therefore, ideas are organized by the collective experience of the group, and they tremendously enhance the effectiveness of the group.

The replicative nature of a system constrains the organization very little, and therefore conforms to the less stringent social model of Hayek (1967) with his "spontaneous order" and to those which operate with rigid hierarchy or "the commanding authority" (Khalil, 1992).

A classification of the ideas has not yet been worked out, but if we define an idea as an organized set of concepts, necessary for achieving a given goal, it is obvious that even a primitive group society had many different ideas simultaneously. For hunting, fishing, and the defense of the group from predators or from other groups, they needed different ideas. It is also clear that the different ideas could not be entirely independent from each other because there are many common behavior elements of these actions, and it is also necessary to coordinate the maintenance and expression of the various ideas. The seed of this coordination is the group as an entity itself. The ideas organize the maintenance and survival of the group, which in turn must harmonize the ideas. Various organizing ideas, such as myths of the origin, legends, and religions emerged. Values and norms appeared.

The group and its idea set form a closed system. Well-organized ideas help the group's maintenance and survival. The group takes care of the propagation of the ideas from generation to generation. Biological and ethological traits of man, like acceptance of group identity, preference of group members, and rejection of non-members (Eibl-Eibesfeldt, 1979b, 1989), and sacrificing someone's life for the defense of the group fit very well with the culturally made ideas about the group. There is an absolute harmony among the individual, the group, and the ideas. Emotional and social stability have been solid for thousands of generations.

The members of a Homo group were few – around thirty to sixty. In such a small group, the acquisition of all ideas by every individual has low cost. Therefore, members of the group learn not only their particular tasks, but also the roles and the necessary actions of the others. This makes the replacement of the contributors very easy. Some studies have found that contemporary group-societies spent most of their time talking (Lee, 1969). This serves for the continuous exchange and refreshment of ideas and concepts and also for teaching the young. This is a "replicative process" showing high levels of compartmentalization and convergence, which are so characteristic to replicative systems (Csányi, 1989a). Ideas maintain and propagate themselves by replicative autogenesis.

The populational nature of the ideas and the groups

An important organizational principle has to be shown. Both groups and ideas are populational entities; that is, they consist of individual components which are bound by some higher functional organization. Components of the group are fellow members – people who are born in or immigrate and are accepted into the group. Therefore the group can be defined only stochastically. In a given moment, all members of a group can be accounted for only artificially and uncertainly. For example, we can consider the newborns, who have not yet acquired the ideas of the group and whose life might be short as members, or we can logically exclude them by restricting memberships to juveniles and adults. It is also important that components of the group are continuously changing by death, birth, immigration, and emigration. The group consists of people as components, but the group is an entity formed above the people, and the definition of its identity is theoretically a difficult problem which I wish only to mention here.

If we examine the ideas closely, their populational nature also shows up. Components of the ideas are the concepts, both linguistic and non-linguistic ones, which exist physically in the brains of the people. Ideas are formed from communicated concepts by a functional organization at the group level. Because the concepts are entities of the nervous system, and they correspond to rather elementary units of behavior or thoughts, it is impossible to determine the exact concept constituents of an idea.

If, for example, we study an ancient craft, like arrow making, it is clear

168

that this craft follows certain technology-technic rules concerning the selection and preparation of raw materials and the sequence of the technological procedures. It cannot be said that only one sequence or set of the concepts results in appropriate products, but small deviations are allowed during the whole technological process, and therefore the idea of arrow making is also only a stochastically characterized entity. An idea is a stochastic set of concepts whose members can fluctuate very much without perceivably changing the effectiveness of the idea.

It is extremely important for our further discussions to emphasize that the stochastic entity of an idea is bound to the physical structure of another stochastically determined entity, the group. Therefore, the action and the effect of an idea is fundamentally influenced by this double stochastic feature of the society.

Abstract components or material entities?

In the usual descriptions of the social sciences, the term idea is used as an abstract entity. I want to emphasize that I use this term entirely differently. All the abstract entities of social systems (e.g., the law system, philosophical and mathematical constructions, ideas, and ideologies) are considered to be the results of the activity of material components in the replicative autogenetic model. Let us take a simple example: A functioning law created in a small group-society. If the law is considered an abstract entity, it raises many methodological problems when the interactions of social components are investigated. A natural scientific point of view, in contrast, allows us to consider the law as a particular system of *memory traces* that has been developed in the brains of the members of the society. Memory traces allow us to recognize each other, to perform our daily activity, and to observe laws.

Culturally we differ from each other by the acquired set of memory traces; to preserve this difference, we try to perpetuate our memory traits by teaching, exemplification, writing, and speaking to the other members, including the following generations. Consequently, memory traces are components of a replicative system. A given law exists in group-society until the system of memory traces creating the law persists in the brains of society members. The way of function and the effects of the law are determined not only by its internal structure, its content, and relevance, but also by biological factors such as the remembering processes of group members, the degree to which memory is able to determine behavior, and the degree to which memory traces can be culturally transmitted to the following generations. These are problems which can be unequivocally investigated and answered by a natural scientific approach. In this circumstance, the law appears as an *effect* of the material system. Consequently, the building blocks of the idea components of our model system have to be the memory traces, which are of material nature. The organized systems of memory traces, the concepts at the individual level, and the ideas at the populational level, develop their effects through manifesting themselves in the particular system of the human body. This is similar to the "meme" concept of Dawkins (1976). He has assumed a multiplication of memory traces analogous to the multiplication of genes.

The nature of the artifacts

Manmade objects are always expressions of ideas, which means that artifacts can also be interpreted as systems of organized sets of rules of behavior. Let us just consider how many rules are followed when we use an instrument as simple as a house door key. I have to take the key with me when I leave and have it with me when I go home. I have to hold it in a given way if I want to open the door; I have to perform a certain motion pattern in the course of turning it in the lock, and different rules apply as to whether or not I will leave the key in the lock. The notion of the key, the lock, the ownership, the concept of fitting together, etc., are also formulated in complex ideas. But the making of an object itself, for example of the key mentioned above, can be described as a series of fixed rules of the production. In the course of preparing the casting mold, the metal, performing the casting, and the rest of the work, the producer will obey well-defined rules, with the object of use being the result of all these steps.

The component class of ideas is contributing to form the component class of the artifacts. The biologically determined usage of objects and tools played an important role in the life of the humanoid primate groups. There are many animals which use various tools; a few of them even make some adjustments on the natural objects which they use. The special linkages which were formed among the tools, the environmental models of the brain, and communication are found only in man (Brown, 1973; Montagu, 1976). A human being is able to imagine various objects; he/she could perform certain processes on this imaginary object in his/her mind. That is, a human being creates the *idea* of the artifacts and transforms this idea into an objectivated form during the making. The idea embodied in the artifact could be transferred back again into the mind of the user of the artifact. In this way, dynamic mutual interactions appear among the component classes of humans, artifacts, and ideas, which built up the human societies. It is noted again that the term idea corresponds to an organized set of memory traces.

There are different ways of creating artifacts. Their shape and structure can be modeled after natural objects or can be invented by applying appropriate rules sequentially. But they are produced usually by "copying" and partially changing an object already in existence. Their production, therefore, can be regarded as a replicative process. The structure of artifacts lends itself to change and recombination. Their production is accompanied by selection. In everyday life, artifacts are able to influence the probability of genesis and existence of each other. Thus a system of artifacts (technology) is capable of replicative autogenesis.

The replicative nature of group societies

Perhaps it is not in question that group-societies can be distinguished on the basis of their sociocultural organization, i.e., on the basis of the relations of their language, customs, belief systems, and the set of artifacts they are using. The most important components of a system such as a group-society are their human members. People are biological beings; therefore, their propagation, birth, and death are parts of a biological replicative process. There is a large difference, of course, between a biological being and a component of a cultural system. The latter has personality, unique individual social relations, and autonomy of a certain degree. But all of these are the products of a socialization process influenced by the sociocultural structure of the group, and they are also part of the replicative process. Language, for example, is transferred from one generation to the following one by copying, i.e., replication. The customs, myths, taboos, and belief systems characterized by the group are also transferred by replicative learning, notwithstanding the rare cases of cultural innovation or cultural transfer.

It is the same with artifacts, if we take a group-society which is more or less isolated and makes its necessary artifacts itself. The artifacts and the necessary knowledge for making them are transferred by copying from one generation to another. There are artifacts with shorter average lifetime, and there are ones with longer than the lifetime of the people, but this fact does not change the replicative nature of the artifact production. Finally, the cultural organization of the group which embodies all the above-mentioned processes and whose lifetime is much longer than the lifetime of any of its components, maintains itself by the continuous renewal of its components and component producing processes – that is, by a genuine "replicative" process (Csányi, 1989c).

Here I want to emphasize again the advantage of the autogenetic replicative model to the autopoietic one, especially in the case of social systems. Replication in the autogenetic model is never identical: Its fidelity in case of the social systems is certainly far from one. The deviations from identity during replication, occasional innovations, outer influences (dissipation), or simply recombinations of already existing components make adaptive changes and cultural evolution possible. Nonidentical replication of the components is the major difference between autopoietic and autogenetic models, and this is the source of the creative power of the sociocultural systems.

171

VILMOS CSÁNYI

From the group-society to the mass society

In group-societies, ideas were organized around group identity, and people carrying these ideas formed a complete unity. A given group was the set of certain people, and at the same time it was also the set of certain ideas. These two components formed the culture of the group. The unity was important because the ethological traits of man concerning group formation, maintenance (attraction to group members, hatred of outsiders, submission to the dominance order of the group, etc.), and ideas converged in the same direction. Group consciousness and the ideas of the group mutually supposed and determined each other on the bases of their stochastic character mentioned earlier.

Mass societies have appeared during the last couple of thousand years of the cultural evolution, and they fundamentally changed the relations among groups and ideas (Csányi, 1990). Ethological traits are unsuitable as bonding forces for the hundred thousands, and later for the many millions of people of modern societies. This is so in spite of the continuous, uninterrupted actions of these factors, because it is well known that a human being could develop strong personal bonds only in groups not exceeding the limit of thirty to sixty people. Bonding forces for larger groups like armies, states, parties, and major religions are provided completely by rule-driven ideas.

Emergence of mass societies also promoted the competition of ideas that has been at a very low level in group-societies. Idea competition led to new forms of self-organization. Ideas in group-societies served practical purposes (technics and technologies), or they supported group identity by means of myths, legends, and primitive religions. Exchange of ideas between societies was only occasional and ineffective, mostly because group-societies are rather closed systems. In modern mass societies, the number of potential idea carriers is enormous, and the acquirement of ideas could occur by new means besides the traditional group framework. Mass communication makes it possible for ideas to unite people who do not compose a real group in the ethological sense.

Apart from its local groups members of various organizations, members of a party's leadership, and the administration do not know each other personally. Ethological factors of their belonging together and commitments are negligible to the processes of the maintenance and evolution of the ideas serving the survival of the given party. People of such a large organization are united by the appropriately organized ideas instead of by group cohesion.

Survival of the ideas of group-societies were granted by early learning and socialization and by extremely strong tradition. Ideas were acquired in childhood. Ideas of mass society compete for the adult members of the society. This change has important evolutionary consequences in the structure and organization of present-day ideas. New kinds of components appeared in the set of linguistic concepts which form the various ideas. These new concepts promote the spreading of the given idea and serve its competition. Missionary function of some modern religions is a good example. Such a role was impossible in the culture of a group-society. Myths of origin of a group-society need not be logical or convincing at all because every member of the group believes it; it is taught by the elderly, and there is no reason to question parts of the myth. Ideas in mass society are continuously challenged. The myths of origin must be supported by science and practice. Logical overall explanations are needed; moreover, we want the possibility of choice among alternatives.

Ideas of common identity in mass society could organize groups of immense size, but only if there are concepts among its constituents which are suitable for maintaining large groups. This led to the appearance of propaganda and ideology as the main tools of the organizations of ideas.

Thus the ideas became the primary group-forming forces, but the ethological group-forming traits of man do not cease to exist. If the nature of human groups makes it possible for the ethological factors to act, they immediately start to do so. Good examples for this were the one-party systems in Russia and Eastern Europe: Administrations, political committees and central committees which were principally ethologically organized, closed human groups, and their activity was only partially controlled by their own ideology.

As we said, the major advantage of groups organized by ideas is the emergence of idea competition, which is the basis, among others, of the development of modern science and also of the modern welfare states. But idea competition has its drawbacks. Group-society has ideas in forms of values and norms which guarantee the undisturbed cooperation, or at least tolerance, of various ideas. In mass societies this harmonizing effect of the values and norms ceases to exist. Ideas appear as entities of choice. The individual must choose ideas from an enormous variety pool to construct his or her personality but there is no comprehensive idea framework accepted by everybody, which could serve his or her unambiguous selection. Alienation of modern man, his insecurity, and his loss of values can be explained by the competition among ideas.

Perhaps this is just a temporary stage, because today new ideas are being formed which have a global nature. The unity of humanity, global peace, global protection of nature, and others emerge, which most probably will form a network of organizing ideas and serve a harmonious environment for others. It will also, of course, result in a closure of the idea-world again.

Levels of organizations in society

Definition of the levels of organization in society is a rather complex issue. In the following we emphasize social systems as physical entities with the

173

components of humans, artifacts, and memory traces (ideas). The first level of organization is the classes of the components themselves, that is humans, artifacts, and memory traces. Here belong the biological organization of the human body, neurobiological organization of the memory traces, and the descriptions of the structure of the artifacts.

Those processes in which these components are renewed belong to the second level of organization. In the case of humans, this organizational level consists of the family, educational institutes, small groups of working places, and political and religious institutions, because these are the most influential in forming human personalities. It is recognized, of course, that the separation of those organizations which have more direct influences from those which have only indirect ones is very difficult if not impossible.

In the case of artifacts, social structures concerned with the design and making of the artifacts belong to the second level, too. In the case of ideas, organizations concerned with communication, education, and artifact making are responsible for the origin and transfer of ideas, and these also belong to the second level. I note here that our insistence on describing society as a physical system yields here, for example, because the origin and interaction of the ideas occur at every level and in every locality of society, but memory traces, the physical bases of the ideas, are produced only in human brains; therefore, the origination of the idea components are always related to communication, learning, and education, that is to building up memory traces.

However uncertain the borders of the second level's organizations are, it is certain that from human personalities, particular ideas and appropriate artifacts, higher levels' structures came into being: Factories, companies, institutions of law, politics, and religions, as well as nations, states, and multinational firms, which are autogenetic replicative organizations. All of these are components of an emerging new *global-system* which is the top level of the social organization.

Social autonomy and creativity

In the course of evolution, it is group-society configurations that defined man's social existence for the longest time. They also influenced his biological evolution, and we can say that species-specific characteristics of man are in an optimal harmony mostly with group-society as a super-structure. The texture of the group-society is based on kinship relations. Individual development is in harmony with the slow alteration of the social structure. The socialization of the individual born into the group is perfect. He completely accepts the conditions that exist in the society, and on becoming adult, he is given the opportunity to climb the social ladder. Values and norms change very slowly, at a pace of generations following one another, if at all.

The harmony of biological factors and a given social structure explain that certain signs of group-societies have prevailed, or they come up sometimes even in mass societies (Csányi, 1992e). In mass societies before the industrial revolution biological family relationships were an essential part of the social structure. The relationships that are new compared to the group-societies appear, in fact, because family relations were not capable any more of organizing the society as a whole. Dependencies based on religion, ownership, and state structure developed. Thus they can be interpreted as a social extension of family relationships. In a society of relatives, an individual is a member of a network of given dependencies; his existence is subject to his relationships, and he is hardly able to change this system of relationships, just like the system of relatives. Feudal society is a typical example. The liege lord is at the top of a group which includes many more people than the number of his relatives, but the relationships are of family character (for example, vassals get certain protection in exchange for their services), with an important exception, namely that the shift of generation characteristic of the group-society is not followed by a change in the seigniory. Vassals do not become liege-lords after a time. Feudal relations are quasi-infantilizing major parts of the society, defining forever their place in the social order of ranks. As mass society, due simply to its size, is unable to completely use the early socialization for conserving a given structure, individuals also appear who reject the superstructure of the society. But it is only after very long development, during only the industrial development in fact, that the idea of social autonomy emerges (Csányi, 1991). Autonomy results in the appearance of individuals and groups which reject the given family and dependence conditions of the society and organize themselves around an independent objective or idea. An autonomous individual is able to choose from the different ideologies, ideas, and social options. The autonomous group, on the other hand, unifies individuals having similar ways of thinking and similar aims, in the interest of some common objective or idea. The acceptance of autonomous ideas is a refusal of monolithic society-organizing ideologies.

The acceleration of modern industrial development has been allowed by social autonomy. The society based on family relationships can only change very slowly, at the pace of generation shifts. The appearance of autonomous groups dramatically accelerated the change in social structure. First of all at the field of production, as a special autonomy of production units, enterprises developed. This comprises a number of factors. The autonomous entrepreneurs' groups recruit their members with no regard to social constraints: They recruit those who, due to their personal character, are able to fulfill a given task, to follow a given target, and to implement a given idea. If society shows tolerance towards the autonomous groups, the competition of these groups can begin, and the ones unable to achieve their goals will collapse and enable other groups of a new composition to rapidly appear. Thus the lifetime of the autonomous groups is usually much shorter than the generation time. A certain selection is also taking place, that means their development will also accelerate. The organizers and executives of a given enterprise create a well-defined organization, and this organization will face the given social conditions. If successfully, it will survive; if it fails, it will disintegrate, without causing too much harm to its participants. And with the participants as units fit for organization, new autonomous groups and new enterprises may form. A recombination and selection of different organizing ideas is taking place this way. Of course, not only companies and enterprises, but also different social organizations, editorial boards, associations, and parties can function on the basis of autonomy. It is worth noting here that the autonomous individual who is able to create autonomous groups is the result of a kind of socialization. Modern industrial societies invest significant energy into developing individual autonomy, as well as the freedom of creating autonomous groups in adult life, or their disintegration in case of inadaptability. Jurisdiction and the political system as a whole should be fit for admitting the autonomy, but this is only one of the preconditions. The other one is a social-scale production of individuals educated to autonomy. Autonomy cannot be introduced from one day to another; it can develop, but in spaces of generations, because production of the human components occurs in such a timescale.

The appearance of autonomy accelerated cultural evolution because it enhanced social creativity by increasing the dynamics of the change of structures on the third levels of social organization.

CONCLUSIONS

The present state of cultural evolution seems transient. In the biological applications of the autogenetic model, it was found that if, on a given level of organization, replicative compartments influencing the probability of each other's genesis develop, then formation of a new organizational level starts, and at the same time the former stability ceases. Conditions for a more-or-less stable replication of the social systems were provided by the emergence of states during historical times.

The early Egyptian, Indian, and Chinese states were stable for thousands of years, although their inhabitants did not live in peace. Replicative systems could replicate in time and space. Besides replicating in time, states can also replicate in space while there is available space. They can conquer territories and colonize them by sending people and ideas, often by using force. Presently, the possibilities for replication in space are practically none. Cultural constraints have emerged which do not allow the complete destruction of the conquered territory and elimination of its inhabitants.

Further evolution of the social systems may continue only if new regulatory mechanisms are created which help to form the coordinated temporal replication of the newly-emerged *global system*, including the biosphere. As autogenesis continues, the fidelity of replication and also the stability of the components of the system increase, but with the formation of the higher global organization, a significant part of their autonomy will be lost. In a final equilibrium the global system and its components might replicate with high fidelity, and then its existence will depend entirely on constant outside, cosmic, conditions.

With the help of the replicative autogenetic model, characteristics of the sustainable development can be inferred. Development of the existing systems might occur through the emergence of new components and disappearance of the old ones. It can be stated that only such component changes can be sustained which allow the replication of the whole global network of the components. Emergence of a radically new component such as the introduction of a new idea or technological product may cause the breakdown of the existing network; therefore, introducing new components needs much care. Only if the network of the functional interactions could be revealed by appropriate studies, the effect of the introduction of new components could be calculated. The replicative model could promote such studies (Pantzar and Csányi, 1991).

REFERENCES

Alexander, E. O. and Borgia, G. (1978) "Group selection, altruism and the levels of organization of life," *Annual Review of Ecological Systems* 9: 469–474.
Artigiani, R., Csányi, V., László, E., and Masulli, I. (1989) "The evolution of cognitive maps: New paradigms for the 21st century," *Futura* 8(2): 32–46.
Bertalanffy, L. (1968) *General Systems Theory,* New York: George Braziler.
Bonner, J. T. (1980) *The Evolution of Culture in Animals,* Princeton: Princeton University Press.
Brown, R. (1973) *A First Language: The Early Stages,* Cambridge, Mass.: Harvard University Press.
Bunge, M. (1963) *The Myth of Simplicity,* Englewood Cliffs, N.J.: Prentice-Hall.
Collett, T. S. (1983) "Sensory guidance of motor behaviour," in T. R. Halliday and P. J. B. Slater (eds) "Causes and effects," *Animal Behaviour,* Vol. 1, Oxford: Blackwell Scientific Publications, 40–75.
Craik, K. J. W. (1943) *The Nature of Explanation,* London: Cambridge University Press. (Reprinted 1952.)
Csányi, V. (1978) "Az evolució általános elmélete," *Fizikai Szemle* 28: 401–417, 441–452.
—— (1980) "The general theory of evolution," *Acta Biologica Hungarica of the Hungarian Academy of Sciences* 31: 409–434.
—— (1981) "General theory of evolution," *Society for General Systems Research* 6: 73–95.
—— (1982) *General Theory of Evolution,* Budapest: Publishing House of the Hungarian Academy of Sciences, 121.
—— (1985) "Autogenesis: evolution of selforganizing systems," in J.-P. Aubin, D. Saari, and K. Sigmund (eds) "Dynamics of Macrosystems", Proceedings,

Laxenburg, Austria 1984, Lecture Notes in Economics and Mathematical Systems No. 257, Berlin: Springer-Verlag, 253–267.

—— (1986) "How is the brain modelling the environment? A case study on the paradise fish," in G. Montalenti and G. Tecce (eds) "Variability and Behavioral Evolution," Proceedings, Accademia Nazionale dei Lincei, Roma, 1983, Quaderno No. 259, 142–157.

—— (1987a) "The replicative model of evolution: A general theory," *World Future: the Journal of General Evolution* 23: 31–65.

—— (1987b) "The replicative evolutionary model of animal and human minds," *World Future: the Journal of General Evolution* 24(3): 174–214.

—— (1988a) "Contribution of the genetical and neural memory to animal intelligence," in H. Jerison and Irene Jerison (eds) *Intelligence and Evolutionary Biology*, Berlin: Springer-Verlag, 299–318.

—— (1988b) "Il modello replicativo dele'evoluzione biologica e culturale," in M. Ceruti and E. László, *Physis: abitare la terra*, Milan: Feltrinelli, 249–260.

—— (1988c) "The replicative model of self-organization: A general theory of evolution," in G. J. Dalenoort (ed.) *The Paradigm of Self-organization*, London: Gordon and Breach, 75–88.

—— (1989a) *Evolutionary Systems and Society: A General Theory of Evolution*, Durham, N.C.: Duke University Press.

—— (1989b) "Origin of complexity and organizational levels during evolution," in D. B. Wake and G. Roth (eds) *Complex Organizational Functions: Integration and Evolution in Vertebrates*, New York: John Wiley & Sons, 349–360.

—— (1989c) "The replicative model of cultural evolution," *Humanbiology Budapest* 19: 83–87.

—— (1990) "The shift from group cohesion to idea cohesion is a major step in cultural evolution," *World Future: the Journal of General Evolution* 29: 1–8.

—— (1991) "Social creativity", *World Future: the Journal of General Evolution* 31: 23–31.

—— (1992a) "Ethology and the rise of the conceptual thoughts," in J. Deely (ed.) *Symbolicity*, Lanham, MD: University Press of America, 479–484.

—— (1992b) "The brain's models and communication," in Thomas A. Sebeok and Jean Umiker-Sebeok (eds) *The Semiotic Web*, Berlin: Moyton de Gruyter, 27–43.

—— (1992c) "Nature and origin of biological and social information," in K. Haefner (ed.) *Evolution of Information Processing Systems*, Berlin: Springer, 257–281.

—— (1992d) "Natural sciences and the evolutionary models," *World Future: the Journal of General Evolution* 34: 15–24.

—— (1992e) "Ethological aspects of human needs," in G. Schaefer (ed.) *Basic Human Needs: An Interdisciplinary and International View*, Frankfurt: Peter Lang, 30–40.

—— (1993a) "Evolution: Unfolding a metaphor. *World Future: the Journal of General Evolution* 38: 75–87.

—— (1993b) "How genetics and learning make a fish an individual: a case study on the paradise fish," in P. P. G. Bateson, P. H. Klopfer and N. S. Thompson (eds) *Perspectives in Ethology*, Vol. 10, *Behaviour and Evolution*, New York: Plenum Press, 1–52.

—— (1994) "Individuality and the emergence of culture during evolution. *World Future: the Journal of General Evolution*, 40: 207–213.

Csányi, V. and Kampis, G. (1985) "Autogenesis: Evolution of replicative systems," *Journal of Theoretical Biology* 114: 303–321.

—— (1987) "Modelling society: Dynamical replicative systems," *Cybernetics and Systems* 18: 233–249.

—— (1988) "Can we communicate with aliens?" in G. Marx (ed.) *Bioastronomy – The Next Steps*, Dordrecht: Kluwer Academic Publishers, 267–272.

Darwin, C. R. (1859) *The Origin of Species*, London: John Murray.

Dawkins, R. (1976) *The Selfish Gene*, New York: Oxford University Press.

Eibl-Eibesfeldt, I. (1979a) *The Biology of Peace and War*, New York: Viking Press.

—— (1979b) "Humanethology: Concepts and implications for sciences of man," *Behavioral and Brain Sciences* 2: 1–57.

—— (1982) "Warfare, man's indoctrinability and group selection," *Z. Tierpsychol.* 60: 177–198.

—— (1989) *Human Ethology*, New York: Aldine de Gruyter.

Glaserfeld, E. (1976) "The development of language as purposive behavior" in S. R. Harnad, H. S. Steklis, and J. Lancaster (eds) "Origins and Evolution of Language and Speech," *Annals of the New York Academy of Sciences*, 280: 212–226.

Gray, W. (1975) "Emotional cognitive structure theory and the development of a general systems psychotherapy," *General Systems* 20: 17–23.

Hayek, F. A. (1967) "Notes on the evolution of systems of rules of conduct: The interplay between rules of individual conduct and the social order of actions," in *Studies in Philosophy, Politics, and Economics*, Chicago: The University of Chicago Press, ch. 4, 66–81.

Ho, M. and Saunders, P. T. (1979) "Beyond neodarwinism: An epigenetic approach to evolution," *Journal of Molecular Evolution* 78: 573–591.

Kampis, G. (1985) "Biological information as a system description," in R. Trappl (ed.) *Cybernetics and Systems '86*, Dordrecht: D. Reidel, 39–46.

—— (1987a) "Some problems of system descriptions. I. Function," *International Journal of General Systems* 13: 143–156.

—— (1987b) "Some problems of system descriptions. II. Information," *International Journal of General Systems* 13: 157–171.

—— (1988) "Information, computation and complexity,' in M. E. Carvallo (ed.) *Nature, Cognition and System I*, Dordrecht: Kluwer Academic Publishers, 313–320.

—— (1991) *Self-modifying Systems: A new framework for dynamics, information, and complexity*, Oxford–New York: Pergamon.

Kampis, G. and Csányi, V. (1987a) "A computer model of autogenesis," *Kybernetes* 16: 169–181.

—— (1987b) "Replication in abstract and natural systems," *Biosystems* 20: 143–152.

—— (1988) "A system approach to the creating process," *IFSR Newsletter* No. 20: 2–4.

—— (1991) "Life, self-reproduction and information: Beyond the machine metaphor," *Journal of Theoretical Biology* 148: 17–32.

Khalil, E. L. (1992) "Hayek's spontaneous order and Varela's autopoiesis: A comment," *Human Systems Management* 11: 101–105.

—— (1994) "Rules," in G. Hodgson, M. Tool, and W. J. Samuels (eds) *The Elgar Comparison to Institutional and Evolutionary Economics, L–z*. Aldershot, UK: Edward Elgar, 253–264.

King, G. A. M. (1982) "Recycling, reproduction and life origins," *Biosystems* 15: 87–89.

Koestler, A. (1963) *The Sleepwalkers*, New York: The Universal Library, Grosset and Dunlap.

Lee, R. (1969) "!Kung bushmen subsistence: An input–output analysis," in P. Vayda (ed.) *Environment and Cultural Behavior*, Garden City, N.Y.: Natural History Press.

Mackay, D. M. (1951–52) "Mindlike behaviour of artifacts," *British Journal of Philosophy* 2: 105–121.

Mandelbrot, B. (1977) *Fractals: Form, Chance and Dimension*, San Francisco: W. H. Freeman and Co.

Maturana, H. R. (1975) *Autopoietic Systems: A Characterization of the Living Organization*, Urbana: University of Illinois.

Maynard-Smith, J. (1969) *The Theory of Evolution*, London: Penguin.

Montagu, A. (1976) "Toolmaking, hunting and the origin of language and speech," in S. R. Harnad, H. D. Steklis and J. Lancaster (eds) "Origins and Evolution of Language and Speech," *Annals of the New York Academy of Sciences* 280: 226–274.

Morowitz, H. J. (1968) *Energy Flow in Biology*, New York: Academic Press.

Morris, D. (1962) *The Biology of Art*, London: Knopf.

Pantzar, M. and Csányi, V. (1991) "Replicative model of the evolution of the business organization," *Journal of Social and Biological Structures*, 14(2): 149–163.

Passingham, R. (1982) *The Human Primate*, Oxford: W. H. Freeman.

Pattee, H. H. (1965) "The recognition of hereditary order in primitive chemical synthesis," in S. W. Fox (ed.) *The Origin of Prebiological Systems*, New York: Academic Press.

Polanyi, M. (1968) "Life's irreducible structure," *Science* 160: 1308–1312.

Prigogine, I. and Stengers, I. (1984) *Order out of Chaos*, New York: Bantam.

Richards, G. (1987) *Human Evolution: An Introduction for the Behavioural Sciences*, London: Routledge and Kegan Paul.

Riedl, R. (1978) *Order in Living Organisms*, New York: John Wiley.

Sebeok, T. A. and Umiker-Sebeok, J. (eds) *1980: Speaking of Apes*, New York: Plenum Press.

Spencer, H. (1862) *First Principle*.

Sterrer, W. (1992) "Prometheus and Proteus: The creative, unpredictable individual in evolution," *Evolution and Cognition* 1: 101–129.

Varela, F. G., Maturana, H. R. and Uribe, R. (1974) "Autopoiesis, the organization of living systems, its characterization and a model," *Biosystems* 5: 187–196.

Zeleny, M. (1977) "Self-organization of living systems: A formal model of autopoiesis," *International Journal of General Systems*. 4: 13–28.

8

HUMAN SOCIETY AS AN EMERGING GLOBAL SUPERORGANISM

A biological perspective[1]

Gregory B. Stock and John H. Campbell

INTRODUCTION

Civilization is made up of human beings and the things they have created. These include buildings, cities and machines, as well as domesticated animals and plants. Other distinctive elements of civilization are primarily organizational – business corporations, public health organizations, governments, and financial markets. All such structures are integrated into a functioning whole capable of maintaining an unprecedented degree of dynamic activity.

A biological perspective sheds light on how this global network functions. The modern developed world can be viewed as an organized biological being, a superorganism in which individual humans play roles analogous to the cells in a multicellular organism. In this view buildings, roads and dams parallel the extracellular tissue components in an animal's body. Even crops and livestock have their organismic counterparts – the intracellular algae that are essential symbiotes in organisms ranging from lichens to corals.

A hundred years ago humanity was fragmented into relatively independent regions, but increasingly, humankind is joined together by a dense web of communication links and trade. Today, locations are linked not only by obvious physical pathways such as highways and phone lines but by a myriad of hidden connections. Unknowingly we walk above pipes and cables, beneath airplane flight corridors and satellite broadcasts, and through radio and television transmissions.

Henceforth, we will refer to this global entity of humanity and its creations as *Metaman*, meaning "beyond and transcending humans." We use the new term to avoid the many associations tied to words such as "society" and "civilization." Metaman functions as an integrated living being in that it possesses a metabolism, is tied together by extensive long-range transports of materials and information and even senses and responds to environmental changes. In short, Metaman functions as a global superorganism rapidly extending across the face of the earth.

The metaphor of society as a living thing is not new. It has been with us since the ancient Greeks, always expressed in ways that reflected the knowledge, philosophy, and vocabulary of the times.[2] In the twelfth century John of Salisbury, inspired by Aristotle,[3] likened society to a creature in which each class played its God-given role. The king was the head, the church the soul, judges and governors the eyes and ears, soldiers the hands, and the peasants the feet.[4] In the mid-nineteenth century, Herbert Spencer in his *Principles of Sociology*, drew a more detailed and systematic analogy between a biological organism and society, which he described as a "social organism."[5] In the early 1900s, Pierre Teilhard de Chardin, biologist and Jesuit priest, linked evolutionary ideas to the concept.[6] He proposed, in both biological and spiritual terms, the growing union of humankind to be an evolutionary transition towards a divine state. More recently, in the 1960s, the evolutionist Theodosius Dobzhansky, extended de Chardin's biological ideas in his book, *The Biology of Ultimate Concern*.[7]

These persons and others have reached for ways of understanding the power, connectedness and dynamics of human society. These qualities, which are becoming more evident every day to even the most casual observer, suggest that a biological interpretation of human society is more than metaphor.

The idea that human society is in reality a superorganism implies that civilization is part of nature rather than separate from it. Moreover, the most notable features of advanced civilization, its complex internal organization, growth, and ability to change can be explained by the concepts of evolutionary biology and physiology. First, modern society is the product of Darwinian evolution and Metaman's continuing evolution is governed by extensions of the same competitive and self-organizing processes that spawned the biological world. Second, analogs to many of the organizational features seen in higher organisms are displayed by Metaman and exist quite simply because they are prerequisites for the existence of any integrated living thing.

Other articles in this volume offer a variety of viewpoints about complex systems, but in developing our biological interpretation of human society, we have deliberately chosen to build from an exploration of the actual working of society rather than from extensions of theoretical abstractions about complex systems. We have done this because we believe that at the present state of understanding about both systems theory and society, our approach yields the richest insights about the nature of human society, its future evolution, and the likely consequences of various real-world economic and social policy options. Thus, throughout this chapter we will be looking at rather familiar activities taking place within modern society and re-interpreting them within a new framework, that of the biological entity we have labelled "Metaman."

PHYSIOLOGY OF METAMAN

The most visible resemblance of Metaman to a superorganism is the organization of its parts into systems corresponding to the physiological ones of animals. These correspondences occur because Metaman has to meet most of the same functional challenges that animals do. It must fuel its activities, repair itself, protect itself from environmental insult, and eliminate whatever toxic by-products it produces. To do this, Metaman has developed digestive, circulatory, excretory, and nervous systems. To clarify the concept of Metaman, we will briefly survey three of these, noting both their parallels with the organs of animals and the ways in which they have been extended in Metaman beyond the organizational constraints present in animals.

Digestion

To survive, all living things must take in raw materials and energy. Metaman ingests and converts large quantities of new materials into its substance for purposes of replacement and growth. Animal and plant matter sustains its human parts while diverse metal ores, petrochemicals, minerals and other raw materials sustain its nonbiological components.

Metaman has discrete systems to assimilate each of these materials. Iron is an example. Its ore is gouged from the earth at hundreds of mines on every continent and hauled to huge nearby smelters. Here the metal is extracted and combined with specified amounts of carbon and other minerals into steel. Sheets, ingots, rods, and other forms are then shuttled to even more numerous factories, where they are fabricated into parts for products ranging from tractors to typewriters.

It is easy to identify the businesses and structures that exist to ingest and digest materials as foodstuffs of Metaman. They are as specialized for their function as is the gastrointestinal tract of an animal. It is also apparent that the digestive system of our planetary superorganism has advanced beyond the simple linear layout of the vertebrate digestive system. Not only does Metaman mine raw materials at widely scattered sites and process them in equally dispersed locales, but its digestive products are more varied than the relatively few forms that serve as metabolic intermediates in our own bodies.

In addition to the materials it incorporates into its structure Metaman consumes fossil fuels and electric power in prodigious quantities to fuel its metabolic machinery. Indeed, the new energy sources that brought the industrial revolution have been critical to Metaman's birth and are essential for its continued evolution. The ability to control and distribute this power by converting it to electricity has been even more critical to Metaman's formation. Metaman is able to exist as an integrated whole by virtue of the telecommunication, computer, and other electronic technologies that allow the coordination of distant activities throughout the world. This coordination in turn brings ever greater specialization within Metaman, and leads to the flow of ever larger amounts of materials among the countless loci of activity in Metaman.

Circulation

For a complex organism to function, it must be able to move materials from one part to another. Metaman's global dimensions require an especially elaborate circulatory system. Vast webs of highways, railways, shipping lanes, and airline corridors crisscross the globe enabling Metaman to shuttle materials among its many parts in hundreds of millions of vehicles.[8] In addition, aqueducts capable of emptying whole rivers convey water for crops, industry, and humans.[9] In the United States alone, more than a million miles of trunk pipelines carry natural gas, and there are four million miles of roadway.[10] These transmission systems integrate the activities of individual persons, businesses, cities, and nations into a functionally interdependent whole.

Watching vehicles move along highways that branch into smaller roadways brings to mind the circulation in our own blood vessels. The comparison is apt but fails to do justice to the full complexity of Metaman's circulation. Animal blood is simply pooled in a central heart and pumped to the periphery. Metaman, however, must move such a complex range of materials from so many sources to so many destinations that no simple flow pattern will suffice.

One major innovation has been for Metaman to ship items directly to specific locations instead of dispersing materials indiscriminately throughout its structure. This circulatory enhancement makes it possible for widely separated organizations within Metaman to cooperate to a degree hitherto unachievable. A clothing manufacturer can depend upon particular companies for its thread, cloth, buttons, packaging. A car can be built progressively in factories on different continents. A small retail store can sell goods from all over the world. This system endows the superorganism with great plasticity because the routing of materials can be modified to readily form and alter collaborations.

In addition to "addressable" routing, Metaman extends the circulatory system of animals in another way. Metaman transports finished products as well as raw materials. This ability permits components of Metaman to specialize their activities to very high degrees. A carpenter building a house installs doors, electrical outlets, tiles, air conditioners, heaters, toilets, sinks, and refrigerators, each fabricated in a specialized factory located somewhere across the globe. Historically, advances in transportation generally have preceded increases in manufacturing specialization and capacity.[11]

Nervous system

The most elaborate part of Metaman's physiology is that which integrates the activities of its many parts into one harmonious whole. The more complex a creature is, the more extensive such coordination must be. Thus, it should be no surprise that a mouse's brain system is more elaborate than an earthworm's ganglion and that Metaman's "nervous system" is immensely more powerful than any animal's. Nevertheless, all sophisticated nervous systems depend on the same four fundamental activities: sensing, conducting information, interpreting, and responding, and are as apparent in Metaman as in animals.

Sensing Metaman has countless sense receptors to monitor its environment and itself, and its sensory capabilities are proliferating rapidly. Radio telescopes detect subvisible radiation from space while nuclear magnetic resonance imagers accurately picture the inside of living tissue. Sensors are placed in spy satellites thousands of miles up in space, in weather stations on the polar ice caps and in earthquake monitors thousands of feet below the surface of the earth. Sensory receptors of every shape and kind generate a flood of data about Metaman's environment. Metaman also monitors its own internal state. Just as an animal must have its proprioception, Metaman needs information about its own activities. Therefore, health organizations track disease incidence, intelligence agencies monitor military capabilities, governments measure industrial production and employment, and companies collect marketing data. Metaman simply could not function as a superorganism without this stream of information about itself.

Human beings, as well as mechanical devices, play an important sensory role in Metaman. Like a dense cloud of complex sensors, they penetrate into everything – watching, interpreting, and recording. But as Metaman orchestrates more and more facets of its economic, social, and intellectual activity, it requires more information than humans alone could possibly provide, so the collection of data is becoming increasingly automated. Computers tally financial transactions, electronic devices record which television programs people watch and automatic counters measure traffic on highways. No individual keeps track of the time we spend on the telephone, although we are billed for each of our calls. Even though all the telephone operators in Italy could not count them, we could discover, if we cared to know, that Italians initiated 785 million minutes of international telephone calls in 1988.[12] Individuals are oblivious to vast domains of monitored data but this information is crucial for Metaman to function.

Transferring the responsibility for collecting information from human to dedicated machine is a significant trend that allows Metaman to sense global conditions beyond the possibilities of individual people. For example, in 1975 the extent of world deforestation could be gauged only by contacting forestry officials in as many relevant countries as possible and assembling their individual assessments into a blurry, incomplete picture. Today, satellites track deforestation by monitoring changing patterns of vegetation throughout the world.[13] Such collective global "vision" is not that of any individual person, but of Metaman as a whole.

Communication   The single most important factor uniting human activity in the developed world is Metaman's rapidly unfolding system of communication. To a large extent this system operates along the same strategies used by higher organisms.

Our body uses two modes of communication: Neurons and hormones. These are closely integrated as two arms of a neuroendocrine system. Nerves mediate rapid direct communication to particular cells in the body. Endocrine hormones broadcast information more slowly throughout the body and coordinate very large numbers of cells into coherent physiological states. For example, sex hormones initiate the changes of puberty; adrenaline prepares various organs for a flight or fight response; and thyroid hormone regulates basal metabolism throughout the body.

Metaman has comparable modes of communication, using both addressed and widely broadcasted information. Telephone lines have an obvious parallel with axons of neurons that send information as propagated electrical impulses to specific targets, but with some major enhancements. Telephones, for example, can directly connect *any* two parties and also transmit much greater information than axons can.

Telecommunication shows how rapidly Metaman's capacity to transmit information is growing. Today, a century after the arrival of the telephone, over 220 million phones in the United States are connected by 1.3 billion miles of telephone line.[14] Internationally, telephone traffic has doubled in just the past four years.[15] Metaman now channels a great variety of messages as electrical impulses through electrical cables, optical fibers, microwaves, satellites, and radio waves. Banks wire money, computers transmit data, stores verify credit, and individuals talk. At any moment some five million pairs of distant elements of Metaman are in dialog within the US and half of that volume of telephone traffic is data transmission rather than voice.[16]

Newspapers, magazines, radio and television are the broadcast arm of Metaman's communication system. They are publicly accessible to any person who cares to tap into their information. Some are localized to various degrees, such as a hometown newspaper or local TV program. Others disseminate information throughout the world.

Interpreting   Sensory data stream continually through Metaman. Some are examined locally while others are passed on to processing centers. For example, an air-traffic control tower locally interprets moment-to-moment airplane traffic and immediate weather conditions. At the other end of the spectrum stock markets interpret diverse and widely scattered information. Buy and sell orders from throughout the world drive price movements, and anything relevant that happens anywhere is soon reflected in a stock's price.

The marketplace is Metaman's most subtle and pervasive mechanism for interpreting information. Where prices are free to rise and fall in response to changing conditions price adjustments and shifts in economic activity are powerful interpreters of diverse information. Just as the price of a stock at any given moment embodies vast amounts of information, so too does the price of a pair of jeans. It integrates information about the cost of labor and material, trends in fashion, the competitive activity of other firms, and the general economic climate. Change one factor significantly and the price of jeans will change. The marketplace is integrating information and interpreting it continually. Moreover, it is a processing system that is massively parallel. At every instant, vast numbers of transactions are occurring simultaneously throughout the economy. This is what makes the market system so powerful and is allowing it to displace other more bureaucratic systems.

Humanity's accumulation of knowledge has been critical to Metaman's evolution. However, instead of growing steadily, the capacity to handle information has jumped several times, with great consequences. The first major leap was brought by language and the creation of oral traditions. Later, the arrival of writing allowed information to be readily stored outside the human mind. Then, printing spread knowledge broadly, and now electronics, especially the computer, is allowing information to be stored in dynamic patterns rather than static ones.

Today, Metaman processes huge amounts of information through human thought, computer calculation, and various combinations of the two in the large organizational networks found in science, government, business, and elsewhere. Each of these cognitive systems is a component of Metaman's "brain."

The human mind, for instance, generally is but a tiny cog in more elaborate structures for interpreting data. Every farmer decides what to plant based on many intricate factors, including long-range weather forecasts, general economic indicators, commodity price projections, and government policies. Thus the farmer, sitting atop a huge pyramid of interpreted data, is but one cognitive element in a global system for making agricultural decisions.

Responding   It is clear that the activities of Metaman are highly integrated. This superorganism exhibits higher level behaviors that are as "purposeful" as the physiology of an organism. For example, just as a human body will actively heal a cut finger, Metaman will mobilize assistance to a city devastated by an earthquake. To appreciate the equivalence of these two processes we must choose the right perspective. Humanitarian aid, though it may arise from the concern of individuals, also is Metaman's purposeful reponse to trauma. After all, our body, too, functions through the actions of individual cells. Each cell has a perfectly good cellular reason for what it does when a finger is injured even though collectively their activities are our body's healing response to the wound. If we monitored the behavior of the individual cells forming a scar, we could explain the particular activities of each in terms of local stimuli ranging from changes in chemical conditions to reception of specific messages from neighboring cells. Yet together, all of these activities would form the larger response of the body as a whole.

"Global warming" provides another example of Metaman's higher level behavior. A rising tide of concern and reaction to this potential problem has emerged quite suddenly during the past decade: Journalists write articles, scientists perform experiments, government bodies debate the issue, environmentalist groups demand action. This is not the program of any individual or group but an organismic response welling up from within Metaman. Indeed, an individual cannot even perceive climatic change on a planetary scale. To detect a half degree of global warming, as has occurred in the past century, requires satellites, thousands of remote sensors and powerful computers to analyze data. *Metaman's* response to this threat is just as purposeful as that of any organism faced with possible danger, even though this superorganism acts slowly by human standards because its size and timescale are very different from our own.

DOES METAMAN THINK?

That Metaman has the functional equivalent of a nervous system suggests the obvious question of whether this planetary superorganism has the capacity to "think." Information flows in the human brain as patterns of electrical and chemical activity that we manipulate in rich, complex ways called thinking. However, the human memory has limited capacity and easily loses information. Civilization overcame these problems by storing information outside the human mind, on physical materials such as paper and film. This furnished unlimited amounts of secure storage, but at a price. Unlike mental representations, information inscribed externally could not be instantaneously retrieved or manipulated. It was static. Now, however, externally stored information is being returned to patterns of dynamic activity, enabling Metaman to manipulate huge amounts of information within its network of global connections: Climate simulations, election tallies, telephone switching systems, global banking systems. These are all elements in a dispersed cognitive system that is in essence the "brain" of Metaman. Moreover, this brain does more than just shuffle and store information, it interprets and processes that information. Such "thinking" may be crude at present but is rapidly growing more complex.

One can even speak of an attention span of Metaman. When we are badly startled, a jolt of adrenaline alerts heart, brain, and other organs to possible danger. Similarly, in Metaman, events such as the 1986 Chernobyl disaster or Iraq's 1990 seizure of Kuwait immediately resonated through the media. Laying hold of the world's attention, these events rapidly provoked diverse and widespread responses ranging from abrupt shifts in financial markets to changes in individual travel plans. Then they slipped out of the world's attention. This resembles the workings of human consciousness. The attention of someone walking along a street may fix briefly on a brightly colored sign, then jump to the face of a stranger and then be seized by the screech of a car's brakes. We suggest that Metaman eventually will possess not only a mind but a consciousness. Indeed, when the mental manifestations of consciousness are understood Metaman may well be found already to be very close to possessing them.

IS METAMAN ALIVE?

Metaman's digestion, circulation, excretion and nervous systems show how deeply this superorganism's "physiology" resembles that of animals. These physiological systems have developed because they underlie processes that are basic to all higher life. There is still no universal consensus on what "living" means; however, life is generally recognized to be a self-perpetuating dynamic state manifesting at least two essential processes. One of these is the regulation of an organism's special internal conditions – homeostasis. The other is evolutionary change. Both are conspicuous in Metaman.

Metaman is increasingly able to regulate its "internal" environment in order to insulate its activities from external climate and weather. Not only do giant dams protect regions from floods and irrigation projects lessen the effects of drought but Metaman also maintains countless local micro-environments tailored to the particular needs of its diverse parts. Even so sturdy a structure as a bridge needs constant painting or it will corrode. The more sophisticated a device is, the more exacting are the conditions in which it must be maintained. Computer chips must be manufactured in ultra-clean rooms and tissue culture requires sterile chambers and cryogenic storage tanks. Homeostasis is so essential a condition for living systems that it almost defines the physical domain of Metaman. The areas and structures of the globe that are part of Metaman can be identified by the constant conditions that Metaman has imposed on them.

A significant aspect of Metaman's homeostasis is to create the comfortable micro-environments for humans. Our homes, factories and offices are heated or cooled to our liking, and artificially lighted to bring us day or night at any hour. Comfortable, sanitary conditions in the workplace and home allow human beings to function optimally in the increasingly complex activities occurring within Metaman.

Another aspect of homeostasis is turnover. Living material is not static but continually replaced. Just as organisms must replace individual molecules, organelles, cells and tissue structures to counter ageing and deterioration, so too, turnover is a conspicuous aspect of Metaman. This superorganism's material is continually replaced at all levels: Crops, machines, buildings, people, and even larger organizational structures. As in animals, replacement occurs across a spectrum of timescales, which sometimes obscures its extent. The world's automobile fleet is replaced in some fifteen years,[17] the turnover of industrial equipment averages under twenty years,[18] and buildings are replaced in fifty to a hundred years. Such turnover is even explicitly recognized in tax codes as depreciation allowances.

In biological systems turnover is distinct from damage repair in that it occurs routinely while the ageing components are still functional. Metaman also is turning over more and more material before it fails. Bus tires are changed before they are threadbare because the expense and danger of a breakdown is greater than the cost of a new tire. Buildings often are torn down not because they are crumbling but to make room for new buildings, and electronic equipment is generally discarded as superior equipment becomes available. A ten-year-old computer seems hopelessly primitive, even if it still works as well as ever. The most advanced parts of Metaman have become throwaway societies that do not keep items in use for their complete lifetime, but instead program their replacement as preventive maintenance or to make room for innovation. This does not mean that Metaman is increasingly wasteful of resources. Just the opposite is true. Biological systems are notable for the efficiency with which they recycle their materials. Cells may turnover but their constituent elements are scavenged and reused. Thus the broad trend towards material recycling and efficiency is one certain to strengthen within Metaman.

EVOLUTION OF METAMAN

An important reason to understand society from a biological perspective is to cope with its staggering rate of change. Often the various changes in society are simply lumped together as "development." Biologists are more discriminating by distinguishing four types of change: Turnover, growth, ontogeny (that is, embryonic development), and evolution. Each has its counterpart in the dynamics of Metaman. We have already discussed turnover, and growth too is straightforward. It is simply an increase in size without significant change in form. Metaman grows when new farm

190

land is brought under the plow, population increases or underdeveloped parts of the world become "westernized." These processes enlarge Metaman by producing more of the same. Metaman has grown across the planet in recent times, drawing ever more of the world into the unified pattern of organization and activity that is the developed world.

Evolution and ontogeny are more creative changes. They produce qualitative change instead of just growth. In multi-cellular organisms these processes are distinct. Evolution is the change across successions of generations of organisms. Ontogeny, which creates the adult form from a fertilized egg, is development within an individual organism. This distinction between evolution and development is not applicable to Metaman. Because it does not (or has yet to) reproduce and continues to exist as a single superorganism,[19] the progressive change within Metaman resembles a process of biological development instead of evolution. However, several key properties of Metaman's progress clearly identify most of its change as evolutionary.

Foremost, Metaman's long-term development is unprogrammed. In contrast, ontogeny is a genetically scheduled process to produce a predetermined end product from a starting egg. The repeated unfolding of a developmental program will give rise to individuals as alike as peas in a pod. Also ontogeny is notably buffered from interference by the environment by various mechanisms. In contrast, evolution is an unplanned and unrepeatable process that is generally thought of as a direct response to environmental contingencies. Some processes within Metaman are carried out according to a development-like program. For example, constructing a new highway is a repeated process identical to many other such efforts. However, the overall progress of civilization has the characteristics of unguided biological evolution rather than an unfolding developmental program.

Metaman's evolution also resembles biological evolution in extending beyond change in physical form to change in the information that underlies form. The development of an egg into a chick is epigenetic – adult cells have exactly the same genetic message as the egg. In contrast, the essence of biological evolution is change in *genetic* constitution with the alterations in phenotype following as secondary consequences. In the case of Metaman, change occurs in laws, building codes, written traditions, scientific knowledge, technological advances, international treaties, genetic constitutions of domesticated animals and plants, and organizational forms, and then the evolution in this information base drives the physical progression of Metaman.

The growth of Metaman has the adaptive quality of evolution, too. Individual multi-cellular organisms can adjust to particular conditions, but their range of adaptability is rigidly circumscribed by their genetics. Although a weasel may turn white in the winter it cannot grow webbed feet or gills if its habitat becomes flooded. To achieve the latter would require evolution. Metaman seems capable of the broader adaptability characteristic of biological evolution.

That Metaman's evolution is adaptive, is seen by its increasing ability to exploit more and more resources and opportunities. Moreover, changes in Metaman are driven by competition, the *sine qua non* of biological evolution.[20] Indeed, Thomas Malthus recognized the role of survival of the fittest even before Darwin formulated his theory of natural selection. However, natural selection engages a superorganism like Metaman differently from plants and animals. This is a necessary consequence of Metaman's enormously greater size, its existence as a single individual instead of a population and its persistence without reproduction. These qualities require Darwinian mechanisms that extend beyond those operating on biological organisms.

As the result of three such extensions, Metaman is evolving millions of times faster than typical organisms. First, Metaman has internalized natural selection: External competition between separate organisms has given way to internal competition among component elements within one superorganism. For example, TV broadcasts compete with print media, and different automobile manufacturers vie with each other. Second, conscious design has supplanted random variation as a source of novelty. New products are invented, corporate reorganizations are planned, and machines are designed. Third, competition among real, material entities (for example, organizations and products) has been joined by that among abstract representations (concepts, ideas, and plans). Thus, the army might conceive a weapon, simulate its operation, find it less effective than an alternative, and abandon it without ever building it.

Internal competition   Metaman is composed of diverse, partially redundant systems which vigorously compete. In doing so they force innovation in each other. For example, several distinct networks serve to transport goods: highway, rail, air, and water. Each provides slightly different but overlapping services. Because they continually struggle to capture old and new business from one another each network must unceasingly push to keep up with the best. Any which fails to do so will shrink or be replaced by its rivals.

The transition in everyday communication from the postal service to the telephone provides a good example of such change, as does the sharp increase in mail-order sales in the United States at the expense of store purchases. Intense internal competition also exists among intangibles such as organizational and management structures. The multinational corporation, for example, has become the globally dominant organizational form in many industries.

Ideas and designs   Competition among ideas and the use of design are the two other major mechanisms of evolutionary change. These allow an organization as large and dynamic as Metaman to evolve rapidly enough to maintain itself in the face of large-scale change. By imagining things-that-are-not, projecting them into an imaginary future and observing their potential performance, Metaman is able to direct its resources to the most promising possibilities. Today competition is increasingly a fierce but bloodless struggle between competing ideas, with the reward of success being physical existence and failure leading not to disappearance but to non-appearance.

So routine and natural does this seem that it is easy for us to overlook its enormous implications. Not only are the time and energy required to develop models and ideas minuscule compared to what would be needed to build real structures, but Metaman can change in anticipation rather than in response to need.

To appreciate these advantages consider the problem of designing an aircraft carrier that will handle well in high seas, accommodate squadrons of aircraft, and satisfy the many other specialized demands of this unique and complex vessel. Imagine "evolving" the carrier by a simple Darwinian process, starting, for instance, with a battleship as a prototype and modifying it and its progeny by incorporating haphazard plan changes into entirely new ships and taking them out to sea for action. The notion seems absurd. Humanity would exhaust the world's iron and oil resources before coming even close to creating a working aircraft carrier. Clearly there is a degree of size and complexity that simply cannot be achieved by ordinary Darwinian evolution. Metaman could not exist were it not evolving by new evolutionary mechanisms.

As Metaman matures it is refining its power to conceive projective models. Computer-aided design enables bridges, buildings, and dams to withstand expected peak stresses, econometric models gauge the anticipated effects of economic policies, marketing models assist in setting production levels, population and traffic projections guide city planners, and impact studies help evaluate environmental effects. These planning techniques are among the fastest evolving aspects of Metaman, and are driving Metaman forward ever more rapidly. It is hard to imagine where they will lead in coming millennia, much less the millions of years previously characterizing significant biological evolutionary change.

THE SWEEP OF MACROEVOLUTION

Advances in evolutionary mechanisms allow Metaman to evolve more rapidly and effectively than any entity ever has before. Their power is so great, in fact, that many biologists hesitate to accept the progress of Metaman as "biological evolution" at all. They reserve the notion for the comparatively feeble way that random mutation and selection is able to operate on biological species. However, this narrow view overlooks the clear connection between civilization and the natural world.

To understand the enormous biological significance of the complex of man, machine, and domesticated plants and animals that is modern civilization we must step back and survey the broad sweep of evolution from life's first beginnings to its present. The most fundamental change, of course, is the appearance of ever more complex forms of life. Bacteria, which evolved early in our planet's history, are simple compared to more recent arrivals. Even the most primitive jellyfish is undeniably more complex than ancient single-celled creatures. This is obvious, but the way complexity has evolved is interesting. It has advanced in abrupt steps in which existing organisms have joined with one another to create larger, composite creatures. Thus, the living world is a hierarchy of levels of complexity, and organisms at each level are not only more complex than ones below, they are actually composed of simpler living forms.

Major transitions to new levels of organization have been exceedingly rare: Only four are known since life's beginnings on the planet. The first was the tight association of biochemicals into bacterial cells some 3.6 billion years ago when the non-living at its most complex gave rise to life at its simplest.[21] Next, simple prokaryotes fused symbiotically into the compound eukaryotic cell, some 1.5 billion years ago.[22] Seven hundred million years ago clusters of these higher cells united into multi-cellular organisms.[23] Now, billions of individual higher organisms are grouping into a social superorganism. This brief recapitulation of macro-evolution shows the enormous significance of human civilization. Life is in the midst of an evolutionary breakthrough as momentous as that which brought the first multi-cellular organisms and at the center of this transition is humanity.

SUPERORGANISMS OR ECOSYSTEMS

We have compared civilization with a biological organism. Some analysts have suggested, however, that society corresponds to an ecosystem instead.[24] The crucial distinction is that an organism is more than the simple sum of its parts. An ecosystem may be cut in half without causing significant effects, except right at the new edges. An impenetrable fence built across a large desert, steppe, or rainforest would not affect its ecology. Also, one part of an ecosystem will be insensitive to a fire, plague or flood raging elsewhere in the ecosystem.

Western civilization is entirely different. A medical breakthrough in the United States, an interest rate hike in Germany, a manufacturing advance in Japan, or a war in the Balkans all send repercussions throughout the civilized world. Cutting America off from Japan or Europe would be as traumatic to the economics of both regions as pulling an earthworm in two

194

would be to that organism. True, the individual parts in both cases would eventually heal when the halves regenerated the missing functional parts. However, a severed Japan or US would undergo a massive reorganization as it re-formed into an autonomous functional whole. As time progresses and global integration continues such partitioning would be increasingly traumatic. Ecosystems offer no parallels. Nor does the earlier world of mankind. Dividing North America down the middle in 1492 would have gone unnoticed to all but a very few of the native inhabitants. Further back in time, cavemen probably would have been oblivious to things happening even fifty miles away.

Looking upon western society as an ecosystem of people ignores the most important dynamics of our economic, political, military, scientific, and technological life. Indeed Metaman is defined by the degree to which western society has progressed from an ecosystem-like organization where interactions were primarily local to that of a superorganism where actions are often felt globally.

IMPLICATIONS

This biological perspective of Metaman has many implications for public policy issues, a few of which we briefly sketch below.

Technology Because Metaman is largely the union of humans and machines, the continued rapid advance of technology is central to its well-being. Essentially, there are no other ways of solving the world's environmental, population, food, and health problems. These are Metaman's problems. The human population is too large to hope to turn back the clock and return to simpler times. Technological progress accelerates change, but the relationship between humanity and technology is inherently a symbiotic one of deep interdependence, not one of conflict. Thus, attempts to block technological progress are not only doomed to eventual failure, they are likely to frustrate rather than aid in the solution of humanity's larger problems.

Energy consumption Metaman's consumption of energy and materials is likely to grow increasingly efficient, but overall consumption is unlikely to be long reduced or even held to current levels. As Metaman's metabolism is refined, its activities are likely to expand, and Metaman's increasing activities will require more energy to fuel them, not less. Thus the long-term solution to humanity's energy problems requires more than conservation. It requires the development of large renewable energy resources to supplement and eventually replace the planet's fossil fuels. As with all other organisms energy will always be critical for keeping Metaman vital.

Change Understanding how Metaman evolves is of more than academic importance; it improves our understanding of the public policies needed to keep a society vital over the long term. For example, Metaman's use of internal competition to evolve suggests the inevitability of internal change within societies and the potential value of enhancing mechanisms that facilitate this process. Metaman is resilient because of the continual creation and destruction taking place within it. Most contemporary institutions, industries, and organizations will eventually succumb to more robust replacements, and such change is a sign of health not of sickness. Thus, in the long run, a society will generally benefit from spending resources to foster growth in new industries and help people migrate towards them, rather than struggling to protect fading industries and the jobs they contain.

International cooperation Metaman is a creature of connections, and it is strengthened by fostering global interdependencies. The major problems humanity faces today are global and cannot be addressed by the action of any individual nation. Policies that promote an illusion of local or national independence from the activities of the rest of the world are likely to be counterproductive. For example, isolation from global trade may temporarily reduce employment problems but cannot permanently solve them. The current difficulties experienced by the economies of India and Argentina illustrate the problems that are spawned by isolation from the larger global economy.

Coordination Biological systems are controlled through a hierarchy of control systems ascending from local to global levels. Such a hierarchy is appearing within Metaman too. It is arising at the expense of other levels of control that evolved before Metaman became a global agency. In particular, the nation-state is in decline and its powers are migrating to both international and local levels. On the one hand, nations are fragmenting under urgent demands for regional autonomy, and on the other they are being transcended by international bodies such as the European Economic Community. These two trends are a natural consequence of Metaman's continuing evolution towards a biological-like hierarchy of control.

The environment Darwinian evolution will no longer be the major influence on the planetary environment. It is Metaman that will increasingly shape the evolution of the earth's biosphere. Even so, the environmental changes taking place today are as "natural" as those of any previous geological era because civilization is a part of nature, not separate from it. Attempts to simply stop human impact on the environment may slow environmental change but alone they will neither arrest it nor effectively direct its course. Humanity must eventually face the choices that come

196

from Metaman's existence and consider the kind of environment it wishes to bring into being.

NOTES

1 A comprehensive exploration of the concepts in this chapter and their broad implications for humanity can be found in Stock, Gregory (1993) *The Fourth Phase: Our Evolving Leap to Metaman*, New York: Simon & Schuster. In the UK (1993) *Metaman: The Merging of Humans and Machines into a Global Superorganism*, London: Bantam Press.

2 For a discussion of the antiquity of this idea see Merchant, Carolyn (1983) *The Death of Nature: Women, Ecology, and the Scientific Revolution*, San Francisco: Harper & Row, ch. 4, "The World an Organism."

3 Book I, ch. 3 and Book VII, ch. 9 of Aristotle's *Politics*, translated by Jowett, Benjamin (1941) in McKeon, Richard (ed.) *The Basic Works of Aristotle*, New York: Random House.

4 John of Salisbury (Bishop of Chartres) (1927) *The Statesman's Book*, selections from the *Policraticus*, written in 1159, trans. Dickinson, John, New York: Knopf, Book V, p. 65.

5 Spencer, Herbert (1897) *The Principles of Sociology*, Vol. 1, New York: Appleton and Co., p. 462.

6 Teilhard de Chardin, Pierre (1959) *The Phenomenon of Man*, New York: Harper & Row. See also Dobson, Edward (1984) *The Phenomenon of Man Revisited: A Biological Viewpoint on Teilhard de Chardin*, New York: Columbia University Press.

7 Dobzhansky, Theodosius (1967) *The Biology of Ultimate Concern*, New York: New American Library.

8 By 1988, there were some 550 million autos, trucks, and buses in the world. Bleviss, D. and Walzer, P. (1990) "Energy for motor vehicles," *Scientific American* 263(3): 103–109.

9 For instance, the Colorado river, which carved out the Grand Canyon, is now reduced to a trickle by the time it crosses into Mexico. By treaty, Mexico is guaranteed only 1.5 million acre feet from the Colorado river's yearly flow of some 13 million acre feet. Reisner, Marc (1986) *Cadillac Dessert*, New York: Viking.

10 *Statistical Abstract of the United States*, US Bureau of the Census, 1990, p. 599.

11 Beniger, James (1986) *The Control Revolution: Technological and Economic Origins of the Information Society*, Cambridge, Mass.: Harvard University Press, p. 204.

12 Staple, Gregory (1990) *The Global Telecommunication Traffic Boom: A Quantitative Brief on Cross-Border Markets and Regulation*, International Institute of Communications, London: Tavistock House South, p. 16.

13 Currently, the best method of measuring deforestation is to assemble large mosaic images covering the rainforests and other areas of interest, digitize the coordinates of the affected areas, and compute the deforestation totals. Cloud-free images of some 95 per cent of the Amazon rainforest are relatively easy to assemble. (Personal communication, Goddard Space Center.)

14 *Statistical Abstract of the United States*, US Bureau of the Census, 1987.

15 *Statistics of Communication Common Carriers*, Federal Communications Commission, Washington, D.C., 1989.

16 *New York Times*, 13 Nov., 1991. The estimate of 50 per cent data transmission is for 1991; within a decade an estimated 80 per cent of telephone traffic will be data transmission.

17 Altshuler, Alan, *et al.* (1985) *The Future of the Automobile: The Report of MIT's International Automobile Program*, Cambridge, Mass.: MIT Press, p. 9.

18 Ausubel, Jesse (1991) "Does climate still matter?" *Nature* 350: 649–652.

19 Metaman's current gropings towards space suggest that one day it will extend its form out into our solar system and beyond. This will be Metaman's reproduction. How far Metaman will eventually spread out into the galaxy, of course, is yet unclear.

20 An entirely different view from Darwinism is that evolution is a process of self-organization. Open systems inherently complexify with time by principles that apply to all systems. Evolution as self-organization has been developed for both social systems (e.g., Hayek, Friedrich A. (1988) *The Fatal Conceit*, ed. W. W. Bartley, III, Chicago: University of Chicago Press) and biological. Proponents of this view stress that the very same principles underlie the emergence of order across all levels of organization. In contrast orthodox Darwinists emphasize the uniqueness of evolution as it occurs in genetic systems.

21 Schopf, J. William (1992) "The oldest fossils and what they mean," in *Major Events in the History of Life*, Schopf, J. William (ed.) Boston: Jones and Bartlett Publishers.

22 For a general discussion of prokaryotes and eukaryotes see Alberts, Bruce, *et al.* (1989) *Molecular Biology of the Cell*, New York: Garland Publishing Inc., pp. 10–26.

23 For a discussion of the early evolution of multi-cellular organisms (metazoans) see Runnegar, Bruce (1992) "Evolution of the earliest animals," in *Major Events in the History of Life*, Schopf, J. William (ed.) Boston: Jones and Bartlett Publishers, ch. 3.

24 Khalil, Elias L. (1990) "Natural complex vs. natural system," *Journal of Social and Biological Structures* 13: 11–31, describes the multiple fundamental differences between an organism (as a natural *complex*) and an ecosystem (as a natural *system*). While some *parts* of Metaman have the relationship to their sub-elements of a "natural system," the global economy, politics and technology above all functions as a "natural complex."

9

NEUROLOGICAL AND SOCIAL BASES OF DOMINANCE IN HUMAN SOCIETY

Henri Laborit

A set is usually represented by a circle, within which smaller circles represent the elements of the set. The elements are not placed randomly with respect to each other, but rather they establish relationships among themselves. These relationships are neither mass nor energy;[1] they are only information, whereas the elements of the set will always be perceived as mass or energy (Figure 9.1). For example, a molecule is composed of a set of atoms, while an organ is a set of cell elements. By combining, organs give rise to systems (cardiovascular, endocrine, nervous, and so forth) and the latter combine to form an organism. By combining, organisms can form social sets, and so forth.

The set of relationships among elements constitutes what is called "Structure" (capital "s"). Humans cannot fully understand all the relationships existing among the elements of a set – in short, its Structure. They can understand only subsets of this set of relationships, i.e., substructures which are a part of the Structure. To put it simply, the basis of ideology is to believe that the structure (lower case "s") describing a subset of the set of relationships in reality constitutes the Structure. Every human group, even every individual, usually abstracts from his or her environment a structure, a subset of the total Structure and generalizes it as if it were the Structure. The symptoms of such pathology include the attempt to impose his or her particular abstraction on the rest of the community.

Thus when you inform me of something, you communicate with me a substructure of the set of structures you have appropriated. In this manner, you try to shape my approach. As a result, I retain at the least traces of your substructure that might affect my approach. In short, the structures we learn are only the elements of a total reality–Structure. It is, thus, of use to determine the largest number of elements of this set of relationships and to understand how they are organized, i.e., what relationships are established among them while still remembering that we might never understand the Structure.

199

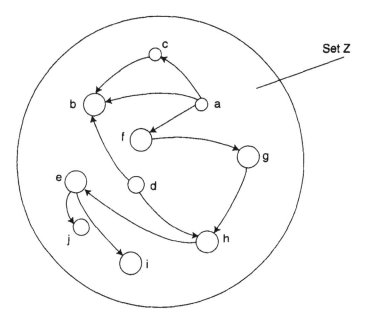

a,b,c,d,e,f,g,h,i,j = elements of set Z
The arrows represent the relationships among the elements of this set.

Figure 9.1 Venn diagram

STRUCTURE-INFORMATION AND MEMORIES

If we accept the etymological sense of information as "shaping," we need to distinguish a "structure-information" and a "circulating-information" (Laborit, 1974b).

The information which shapes an organism we have called "structure-information." It will enable us to distinguish a man from an elephant. It does not circulate and is relatively invariant. It is transmitted to another timescale by reproduction and the genetic code. From the standpoint of structure-information, the individual can be coarsely considered as a closed system. It is a system which is open to the circulation of matter and energy and to circulating-information, but its constituent elements must retain certain invariant relationships among themselves.

Structure-information constitutes what we may call a memory, whose form persists with time. For example, structure-information may be monuments, books, phonographs, records, or films, whose elements (stones, letters, grooves, images) have been organized by man and have retained this organization with time. Structure-information in biology also leads to the formation of memories such as genetic memory, immune memory, or nervous memory. We have long been aware that atoms participate in the formation of deoxyribonucleic acid, the basic component of genes, capable of transmitting the form of the individual of a species from generation to generation. But as long as we did not know the way in which these atoms were organized in space, i.e., in the form of a double helix, nothing was understood of the transmission of genetic characteristics. This organization of atoms in living systems, which requires a constant supply of solar energy to maintain its structure-information, constitutes metastable organizations of the elements of a set.

Metastable organizations characterize for us what Khalil (1990) calls "configuration" and Prigogine (1984) labels "dissipative structures." For example, the formation of an antibody for immune defense, in other words the recognition of elements foreign to the organism, constitutes a molecular form which is a particular specific protein, in addition to being a memory. Similarly, nervous influx through neural chains, which leaves behind a trace of their passage, also in the form of a protein synthesis which will code neural factors, is, indeed, a shaping process. In the same way as in the course of immune memory, there is synthesis of specific proteins; thus there exists the appearance of molecular forms and of molecular organizations whose persistence will be, as is generally admitted today, the source of long-term memory.

In contrast to genetic memory, which transmits the structure-information of a species from generation to generation, the memory of an organism will disappear with its death. In the case of humans, it can survive and also be transmitted from generation to generation as a result of a new structure-information, which becomes circulating-information between different individuals and generations. When you communicate a piece of information to me, this information circulates from you to me, from one point to another in space–time. It is initially a structure-information particular to your personal brain, but you will employ means capable of transmitting this information to others. To do so, you are going to create a new structure-information external to you, the sentence, but it will be shaped by your cerebral structure-information. The latter is the result of your learning, training, and experience. This leads us to the problem of semantics, which we have not yet envisioned.

STRUCTURE-INFORMATION AND ORGANIZATION LEVELS

A message requires the creation of structure-information which constitutes the signifier. In order to send a piece of information from Paris to Montreal, I have to combine words. I cannot place them haphazardly but must do so in a particular order. According to syntax and grammar, I combine the words into a sentence which will be the order or structure of the signifier. In other words, the order of a sentence is the set of relationships existing among the elements of this signifying set. The set of elements, letters, words, and sentences constituting the signifier (material requiring a certain energy to be transmitted, regardless of the channel used for the transmission) makes up semantics. In turn, semantics, the meaning of the message, transforms and shapes the nervous system of the receiver. In order to do this, it is evident that the sender must organize the signifier according to code, which is also used by the decoder, the receiver of the message. If I send you a message in French, and the only code you know is Chinese, the exchange of information between us will be relatively scant at best. Finally, this information we call "circulating" is not limited to communications between organisms, i.e., at the social level, but is found at various levels of organization that we will now consider.

Several decades ago, Laborit (1963a) drew attention to the fact that living organisms are structured by organization levels. The number of these organizational levels is an expression of complexity. To cite only a few of these organizational levels, atoms combine to form a molecular set. These molecules are the elements of a new set, e.g. enzymatic. These molecular groups, enabling an enzymatic reaction to occur, combine in subcellular organelles such as mitochondria, the nucleus, the Golgi apparatus, the endoplasmic reticulum, membranes, and so on. These subcellular organelles, such as microtubules and microfilaments, constitute a cellular set − the cell. Cells which have the same function constitute organs. These organs in turn cooperate to constitute systems, which together assure the structure of an organism.

Each of the organizational levels enumerated above can be isolated by the experimenter from the organizational levels surrounding it of which it is an element. Once isolated, its function can be better examined by varying only one factor of this function at a time. But it must be remembered that once this organizational level is put back into the system containing it, it will not function exactly the same way that it did when it was isolated in the laboratory. Certain factors were ignored; however, comparing the function of this isolated organization level and the function of the same level when it is incorporated, we can progressively discover the design factors and better understand its functioning when it is incorporated. This means that although it is important to determine the structure of an organizational level, it is perhaps more important to detect the relationships it establishes with its own organizational levels.

An organizational level can function alone since it, in turn, includes a number of other underlying organizational levels. It may thus be considered as a regulator whose effect controls − generally negatively − the value of factors by a feedback loop. When it is placed in a normal situation − the system of which it is normally a part − this regulation will be controlled by information reaching it from the surrounding system. The regulator (Figure 9.2) is thus transformed into a servomechanism. The experimenter may cut

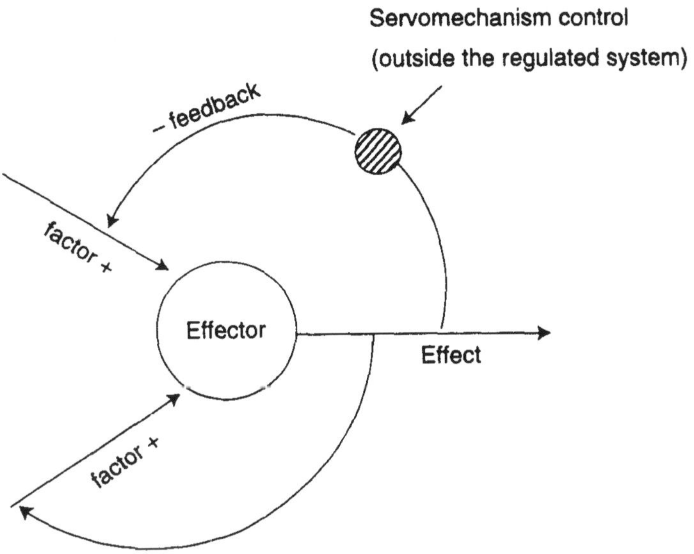

Figure 9.2 Regulated system

the servomechanism – the outside command of the system he is working on – in order to analyze what can be observed or experimented on at a single level isolated from the Structure. There must be communication and circulation information between each organizational level such that the organic set can function harmoniously from one organizational level to another, and above all can maintain its own structure.

Thus, circulating information-messages exist between each organizational level which will control the functional activity of each. The nervous system and the endocrine system are, without doubt, the two principal means used by an organism, assuring its autonomy in a different environment. Each organizational level is thus a closed system at the level of its structure-information, but this is also what enables a heart, liver, intestine, and, in general, organs belonging to systems, to function alone. This is also what enables cultured cells to be isolated, or, after destroying their cellular structure, what enables researchers to study the functioning of isolated organelles such as mitochondria.

In addition, the endocrine system has the characteristic advantage of conveying information to certain cell groups in order to transform their functional and metabolic activity in a direction favorable to the maintenance of the structure and functional activity of the set of the organism within its environment. This is also why hormones secreted by endocrine glands were called "chemical messengers."[2] Each is represented by molecules with a particular structure, and the signifier it constitutes must be able to be decoded by other entities conforming to their structure –

complementary entities we call receptors. This enables us to understand why only cells equipped with receptors capable of understanding the message of a particular hormone will be able to respond to the message it carries. We find the same problem with regard to language communication.

Furthermore, the receptors are generally located in or on cell membranes and will transmit the information to a "second messenger," which will transmit this biochemical message to the metabolic factory, which is in the cell. It follows from these concepts that although each organizational level is a relatively closed system in terms of its structure, it is linked to all the organizational levels. By nesting in each other, the organizational levels constitute the entire organism as a result of a system of communication. This enables each organizational level to maintain its own structure by participating in the maintenance of the overall structure of the organism. Thus, by maintaining the overall structure of the organism, the structure of each organizational level can be maintained.

Thus, too, at the level of structure-information, opening can be done only by inclusion into a system assuring the control of functioning of the organizational level considered. In terms of thermodynamics (mass and energy), however, living organisms which have chloroplasts are open systems into which solar photon energy flux flows and is transformed into chemical molecules by photosynthesis. These transformed chemical molecules, or foods, will supply the required energy, initially, for the structural maintenance of each element at each organizational level, and indirectly will permit the functional and thermodynamic activity of each organizational level participating in functional activity – the movement of the whole organism. It follows that the only reason for being a being is to be, i.e., to maintain structure-information in relation to a less-organized environment.[3]

Another communication system is the nervous system. It functions as a link between the different organizational levels we have spoken of, but it also has a liaison role between the entire organism and its environment. The nervous system participates in the maintenance of structure-information of the whole organism in which it is incorporated by controlling the environment via action. In order to carry out this control, the nervous system must be aware of the well-being or discomfort of the entire cellular community in which it is situated. In addition, it must be informed of what is happening in the environment. Once the nervous system integrates these two sources of information, especially that coming from within the organism, it can inform specialized cells – muscle cells – in such a way that the organism is mobilized within the environment in order to act upon that environment. The organism is also mobilized to maintain well-being, i.e., the structure-information of the organism.

BIOLOGICAL BASES OF BEHAVIOR

Our nervous system distinguishes us from plants. Flowering plants cannot move quickly, and are obliged to wait for the wind or an insect to bring pollen from anther to stigma in order to reproduce, unless they are self-pollinating. Animals with a nervous system, on the other hand, move in their environment and achieve motor autonomy.

A nervous system is used only to act in space. Our cells bathe in a liquid, a part of which circulates, viz., the blood. The cells constituting an organism will remove substrates from this internal medium, enabling them to maintain their structure and discard waste. This is what Claude Bernard (1878) called "the constancy of conditions to maintain life" in our internal milieu, i.e., the "homeostasis" of Cannon (1932). Our internal milieu, however, is in constant change: What Sigmund Freud called the "principle of pleasure" is linked to the reestablishment or maintenance of homeostasis balance. If you have not eaten for three days, you will be happy to absorb food. This concept of homeostasis or of pleasure is thus the maintenance of a complex organization, from the level of the molecule up to that of the individual.

The primitive nervous system, represented by the hypothalamus and brain stem in higher animals, is informed of changes in cellular life by cells of the internal milieu. It is informed that at certain times all is well, and that at others, it is not. In addition, changes in the environment will affect the sensory organs of sight, hearing, and so on. This will cause sensory nervous stimuli, which will encounter the preceding stimuli in the same primitive region of the nervous system. This region will be informed of all that is happening in the cellular colony – well-being or discomfort – and of what is happening on the outside. The nervous system will then inform a number of muscular structures, which will enable the organism to act upon the environment and to close the loop in such a way as the equilibrium of the internal milieu is reestablished by this control of the environment (Figure 9.3).

Regarding the nervous system in question, it is first and foremost only the means of acting upon the environment-preserving structure and controlling the characteristic of the environs, thus obtaining maximal organic well-being. MacLean (1949) called the primitive brain "reptilian brain." It supplies a programmed response which cannot be improvised upon. Starting with the earliest mammals, we find a second brain added to the first – the limbic system.

In agreement with MacLean, most authors believe the limbic system to be the affective system, although I prefer the term memory. A newborn baby will not hate the person who has forgotten to feed him or who pinches him. He does not know that a person is responsible for these actions. He suffers, but he is not "affected"; he has no feelings. To have

205

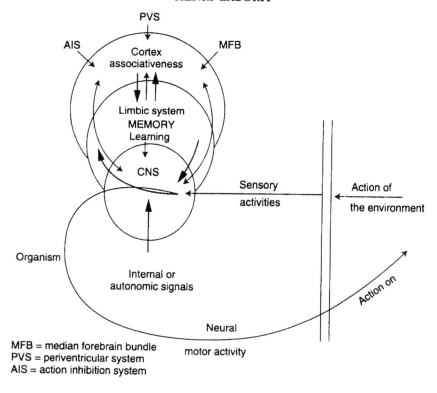

Figure 9.3 Organism–environment interface

feelings, one must first learn that one exists; it is necessary to have constructed one's body scheme and to realize that one is different from one's surrounding environment. It is necessary to have learned that some things are unpleasant and that others are pleasant. Only then can the entire range of feelings of joy, hate, and love be experienced.

How does this learning occur? Nervous stimuli which were initially localized in the primitive system reach the limbic system, leaving traces at the point of contact between two neurons called the synapse. Neural stimuli are conducted by molecules contained in vesicles and released into the synapse. It is known how these chemical mediators are synthesized: There are metabolic pathways leading to their production, storage, release, and destruction. In addition, we now have a vast pharmaceutical armamentarium to act on the metabolism of molecules mediating nervous influx.

Since the passage of a neural stimulus from one neuron to another occurs by the release of these molecules, we have means of acting on the functioning of the nervous system and thus on behavior.

Memory also has molecular bases. It is built around protein molecules synthesized by neurons, which will code synapses. Thus, when an analog stimulus penetrates this system, it passes preferentially via previously coded paths. In the laboratory, we can use chemicals which act on protein synthesis to attenuate or augment this memory. But the memory of a pleasant experience does not affect the same nervous pathways and does not involve the same neural influx chemical mediators and the same systems of transducing membrane signals within neurons as does the experience which leads to action inhibition (Zerbib and Laborit, 1990).

Memory is not specifically human. A dog can recognize its former master ten or twelve years later, simply by his odor. Immune memory, which remembers the encounter with an infectious agent, also occurs partially by the synthesis of protein molecules and antibodies and is intimately related to nervous memory (neuro-immuno-modulation).

In addition, there is one type of memory of utmost importance: that accompanying the phenomenon of imprinting. The brain is immature at birth; in other words, all synaptic connections between neurons have not yet been developed. They will develop as a function of the number and variety of stimuli reaching the central nervous system during the first months and years of life. This has two consequences: One, the importance of the environment in the early organization of a brain is fundamental. Multiple experimental findings, gathered by direct observation of neuronal interconnections and of behavior, have confirmed the importance of the environment. Second, synaptic connection forms are permanent and persist through the entire life. Freud saw the importance of the first months and first years of life in the constitution of a human personality. Konrad Lorenz and other ethologists have shown the stability of nervous structures induced at this time, which they called the "imprinting period."

Moreover, the cortex is highly developed in man, in particular at the level of the orbitofrontal lobes. The outside world enters through separate sensory channels. The baby just born and who does not yet know that he is in an environment different from himself, feels and memorizes visual, auditory, tactile, osmic, and gustative sensations. These sensations follow different nervous pathways and also arrive in different regions of the cortex. "Associative" neurons will join these different brain regions, mobilized by the action of the object, and as a result of the concomitance of sensations gathered from it will enable the realization of the "concept of object."

In her first years, the child associates pleasure she feels when basic needs are tended to with other sensations: Contact with the mother, odor of the mother, and so on. During the first three years, she will progressively realize that she is not the world. She will discover her limits in space through a learning process. At the beginning, she is not conscious of her body scheme. This consciousness will develop with time by a memory process. When she realizes that her mother is not included in her "me-all" mentality, when she realizes that her mother is the wife of the father and the mother of siblings, she discovers unhappy love, jealousy, and in the case of a boy, the Oedipus complex.

These different stimuli which leave traces in the nervous system code different nerve pathways. Man is distinguished from animals only by the existence of more highly developed associative lobes, which combine underlying nerve pathways coded by memory in a different way from that imposed by the environment. This is called "imagination." When associative processes enable the manipulation of concepts, not objects, by the use of language, creativity becomes considerable. A newborn baby cannot imagine anything since he has learned nothing. The more the baby memorizes after birth, the more his cortical associative systems will have rich material to create new structures, new subsets of relationships – the structures of imagination.

Working hypotheses remain to be tested against experimentation. They are also possible escapes from reality into a bearable world – a product of imagination. It is the world of desire, while memory alone can lead only to envy. An animal cannot desire "an unknown woman whom I love and who loves me, and who each time is not exactly the same, not exactly someone else, and loves me and understands me" (Verlaine, 1978). The animal lacks an orbito-frontal cortex to associate its past experiences in an imaginary process "of a strange and penetrating dream." In order to imagine, however, it is important not to remain imprisoned in acquired automatic actions of motor functions, language, and concepts, which must be constantly questioned. Without this, we duplicate rather than create.

In order to act, these brains, which are superimposed, must function together, and certain nerve pathways will permit this. Olds and Milner (1954) in the United States described the median forebrain bundle (MFB), as the "reward bundle."

There exists another, deeper bundle, called the periventricular system (PVS), which is a punishment system. Since 1970, I have studied a third neuronal system, which I named the AIS, or action inhibition system (Laborit, 1986). Briefly (Figure 9.4), a first bundle is involved when we obtain pleasure in such a way that we will renew the action leading to pleasure after memorizing it. A second bundle is that of punishment, whose stimulation causes flight or fight: Flight first – fight when flight is impossible. Courage is a socioculturally learned experience. When flight or fight is effective, it is used repeatedly, since it is an innate system. When effective, it resets the reward circuit, since avoiding punishment is also a reward.

Action inhibiting system

At the end, when we can no longer fight or flee, we use the AIS. This is the origin of mental, infectious, and tumorous pathologies when the situation persists. The action-inhibiting system triggers the release of adrenocortico-

208

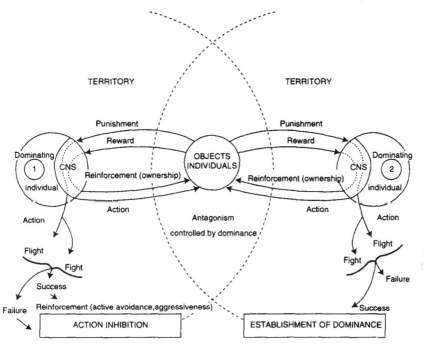

Figure 9.4 Origin of action inhibition system (AIS)

tropin hormone (ACTH) by the pituitary gland, and that of glucocorticoids by the adrenals. In particular, cortisone release blocks the immune system, and when this system is inhibited, we are exposed to the action of any pathological factor. Diseases of modern civilization are diseases of action inhibition: High blood pressure, stomach ulcer, nervous depression, absenteeism, fatigue, insomnia, and so forth. Depressed patients have elevated blood cortisol levels. Similarly, it is known that cortisone prevents the appearance of paradoxical sleep and causes retention of water and electrolytes. But this system also causes the release of a neurohormone: Norepinephrine. While epinephrine, the fight or flight hormone, is released by fear, norepinephrine is a vasoconstrictor for all blood vessels, resulting in high blood pressure, cerebral hemorrhage, and so forth.

This action-inhibiting system thus controls behavior in a social environment. This action inhibition triggers and is accompanied by anguish.

What are the mechanisms of action inhibition? According to the Freudian interpretation, a hypothalamic impulse clashes with limbic sociocultural learning: The id vs the super-ego. The inhibition also results from a deficit of information: We do not know how to classify an event; we do not know how to act with respect to it because we have never experienced it.

In addition, it is the overabundance of information from the mass media concerning events that we cannot classify by organizational levels and on which we cannot act. Its abundance and propagation is favored by the urban environment. Action based on ideology gives the illusion of offering a solution to action by narrowing the field of understanding. Here again, it is specific human anguish which results from the imaginary construction of a painful scenario, an event which may never occur, but which we fear without being able to act in advance to prevent it. It is also fear of death, which is fundamental. We know that death will come one day, but we have an information deficit concerning its time, factors, pain, what comes next. This is the basic cause of anguish. Modern societies attempt to hide it in order to protect the production of goods. This is what is favored by urbanization, while drawing the individual further from natural harmony with the environment.

Thus, rewarding action inhibition and its corollary anguish can be the origin of the pathological development of syndromes such as neurosis, drug addiction, aggressiveness, and suicide. We should also speak of the origin and role of language, which is a way of acting on others, but this is beyond the scope of our subject.

Finally, creativity and psychosis often follow each other or are inter-mingled. Insanity occurs via profound biological disturbances. When it sets in, however, the insane person often finds a favorable biological equili-brium, since he is no longer among us, but rather in an imaginary world. The insane contract cancers less often than the normal population and appear to be effectively protected against infections. It is entirely possible to be in agreement with the social code and climb the ladder of the hierarchy, thereby becoming a prosperous and respected individual cov-ered with honors. But usually such a person is not true to his unconscious impulses and so can suffer and be in the state of action inhibition that leads to various pathological situations. In more general terms, social conformity can be antagonistic to health and welfare.

FROM BIOLOGY TO SOCIOLOGY

Without invoking analogy, but rather with casual observation of facts, we can conclude that the concept of complexity or organizational level will enable us to enter into the domain of the humanities, viz., psychology, sociology, economics, and politics.

Here is a living human being with a nervous system that can be used to act only in space or "territory." If space is empty, he/she would have no reason to act. One will act on objects and individuals within space. When he/she encounters objects and individuals which furnish pleasure, the person will repeat the strategy which led to satisfaction. This is possible only if the objects and individuals remain available. If they cause pain, the receiver will flee. When flight is not possible, fight ensues, and when neither are possible, the individual will enter action inhibition.

Competition would arise if, in the same space, there is another person who desires reward by repeating a proven strategy. Among animals, the strongest wins. Among humans, this was also true for a long time. Studies by ethologists (Bateson and Klopfer, 1978) have shown that dominant–dominated "diads" were not always the rule, and that, sometimes, triads of fairly complex combinations played a part in the establishment of these hierarchical scales. The dominated animal often becomes sick (high blood pressure, weight loss, gastric ulcer, infections) and occasionally dies.

What happens in the case of humans? Apparently, the only point distinguishing us from animals is the presence of associative zones in the orbito-frontal cortex. At the beginning, when a human being hewed a stone, he passed information on to matter. He undoubtedly did this by proceeding to associations of memorized experiences. He thus discovered that he could better defend himself with his cut stone than with his bare fists.

Humans proceed by a working hypothesis which is corrected by positive or negative experimentation. Paleolithic humans were undoubtedly the only polytechnic engineers who ever existed: In order to survive, they had to know the entire technical corpus at that time. Every human was a hunter and had to know all the technologies invented by the species. His/her information-creating brain could "inform" and "shape" matter. Matter which was transformed by work, depending on the geoclimatic environment, soon furnished surpluses which could be exchanged – the rise of trade. The origin of the search for dominance generally could be traced to the possession of surplus goods.

Language first gave to each object its verbal counterpart, making possible the elaboration of sentences. This gave humans access to conceptual imagination – the creation of new structures enabling them to check a hypothesis against its coherence not only with the non-human world, but also with the experience of others, i.e., cross-experimentation. Starting with abstraction, it was possible to invent a new abstract world, exchangeable and freed from objects, which could come to life again in group communication. In addition, the brain of humans at birth is immature with few synaptic connections. It is progressively formulated and developed by the language emanating from others. This is what makes us say that we are merely the reflection of others, the living as well as the dead, via tradition (Laborit, 1970). The development of the brain by the use of language is made possible as a result of our genetic combinations and of our learning experiences in life. Noam Chomsky (1965) argues that humans possess an innate ability to formulate sentences. Human cerebral structures exist, but they have to be coded in such a way that they become useful.

Once we understand the role of language, it is easier to see the importance of modern telecommunications. It contracts space by bringing a distant correspondent close to our ears and eyes. By contracting space, it contracts the time our message would have taken to come from our communication partners. The appearance of language did exactly this, but it did so at the level of generations. Starting with language, the time and experience of man could be transmitted and accumulated. Time passed more slowly for our ancestors than it does for us. Social time thus accelerated in comparison to biological time. This undoubtedly constitutes an important factor in conflicts between generations.

A great moment in the history of the species was the passage from the paleolithic to the neolithic mode of subsistence. The reason for this passage is in all likelihood the climatic changes occurring at the end of the last glaciation. The climate of the northern hemisphere became much milder, the main characteristic of such a climate being the succession of seasons – summer followed by winter. The mildness of such a climate can be appreciated only in summer – the prior difficult climatic conditions being found in winter. Our distant ancestors had suffered from this for a long time. Their imagination enabled them to escape it. Agriculture and husbandry enabled silos to be stocked in summer and fresh meat and grass reserves to be available during the winter. The gratifying object – the reward that is necessary for survival – was no longer dispersed in nature, but was collected and assembled in a territory.

The concept of property was born – property that had to be defended against all sorts of predators starting with other, less technically advanced, human groups. Neither in the first neolithic societies nor in most animal societies does there exist, in all likelihood, an innate *instinct* of property and defense of territory. Rather, the desire to possess a property is the result of reward – the protection of biological equilibrium and pleasure.

This thesis is supported because certain ethnic groups migrated at the same time, the beginning of the neolithic era, to certain regions of the globe in which the geoclimatic environment enabled them to ignore the fear of extinction – as in the case of the South Pacific islanders. These people apparently had no idea of the concept of property or defense of territory until humans from the 45th parallel of the northern hemisphere recently taught them.

At the opposite end of the climatic scale, among Eskimos for example, there is also almost an absence of aggressiveness and possessiveness. The survival of these ethnic groups has remained just as precarious as that of our paleolithic ancestors. The concept of property, and the consequent search for dominance and aggressiveness, do not appear to depend on an innate characteristic of the human nervous system. Rather, they depend on learning conditioned by the uncertainties of supplies in specific geoclimatic niches in which certain ethnic groups developed.

One way to look at agriculture is as a way of rapidly transforming solar energy into calories, which could assure the maintenance of structure-information of human organisms (Laborit, 1963b). The transformation shapes the "information" of solar energy. In addition to mass (raw materials) and energy, information also appeared with the first humans. Matter and energy have always been available to the human species, but what was lacking at the beginning was the technical information necessary to shape them. However, this information has long been used to transform matter. The halter is a recent invention which played an important role in the transformation of solar energy. The instruction manual for the use of animal energy for transport and work took a long time to be written.

Agriculture and husbandry, which ought to have afforded abundance and decreased work, in reality only transformed the form of human activity (Laborit, 1974b). They partially decreased thermodynamic work and increased informational work. Free time available in winter, as a result of accumulated reserves, was increasingly filled with informational work. We also witness that practical sciences timidly began their appearance: useful geometry, useful mathematics, useful physics. It was above all village settlements, sedentariness, that was the origin of technical specialization (Mumford, 1964).

Over the centuries these first village dwellers forgot the use of arms. There was no longer a need for arms to survive or to defend against carnivorous predators. Groups remaining at the paleolithic stage – hunters – still used arms. In these hunters, the desire for accumulated food reserves explains why the first cities were organized and defended against the human predators wishing to rob their reserves. Gimbertas (1978) showed that the first neolithic civilizations of ancient Europe were matrilinear, egalitarian, and unarmed. They were conquered by Caucasian paleolithic horsemen-hunter peoples. Hierarchies were established. Predatory aggressiveness allowed leaders responsible for community safety to recruit soldiers; priests to manipulate myths and assure the community the protection of kindly gods; scribes to keep records; blacksmiths to forge arms and plowshares; and peasants to assure nourishment for the entire population. With human predatory aggressiveness, nothing remained to forestall the birth of competitive aggressiveness – the rise of private property and dominance.

Dominance, which became necessary in order to access private property, soon developed less exclusively through physical strength and more and more through the acquisition of technical information. A great demographic leap followed the improved conditions of life, and the initial territory became insufficient to ensure survival. Consequently, pacifist societies became warlike in order to conquer neighboring territories, seeking new resources and rewarding objects.

In more recent times, society has reached a similar impasse. With the modern development of trade, the aristocrats had fewer reasons to dominate. This called for the bourgeois revolution. It is better to have capital than blue blood in order to acquire the means of production – the possession of rewarding objects and power.

Competition and dominance

The recent invention of the steam engine, followed by the shaping not only of matter but also of different resources of energy, progressively led to the dominant rise of technocrats, who invented the machines, and bureaucrats, who organized production relationships. The strength of the manual worker and the skill of the craftsman became increasingly marginal with the rise of factory-produced goods. Technological progress of society became dependent on those reaching a high level of abstraction in their professional activity, since the formulas of physics and mathematics were used to invent the technology.

To put it simply, those who organize production appropriate technology for greater dominance. Nations poor in energy and raw materials must purchase these products elsewhere. Imports of raw materials can be paid for by exports of manufactured goods. This has given rise to unequal terms of trade. There was little chance to discover the laser in the Republic of Andorra or in Liechtenstein.

It is competition which is rarely questioned – often, on the contrary, sanctified – that has governed human progress for more than twelve thousand years. Anguished by a dangerous world they do not understand, human beings have slowly discovered the laws of the inanimate world. In this manner, they are believed to be the rulers of nature.

Even the field of scientific theories is not spared. It also appears to provide the indisputable basis of competition. Darwinism teaches us that all evolution occurs via a fight for life, leading to the survival of the fittest, or more discreetly of the best "adapted." In human society, this means adaptation to a pseudo-milieu of dominance hierarchy by humans. In light of facts that scholars, including Kropotkin (1978), have gathered, we could say that evolution was possible mainly through "mutual aid." The example of symbiosis between mitochondria and primitive anaerobic forms (see review of Lynn Margulis, 1965, Charles Mann, 1991), as well as the transition from uni-cellular to multi-cellular forms where task specialization occurs, would suffice to show the importance of cooperation – as opposed to dominance – in the course of evolution.

We have proposed (Laborit, 1974b, pp. 46–50) that symbiosis is more important than mutation in the course of evolution. It is true that every time a new organization level has been reached, competition and the struggle for life took the lead. At this stage of the human species, however, competition and domination may have reached dangerous levels.

214

Competition and hierarchies

One has to be careful how to use the term hierarchy when speaking of organizational levels. As Khalil (1990) states, "the word hierarchy is scantily used in academic discussion, probably because it connotes aristocratic and eschatological justification of political inequality." For this reason, we have proposed (Laborit, 1974, pp. 118–127) to distinguish "function hierarchy" and "value hierarchy."

In an organism, all organs, all cells, all molecules work for their own maintenance and the maintenance of the Structure. Each of these elements alone commands nothing; each merely informs and is informed. There are no hierarchies of power, but rather those of organization. The term hierarchy in this case should be abandoned, since it is difficult to rid it of any value judgment. Thus, it should be replaced by "organizational levels."

At the social level, the search for and establishment of dominance lead to power hierarchy, whose value depends on the men and the social group which establishes it. This fact results from the competing search for reward, with the multiple outcomes we have described. But it is also the result of the persistent ignorance of the mechanisms governing human behavior in social situations. The functioning of the human nervous system uses a large number of organizational levels, from molecules to behavior. The ignorance of the various levels enables logical speech to find linguistic alibis for the unconscious human problem. But logical speech is also the expression of complex biological processes that generate human behavior. One might expect that the generalization of this knowledge could cause one to be wary of logical speech, which very well could be an obfuscation of reality.

It is not a question of returning to the paleolithic pre-dominance era. Rather, it is about changing the aim of humans, viz., the search for domination through economic means. It is hoped that the day will come when societies will furnish each individual, from his infancy and throughout his life, with sufficient information on the human potential – the mechanism of which would enable him to think freely. When this happens, the daily life of humans would have a chance of being transformed. In this manner, alienation and isolation would give way to organization without dominance hierarchy.

NOTES

1 The recent concept of quantum vacuum nevertheless leads to the presumption that at the level of elementary particles those which are called "virtual particles" can establish energy relationships.

2 The immune system can be considered as both a sensory system sensitive to microscopic stimuli and an endocrine system releasing numerous hormones.

3 In other terms, the goal is to combat the second principle of thermodynamics,

the increase in entropy, by using solar energy (Laborit, 1963a), i.e., solar entropy which is the characteristic of dissipative structures.

REFERENCES

Bateson, P. P. G. and Klopfer, P. H. (1978) *Perspectives in Ethology*, Vol. 3, *Social Behavior*, New York: Plenum Press.

Bernard, C. (1878) *Leçons sur les phénomènes de la vie communs aux animaux et aux végétaux*, Paris: Ballière.

Cannon, W. B. (1932) *La sagesse du corps*, New York: W. W. Norton and Co.

Chomsky, N. (1965) *Aspects of the Theory of Syntax*, Cambridge, Mass.: MIT Press.

Gimbertas, M. (1978) "La fin de l'Europe ancienne," *La Recherche, Paris*, 9(87): 228–235.

Khalil, E. L. (1990) "Natural complex vs. natural system," *Journal of Social and Biological Structures* 13(1): 11–31.

Kropotkin, P. (1978) *L'entr'aide, un facteur de l'évolution*, Paris: Ed. L'entr'aide.

Laborit, H. (1963a) "The need of generalization in biological research. The theory of 'ensembles' or sets," Annual Korzybski memorial lecture, New York (1963), in *Agressologie* 4: 551–560.

—— (1963b) *Du soleil à l'homme. L'organisation énergétique de structures vivantes*, Vol. 1, Paris: Masson et Cie.

—— (1968) "Biologie et structure," Coll. *Idées*, Paris: Gallimard.

—— (1970) *L'homme imaginant*, Paris: Union Générale d'Edition. coll. 10/18.

—— (1974a) "Proposition d'un modèle intégré des comportements normaux et anormaux à partir de données biochimiques, neurophysiologiques, éthologiques, cliniques et sociologiques," *Annales Medico-Psychologiques* 1(1): 47–60.

—— (1974b) "La nouvelle grille," Paris: Coll. *Libertés 2000* Laffont. English translation (1977): "Decoding the human message," London: Allison and Busby; New York: Martin's.

—— (1986) *L'inhibition de l'action* (2nd ed.), Paris: Masson et Cie.

—— (1988) *Dieu ne joue pas aux dés*, Paris: Grasset.

MacLean, P. D. (1949) "Psychosomatic disease and the visceral brain. Recent development bearing on the Papez theory of emotions," *Psychosomatic Medicine* 11: 338–353.

Mann, C. (1991) "Lynn Margulis. Science's unruly earth mother," *Science* 252: 378–381.

Mumford, L. (1964) *La cité à travers l'histoire*, Paris: Seuil.

Olds, J. and Milner, P. (1954) "Positive reenforcement produced by electrical stimulation of septal area and other regions of rat brain," *Journal of Comparative and Physiological Psychology* 47: 419–427.

Prigogine, I. (1984) "Nouvelles perspectives de la complexité," Science et pratique de la complexité: Actes du Colloque de Montpellier, La Documentation Française, 129–141.

Verlaine, P. (1978) *Poèmes saturniens* Paris: Editions du Cerf.

Zerbib, R. and Laborit, H. (1990) "Chronic stress and memory: implication of the central cholinergic system," *Pharmacology, Biochemistry and Behavior* 36: 897–900.

10

THE PROPENSITIES OF EVOLVING SYSTEMS

Robert E. Ulanowicz

INTRODUCTION

The fundamental problem with the prevailing scientific worldview is its glaring inadequacy to address living systems. Such an audacious assertion, coming from anyone but the most notable of philosophers, would deserve to be dismissed immediately. But it is, I believe, an accurate summary of a small monograph written recently by one of the preeminent thinkers of our time, Sir Karl Popper (1990).

Popper is perhaps best known for his contributions to logical positivism, although he himself takes credit for "killing" the movement (Popper, 1974). Then there are his engrossing debates with Kuhn, Lakatos and Feyerabend concerning the nature of science. But what has been obscured by these more renowned exploits is Popper's origins as a biologist, and it is to the subject of living systems that he returns in his latest work, *A World of Propensities*. Popper expresses strong misgivings about popular accounts of evolution. Cast as they are solely in terms of proximate and mechanical causes, current narratives on evolution seem inadequate to address its very nature and direction. To grasp the essence of evolution, Popper argues, requires an "evolutionary theory of knowledge," the beginnings of which he proceeds to outline.

While I have never been a disciple of the positivist school of thought, I find much in Popper's latest thinking that lends support to my own inclinations. In fact, I will attempt to show how his recommendations lead quite readily to an alternative image of natural causation that I have espoused elsewhere (Ulanowicz, 1986, 1989, 1990, 1991). Of course, opinions are one thing and quantitative science is quite another. So in good Popperian fashion I will attempt to go even further and provide the reader with mensuration formulae that could be employed by anyone wishing to falsify my very contentions.

ROBERT E. ULANOWICZ

A WORLD OF PROPENSITIES

To Popper the world is not closed. More precisely, it is not a deterministic clockwork, as Descartes would have had us believe. Rather it is composed of "propensities" – the tendencies that certain processes or events might occur. He gives as an example the estimation of the probability that a given individual will survive until twenty years from the present, say to a particular day in 2016. Given the age, health and occupation of that individual, it is possible to assign a probability for survival until 2016. As the years pass, however, the probability of survival until the set date does not remain constant. It may increase if the person remains in good health, decrease if accident or sickness should intervene, or even fall irreversibly to zero in the event of death.

How does any of this differ from the conventional notion of probability? In two crucial ways: First, Popper holds that there is no such thing as an absolute probability. That is, no probability exists purely in isolation; each is contingent to a greater or lesser extent upon circumstances and interfering events. This is manifestly clear in the cited example of an individual's life course. It is mostly ignored, however, in classical physics, where one deals largely with events that are nearly isolated.

What in physics are called "forces," Popper sees as propensities of events in near isolation. A clear example is the mutual attraction of two heavenly masses for each other. The absence of interfering events in such a case allows for very precise and accurate predictions. When only well-defined forces are at play, the propensity of any effect given its particular cause approaches unity. This certainty is expressed as a deductive relationship between cause and effect. However, as the example of twenty-year survival shows, events are rarely isolated and subject to deductive analysis. Hence, forces are very special and degenerate examples of more general agencies that Popper calls *propensities*.

The problem with contemporary biology is that it attempts to extrapolate backwards from the narrow, deterministic, ethereal realm into that of more common experience. Descartes and Newton gave us the world as universal clockwork, a notion that reigned almost two centuries in physics and still permeates biology (viz. the influence of Newtonian thought upon Darwinism, Weber *et al.*, 1989). The very essence of the scientific method, according to Popper, is to create "at will, artificial conditions that either exclude, or reduce to zero, all the interfering and disturbing propensities."

At this point the reader might object that current theories of evolution hardly seem deterministic. After all, chance and probability play a large role in the neo-Darwinian narrative. However, the probabilities invoked there are of an absolute nature. Furthermore, the role of chance is relegated mostly to mutations that occur at the moment of genetic reproduction. From there the new organism enters a world that is assumed to be Newtonian, until the

218

inception of the next generation (Depew and Weber, 1995). Without much exaggeration, the prevailing outlook on evolution is one that splices a causal theory derived at the scale of the heavenly orbs onto the assumption that the world at molecular scales is purely stochastic. The dogma is that cause may originate at these extremes and propagate inward towards the scales of more immediate experience, but we are specifically enjoined from entertaining the notion that causes may arise at intermediate levels.

Popper is decrying this disjointed view of reality and urges us to rethink our attitudes toward causality. He is suggesting that there is something between the "all" of Newtonian forces and the "nothing" of stochastic infinitesima. "Propensities" spontaneously appear at any level of observation because of interferences among processes occurring *at* that level. This hypothesis highlights Popper's second distinction of propensities from common probabilities. Propensities are not properties of an object, rather they are *inherent in a situation*. The reality of propensities derives from the circumstances or the context in which processes occur. The mutual attraction of two heavenly bodies occurs in a context that is almost vacuous – not so the fall of an apple from a tree. "Real apples are emphatically not Newtonian apples," according to Popper. When an apple will fall depends not only upon its Newtonian weight, but also upon the blowing wind, and the whole process is initiated by a biochemical process that weakens the stem, etc.

It makes no sense to Popper to speak of a propensity in abstraction from its surroundings, which in turn are affected by other propensities. Sidney Brenner, in trying to map genetic sequences onto the characteristics of phenotypes, said it very convincingly (Lewin, 1984):

> At the beginning it was said that the answer to the understanding of development was going to come from a knowledge of the molecular mechanisms of gene control . . . [but] the molecular mechanisms look boringly simple, and they do not tell us what we want to know. We have to discover the principles of organization, how lots of things are put together in the same place.

Popper provides a major clue how to begin to understand the principles of organization: "We need a calculus of relative or conditional probabilities as opposed to a calculus of absolute probabilities."

A CALCULUS OF CONDITIONAL PROBABILITIES

Popper posits the tantalizing notion of propensity as a generalization of the concept of force, but he does not explicitly show how to quantify propensities. Precisely what calculus of conditional probabilities pertains when "lots of things are put together in the same place"? But if we follow

Popper's lead in a very literal way, we discover that much of his calculus already has been developed.

Conditional probabilities have probably been encountered by most readers. In a system consisting of multiple processes, one might identify a suite of potential "causes", call them $a_1, a_2, a_3, \ldots, a_m$. Similarly, one may cite a list of observable "effects", say $b_1, b_2, b_3, \ldots, b_n$. One could then study the system in brute empirical fashion and create a matrix of frequencies that contains as the entry in row i and column j the number of times (events) that a_i is followed immediately by b_j. A table showing the hypothetical number of times that each of four causes was followed by one of five outcomes is shown in Table 10.1. For the sake of convenience exactly 1,000 events were tabulated. This allows us to use the frequencies of joint occurrence to estimate the *joint probabilities* of occurrence simply by moving the decimal point to the left. For example, of all the events that occurred, in 19.3 per cent of the cases cause a_1 was followed by effect b_2, and in 2 per cent of the cases a_4 was followed by b_4, etc. We denote these joint probabilities as $p(a_i, b_j)$.

Listed in the sixth column are the sums of the respective rows. Thus, a_1 was observed a total of 269 times, a_2, 227 times, etc. Similarly, the entries in the fifth row contain the sums of their respective columns. Effect b_4 was observed 176 times, b_5, 237 times, etc. These marginal sums are estimators of the *marginal probabilities* of each cause and effect. Thus, 26.3 per cent of the times a cause was observed, it was a_3, or 17.6 per cent of the observed effects were b_4. We denote the marginal probabilities by $p(a_i)$ or $p(b_j)$.

A *conditional probability* is the answer to the question: "What is the probability of outcome b_j given that 'cause' a_i has just occurred?" The answer is easy to calculate. For example, if $i = 2$ and $b = 5$, then a_2 occurred a total of 227 times, and in 175 of those instances the result was b_5. Therefore, the conditional probability of b_5 occurring, given that a_2 has happened, is estimated by the quotient 175/227 or 77 per cent. In like manner, the conditional probability that b_4 happens, given that a_1 has just transpired, is 4.1 per cent, etc. If we represent the conditional probability

Table 10.1 Frequency table of the hypothetical number of joint occurrences that four "causes" ($a_1 \ldots a_4$) were followed by five "effects" ($b_1 \ldots b_5$)

	b_1	b_2	b_3	b_4	b_5	*Sum*
a_1	40	193	16	11	9	269
a_2	18	7	0	27	175	227
a_3	104	0	38	118	3	263
a_4	4	6	161	20	50	241
Sum	166	206	215	176	237	1,000

Table 10.2 Frequency table as in Table 10.1, except that care was taken to isolate causes from each other

	b_1	b_2	b_3	b_4	b_5	*Sum*
a_1	0	269	0	0	0	269
a_2	0	0	0	0	227	227
a_3	263	0	0	0	0	263
a_4	0	0	241	0	0	241
Sum	263	269	241	0	227	1,000

that b_j happens given that a_i has occurred by $p(b_j|a_i)$, then we see the general formula $p(b_j|a_i) = p(a_i, b_j)/p(a_i)$.

It is well to pause at this point and consider what sort of system might have given rise to the frequencies in Table 10.1. Unless the observer was unusually inept at identifying the a_i and b_j's, then the system did not behave in strictly mechanical fashion. We see that most of the time a_1 gives rise to b_2, a_2 to b_5 and a_4 to b_3. But there is also a lot of what Popper calls "interference" – situations like those in which a_4 yielded b_1, that were occasioned either by some external agency or by the interplay of processes within the system. One also notices that there is ambiguity as to the outcome of a_3.

If it were possible to isolate individual processes and study them in laboratory-like situations, then something like a mechanical description of the system might ensue. For example, we might discover that if we take great care to isolate processes, a_1 always yields b_2, a_2 gives b_5, a_3 invariably results in b_1 and a_4 in b_3. The same frequency counts for a collection of isolated processes could look something like that in Table 10.2. Knowing a_i immediately reveals the outcome b_j in mechanical, lockstep fashion. As Popper noted, the conditional probabilities of force-effect pairs are all unity, or certainty. What is also interesting in Table 10.2 is that b_4 is never the outcome of an isolated cause. One surmises that in the natural ensemble, b_4 is purely the result of interaction phenomena.

There is assuredly nothing new about conditional probabilities. Bayes defined them in the eighteenth century. What is decidedly of more recent origin is Popper's sought-after "calculus of conditional probabilities," i.e., information theory. Now the word "calculus" probably associates freely in the minds of most readers with Newton's or Leibniz's methods for studying changes in algebraic quantities. One uses the operations of differential calculus to quantify the rate of change of an algebraic function at a given point. What too few realize is that the relationship of information theory to probability theory is strictly analogous to that which differential calculus bears to algebra. Information theory was created to quantify the results of a change in probability assignment. In fact, Tribus and McIrvine (1971) proposed as the definition of information, "anything that causes a change in probability assignment." Seen in this way information theory bears an organic relation to probability theory. This fact is tragically ignored by so many ecologists and economists, who regard probability theory as their bread and butter, but perceive information theory as something unrelated and totally useless. (One could go even further and regard probability theory as deriving from information theory, as Li and Vitanyi (1992) did.)

What should be clear from the way I introduced conditional probabilities is that they represent revisions in probability assignments. For example, delete any knowledge of "causes," and the probability that one observes outcome b_5 is identical to its marginal probability, or 23.7 per cent. However, knowing that a_2 has just occurred allows us to revise that estimate (upwards in this case) to a 77 per cent chance that b_5 will now happen. The same knowledge about a_2 induces us to amend the probability that b_2 will transpire downward from 20.6 per cent to 3 per cent, etc.

It remains to relate the calculated change in probability assignment to the degree of information which it conveys. The difficulty in so doing is that information cannot be directly quantified. Rather, it can be gauged only indirectly in terms of the disappearance of its opposite, or what is variously called "uncertainty" or "surprisal."

A connection between the probability of an event occurring and the subjective response such happening evokes (surprise) is made mathematically via the logarithmic operator. More precisely, one's surprise at a particular outcome is assumed to be proportional to the negative logarithm of the probability that that outcome will transpire. Thus, if $p(b_j)$ is the a priori probability that b_j will occur, then our surprisal when it happens is measured by $-\log p(b_j)$. This measure accords with intuition insofar as whenever one is absolutely certain that b_j will occur (i.e., $p(b_j) = 1$), then one's surprisal is identically zero. Conversely, if $p(b_j)$ is very small (near zero), one is very surprised whenever it does turn up. In the latter case $-\log p(b_j)$ is high.

If surprisal prior to knowing anything about the a_i is set to $-\log p(b_j)$, then it follows that surprisal after the particular a_i is revealed should become $-\log p(b_j | a_i)$. Any decrease in surprisal would be equal to the difference between the a priori and a posteriori surprisals, i.e.,

$$-\log p(b_j) - [-\log p(b_j | a_i)]$$

or, more simply,

$$\log [p(b_j | a_i)/p(b_j)].$$

Every combination of i and j makes such a contribution, some of which may be negative in value. However, when each term is weighted by the joint probability that i and j occur in combination, the weighted terms all sum to yield a nonnegative overall measure of information contained in the system of processes,

$$I = \sum_{i=1}^{m} \sum_{j=1}^{n} p(a_i, b_j) \log[p(b_j \mid a_i)/p(b_j)].$$

The formal name for the quantity I is the *average mutual information*. I increases in systems that are highly defined and that approximate mechanical behavior, and decreases as interference and ambiguity increase. For example, the value of I for Table 10.1 is 0.96 bits, whereas it increases to 2.00 bits for the more highly articulated system in Table 10.2.

A NEW VIEW OF CAUSALITY

A calculus of conditional probabilities already exists, and it can be used to differentiate between strictly mechanical and more complex behaviors. But we have yet to capture the full import of Popper's propensities. He lays great emphasis, for example, on skewed behavior, such as might be exhibited in a pair of loaded dice or an uneven roulette wheel. As mentioned, he cites the need for a new view of causality, implying that the Newtonian categories of material and efficient causes are somehow insufficient for describing evolving systems. However, there seems to be little in our derivation of the "calculus of conditional probabilities" that would seem to justify his attitudes. We therefore ask whether there is anything special that could happen when "lots of things are put together in the same place" that might impart a preferred direction to evolutionary behavior?

When a process occurs in proximity to another, there are three qualitative effects each could have on the other. It could augment the other process (+); it could decrement it (−); or it could have no effect whatever (0). When one considers the reciprocal effect of the other process on the given one, there are nine pairs of possible interactions, e.g. (+−), (−0), (−−), etc. I wish to concentrate on the peculiarities of one type of interaction, namely, mutualism (++).

When manifested in a system of chemical reactions, mutualism is called "autocatalysis," a term which I shall retain as applying to more generic systems (e.g., ecosystems, economic networks, etc.). Autocatalysis is not limited to interaction pairs, but also can pertain to cycles with one or more intermediaries. For example, Figure 10.1 is a schematic representation of a four-member autocatalytic loop. An increase in the activity of any member in this loop engenders increments in the activities of all other "downstream" elements (including itself). Thus, an increase in the activity of A leads to a growth in the level of activity B, which in turn causes the rate of C to rise, and so forth, until the effect propagates back to its origin, A, i.e., it becomes self-reinforcing.

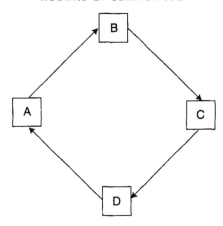

Figure 10.1 A four-member autocatalytic configuration (two intermediaries)

Most unfortunately, conventional wisdom regards autocatalysis simply as a mechanism. This outlook reflects the deterministic mentality that Popper justifiably takes to task. Autocatalysis is not mechanical in nature. It possesses intriguing properties, several of which are quite incompatible with the concept of mechanism (Ulanowicz, 1989).

To start with, autocatalytic configurations, almost by definition, are *growth enhancing*. An increment in the activity of any member engenders greater activities in all other elements. The feedback configuration results in an increase in the aggregate activity of all members engaged in autocatalysis greater than what it would be if the compartments were decoupled.

Although the growth characteristics of autocatalysis are widely accepted it often is not recognized that an autocatalytic configuration also exerts *selection pressure* upon the characteristics of all its constituents. If a random change should occur in one member such that its catalytic effect upon the next compartment is accelerated, then the effects of that alteration will return to the starting compartment as a reinforcement of the new behavior. The opposite also holds – should a change in an element decrement its effect on downstream elements, it will be reflected upon itself in negative fashion. Thus, inherent within autocatalysis is an *asymmetry* that ratchets all participants to ever greater levels of performance. It is just such skewedness that accounts for Popper's loaded dice. In Newton's scheme every action has an equal and opposite reaction. In the world-at-large, autocatalytic configurations impart a definite sense (direction) to the behaviors of systems in which they appear.

Matters become even more unconventional when one realizes that an autocatalytic loop can define itself as the focus of a *centripetal* flow of material and resources. To see how this could happen, one need only consider the particular case where a change in a compartment accidentally

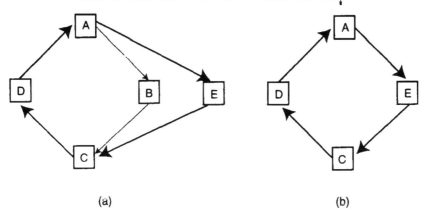

Figure 10.2 The replacement of B by E in the loop shown in Figure 10.1

brings more necessary resources into it, thereby allowing it to operate at an elevated level. By the argument in the preceding paragraph, such acquisition will be rewarded. Because this selection pressure favoring the acquisition of resources applies to all members of the configuration, the loop will become an attractor of material and energy from the world around it. Taken as a unit, the autocatalytic cycle is not simply reacting to its environment, it also actively creates its own domain of influence.

The evolutionary propensities of autocatalysis also delimit the ways in which the participants in the process configuration may be replaced. For example, if A, B, C, and D are four sequential elements comprising an autocatalytic loop, and if some element E: (1) appears by chance, (2) is more sensitive than B to catalysis by A, and (3) provides greater enhancement to C than does B; then E either will grow to dominate B's role in the loop, or will displace it altogether (Figure 10.2). Alternatively, if B should happen suddenly to disappear for whatever reason, it is, in Popper's own words, "always the existing structure of the . . . pathways that determines what new variations or accretions are possible."

By simple induction, one may proceed from replacement of B by E to the successive replacements of C, D, and A by, say, F, G, and H, until the final configuration, E–F–G–H, contains *none* of the original elements. In this sense the action of the autocatalytic loop over the long term becomes immaterial of its particular constituents. Even more importantly, the duration of the autocatalytic form is usually *longer* than that of its constituents. Lest this sound too bizarre, the reader should realize that one's own body is composed of cells (with the exception of neurons) that, on the average, did not exist seven years ago. The residences of most chemical constituents in the body are usually of even shorter duration. Yet most readers will be recognized by friends they haven't met in the last ten years.

225

ROBERT E. ULANOWICZ

By now it should be clear that autocatalysis is no passive mechanism. The emergence of selection pressure, centripetality and persistence, taken together, bespeak of a degree of autonomy from material constitution and mechanical constraint. Attempts to predict the life course of an autocatalytic configuration by ontological reduction to material constituents and mechanical operation are doomed over the long run to failure. If one persists in maintaining that only material and mechanical causes are legitimate for explanation, then one will remain trapped in Tolstoy's conundrum, ". . . the cause of the event is neither in the one nor in the other. . . . Or in other words, the conception of a cause is inapplicable to the phenomena we are examining."

Popper was right, we do need a new conception of causality if we are to accommodate propensities such as are engendered by autocatalysis. To see why radical change is necessary, it helps to regard causality in a hierarchical framework. For example, in the Newtonian world we are used to observing a system at a particular level and explaining its behavior in terms of its material and mechanical components, i.e., the "bottom-up", or reductionistic approach of conventional systems analysis. Although it is usually not accorded the same emphasis, we are also familiar with the "top-down" influence that may be exerted on a system via its "boundary conditions," e.g., its environment (which often is dominated by the experimenter).

Absent from our conceptual inventory is the possibility that causation can appear *at* the focal level of observation. However, this is exactly how autocatalysis operates! Its agency is inherent in the configuration of processes *at* the scale of observation and does not derive from other levels. Of course, an autocatalytic system continues to be constrained and influenced from above and below, but I hasten to emphasize that at the same time it is the origin and locus of influence that subsequently can propagate both up and down the scale of events.

The reader will note that the agency of autocatalysis derives not from the entities composing a system, but rather from the spatial and temporal juxtaposition of processes that transpire among the elements, i.e., the kinetic *form* of the system. For this reason I have elsewhere called this agency a "formal cause." In so doing I borrowed from the lexicon of Aristotle, although I hasten to point out that the formal agency of autocatalysis differs appreciably from the formal cause posited by Aristotle.

QUANTIFYING PROPENSITIES

Most of the ideas advanced by Popper in his latest monograph now have been elaborated. It remains to bring them all together for the purpose of defining "propensity" in clear and quantitative terms. To do this it becomes necessary to point out that we have been implicitly regarding systems as networks of connecting processes. To be sure, any system has identifiable material components, such as individual cells, organisms, populations, species, economic sectors, or whatever. But more importantly, these entities affect one another over threads of communication that constitute processes, e.g., exchanges of material or energy, exchanges of money, spatial displacements, exchanges of explicit information, etc. The focus in evolutionary thinking must be upon networks of processes. As Popper so delightfully put it, "Heraclitus was right: we are not things, but flames. Or a little more prosaically, we are, like all cells, *processes of metabolism*, nets of chemical processes, of highly active (energy-coupled) chemical pathways."

The problem with networks of processes is that often they are very difficult to quantify. For one, the sheer multitude of exchange processes usually makes the accumulation of sufficient data a formidable task. Then some exchanges simply don't lend themselves to easy mensuration – like the effect a bird's colors and morphology have upon its prey, predators and comensals. For this latter reason it is best to limit further discussion to networks of palpable exchanges, like those of energy, material or cash. In considering only palpable media the assumption is made that the effects of other, harder to measure properties are implicit in those flows we do measure. For example, the color of a population of birds could affect how successful its members are at capturing prey and how often they are eaten in turn. Both of these processes constitute palpable rates of exchange. This reduction bothers some ecologists who eschew the expression of intangibles in such "brute" terms (Engelberg and Boyarsky, 1979). Economists seem to have fewer scruples about expressing the world of human activities as a matrix of material transactions!

The relative availability of data in the fields of economics and ecology is likewise disparate. Input–output tables of commodity flows among hundreds of economic sectors abound. By contrast, quantified networks of ecological exchanges are few and usually treat communities with but several compartments, although networks of ecosystems with twenty to forty elements are beginning to appear (see Baird and Ulanowicz, 1989).

The key question to ask about networks of exchanges is how might autocatalysis tend to affect patterns of exchange among system elements? From the foregoing discussion we see its effects are basically twofold: First, autocatalysis tends to increase the aggregate amount of system activity. To quantify this effect, we let T_{ij} represent the measured transfer of medium from compartment i to compartment j. Then the aggregate community activity in an n-compartment system can be expressed as

$$T = \sum_{i=0}^{n} \sum_{j=1}^{n+1} T_{ij}$$

where the index value 0 (zero) identifies the source of imports from outside the system, and the value $n + 1$ designates the destination of exports out of the system. In the parlance of economic input–output analysis T is called the "total system throughput." It is a sibling variable to the gross com-

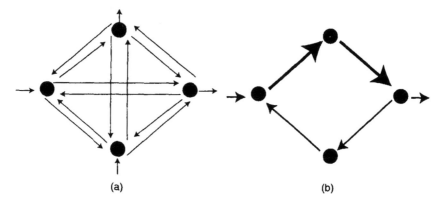

Figure 10.3 A schematic representation of the effects of autocatalysis: (a) before; (b) after.

munity (or national, as the case may be) output. Hence, one effect of autocatalysis is to increase T, the "size" or extent of the system.

The other visible effect of autocatalysis is to streamline the topology of interconnections (processes) in a way that abets those transfers that more effectively engage in autocatalysis at the expense of those showing little or no participation. In effect, as autocatalysis progresses, the network will tend to become dominated by a few intense flows. Schematically, this tendency is depicted in Figure 10.3.

In order to quantify these topological changes, one should notice that the exchange T_{ij} can be arrayed as the entry in row i and column j of a two-dimensional matrix. Then the effect of pruning connections and augmenting those remaining will be depicted as something like the transition from Table 10.1 to Table 10.2. Because flows represent aggregate discrete transfers, or events, it is only natural to estimate probabilities in terms of measured flows (viz. Rutledge *et al.*, 1976). Toward this end, we identify $p(a_i, b_j)$ with the probability that a quantum of some medium leaves i and enters j. Because T is the aggregate of all such system transfers, we can estimate $p(a_i, b_j)$ by T_{ij}/T. Similarly, $p(b_j)$, the probability that a quantum enters element j, will be estimated by $(\Sigma_p T_{pj})/T$. Finally, the conditional probability $p(b_j|a_i)$, that a quantum enters j after having left i, is approximated by $T_{ij}/(\Sigma_k T_{ik})$. Substituting these estimators into the definition of the average mutual information yields

$$I = \sum_{i=0}^{n} \sum_{j=1}^{n+1} (T_{ij}/T) \log(T_{ij}T/[\Sigma_p T_{pj}][\Sigma_k T_{ik}]).$$

That is, the average mutual information, I, quantifies the degree to which autocatalysis (and possibly other agencies) have organized the flow structure.

The reader will notice that I is an intensive and dimensionless quantity, i.e., it depends on the system topology but not on its physical extent. However, it has been argued above that the effects of autocatalysis are both extensive and intensive – it tends to increase both the size and the organization of the flow structure. Therefore, following the lead of Tribus and McIrvine (1971), who urge information theorists to attach physical dimensions to their indices, we scale I by T to yield a network property called the system ascendency,

$$A = T \times I = \sum_{i=0}^{n} \sum_{j=1}^{n+1} T_{ij} \log(T_{ij}T/[\Sigma_p T_{pj}][\Sigma_k T_{ik}]).$$

To summarize, autocatalysis is hypothesized as a formal agency that imparts a preferred direction to evolving systems. That is, in the absence of major perturbations, *autonomous systems tend to evolve in a direction of increasing network ascendency.*

Evolution as increasing ascendency, which appeared here as a deductive consequence of several assumptions concerning autocatalysis, originally was formulated as a phenomenological description that encapsulated diverse trends in ecological succession (Ulanowicz, 1980). Specifically, more developed ecosystems are usually comprised of a larger number of elements (species), which, in the aggregate, exchange more material and energy among themselves over less equivocal routes. Furthermore, as ecosystems undergo succession, they decrease both their losses to the external world, as well as their dependencies on imported resources (Odum, 1969). Taken individually, these changes all result in increases in a system's network ascendency. Elsewhere, I have argued that increasing ascendency also portrays development in economic systems (Ulanowicz, 1986).

A word of caution: Although natural progression appears to give rise to increasing ascendency, it does not follow that a system's robustness should be equated to its ascendency. With increasing ascendency may come greater vulnerability to external perturbations. Furthermore, disorder and redundancy, elsewhere called system overhead (Ulanowicz, 1980), actually can contribute to system persistence. Overhead may act as a reservoir of potential adaptations available for the system to implement in response to novel perturbations.

It would not be incorrect to say that evolving systems exhibit a propensity toward higher ascendencies. However, one can be even more precise. Ascendency is, after a fashion, a surrogate for overall system efficiency – an index of system performance. If the constituent flows are measured in terms of energy, then the resulting A has the physical dimensions of power. In fact, it was first formulated as a rough analogy to the thermodynamic Helmholz work function (Ulanowicz, 1980, 1986).

229

Power functions play a prominent role in the thermodynamics of irreversible processes. For example, Onsager (1931) showed how the entropy production of a system always could be written as the sum of terms, each of which is the magnitude of a constituent flow times its conjugate thermodynamic "force." Consider, for example, several electrolytes moving in a solution under the influence of a voltage gradient. The first set of conjugate products would be the diffusive flux of each species times the negative of its gradient in chemical potential (diffusive "force"), and the second would be the electrical flux of each ion times the negative of the imposed electrical gradient (the coulombic force). One need only sum all such products to calculate the system's rate of dissipation. The same formal procedure with a change in sign applies as well to power *production* or "work" functions.

Elsewhere, I have remarked how ascendency is, in formal terms, a power function (Ulanowicz, 1986). The system ascendency is the sum of products, each of which consists of a flow magnitude times a logarithmic term. In a formal sense one could identify the logarithmic term with the thermodynamic "force" that the system context exerts upon the resultant flow. However, I have never been comfortable with the notion of generalized thermodynamic forces, mostly because they cannot be formulated (or even identified!) for anything but the simplest of physical systems.

Popper now affords the overarching perspective: Those agencies we identify as forces are but a small and degenerate subset of a larger class of actors – propensities! More generally speaking, things are not always compelled (forced) to happen, but there is a greater or lesser tendency that they transpire. When "lots of things are put together in the same place," there is a propensity for or against particular events to occur.

We are led formally to identify the logarithmic terms in the ascendency with the propensities for their conjugate process to occur. Rather than formulate the propensities in terms of flows, it is better to define them more generally in terms of joint and conditional probabilities. Accordingly, we let P_{ij} be the propensity for event i–j to occur within the context of the given system. P_{ij} may be written as any one of three equivalent expressions:

$$
\begin{aligned}
P_{ij} &= \log[p(b_j \,|\, a_i)/p(b_j)] \\
&= \log[p(a_i,\ b_j)/p(a_i)p(b_j)] \\
&= \log[p(a_i \,|\, b_j)/p(a_i)].
\end{aligned}
$$

Thus, all one needs to calculate the propensities in a system is a table of joint occurrences that categorizes a sufficient number of observations on its behavior.

This definition of propensity also makes intuitive sense. If a_i and b_j are completely independent, then $p(a_i,\ b_j) = p(a_i) \times p(b_j)$, and $P_{ij} = 0$. A value of $P_{ij} > 0$ means that the associated process has that particular propensity to happen *in the given system context*. For any prescribed system configuration the count of $P_{ij} < 0$ is usually small, especially in systems that are the result of natural evolution. The processes with negative P_{ij} do not coordinate well with the prevailing system kinetics. There is a degree of selection pressure against their happening. That they nevertheless occur is due either to chance disturbance, or to a particular limiting factor that has not been included in the system description. (For example, a particular predator–prey interaction may have a negative propensity when interactions are measured in terms of carbon flows; however, this may mask the possibility that this prey provides essential nitrogen to the predator. As mentioned earlier, processes with low or negative propensities may become major players in a system's adaptation to unforeseen changing external conditions.)

AN EMERGING EVOLUTIONARY SYNTHESIS

Popper may have been unaware of the extent to which his desiderata already are part of emerging evolutionary theory. His sought-after "calculus of conditional probabilities" is extant in current information theory, which may be used to facilitate a quantification of propensities that accords well with observable trends in evolving systems.

Some readers might object (in good Popperian tradition) that the principle of increasing ascendency and its attendant calculus of propensities are seeming tautologies. Just how tautologous they really are is a matter of hierarchical perspective. Rather than contend the issue, however, I am content to point out that, tautologous or not, ascendency makes quantitative that which heretofore was only descriptive. The same critics could as well argue that the laws of thermodynamics are only tautologies, but it is hard to deny their power in making explicitly quantitative that which had been only intuitive. Beyond regretting death and taxes, one may now aspire to measure the entropy productions that thereby ensue.

Similarly, ascendency provides the ecologist with a gauge of ecosystem status. In the event of perturbation, the size and trophic organization of the ecosystem can now be measured before and after the fact. The ascendency and its related variables give the economist tools that are more powerful than the gross community product for judging the vitality of an economic system. The propensities of individual economic exchanges can be calculated to indicate how well that activity accords with the economic community at large.

Perhaps even more importantly, the theories of ascendency and propensity could impart significant momentum to a new and more dynamic worldview. For science today is truly schizophrenic in its view of nature. At one extreme is the model of the world as a universal clockwork – the Cartesian and Newtonian attitude that everything is connected in rigid and deterministic sense to other elements of the universal machine. At the other extreme is the disconcerting inference from quantum physics that, at its core, nature is chaotic and without form.

Like Lucretius, who saw only atoms and the void, prevailing dogma provides no middle ground between the motion of the planets and the vagaries of quarks. When contemporary science applies its models to living systems, the fit is usually awkward – like the shell game of neo-Darwinism that distracts the observer from the agencies at hand by oscillating between the realms of molecule and machine.

In contrast, Popper, and others such as Peirce and Prigogine, are assuring us that the living world at the level of more immediate experience is amenable to scientific narration and quantification. Furthermore, causes of behavior there do not originate only at the edges of life and propagate inward – they can appear within its very fabric! Living beings are neither automata nor epiphenomena; some degree of autonomy is proper to each organism.

To the strict determinist, this idea of an open universe was too horrible to contemplate, like staring into the yawning abyss. They might concede that probabilities could be useful in describing confusing situations, but would argue that behind an indeterministic appearance, there lies hidden a deterministic reality. This was the motivation behind Einstein's famous quotation, "God does not play dice!" It appears that Popper is now responding to his hero: "God plays dice all right. But not to worry – they're loaded!"

ACKNOWLEDGMENTS

I am greatly indebted to Dr Arne Freimuth Petersen at Copenhagen University, who made a generous gift of Popper's book to me. Accompanying his present was the admonition that Popper's notions provided a better backdrop for my own theories than the one I had been using. I at first resisted his suggestion, and still have reservations about much of Popper's work. However, I hope this essay will give *de facto* testimony to the wisdom of Dr Petersen's advice. I also wish to thank John Collier, Elias Khalil, Kenneth Tenore, Marie Ulanowicz and Bruce Weber for offering suggestions helpful in revising an earlier draft of this chapter. Mrs Jeri Pharis typed the several copies of the evolving manuscript.

REFERENCES

Baird, D. and Ulanowicz, R. E. (1989) "The seasonal dynamics of the Chesapeake Bay ecosystem," *Ecological Monographs*, 59: 329–364.
Engelberg, J. and Boyarsky, L. L. (1979) "The noncybernetic nature of ecosystems," *The American Naturalist* 114: 317–324.

Depew, D. J. and Weber, B. H. (1995) *Darwinism Evolving: Systems Dynamics and the Genealogy of Natural Selection*, Cambridge, MA: MIT Press, p. 588.

Lewin, R. (1984) "Why is development so illogical?" *Science* 224: 1327–1329.

Li, M. and Vitanyi, P. M. B. (1992) "Inductive reasoning and Kolmogorov complexity," *Journal of Computer and System Sciences* 44(2): 343–384.

Odum, E. P. (1969) "The strategy of ecosystem development," *Science* 164: 262–270.

Onsager, L. (1931) "Reciprocal relations in irreversible processes," *Physical Review* 37: 405–426.

Popper, K. R. (1974) "The philosophy of Karl Popper," Vol. XIV, Book I, In P. A. Schlipp (ed.) *The Library of Living Philosophers*, LaSalle, Ill.: Open Court.

—— (1990) *A World of Propensities*, Bristol: Thoemmes.

Rutledge, R. W., Basorre, B. L. and Mulholland, R. J. (1976) "Ecological stability: an information theory viewpoint," *Journal of Theoretical Biology* 57: 355–371.

Tribus, M. and McIrvine, E. C. (1971) "Energy and information," *Scientific American* 225(3): 179–188.

Ulanowicz, R. E. (1980) "An hypothesis on the development of natural communities," *Journal of Theoretical Biology* 85: 223–245.

—— (1986) *Growth and Development: Ecosystems Phenomenology*, New York: Springer-Verlag..

—— (1989) "A phenomenology of evolving networks," *Systems Research* 6: 209–217.

—— (1990) "Aristotelean causalities in ecosystem development," *Oikos* 57: 42–48.

—— (1991) "Formal agency in ecosystem development," in M. Higashi and T. D. Burns (eds) *Theoretical Studies of Ecosystems: The Network Perspective*, Cambridge: Cambridge University Press, pp. 58–70.

Weber, B. H., Depew, D. J., Dyke, C., Salthe, S. N., Schneider, E. D., Ulanowicz, R. E. and Wicken, J. S. (1989) "Evolution in thermodynamic perspective: An ecological approach," *Biology and Philosophy* 4: 373–405.

11

SYNERGETICS AS A BRIDGE BETWEEN THE NATURAL AND SOCIAL SCIENCES

Hermann Haken

WHAT IS SYNERGETICS ABOUT?

For a long time, it seemed that science was being split into more and more disciplines, and that there would be no unifying principles at all. Over the last couple of decades, however, this trend has been changing. A number of attempts are being made, aiming at building bridges among the different sciences. Synergetics may be considered as one of these bridges. I coined the term "synergetics" over twenty years ago (Haken, 1969, 1971) in order to characterize an interdisciplinary field of research that did not exist at that time. When we browse through different scientific disciplines, we will find that quite often they deal with the following problem: The objects of research are composed of individual parts, which by their cooperation may produce spatial, temporal, or functional structures. Let us consider a few simple examples. In physics, molecules may form a liquid which may exhibit different kinds of motions. In chemistry, specific kinds of molecules may undergo reactions by which macroscopic patterns, e.g., in the form of spirals or concentric rings, are formed. In biology, the individual cells constituting organisms cooperate in a highly organized fashion. High cooperation can also be found in animal societies, in human economy, or in human society. It is important to stress that these structures are not imposed from the outside, but that they are fully organized by the system itself, that is, we are considering self-organizing systems. As far as physics, chemistry, and biology are concerned, synergetics focuses its attention on open systems whose functioning or organization is maintained by a more or less continuous input of energy and/or matter into the system.

The question I asked some twenty years ago was whether general principles governing self-organization, irrespective of the nature of the individual parts of a system, exist. At least at that time, this question must have sounded rather far-fetched because subsystems may be as diverse as atoms or molecules in physics and chemistry, cells in biology, or animals or humans in a society. But actually, this question could be answered positively for large classes of systems. As one may guess, a price had to be paid for the generality of the applicability of these principles. The price is that we have to focus our attention on those situations in which the macroscopic properties of a system change qualitatively. What is meant by this statement will become clear by means of the examples I am providing below.

The principles governing self-organization have been revealed in a rather comprehensive, rigorous mathematical theory which has been published in some of my books (Haken, 1983a, 1983b, 1988). This is certainly not the place to describe these mathematical theories. All I want to say here is that the statements made are statements on structural relationships. It is important to stress at the very beginning that I am not advocating any physicalism in which we try to transfer concepts of physics to other disciplines – say sociology. Rather, what we are doing here is to exemplify the mathematical relationships by simple examples, some of which belong to physics.

THE LASER PARADIGM

Let us begin with an example of general principles in the field of physics. This example has both an advantage and a disadvantage. Its advantage is that the concepts can be deduced in every detail and the predictions made because the theory has been checked experimentally. The disadvantage may be that a sociologist not familiar with physics will not appreciate the stringency of the conclusions; rather, he may even argue that a society is extremely complex and a rather soft system. For this reason, we shall discuss these points later in more detail. But let us start with our simple example and show why it is so pertinent for the spontaneous formation of structures or, in other words, for self-organization.

A simple example of a laser is provided by a gas laser. A glass tube is filled with a gas comprised of atoms. At the end faces of the glass tube, two mirrors are mounted. They serve to reflect light waves running in an axial direction to interact strongly with the atoms of the gas in a way which we shall describe below. An electric current sent through the gas excites the individual atoms energetically. After an excitation, an individual atom acts as a miniature radio antenna by emitting a wave train of light (instead of a radio wave). If the current is weak, only a small percentage of the atoms becomes excited. Each of them emits an individual wave train which can be visualized as throwing a pebble into water, creating a water wave. When several atoms are excited, it is as if we are throwing a handful of pebbles into water, and a wildly excited water surface will emerge. However, when we increase the current, more and more atoms will get excited. Suddenly a new phenomenon occurs: namely, instead of the many independent wave trains, a practically continuous giant wave emerges. In other words, the microscopic chaos of the original emission of light is replaced by macroscopic order. How is this achieved? As was shown by Einstein (1917) at the beginning of this century, an excited atom may not only spontaneously emit a wave train, but it can also be forced by a wave train impinging on it to give its energy to that wave train so that the latter is enhanced. When several excited atoms are hit one after the other by a wave train, quite evidently a light avalanche will be generated. A subtle point must be considered, however. Namely, as it develops, different kinds of wave trains act differently upon the atoms. A particular wave train is more efficient to force an atom to enhance its strength than are other wave trains. In this way, a competition between different avalanches occurs and one specific amplified wave wins the competition. Some kind of Darwinism (of the nonintentional kind) of the inanimate world is at work here.

Now the important concepts of synergetics enter. Once a light wave has won the competition, it forces all the atoms to deliver their energy to it. At the same time, the electrons in the atoms are forced to oscillate in a highly ordered fashion prescribed by the emerging light wave. Thus, the light wave that evolves describes both the order in the system and also gives orders to the individual atoms, i.e., to the individual parts. This is why we call this quantity the order parameter. At the same time, we realize the existence of a circular causality. The order parameter enslaves the individual atoms, whereas the individual atoms support the order parameter. The behavior of one conditions the behavior of the other subsystem. When we disturb the order parameter "light wave," it can return to its former state only after a rather long period of time. The subsystems, namely the atoms, on the other hand, relax very quickly after any perturbation. Order parameters and enslaved subsystems are thus distinguished by different timescales of their individual adjustments.

This will be an important criterion for the applicability of the concept of the order parameter and the slaving principle. As the mathematical theory reveals, the transition of the microscopic state to the highly ordered state of laser light can be described thus: The order parameter behaves as if it is a ball moving in a landscape. If the electric current is small enough, the landscape has the form shown in Figure 11.1.

After each emission of a light wave train, the ball will relax towards its equilibrium value, i.e., the order parameter relaxes to zero and shows only fluctuations around its zero value. However, when the current exceeds a critical value, the landscape is deformed into Figure 11.2, which apparently has two minima. (Actually, in the laser case, the situation is still more complicated, but for our purposes, it will be sufficient to treat the present case). Quite evidently, the former value "zero" of the order parameter has become unstable and is replaced by two new stable equilibrium points at the bottoms of the valleys. Of course, the system can go to only one of the two valleys, i.e., it has to break the symmetry. Now a very important but subtle point comes into play, namely, what causes the system to go to one

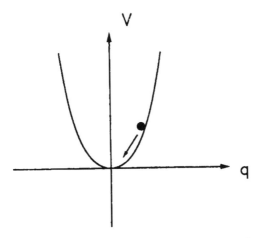

Figure 11.1 Visualization of the behavior of an order parameter q by means of the position of a ball moving in a hilly landscape with one valley

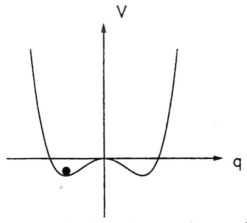

Figure 11.2 Same as Figure 11.1, but the landscape now has two valleys with two bottoms

or the other minimum? This is achieved by an initial spontaneous emission of a wave train which, according to quantum theory, cannot be predicted. Thus, a chance event at a microscopic level determines which course the system will take on the macroscopic, observable level.

Another phenomenon is of fundamental importance, namely that when the current is increased from below to above its critical value, the curve of Figure 11.3 becomes very flat close to the equilibrium point. The ball, however, is still subject to fluctuations. Because the restoring force in such a flat potential is extremely small, the ball will feel strongly the fluctuations

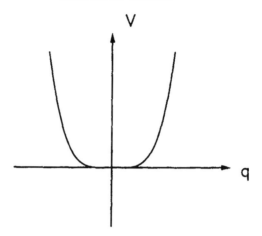

Figure 11.3 When a control parameter is changed, there is an intermediate situation between Figures 11.1 and 11.2, where there is still only one valley but with a very broad bottom

to which it is exposed. Its amplitude will oscillate strongly; we are thus dealing with so-called critical fluctuations. When the ball is pushed away from its equilibrium point, because of the very small restoring force, it will relax very, very slowly to its equilibrium value. This phenomenon is called critical slowing down.

When the electric current is increased more and more, the previously established ordered light wave may become unstable and may be replaced by other phenomena, e.g., by regular light flashes or by so-called deterministic chaos. In these cases, not just one but several order parameters occur, and their interplay determines the total behavior of the laser. This example allows us to formulate the results of the abstract mathematical theory of self-organizing systems in the following way: A change of rather unspecific conditions, in the laser case namely the power of the electric current, may cause the system to undergo a qualitative change on a macroscopic scale. In technical terms, the old state, e.g., the microscopic chaotic state, becomes unstable and is replaced by a new state – in our case, the laser light state. At the instability point, one or a few order parameters occur. They enslave the individual parts of the system and thus create a specific structure within the system. At instability points in general, the system has the choice of several possibilities; which one is realized depends upon microscopic fluctuations. In the transition region, critical slowing down and critical fluctuations occur. These concepts and the corresponding mathematical tools have been applied either to explain or to predict a variety of phenomena in physics, such as structure formation in fluids, in plasmas, in semiconductors, and so

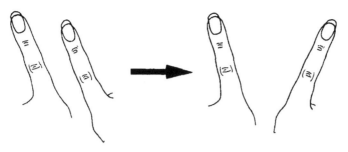

Figure 11.4 Transition from a parallel finger movement to an antiparallel symmetric one

on. But this is not our concern here; we want rather to proceed to biology, psychology, the computer sciences, and sociology.

BIOLOGY: THE FINGER MOVEMENT PARADIGM OF KELSO

As we all know, humans and higher animals are composed of billions of cells of different types such as muscle cells, nerve cells, tissue cells, and others. They have to cooperate in a highly organized fashion, so as to produce morphogenesis, locomotion, movements, feeling, heartbeat, and blood circulation among others. Quite clearly, such highly organized co-operation must occur at the cognitive level. What are the principles behind this high coordination? An experiment done by Scott Kelso (Kelso, 1989) may serve as a fundamental paradigm. A few years ago, Scott Kelso visited me and told me about the following experiment: He asked test persons to move their fingers in parallel and then asked them to move their fingers more and more quickly. Suddenly, the finger movement changed quite involuntarily from the parallel to the antiparallel, i.e., symmetric configuration (Figure 11.4). Quite clearly, what happens here is a qualitative change of a system on a macroscopic level, or, in other words, a phase transition.

Can we apply the concepts of synergetics to this experiment, and can we model its features? Quite clearly, the relative position of the fingers or, in more technical terms, the relative phase between the oscillating fingers, suggests itself as the adequate order parameter. In the simple case of a single order parameter, one may try to construct a landscape describing its movement. Such a landscape can be easily devised by simple arguments that I will not repeat here (Haken *et al.*, 1985). As it develops, the landscape has the form shown in Figure 11.5 and undergoes a series of slight deformations when the speed of the finger movement is increased from the upper left to the lower right corners. From the qualitative point of view, a number of predictions can already be made. Namely, when the situation

239

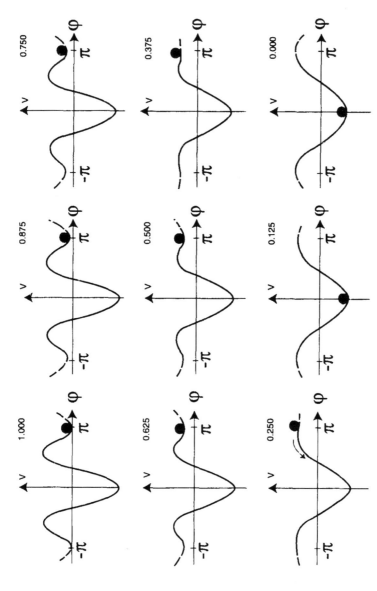

Figure 11.5 The landscape describing the behavior of the relative phase of the finger experiment. In the upper left corner, the finger movement is still slow, and the system is in a stable state in the upper right valley, as indicated by the ball. With increasing speed of the finger movements, the landscape is deformed until in the middle row, on the right-hand side, the unstable situation is reached, and a little push now can cause the ball to fall down to the absolute minimum corresponding to the antiparallel finger movement. With a still higher speed of finger movement, the lower minimum is the only minimum available

of the middle row, right-hand side of Figure 11.5 is reached, the position corresponding to the parallel finger movement becomes unstable; the ball will fall down to the absolute minimum and stay there. This corresponds to the symmetric finger movement. When a person moves his or her fingers quickly in the symmetric mode, and then is asked to slow the finger movement down, the ball will, of course, stay at the absolute minimum. This prediction could easily be checked by Kelso and verified. This is the effect of hysteresis that is well known in physics. In the case of hysteresis, the state of a system depends on its past history. For instance, when a ferromagnet is subjected to an external magnetic field, the magnetization may become parallel to the magnetic field at a specific field strength. When we reverse the field, the magnetization will switch again, but at a different field strength than before. In other words, the ferromagnet has retained some kind of memory of what happened to it previously.

But as we have observed earlier, close to the instability point, critical fluctuations and critical slowing down must be expected (Schöner et al., 1986). By careful measurements, Kelso could show that the relative phase undergoes pronounced fluctuations in the transition region, and that it can also show the phenomenon of critical slowing down (Schöner et al., 1987) once the finger movement is disturbed. Our model can be cast in a mathematical form so that these statements can be made quantitative. This is, however, not our concern here. What is important is the following statement: It has often been argued that our brain is a computer which, by specific programs, steers the motion of our extremities and our other functions. However, the picture we are drawing here is quite different. It strongly suggests that a biological system is a self-organizing one when it coordinates the movements of its extremities. The concept of a computer program could not explain how critical slowing down and critical fluctuations arise. Rather, these features are typical for self-organizing systems. A variety of experiments presently being undertaken shows that this interpretation of biological coordination holds in a variety of cases.

THE APPLICATION TO COMPUTER SCIENCE: THE SYNERGETIC COMPUTER FOR PATTERN RECOGNITION

How far do the concepts of order parameters, slaving principle, and so on reach when we are dealing with complicated patterns? Remember that the slaving principle allows us to introduce a considerable compression of information into complex systems because it permits us to express the behavior of the numerous components of a system by order parameters. To demonstrate the power of the order parameter concept, we constructed the "synergetic computer," based upon principles of synergetics that allow for pattern recognition. Since this computer has been described elsewhere in

241

Figure 11.6 A well-known example of an ambivalent picture: vase or faces?

Figure 11.7 Another example: old or young woman?

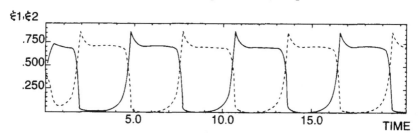

Figure 11.8 Results from a computer simulation of the perception of ambiguous figures. Along the abscissa time is plotted, whereas the ordinates ξ_1, ξ_2 represent the size of the order parameters corresponding, say, to the vase or the faces. The oscillation between these two percepts can clearly be seen

242

great detail (Haken, 1990), we shall not dwell on any details but rather stress the salient features. The basic idea is that a specific pattern is described by its order parameter and the slaving principle, by which the system is brought into the state prescribed by the order parameter. Once a set of features, e.g., the eyes and the nose, are given, the system generates its order parameter which competes with order parameters to which other noses or eyes belong. This competition is eventually won by the order parameter connected with the presented nose and eyes. Once the order parameter has won the competition, it is able to restore the whole pattern. The original relationship between each order parameter and its pattern is determined by a learning procedure.

The order parameter concept is thus a highly powerful tool in constructing a new type of computer which actually can be fully parallelized to act as a competitor to the presently discussed neural computers. It may be worthwhile to elucidate similar features, and differences, between neural and synergetic computers. Both concepts aim at realizations of computers by computer architectures in which computations occur in parallel within specific basic cells. In neural computers, these cells have only two internal states – namely, on and off. A switch from the off-state to the on-state occurs if the input signals from the other cells exceed a certain threshold. The cells of the synergetic computer may occupy a continuum of states. Their activity depends smoothly, in a nonlinear fashion, upon the input from the other cells. In contrast to neural computers, a complete learning theory of synergetic computers exists. Its performance leads to unique results, whereas in neural computers difficulties still need to be overcome, such as the appearance of so-called spurious states.

We mention here only that the order parameter concept allows us to make connection with Gestalt theory, originally formulated by Wertheimer and Köhler (Köhler, 1920) and that it allows us to describe a number of detailed experiments in the field of psychophysics on ambiguous figures, as shown in Figures 11.6–8. After we have developed some confidence in the concepts of order parameters and the slaving principle, let us now turn to the so-called softer sciences, which actually will produce hard problems. I will take the example of sociology, though a number of remarks will also apply to economics and possibly ecology.

ORDER PARAMETERS AND THE SLAVING PRINCIPLE IN SOCIOLOGY

Let me begin with a provocative statement. In my opinion, the concept of order parameters and the slaving principle will become central issues in sociology. Let us consider some typical order parameters in society. A language certainly survives longer than any individual. When a baby is born, he or she is subjected to the language of his or her parents and

243

later to that of other people of the same nation. When grown up, the individual carries the language further. In technical terms of synergetics, the baby is enslaved by the language. How much we are saturated by our mother tongue becomes clear when we visit other countries. There is by no means a one-to-one correspondence among words in different languages, and there are a great variety of subtleties that cannot be translated properly. This becomes particularly evident when we try to translate poetry. At the same time, language provides us with a powerful means of communication among members of the same nation. How much we are influenced by a language also becomes evident when we consider different accents. For instance, in the United States, one cannot distinguish between people only from the north or the south. A skilled person can even tell, by listening to somebody from New York, in which part of New York he or she was raised. Generally speaking, language establishes an identity among a certain class of people and, at the same time, serves to distinguish them from other people. Clearly then, language is a typical order parameter.

Another order parameter is national character. Whether one may define a national character or not was beautifully discussed by Gregory Bateson some decades ago (Bateson, 1944). It is still worth reading his article. As he points out, a national character is brought about by the evolution of attitudes of people interacting with each other. He characterizes national character not by single properties but by dual properties such as dominance or obedience. Bateson was, of course, not aware of synergetics, which came into existence only later. From his definition of national character, one can easily deduce that it has all the properties of an order parameter.

Another order parameter is "ritual." Rituals serve to identify a group and to discriminate that group from others. The external form of a ritual is not at all important. All that matters is that the ritual is done within a specific group of people only. In the ritual, a newly-born baby or a youngster becomes a member of that group. Another order parameter is the kind of state, such as democracy, dictatorship, and possibly others. The set of laws constitutes an order parameter. Law is the outcome of a typical collective effect. Quite a number of laws can be interpreted as means to resolve conflicts originally at an individual level by collective regulation. To give a simple example: When a couple marries, it is not obvious at all whether the husband and wife will adopt the husband's or the wife's name. This solution can be negotiated at a personal level between the two married people, but the conflict can be resolved by a law stating, for example, that the family has to carry the name of the husband. Considering some less serious issues, we may state that fashion is an order parameter. Another order parameter is public opinion, though difficult interplay among individuals, mass media, government, and so on, obtains.

When I use the term "slaving principle" or "enslavement" for relationships betwen individuals and the order parameters, sociologists are quite often shocked. They tell me that individuals have a free will and may certainly choose, so to speak, their order parameter quite freely. A friend of mine has suggested replacing the word "enslavement" by "consensualization." A good way out of our dilemma may be a careful distinction between "rules" and "principles" as developed in the article "Natural complex vs. natural system" by Elias L. Khalil (Khalil, 1990), and I hope to return to this issue at a later occasion. Since with this issue we are coming to the heart of the relationships between individuals and society, let us discuss it further. First of all, one cannot deny that there are strong cases for an influence of order parameters on individuals. Such a case is certainly prescribed by language – possibly also by rituals. It is certainly true that joining a religious movement is voluntary. However, we know quite well of recent examples how strong the pressure of a group can become upon an individual, even leading to collective suicide in the extreme case. Another reason why I wish to retain the word "enslavement" is based on the following observation: One may ask how it was possible that Germany so easily became a prey of Nazism. In my opinion, this was again a collective effect, where people looked at each other, and each individual followed the other. This is a typical cause for an instability which may lead to anything – even to criminal acts. I think it is very important to make people aware of the collective effects of their enslavement mechanisms so as to counteract these early enough. These mechanisms are linked up, for instance, with national characteristics such as obedience.

Let me list a few other order parameters, for instance in companies. One of them is corporate identity; another is social climate within a company. Why, in our opinion, is the concept of the order parameter so important? Because it points to the way we may or may not change an order parameter. Let us consider the social climate within a company. One cannot give a command such as be friendly to each other to the individuals. The social climate has evolved and when newcomers enter the company, they are subjected to the social climate and enslaved by it. As we have learned in synergetics, order parameters cannot be changed by the action of an individual (subsystem), but rather by the change of external conditions – in the present case by a change of the general frame of working conditions.

Before we discuss the mechanisms of changes in more detail, let us list a few other order parameters from other fields, namely economics and science. The important role of slowly varying variables (in synergetic terms, the order parameters) and fast varying variables was clearly stated in the important book by Paul Samuelson (Samuelson, 1947). This distinction also plays an important role in a recent work by Wei-Bin Zhang (1991). In his well-known book *The Structure of Scientific Revolutions*, Thomas S. Kuhn (1970) introduced the terms "paradigm" and "changes of paradigms." Scrutinizing his book, we readily observe that his paradigms are also the order parameters of synergetics.

Let us now discuss "mechanism of changes." Let us ask the question: Can an individual change the order parameter, or under what condition can he or she change it? Let us take a concrete example. Can an individual start a revolution? In my opinion, there is a clear prerequisite: namely, the whole situation must be close to an instability. In politics, such instabilities may be caused by long-lasting economic depressions, many acts of terrorism, loss of credibility of a specific form of state, and so on. Only under such conditions may a revolution begin. However, as the mathematical theory of synergetics illustrates, there may be different realizations beyond the instability point. Which one will be reached depends upon small fluctuations or, in the present case, on a decisive group of individuals who will drive the destabilized system into the new state. From this point of view, a revolution is a two-step process consisting of destabilization and then the decisive fluctuation driving the system into a specific new stable state. During such a transition, typical phenomena known in synergetics as critical fluctuation and critical slowing down occur. These are phenomena which we can clearly observe now in the decay of the former Soviet Union. But from general principles of synergetics, it follows that the further course of this system is not at all evident. One must not expect that, for instance, democracy will now be established automatically in all parts of that decayed union. Which new kind of state will emerge in each case is a very subtle question which depends upon individuals, but which hopefully may also be influenced by external means, e.g., by the kinds of economic support given.

An important issue is, of course, whether one can do experiments on the formation of order parameters in society. In this respect, an early experiment by Solomon Asch (Asch, 1952) seems to be both relevant and important. Solomon Asch made the following test: He had about ten test persons; however, only one of these was a real test person. The others were his helpers, but that was not known to the real test person. Now he showed the group three lines of different lengths and asked the group: "Which one is the longest line?" His helpers gave the correct answer, and the test person did too. Then he repeated the experiment, and his helpers gave a specific wrong answer. In this case, about 60 per cent of the test persons changed their opinion and agreed to the wrong answer of the helpers. For me, this was a clear indication of how easily people can be influenced regarding their opinion formation. In my opinion, such a formation of a collective opinion (an order parameter) is still more pronounced if a situation becomes truly difficult and complex. When I discussed these results of my interpretation with a sociologist, to my surprise he denied the applicability of the results of Asch's experiments to social issues. He said, "In the situation caused by Asch, the test person wanted to be sociable. If there were, however, really important issues, then the test person would develop his or her own opinion." I quote my conversation because it shows the limits of the possibility of having an interdisciplinary talk. What seemed to me quite obvious was entirely denied by the other person.

I hope my above points illustrate the limits of predictability. When a system is destabilized, we cannot predict, at least in general, which new stable state it will become. This depends on very subtle events. Nevertheless, before such an instability point is reached, there are indications for its occurrence, namely critical fluctuations and critical slowing down. In retrospective, these critical fluctuations could be clearly observed before the German Democratic Republic broke down, by, for instance, mass demonstrations.

THE ROLE OF CHAOS THEORY

More recently, it has become fashionable to apply chaos theory to events in society and the economy, to mention two examples. First of all, we must bear in mind that chaos theory applies only when the so-called dimension of a system is small, or when only a few degrees of decisive freedom exist. But how can a complex system such as a society or a market exhibit only a few degrees of freedom if so many individuals are involved? The answer is provided by synergetics, according to which the degrees of freedom are the order parameters. But, in general, these degrees of freedom are not explicitly known in chaos theory; rather, we have only one or a few indicators, e.g., the gross national product. A number of methods have been developed mathematically to reconstruct the dynamics of a chaotic system once the time evolution of one variable is known. In such a case, one may determine so-called fractal dimensions and Lyapunov exponents, the latter being a measure for how long a time we may predict the time development of such a system. But there is the following crucial point: In order to derive the above-mentioned quantities, the observed time series must be long enough. There is no case known to me in which this condition is fulfilled in the economy, society, or even in weather forecasting. Thus chaos theory can give us some qualitative hints, but I think a search for underlying models giving quantitative agreement with observed data will be in vain.

I am very sceptical about quantitative predictions for complex systems, such as economic and social ones. While it may seem necessary to make such predictions, we must be also aware of their great limitations. The only way out is to steer a system continuously and softly by setting conditions again and again so that it can smoothly self-organize into a hopefully optimal state. This then leads to the question of control parameters, which in the economy may be interest rates, the amount of cash flow, and so on. But the discussion of these issues is beyond this chapter.

HERMANN HAKEN

CONCLUDING REMARKS

I have tried to show how the same principles can be applied to quite a variety of disciplines dealing with self-organizing processes in complex systems. The systems treated ranged from physics to sociology. Because of the analogies thus unearthed, it becomes possible to model phenomena in complex systems, for instance, by computer procedures. It should be stressed that I constrained myself in the above chapter to the conceptual level; the level at which concrete models are produced has been described in a variety of volumes of the Springer Series in Synergetics lectures.

REFERENCES

Asch, Solomon E. (1952) "Group forces in the modification and distortion of judgements," in *Social Psychology*, New York: Prentice-Hall Inc., 452.
Bateson, G. (1944) "Morale and national character," in *Civilian Morale. Society for the Psychological Study of Social Issues*, Second Yearbook, ed. Goodwin Watson, Boston: Houghton, Mifflin Co. (for Regual and Hitchcock, New York) 71–91.
Einstein, A. (1917) "Zur Quantentheorie der Strahlung," *Physik Zeitschrift* 18: 121.
Haken, H. (1969) Lectures at Stuttgart University, in H. Haken and R. Graham, (1971) *Umschau* 6: 191.
—— (1983a) *Synergetics, An Introduction*, 3rd edn, Berlin: Springer.
—— (1983b) *Advanced Synergetics*, Berlin: Springer.
—— (1988) *Information and Self-Organization*, Berlin: Springer.
—— (1990) *Synergetic Computers and Cognition*, Berlin: Springer.
Haken, H., Kelso, J. A. S., Bunz, H. (1985) "A theoretical model of phase transitions in human hand movement," *Biological Cybernetics* 51: 347–356.
Kelso, J. A. S. (1989) "Phase transitions and critical behavior in human bimanual coordination," *American Journal of Physiology: Regulatory, Integrative and Comparative Physiology* 15: R1000–R1004.
Khalil, E. (1990) "Natural complex vs. natural system," *Journal of Social and Biological Structures*, February, 13(1): 11–31.
Köhler, W. (1920) *Die physischen Gestalten in Ruhe und im stationären Zustand*, Braunschweig: Vieweg.
Kuhn, Thomas S. (1970) *The Structure of Scientific Revolution*, Chicago: University of Chicago Press.
Samuelson, Paul (1947) *Foundations of Economic Analysis*, Cambridge, MA: Harvard University Press.
Schöner, G., Haken, H., and Kelso, J. A. S. (1986) "A stochastic theory of phase transitions in human hand movement," *Biological Cybernetics* 53: 442.
Schöner, G., Haken, H., Kelso, J. A. S., and Scholz, J. P. (1987) "Phase-locked modes, phase transitions and component oscillators in biological motion," *Physica Scripta* 35: 79–87.
Zhang, Wei-Bin (1991) *Synergetic Economics*, Berlin: Springer.

12

THE PROBLEM OF OBSERVABLES IN MODELS OF BIOLOGICAL ORGANIZATIONS

Howard H. Pattee

INTRODUCTION

The concepts and methodologies of physics have provided powerful tools that are useful for modeling biological and social systems. However, all models have limited domains, and the classical question always arises: Are the methodologies of physics adequate to model *all* the domains that characterize living organizations? I will discuss a domain where they are not. This is the domain characterized by epistemic functions like observation, classification, recognition, and measurement, that existing physical theory, in order to be universal, has excluded by principle. Physical theory is designed to be observer-independent, whereas living organisms must continually discover new observables to survive and evolve. I am not claiming that some physical description of all biological activity is not possible. Insofar as laws are universal, such a formal reductionist description is certainly possible, at least in principle. However, such a detailed description cannot derive or reveal the significant observables at the level of function. This is the case even within physical theory itself, where the choice of observables and the process of measurement is not derivable from physical laws.

The modern programmable computer is apparently not restricted by physical laws and is therefore a more general modeling tool. Anyone who wishes to "reduce" biological behavior to a detailed physical description will find computers essential. However, the programmable computer was also designed to be universal, which requires that its internal operations be totally syntactic, isolated from physical analogs and any observational or measurement functions. In other words, universality in computation requires complete syntactic control in a formal symbol system. After discussing the limitations of the universality of physics and the different universality of computation, I will show why concurrent, distributed networks now used mostly for brain models, are necessary for modeling the statistical, epistemic classifications and the complex, autonomous observations that have evolved in biological organizations. Such autonomous network models are also needed for a theory of observables in physics.

THE NATURE OF OBSERVABLES IN PHYSICAL THEORY

The domain of physics is restricted to those laws that are expressible in a mathematical formalism and that satisfy invariance principles that keep the laws independent of the state of the observer. Classical physics studies the laws of universal and inexorable events that we feel "could not have happened any other way," as Wigner (1964) expresses it. Quantum theory has lost this classical determinism but is even more structured by invariance or symmetry principles that assure the minimum influence of the observer on the formalism and the results of measurements. Quantum theory also differs from classical theory in the way the observables enter the formalism, but in both theories there is in every application a clear distinction between the constructs that are treated as measurable observables and those that are not.

This artificial separation of observable and imaginary constructs is embodied in the practice of physics by keeping the laws (expressed in a formal symbol system) and initial conditions (obtained by measurements) operationally distinct. The laws are represented by the equations of motion that define the family of patterns that can be calculated, and the measurements provide the initial conditions that specify which pattern corresponds to the world. Thus, the actual values of observable constructs can be grounded only by measurements, while the values of non-observable constructs can be obtained only by calculations. In practice, all scientists following this paradigm know without ambiguity whether at any moment they are making measurements or doing calculations.

Ideally, this separation guarantees that all the relevant contacts between the formal syntactical aspects of the model and the world occur *only* during the measurement process. That is, the model is related to the world only through explicit observables. All other aspects of the model are essentially imaginative constructs that, beyond generating predictions, appear to be ontologically moot, and are justified only by highly informal metaphysical interpretations, and by aesthetic values such as simplicity, coherence, and elegance.

One of the first statements of this idealized view of formal theories was given in 1894 by Hertz (1956) in the introduction to his *Principles of Mechanics*:

> We form for ourselves images or symbols of external objects; and the form which we give them is such that the necessary consequents of the images in thought are always the images of the necessary consequents in nature of the things pictured. . . . With the things themselves they

are in conformity in *one* important respect, namely, in satisfying the above requirement. For our purpose it is not necessary that they be in conformity with the things in any other respect whatever. As a matter of fact, we do not know, nor have we any means of knowing, whether our conceptions of things are in conformity with them in any other than this *one* fundamental respect.

By "*one* fundamental respect" Hertz did not mean that only one model was possible, since he stated that, "One image may be more suitable for one purpose, another for another." His point was only that whatever image we use, the image has no verifiable truth value except at the perceived or measured "consequents."

This principle that establishes a sharp cut between the world and any formal or syntactic model of the world, also implies that any two formalisms that give the same measurable predictions are operationally equivalent. Two well-known examples of formally equivalent, but conceptually distinct models are the variational view and differential-equation–initial-condition view of trajectories, and the Schrödinger and Heisenberg descriptions of quantum mechanics. Of course, the conceptual and aesthetic differences between these formalisms, as in all formalisms, play an essential role in our choice of theory (e.g. Polanyi, 1958). Quantum theory is exceptional because its non-observable constructs are so completely imaginary that they appear to have no commonsense interpretation. This contributes to the view, as expressed by Wheeler (1982), that, "No elementary quantum phenomenon is a phenomenon until it is a recorded phenomenon" (i.e., the results of a measurement).

THE NATURE OF OBSERVATION IN LIVING ORGANISMS

Organisms have evolved and learned to recognize patterns by direct sensing or perceptions that are far more numerous and complex than physical observables. These natural observables are selected because of their survival value, which often means that patterns must map to immediate actions rather than computations. Consequently, the organism's measurement process is normally a *classification* of patterns that allows immediate decisions rather than the quantitative values necessary for computation. There are, of course, some elementary observables, like length, time, force, and temperature that have quantitative physical measurement procedures that naturally correlate with our senses. These direct perceptions are usually felt to be closer to what we call reality than other physical concepts like potentials, vector fields, spins, and wave functions. This is a reasonable and useful belief for everyday survival, but nevertheless from the physicist's point of view it remains only a metaphysical belief, since "reality" is not an

251

observable of any physical theory. Fortunately, the predictive value of physical theory does not depend on which metaphysical view of reality we may prefer.

For many years I have used generalized epistemic operations like observation, detection, recognition, measurement, and control as the essential type of function that distinguishes living from non-living organizations (Pattee, 1967, 1972, 1982). Survival requires the discovery of the significant patterns in the environment that can improve the organism's control stategies. This recognition-control behavior is required for survival at all levels from genes to brains, and from families to societies. On the other hand, as I discussed above, physical theory, while depending on well-defined observables, says nothing about how the significant patterns are discovered or selected, nor does the concept of control play any role in describing physical laws. Furthermore, the sharp separation between laws and measurements required by the universality of physical theory is not a characteristic of natural biological recognition-control processes.

My use of words like "observe" and "recognize" here must be generalized beyond their contextual senses in the several disciplines with which they are normally associated. Since I need to discuss the evolution of these functions, I always try to define the simplest cases. For example, I mean by an observer any system that recognizes patterns that subsequently are used to control actions. There are no special words or concepts for the most primitive cases. What is the simplest recognition process? What is the simplest control process? What is the simplest model?

These concepts are normally used at the cognitive level where we speak of recognizing patterns and performing controlled actions based on an intervening model. However, this same language can also be used at the molecular level to describe enzyme catalysis. The enzyme binds (recognizes) its specific substrate and catalyzes (controls) a specific reaction. There is no intervening model in this case, unless it is the structure of the enzyme molecule itself. My use of recognition and control at the enzyme level is not metaphorical. In both cognition and catalysis, the essential requirement for recognition-action or measurement-control function is that the mapping from pattern to action is arbitrary, or gratuitous, in Monod's (1971) sense. Any pattern can be coupled to any action depending on the structure of the cognitive model or the enzyme. If this were not the case, that is, if the measurement-control relation "could not have happened any other way," then it could be described as a law.

Reductionists will of course claim that there is a valid physical description in terms of laws of any imaginable recognition, measurement, or control device, especially at the enzyme level. They would say that the apparent arbitrariness is simply a lack of a complete theory. This is a half-truth. While a lawful description is certainly possible in principle, no such description can define its own initial conditions. Therefore, as von

Neumann (1955) pointed out long ago, such a description in terms of laws alone cannot describe the necessary *function* of measurement and only leads to an infinite regress of increasingly complex lawful descriptions until terminated at some stage by functional measurements that are not describable by laws.

THE NATURE OF MEASUREMENT IN PRIMITIVE ORGANISMS

It is still reasonable to question the use of such high-level terms as "measuring device" and "model" for a structure as simple as an enzyme. In normal usage, both concepts imply a much richer context. I have argued that the simplest context that would allow the normal use of epistemic concepts like measurement and observer is an organization that can construct the measuring device and use the results for its survival. In other words, measurement is not distinguishable by the local behavior of any mechanism. To qualify as a measuring device, it must have a function, and the most primitive concept of function implies improving fitness of an organism. Thus, observation and measurement require an organization that (1) constructs the measuring device, and (2) uses the results of the measurements. This requirement I have called the *semantic closure principle* (Pattee, 1982). This provides an objective criterion for distinguishing measurements and observations from other physical interactions. Only organizations with this semantic closure property should be called observers. The cell is the simplest natural case of an observing system. According to this view, simple artifacts that we commonly call measuring devices, like rulers, pendulums, and thermometers, are not intrinsically measuring devices but perform the measurement function only by virtue of their role in the semantic closure that involves a human constructor, user, and interpreter. Of course, the same semantic closure requirement holds for simple, artificial controls, like governors and thermostats.

There are many relatively simple biological recognition-action structures that might suggest a primitive kind of model. For example, seedlings detect gravity and light, and by converting these input observables to specific rates of growth, they control their morphology. A physiologist might prefer to call such tropisms a stimulus-response action and reserve the concept of model for a more complex relation between recognition and action. A cybernetician, on the other hand, would claim that the seedling has a model of its world, however primitive (Ashby, 1956). In higher organisms, we can recognize the nervous system as the physiological structure with the primary function of mapping sensory inputs from various receptor organs to output actions of muscles, and we often restrict the idea of model to mappings or representations in the brain. However, in the context of the more or less gradual process of evolution, we do not learn much about primitive necessities for function by looking only at highly evolved organisms. There is generally more explanatory power in studying the origin of functions. What are the minimum requirements for this modeling relation in organisms?

An engineering description of a modeling relation would include at least three functions:

(1) detection, recognition, or measurement that transforms a physical pattern into model inputs. In organisms these are usually called receptors or sensory organs;

(2) the model itself that establishes the particular input/output relation; and

(3) the effectors that are controlled by the output of the model and that interact again with the physical environment.

This very general description might apply to the seedling example as well as the brain, but how do we make these divisions? Are these three functions intrinsic within all organisms themselves, or are they simply a convenient and conventional partition based on the physical and engineering paradigms of a model?

The practical criterion for choosing where the world ends and the measurement begins is simple, since the boundaries of organisms are usually sharp. But how do we determine where the measurement ends and the model begins? How do we determine when the model ends and the control begins? Since evolution is a more or less gradual process, the simpler the organism, the less clear these distinctions become, but even in organisms with cells that are highly differentiated physiologically, it is not obvious how detection, modeling, and control should be functionally differentiated.

SOME GENERAL CRITERIA FOR MEASUREMENT PROCESSES

These questions might suggest that it is the gradualism of evolution that makes it difficult to establish boundaries between measurements and model. However, since these same questions have not been answered clearly, even in the case of simple, artificially designed physical measurements, it is clear that gradualism is not the problem. How we should separate what we see as only physical interactions of an organism from perception remains a classical and still controverial problem in psychology. How do we determine the nature of what is observed; that is, how do we distinguish illusions and apparitions that are also observables? When do the various physical stimuli on the receptors become a recognized pattern in the brain?

There are many suggestions on how to objectify the measurement process. One strong criterion used in physics is that the completion of a measurement occurs only when a result has been recorded (see quotation of Wheeler, 1982, above, p. 251). A record implies some kind of memory, but there are many types of records and many types of memories with all degrees of permanence – e.g., chalk marks, the grains of a photographic plate, magnetic tape, short- and long-term memory in the brain, etc. This criterion does not apply easily to the example of seedling growth, since there is no obvious record of interactions with light or gravity.

A weaker and more general criterion for a measurement is that the completion of a measurement *changes the probability* of selective future events. This implies that the result of a measurement gives us new information that updates our calculations of the probability of events. Boltzmann was probably the first to relate entropy to missing information, and Szilard (1929) showed qualitatively how a measurement by an observer can decrease the entropy of the system under observation. Of course to satisfy the second law of thermodynamics, the measuring device itself must have a corresponding increase in entropy, but it is not the system under observation.

Note that this criterion applies to seedling growth, since changing the rate of selected directions of growth amounts to a change of probabilities. This criterion also applies to enzyme catalysis that is defined as a statistical bias on rates of specific reactions. This broad criterion even appears to apply to natural selection, which can also be defined as a statistical bias on the relative rates of survival of hereditary units (Williams, 1966). However, natural selection has no measuring device, unless it is the entire ecosystem, and I would exclude that by the semantic closure principle, since the individual organism (or observer) cannot be said to construct its ecosystem.

This selective statistical bias criterion for measurement also distinguishes the semantic interpretation of information from Shannon and Weaver's (1949) syntactic definition in which measurement processes play no role. The use of Shannon information measure is entirely arbitrary or gratuitous for any physical system for which the concept of fitness or function has no meaning, or for which "useful" work is not defined, since in these cases, information and entropy are formally interchangable. However, information arising from measurement must be distinguished from system entropy, since it can be "usefully" applied as a statistical bias (control) of the system's behavior, as in the Maxwell demon case. Of course, this distinction will remain largely arbitrary until we have a more objective criterion for when a measurement is completed.

THE EVOLUTION OF NON-OBSERVABLE CONSTRUCTS

Fortunately we do not have to solve the measurement problem in order to understand other important conditions that make the results of measurement more effective for survival and adaptation. Evolution has gradually

255

differentiated and improved all functional organs, but the receptor and effector organs that interact directly with the world have strict functional limits determined by natural laws. For example, the sensitivity of detectors is limited by noise, and the forces of effectors by the strength of materials. Such physical limits are approached in the receptors and effectors of many species. Consequently, after approaching these physical limits of input/output transducers, the only significant adaptations left are those occurring in the nervous system.

We recognize two types of brain models: instinctive models, or those inherited primarily from genetic instructions, and acquired models based on individual learning. What is epistemologically significant about primitive instinctive models is that there is little meaning to the distinction between non-observable constructs and observables or between literal and metaphorical models. The only possible test of an instinctive model is natural selection, and natural selection cannot distinguish imaginary constructs from measured observables in the organisms' models. The only evolutionary distinction that can be made between models is between their relative survival rates.

By contrast, our learned cognitive models are evaluated by how well they perform more limited, local functions. Usually these functions are tacit or poorly defined, although clearly the choice of function and quality of the model cannot evade natural selection. Physical models are exceptional because the observer-free universality principle and the separation of laws and measurements are explicit. Man has acquired enormous power from these principles, but still it is not obvious that such power improves his chance of survival as a species. Of course we have no way of knowing at what stage of evolution imagination and myth became components of models important for survival. Certainly it was a gradual process, as it is in infant intellectual development.

One of many possibilities is that imagination improved on stategies of deception as well as its detection. How could this occur? Since deception, as well as its recognition, is already built into primitive instinctive strategies, to improve on these instincts would require a model of deception that can take into account learned experiences about deception. Any great improvement on instinctive models of deception could not consist of only direct observables, since some forms of deception are based on missing observables. In other words, a good model of deception must be made up of non-observable constructs. The same stategy works for discovering laws, even if nature is not deceitful.

In any case, whatever the survival functions of primitive imagination, it is this ability to invent mythical images or non-observable constructs that has, along with larger memories and more rapid learning, so effectively enlarged the domain of models. This domain of imaginary structures is apparently endless and has evolved through all levels of meaning from vague and illusory images; from primitive dance to natural language, with its rich myths, metaphors, and fictions; and only very recently, on an evolutionary scale, to the invention of number, mathematics, and the precise syntactic structures and rules of formal symbol systems. Modern physical theory now, more than ever, consists largely of these imaginative mathematical constructs that conform to reality only in Hertz's "*one* fundamental respect" that the observables agree at the points of completed measurements.

SEQUENTIAL VS COHERENT HYBRID MODELS

The short-term historical evidence would suggest that models that depend either too much on imagination or too much on direct observation and measurement do not survive as well as hybrid models that use the advantages of both. That is, purely imaginary or mythical models, although they may correctly predict some events, carry so many gratuitous, fictitious concepts that they also incorrectly predict most other events. On the other hand, models based only on direct observation and measurement with literal, unimaginative interpretations will generate only local extrapolations and miss the predictive and explanatory power of universal laws that are guided by unobservable, logical, and aesthetic principles. Of course myths and aesthetic principles are themselves undoubtedly influenced by primitive genetic models (Casirer, 1957; Piaget, 1978).

What are the stategies for combining observables and non-observables in a hybrid model? As I have described above, physical theory is one extreme stategy that tries to formalize all non-observables so that they are invariant with respect to observers. This syntactical formalism of laws is semantically grounded only by discrete sequences of measurements performed at times or intervals that are necessarily unpredictable by the theory. One way to say this is that the formal structures of laws form *coherent, rate-dependent* dynamics established by a universal time parameter. The computation of laws requires discrete symbols and *rate-independent* discrete steps. It is the measurement process that maps continuous dynamics into discrete, rate-independent (recorded) symbols. The invariance principles also demand that the measurement event cannot be described by this coherent dynamics, since the time of measurement is the observer's choice. Measurement in physical theory is therefore incoherent, and must be a non-dynamical, sequential process (von Neumann, 1955).

A second less principled stategy of hybrid models is characteristic of the engineering and cybernetic disciplines where the purpose of models is to control the behavior of artificial systems according to intelligently designed functional specifications. In engineering, finding physical laws is not the problem. The laws are assumed, and the problem is to find machines that constrain these laws to fulfill the required function. In these applications, observables are chosen according to their value as *control* parameters for attaining the specified function. Unlike measurements in physics, which are discrete and relatively infrequent, engineering measurements used for control are often made continuously, as in servomechanisms. Measurement in this case becomes a coherent part of the dynamics. Since this type of control is also characteristic of living organisms, they appear to be much more amenable to description by engineering models than by fundamental physical models. However, engineering models also partition the measurement, model, and control functions in constructing machines. Also, as Polanyi (1968) has emphasized, all machines are designed only as prosthetic devices by organisms with brains, and therefore engineering models seldom have any explanatory power for the origin of observables.

COMPUTER MODELS

The most recent addition to scientific modeling tools is the programmable computer. Computers can represent complex behavior that in some ways is beyond the capacity of the brain, and therefore the significance of computer models is sometimes difficult to evaulate. A new appreciation of nonlinear dynamical behavior (strange attractors, chaos, cellular automata, fractals, etc.) has resulted from computer experiments that have caused us to reconsider our views of determinism and random behavior, as well as our choice of significant observables in complex systems. As a result of these computational discoveries, we are more willing to consider the possibility that much detailed biological and social behavior is, in principle, unpredictably complex.

However, the discovery of new observables remains outside the domain of computer programs and requires the pattern-recognizing skills of an intelligent observer. Such "empirical" computations are more accurately interpreted as analogs or artificial worlds in which an outside observer can discover predictable statistical relations and patterns of behavior that would otherwise be undetectable or unrecognizable. All programmable computational processes require that the inputs are already in symbolic form (i.e., all observables have been chosen, and all measurements have been completed), so that the measurement problem does not arise. Therefore, the programmable computer itself cannot be classed as a hybrid model, since the distinction of observable and non-observable, if it is made at all, must be made by an interpreter outside the computer. At the cost of having no intrinsic contact with the world, programmable computers are symbolically universal. Programmable computers can therefore simulate anything that can be defined symbolically, but insofar as a computation is purely syntactic, its operation should not be called a *theory* of anything. Of course, the same is true of any purely formal mathematical symbol system.

LIMITS OF UNIVERSALITY IN PHYSICAL AND COMPUTATIONAL MODELS

Both physical and computational models are often described as universal, a description which is used frequently as an argument for reductionism in both types of models. However, "universal" has a different meaning in each case, and both are strictly limited. In physical theory, the concept of physical law is universal only with respect to the defined observables. As I discussed above, all candidates for a law must, in principle, apply everywhere and at all times, i.e., under all conditions of observation. This is not a demonstrable fact but an epistemological requirement to distinguish what we call objective reality from an individual's local perceptions. The reductionist's claim that all possible observables are derivable from the atomic observables of physical laws remains a metaphysical faith, since not even in physics are observables at any level derivable from the laws.

Computational universality has nothing to do with observables in the physicist's sense, but it is a purely formal statement about equivalent processes of unambiguously rewriting strings of discrete symbols. The term "universal" arose from Turing's discovery of his universal machine that could imitate the computation of any definable Turing machine. This formal concept of "machine" was extended by proofs that other types of symbol-string rewriting rules were equivalent to Turing's universal machine and by the Church–Turing informal thesis that the concept of effective computability did not extend beyond these equivalent formalisms.

Both of these "universal" models have intrinsic limitations that are well known but not always interpreted in the same way. In physics, there are the uncertainty relations that assume quantum mechanics is a complete description (i.e., no hidden variables), but in which determinism is proved impossible by limitations on the precision of simultaneous measurement of conjugate observables (e.g., position and momentum). A kind of converse limit occurs in formal systems that assume determinism (i.e., effective computability), but in which completeness is proven impossible (i.e., non-computable functions exist).

These limitations have been used as escapes from the classical determinism of laws and computation that to some appear necessary for modeling emergence of novel traits, creativity, and the unpredictable behavior characteristic of life. The oldest attempts to escape from classical physical determinism invoke the probabilistic interpretation of quantum mechanics. Gödel incompleteness (see, e.g., Nagel and Newman, 1956) has been used as an escape from syntactic determinism, and as evidence that minds are not machines. More recently the idea of symmetry-breaking instabilities has been added to escape theories (e.g., Prigogine and Stengers, 1984), and the newest escape from determinism is non-computable chaotic dynamics (e.g., Ford, 1989). There are many other ideas on the inadequacy of the physical and computational paradigms for models of life that are too lengthy to be described here (e.g., Lockwood, 1989; Penrose, 1989; Rosen, 1991; Cariani, 1992).

These are all profound limitations, and yet if they could in some way be evaded or overcome, I do not see that the problem of discovery of observables and the arbitrariness of measurement would be resolved. According to my view here, ideas like determinism and chance fall within the enormous class of non-observable constructs that may be conceptually useful for some models and only confusing for others. My point is that whether one or another non-observable construct is appropriate for a model depends on the *observables* chosen for the model. In other words, it can only be of metaphysical concern whether one model of a system uses deterministic constructs and another model of the "same" system uses stochastic constructs as long as the observables of the two models are different. This view is not new. Such complementary models are well known in the reversible mechanical and irreversible thermodynamical descriptions of a system of particles and in quantum mechanics, where the *necessity* of such incompatible constructs is the basis of Bohr's (1927) complementarity principle.

CONCURRENT DISTRIBUTED NETWORK MODELS

The renewal of interest in concurrent, distributed network computer architectures (e.g., Anderson and Rosenfeld, 1988) is in part the result of the superiority over traditional programmed computers to perform *classifications*, and that is one necessary condition for an organism to discover a new observable. What does this mean? Logically, a classification requires a many-to-one mapping, and to realize this in a physical system means that the classes correspond to statistical stationary states reachable from many initial conditions. This idea that a local statistical equilibrium could correspond to a class of input patterns was a key motivation for many distributed network models of cognition (e.g., Hopfield, 1982).

In addition to their potential as models of cognitive activity, network models would appear to apply to a wide variety of biological and social models. Living organizations are highly interconnected as networks at many levels, from the metabolic networks of enzyme-catalyzed reactions, multicellular organisms, and social groupings, to ecological networks. All of evolution has occurred in such metabolic and ecological networks. Kauffman (1991) and others have shown how such network models can be instructive from the molecular level of evolution, even though we do not know the detailed connectivity of such networks, since even random networks exhibit robust generic behaviors that accomplish a type of statistical self-organization that is necessary for the appearance of autonomous classifications.

Some computationalists try to interpret networks as only another architecture that realizes the logical computation of a univeral Turing machine. This is based on the invention of codings that show formal computational equivalence, but this view ignores the fact that new codes and different architectures can generate new patterns and statistical observables that have no meaning at the formal symbol-rewriting level. A more physical interpretation of networks is that they represent a statistical dynamical system that, like all dynamical systems, is representable by suitable programming of a univeral computer (e.g., Smolensky, 1988).

Ironically, the idea of logical computation was initially motivated by the desire to understand thought rather than physical laws. Descartes and Leibniz believed that computation could represent thought itself, and many of the founders of the modern programmable computer were first motivated by their interest in logic and the brain. McCulloch and Pitts, who knew their neurophysiology, were trying to see if brains could be modelled as a network of logical elements; so were von Neumann and Weiner. The later, well-known contributions to computer engineering by these men was first motivated by the practical computational problems of World War 2, rather than attempts to model the brain (Weiner, 1948).

In spite of these roots of computer theory in attempts to model brains as networks and von Neumann's (1958) cautions that the brain was "not digital, but statistical," and that "the language of the brain [is] not the language of mathematics," the next generation who founded the field of artificial intelligence ignored these original, biologically based network concepts and postulated the logical, programmed computer, which had been originally engineered to do numerical computations, as the model of all cognitive activity. The fundamental physical concepts of observables and measurements were completely excised from the domain of cognitive models by *the physical symbol system hypothesis* (Newell and Simon, 1976) that defined intelligent action as programmable, symbolic computation. Logical programmed computation became the dominant model for thought for over two decades, largely eclipsing network models. Logical programming was, of course, supported by the rapid growth of sequentially programmed computer architectures and hardware technologies.

The reasons for the rather sudden revitalization of network models are not obvious and involve many complex people and events (e.g., Papert, 1988; Dreyfus and Dreyfus, 1988; Rumelhart and McClelland, 1986). However, it is clear that several fundamental papers that influenced network research were written by physicists (Cooper, 1973; Little and Shaw, 1975; Hopfield, 1982) who saw networks as *analogs* of physical systems, not as logical computers. The fact that network dynamics is computed by discrete symbol manipulation is a matter of technical speed and precision, just as it is in calculating the orbits of celestial bodies. Their discovery of interesting observables in network patterns occurred by the same cognitive processes that interesting observables are discovered in the real world.

THE COMPLEMENTARITY OF PHYSICAL AND NETWORK MODELS

Distributed networks are a promising model for exploring how new observables are discovered, because they can autonomously classify patterns. However, an observable is more than a classification. If we say that observables are that part of a model of the world that can be measured or recognized, we are slipping into the dichotomy of physical theory that separates the measurement from the model. Recall that the principle requiring this dichotomy was that physical models be observer-independent or objective. But objectivity is seldom a biological requirement for survival. In fact, our individuality is based on our separate memories and models that are uniquely observer-dependent or subjective.

We can imagine two ideal types of models that are complementary: one type for discovery of universal laws, and the other type for controlling individual actions. In Ryle's terms, one type of model for "knowing that" and another type for "knowing how." It is only because of the epistemological requirements for objectivity and universality that the ideal discovery model requires observer-independence. This in turn requires strict separation of the *actions* of individual observers, which included making measurements, from universal laws.

In contrast, the ideal control model benefits the individual and has no requirements for objectivity or universality. Therefore it need not separate measurements, models, and actions. These categories may not even be appropriate for describing the behavior of a brain's distributed networks that continuously modify their complex inputs and generate output patterns or equilibria. How can one say when measurement ends and modeling begins when these functions are concurrent and distributed? How can observables be distinguished from imaginary constructs if neither is localized in the network?

And yet it is clear that some activities in the brain allow us to invent observable and non-observable constructs, to imagine the sharp classifications that allow physicists to separate laws and measurements, and that allow mathematicians to imagine the crisp, formal symbol systems with which we calculate. Physical theory attends explicitly only to the universal laws but cannot explain the discovery of observables and the measurement process without also attending to models of the observer. Biological theory will need to attend more to distributed network models to explain emergence of observables in evolution and learning, but this must include the origin of objective models. I conclude that a complete description of either living or inanimate behavior is not possible without the other. Both types of

262

models are required – observer-independent and observer-dependent. These models are complementary in Bohr's sense that neither type of model is derivable from or reducible to the other, and both are necessary for understanding physical laws and life.

REFERENCES

Anderson, J. A. and Rosenfeld, E. (1988) *Neurocomputing: Foundations of Reasearch*, Cambridge, MA: MIT Press.

Ashby, R. (1956) *An Introduction to Cybernetics*, London: Chapman & Hall.

Bohr, N. (1927) The 1927 Como Lecture, reprinted in *Nature* 121: 580.

Cariani, P. (1992) "Emergence and artificial life," in C. Langton, C. Taylor, J. Farmer, and S. Rasmussen (eds) *Artificial Life, Vol. II*, Santa Fe Institiute Studies in the Sciences of Complexity, Redwood City, CA: Addison-Wesley, 775–797.

Casirer, E. (1957) *The Philosophy of Symbolic Forms. Vol. 3: The Phenomenology of Knowledge*, New Haven, CT: Yale University Press.

Cooper, L. N. (1973) "A possible organization of animal memory and learning," in B. Lundquist and S. Lundquist (eds) *Proceedings of the Nobel Symposium on Collective Properties of Physical Systems*, New York: Academic Press.

Dreyfus, H. L. and Dreyfus, S. E. (1988) "Making a mind versus modeling the brain: Artificial intelligence back at a branchpoint," *Daedalus* 117: 15–43.

Ford, J. (1989) "What is chaos that we should be mindful of it?" in P. Davies (ed.) *The New Physics*, Cambridge: Cambridge University Press, 348–371,

Hertz, H. (1956) *The Principles of Mechanics*, Introduction, New York: Dover, 1–2. (Orig. German edn, 1894.)

Hopfield, J. J. (1982) "Neural networks and physical systems with emergent collective computational abilities," *Proceedings of the National Academy of Science* 79: 2554–2558.

Kauffman, S. (1991) *Origins of Order: Self-Organization and Selection in Evolution*, London: Oxford University Press.

Little, W. A. and Shaw, G. L. (1975) "A statistical theory of short and long term memory," *Behavioral Biology* 14: 115–133.

Lockwood, M. (1989) *Mind, Brain and Quantum*, Oxford: Blackwell.

Monod, J. (1971) *Chance and Necessity*, New York: Alfred Knopf.

Nagel, E. and Newman, J. R. (1956) *Gödel's Proof*, New York: New York University Press.

Newell, A. and Simon, H. (1976) "Computer science as an empirical enquiry," *Communications of the Association for Computing Machinery* 19: 113–126.

Papert, S. (1988) "One AI or many?" *Daedalus* 117: 1–14.

Pattee, H. H. (1967) "Quantum mechanics, heredity, and the origin of life," *Journal of Theoretical Biology* 17: 410–420.

—— (1972) "Physical problems of decision-making constraints," *International Journal of Neuroscience* 3: 99–106.

—— (1982) "Cell psychology: An evolutionary approach to the symbol-matter problem," *Cognition and Brain Theory* 5(4): 325–341.

—— (1988) "Simulations, realizations, and theories of life," in C. Langton (ed.) *Artificial Life*, Santa Fe Institute Studies in the Sciences of Complexity, Redwood City, CA: Addison-Wesley, 63–77.

Penrose, R. (1989) *The Emperor's New Mind*, Oxford: Oxford University Press.

Piaget, J. (1978) *Behavior and Evolution*, New York: Pantheon.

Polanyi, M. (1958) *Personal Knowledge*, New York: Harper & Row.

—— (1968) "Life's irreducible structure," *Science* 113: 1308–1312.

Prigogine, I. and Stengers, I. (1984) *Order out of Chaos*, New York: Bantam Books.

Rosen, R. (1991) *Life Itself*, New York: Columbia University Press.

Rumelhart, D. and McClelland, J. (1986) *Parallel Distributed Processing*, Cambridge, MA: MIT Press, ch. 1.

Shannon, C. and Weaver, W. (1949) *The Mathematical Theory of Communication*, Urbana, IL: University of Illinois Press.

Smolensky, P. (1988) "On the proper treatment of connectionism," *Behavior and Brain Sciences* 11: 1–74, and continuing commentary (1990) ibid. 13: 399–412.

Szilard, L. (1929) "Über die Entropieverminderung in einem thermodynamischen System bei Eingriffen intelligenter Wesen," *Zeitschrift für Physik* 53: 840–853.

von Neumann, J. (1955) *The Mathematical Foundations of Quantum Mechanics*, Princeton: Princeton University Press.

—— (1958) *The Computer and the Brain*, New Haven, CT: Yale University Press.

Weiner, N. (1948) *Cybernetics*, Cambridge, MA: MIT Press.

Wheeler, J. A. (1982) "Bohr, Einstein, and the strange lesson of the quantum," in R. Elvee (ed.) *Mind and Nature*, New York: Harper & Row, 9.

Wigner, E. (1964) "Events, laws, and invariance principles," *Science* 145: 995–999.

Williams, G. C. (1966) *Adaptation and Natural Selection*, Princeton, NJ: Princeton University Press, 22.

INDEX